T0305515

The Connectivity of Innovation in the Construction Industry

The construction industry is currently experiencing accelerating developments concerning societal demands along with project complexity, internationalization and digitalization. In an attempt to grasp the consequences of these demands on productivity and innovation, this edited book addresses how innovation is likely to take place with a more long-term perspective on the construction sector.

While existing literature focuses on organizational discontinuity and fragmentation as the main reasons for the apparent lack of innovation in the industry, this book highlights the *connectivity* of construction actors, resources and activities as fundamental for understanding how innovation takes place. Through 15 empirically grounded chapters, the book shows how innovation is part of construction processes on various levels, including project, firm and industry, and that these innovation processes are characterized by organizational and technological connectivity over time.

Written by European business management scholars, the chapters cover empirical cases and examples from both a multi-organizational and a multi-international perspective in terms of covering the viewpoints of different industry actors and the contexts of several different European countries including: Sweden, Norway, the UK, Italy, France, Hungary and Poland. By illustrating how connectivity is part of innovation processes in the creation of single-product innovations, of various innovations within and across projects, as well as a fundamental aspect of the processes in which innovations cross nations, the book provides a new angle on how to understand construction innovation and where the industry might (or needs to) be heading next.

This book is essential reading for anyone interested in construction management, project management, engineering management, innovation studies, business and management studies.

Malena Ingemansson Havenvid is Associate Professor in construction project management at KTH the Royal Institute of Technology in Stockholm. Her research places an inter-organizational perspective on innovation and technology development in various industries, nowadays foremost in construction. She has published in *Construction Management and Economics, Technovation, Industrial Marketing Management, Journal of Business and Industrial Marketing,* and *The IMP Journal.*

Åse Linné is a researcher at Uppsala University, and her main research interest is related to understanding innovation and renewal in various industries. She has published in the following journals: *Construction Management and Economics, Industrial Marketing Management* and *The IMP Journal.*

Lena E. Bygballe is Associate Professor at the Department of Strategy at BI Norwegian Business School and head of BI's Centre for the Construction Industry. With an inter-organizational perspective, her research focuses on innovation, organizational development and project delivery models in the construction industry. She has published in *Construction Management and Economics, International Journal of Project Management, Industrial Marketing Management, Journal of Purchasing and Supply Management,* and *The IMP Journal.*

Chris Harty is Professor of Technology and Organisation and head of the School of the Built Environment at the University of Reading. His research contributions are in the areas of understanding innovation in the built environment and organizational processes, applying socio-technical systems oriented approaches to organizations and projects, and the design, implementation and use of information systems, and he has published widely in these areas.

Spon Research

Publishes a stream of advanced books for built environment researchers and pro-fessionals from one of the world's leading publishers. The ISSN for the Spon Research programme is ISSN 1940–7653 and the ISSN for the Spon Research E-book programme is ISSN 1940–8005.

Trust in Construction Projects
A. Ceric

New Forms of Procurement
PPP and Relational Contracting in the 21st Century
M. Jefferies and S. Rowlinson

Target Cost Contracting Strategy in Construction
Principles, Practices and Case Studies
D.W.M Chan and J.H.L. Chan

Valuing People in Construction
F. Emuze and J. Smallwood

Funding and Financing Transport Infrastructure
A. Roumboutsos, H. Voordijk and A. Pantelias

Sustainable Design and Construction in Africa
A System Dynamics Approach
Oluwaseun Dosumu and Clinton Aigbavboa

Making Sense of Innovation in the Built Environment
Natalya Sergeeva

The Connectivity of Innovation in the Construction Industry
Edited by Malena Ingemansson Havenvid, Åse Linné, Lena E. Bygballe and Chris Harty

For a full list of titles in this series, please visit www.routledge.com

The Connectivity of Innovation in the Construction Industry

Edited by Malena Ingemansson Havenvid,
Åse Linné, Lena E. Bygballe
and Chris Harty

Routledge
Taylor & Francis Group
LONDON AND NEW YORK

ENRIC
European Network for Research on Innovation in Construction

First published 2019 by Routledge

2 Park Square, Milton Park, Abingdon, Oxon OX14 4RN
605 Third Avenue, New York, NY 10017

Routledge is an imprint of the Taylor & Francis Group, an informa business

First issued in paperback 2021

Publisher's Note

The publisher has gone to great lengths to ensure the quality of this reprint but points out that some imperfections in the original copies may be apparent.

British Library Cataloguing-in-Publication Data
A catalogue record for this book is available from the British Library

Library of Congress Cataloging-in-Publication Data
Names: Havenvid, Malena Ingemansson, editor. | Linnäe, êAse
    (êAse Kristina), 1974– editor. | Bygballe, Lena E. (Lena Elizabeth),
    1975– editor. | Harty, Chris, editor.
Title: The connectivity of innovation in the construction industry /
    [edited by] Malena Ingemansson Havenvid, êAse Linnâe, Lena E.
    Bygballe and Chris Harty.
Description: Milton Park, Abingdon, Oxon ; New York, NY : Routledge,
    2019. |
Series: Spon research | Includes bibliographical references.
Identifiers: LCCN 2018055240 | ISBN 9780815363224 (hardback) |
    ISBN 9781351110198 (ebook)
Subjects: LCSH: Construction industry—Technological innovations—
    Europe. | Construction industry—Europe—International cooperation.
Classification: LCC HD9715.E852 C66 2019 | DDC 624.068/4—dc23
LC record available at https://lccn.loc.gov/2018055240

ISBN: 978-0-8153-6322-4 (hbk)
ISBN: 978-1-03-217829-5 (pbk)
DOI: 10.1201/9781351110198

Typeset in Goudy
by Apex CoVantage, LLC

Contents

Contributors

Silvia Biraghi
Assistant Professor of Management Sciences
LABCOM, Economics and Management Sciences, Università Cattolica del
Sacro Cuore, Italy
Silvia Biraghi, PhD, Italy, Assistant Professor of Management Sciences. She
teaches corporate communication and consumer-brand relationships. She conducts qualitative research in the field of client–agency relationships, consumer
culture and branding, societal perspectives on corporate intangibles.

Lena E. Bygballe
Associate Professor
Department of Strategy and Entrepreneurship, BI Norwegian Business School,
Oslo, Norway
Lena Elisabeth Bygballe is Associate Professor at the Department of Strategy at BI
Norwegian Business School and head of BI's Centre for the Construction Industry. With an inter-organizational perspective, her research focuses on innovation, organizational development and project delivery models in the construction
industry. She has published in *Construction Management and Economics*, *International Journal of Project Management*, *Industrial Marketing Management*, *Journal of
Purchasing and Supply Management* and *The IMP Journal*.

Florence Crespin-Mazet
Professor
Kedge Business School, Toulon, Marseille, France
Professor of Business-to-Business Marketing, Florence Crespin-Mazet has specialized in the field of project marketing and negotiation of complex solutions.
She carried out her PhD at the University of Manchester on the issue of
co-development and partnering as a marketing strategy in the construction
industry. She has published in *Decisions Marketing, Industrial Marketing Management, The IMP Journal, Journal of Purchasing and Supply Management, Management
Decision, Management International, Management & Avenir* and *Marketing Review
Saint Gallen*.

Rossella C. Gambetti

Associate Professor of Management Sciences

LABCOM, Economics and Management Sciences, Università Cattolica del Sacro Cuore, Italy

She teaches corporate communication and brand management. Among research topics, communication of big construction projects, consumer culture and branding with a focus on interpretive research methods, social constructionist perspectives on intangible asset management.

Håkan Håkansson

Emeritus Professor

Department of Strategy, BI Norwegian Business School, Oslo, Norway

Emeritus Professor and one of the founding members of IMP. He has published a number of books and articles about business relationships and networks. His current research interest is development issues, including innovations in business networks.

Chris Harty

Professor

School of the Built Environment, University of Reading, the UK

Chris Harty is Professor of Technology and Organisation and head of the School of the Built Environment at the University of Reading. His research contributions are in the areas of understanding innovation in the built environment and organizational processes, applying socio-technical systems–oriented approaches to organizations and projects, and the design, implementation and use of information systems, and he has published widely in these areas.

Malena Ingemansson Havenvid

Associate Professor

Department of Real Estate and Construction Management, KTH The Royal Institute of Technology, Sweden

Malena Ingemansson Havenvid is Associate Professor in Construction Project Management at KTH The Royal Institute of Technology in Stockholm. Her research places an inter-organizational perspective on innovation and technology development in various industries, nowadays foremost in construction. She has published in *Construction Management and Economics, Technovation, Industrial Marketing Management, Journal of Business and Industrial Marketing* and *The IMP Journal.*

Erzsébet Hetesi

Professor

Institute of Business Studies University of Szeged, Hungary

She was a founding member of the International Association on Public and Nonprofit Marketing. She is member of the editorial board of the journal *International Review on Public and Nonprofit Marketing.* Her current research interests are related to non-profit marketing and the dynamic relationship capabilities of organizations.

Will Hughes
Professor
Professor of Construction Management and Economics
School of the Built Environment, University of Reading, the UK
Will Hughes is interested in commercial processes of structuring, negotiating, recording and enforcing business deals in construction. His researches are positioned in the construction sector, covering contracts, design, organization and procurement. He was an editor-in-chief of *Construction Management and Economics* for 25 years and author of several textbooks on contracts and procurement issues.

Mårten Hugosson
Associate Professor
Department of Organisation, Leadership and Management, Inland Norway
   University of Applied Sciences, Norway
Mårten Hugosson has, among other areas, done research on relationship-oriented strategy formation within the wood building supply chain. Education-wise, he has given courses on a variety of management-related subjects, including knowledge management and business strategy.

Kajsa Hulthén
Professor
Department of Technology Management and Economics, Chalmers University
   of Technology, Sweden
Kajsa Hulthén is Professor in Supply Chain Management (SCM) at Chalmers. Her research focuses on structural and dynamic aspects of supply and distribution networks. The research takes an inter-organizational approach, focusing on business networks, and issues of interest are efficiency, effects of changes in division of labour and actor roles in business networks. She has published in *Construction Management and Economics, Engineering, Construction and Architectural Management, Industrial Marketing Management, Journal of Cleaner Production, Journal of Business Research, Journal of Purchasing and Supply Management* and *The IMP Journal*.

Carmel Lindkvist
Post Doc, Dr
Architecture and Planning Department, Norwegian University of Science and
   Technology, Norway
Carmel Lindkvist has spent 14 years working in the UK (University of Reading) and Norway (NTNU) researching and publishing on facilities management and sustainable approaches to building. She draws on organizational management theories to understand the interplay of practices, clients and end users involved in the construction industry. Her portfolio of research projects includes EU FP7 Near Zero Energy Neighborhood and London 2012. She has published in many journals, which include *Engineering Project Organisation Journal* and *Technological Forecasting and Social Change*. In addition to her research, she lectures on facilities management and research methods.

Åse Linné
Researcher
Department of Engineering Science at Division of Industrial Engineering and
    Management, Department of Engineering Sciences, Uppsala University,
    Sweden
Åse Linné is a researcher at Uppsala University, and her main research interest is related to understanding innovation and renewal in various industries. She has published in the following journals: *Construction Management and Economics*, *Industrial Marketing Management* and *The IMP Journal*.

Tibor Mandják
Professor
EM Normandie (Normandy Business School), France
Tibor Mandják, Doctor Habilitatus, PhD, research professor at the EM Normandie in France, former director of the Hungarian IMP Research Centre (hIMP). Mandjak's current research interests are inter-organizational questions, international business relationships and networks and multidisciplinary approaches of business-to-business marketing. He has published in *Industrial Marketing Management*, *Journal of Business and Industrial Marketing*, *The IMP Journal* and IMP Conference Proceedings.

Tomas Nord
Senior Lecturer
Department of Management and Engineering, University of Linköping,
    Sweden
Tomas Nord has, among other areas, done research on strategic positioning of firms manufacturing wooden building components. As regards education, he has given a variety of courses in management and industrial economics.

Finn Orstavik
Associate Professor, Dr Philos.
Department of Business, History and Social Science; School of Business,
    University College of South-East Norway, Norway
The author holds a doctorate in Sociology from the University of Oslo and has published extensively in international journals and books, on innovation theory, on construction innovation and on sectorial innovation policy and practices. His core interest is in innovation sociology, and he teaches courses on innovation, innovation management, globalization, as well as qualitative methods and sociological theory. In the period 2007–2013, he directed a large, cross-sectorial research project on knowledge processes and innovation in construction and is active in international research collaborations in this area.

Milena Ratajczak-Mrozek
Associate Professor
Poznań University of Economics and Business, Department of International
  Marketing, Poland
She is Associate Professor in the Department of International Marketing
at the Poznan University of Economics and Business. Her main areas of
research include the analysis of company relationships and cooperation in
an international setting, as well as competitive advantage in the global market. She focuses on the analysis of both SMEs and large multinationals from
the high-technology and furniture industries. She has served as the guest
editor of the special issue of *Industrial Marketing Management* and *The IMP
Journal*.

Balázs Révész
Associate Professor
Institute of Business Studies, University of Szeged, Hungary
His research interests include business and industrial marketing, relationship
marketing, and customer relationship management. He has presented at several
marketing conferences (including EMAC, IMP and IPSERA). He served as the
guest editor of the special issue on Purchasing Orientation of *Journal of Business
and Industrial Marketing*.

Natalya Sergeeva
Associate Professor in the Management of Projects
The Bartlett School of Construction and Project Management, University Col-
  lege London, the UK
Dr Natalya Sergeeva is Associate Professor in the Management of Projects at
the Bartlett School of Construction & Project Management, University College
London, England. She holds a PhD degree from the School of Construction Man-
agement and Engineering, University of Reading. Natalya's work is published in
*Industrial Marketing Management Journal, International Journal of Project Manage-
ment, Project Management Journal, International Journal of Innovation Management,
European Journal of Innovation Management, Creativity and Innovation Management
Journal*.

Judit Simon
Professor
Institute of Marketing and Media, Corvinus University of Budapest, Hungary
Simon's teaching and research interests are marketing research, business-to-business
marketing and health care marketing. She is professor and head of the Hungarian
IMP Research Centre. She has publications in *Industrial Marketing Management,
Industrial Management and Data Systems, The IMP Journal* and the *IMP Conference
Proceedings*.

Per Søberg
Head of department and Associate Professor
Department of Business Administration, Inland Norway University of Applied
  Sciences, Norway
Per Søberg teaches management accounting and control and has working
experience from the construction business.

Lars Stehn
Professor of Construction Management and Building Technology
Department of Civil, Environmental and Natural Resources Engineering,
  Luleå Technical University, Sweden
Research interest primarily concentrated on construction efficiency covering
strategic and construction management, industrialized construction and construction system development. For the last 15 years, Lars has been responsible for
several large R&D programs on integrated technical and business development
in the Swedish construction sector.

Kristin Stevik
Vice Dean of Education and Assistant Professor
Inland School of Business and Social Sciences, Inland Norway University of
  Applied Sciences, Norway
Kristin Stevik teaches economics and engages in cross-curricular research and
teaching projects.

Viktoria Sundquist
Senior Lecturer
Department of Civil and Environmental Engineering, Chalmers University of
  Technology, Sweden
Viktoria Sundquist, PhD, is Senior lecturer in Construction Processes and Organizing at Chalmers. Her research deals with interaction processes in business networks,
with a main interest in change and dynamics in relation to purchasing, logistics
and organizational innovation. Research includes studies of changes in division of
labour and collaboration forms and subsequent effects on efficiency and innovation. She has published in *Construction Management and Economics*, *Engineering*,
Construction and Architectural Management and *Industrial Marketing Management*.

Zsuzsanna Szalkai
Associate Professor
Department of Management and Corporate Economics, Budapest University of
  Technology and Economics, Hungary
Zsuzsanna Szalkai has more than ten years of research experience in health care
and pharmaceutical marketing in Hungary. PhD dissertation was written in this
field in 2004. She is a co-founder of the Hungarian IMP Research Centre. She
has publications in *Industrial Marketing Management*, *The IMP Journal* and the
IMP Conference Proceedings.

Kjell Tryggestad
Professor
Department of Business Administration, Inland Norway University of Applied Sciences and Associate Professor at the Department of Accounting, Copenhagen Business School, Norway and Denmark
Research interests span the role of management technologies in strategic and organizational change and the design and delivery of sustainable innovations in health care and the built environment. He has published on these topics in books and journals within accounting, construction and project management, organization/sociology, and marketing. His research is informed by actor-network theory, supplemented with fieldwork and case studies of the unfolding empirical processes and practices.

Alessandra Tzannis
Lecturer in Marketing
CENTRIMARK, Economics and Management Sciences, Università Cattolica del Sacro Cuore, Italy
Alessandra Tzannis, PhD, is Lecturer in Marketing and Service Marketing. Research topics regard quality, customer satisfaction, innovation, service process and network analysis, in particular dedicated to the health care context with a focus on qualitative methodology.

1   In pursuit of a new understanding of innovation in the construction industry

The significance of connectivity

Malena Ingemansson Havenvid, Åse Linné,
Lena E. Bygballe and Chris Harty

The forming of a European research network

On the 25th and 26th of April 2013, 16 academics met at BI, the Norwegian Business School in Oslo. They came from different institutions and departments across Europe and from different disciplines but with a common interest in construction innovation. They especially held in common interest in the variety of types and scales of innovation activities in the construction industry, and the connections between products, processes, resources, projects, firms, sectors and nations influencing these activities. The title of the workshop was "On How the Construction Industry Is Organised to Deal with Innovation."

Innovation in construction is in many ways a well rehearsed area and the subject of hundreds if not thousands of conference and journal papers, books and reports. But the coming together of disciplines across built environment, organisation and management, social science and engineering was quite innovative in itself, as was, to some extent, the focus on *connections* over either specific instances of innovation or the development of system-level theories of innovation.

One of the anticipated outcomes from this meeting was the development of a shared methodological platform, from which researchers across Europe could undertake individual (and individually relevant) studies yet produce robust and comparable data. These would be on levels of innovation, on types and features of innovation networks, on measuring the value and success of innovation – a standardised innovation barometer if you will – to apply across European sectors. This would be a significant step forward in not only our understanding of innovation in construction but also generating real impacts on construction in supporting successful innovation activities.

This, of course, was doomed to fail. The benefits of different research traditions and interests across an interdisciplinary group – of multiple lenses held up to the same issues – bring the drawbacks of contested epistemological positions, theoretical incompatibility and irreconcilable units of analysis. Interdisciplinarity comes at the expense of homogeneity in approach.

But all was certainly not lost, and several actions emerged from this meeting, the most important being to meet again. Another was to use (and expand) the group in order to look for meaningful and coherent collaborations across disciplines, approaches and national boundaries. Yet another was to provide a peer support network on emerging publications or ideas for future research projects. So a programme of workshops every six months began, each hosted at a different institution and in a different country, some with particular themes or intentions, others as a more open forum for furthering discussions.

Since the first meeting in Oslo, ENRIC (European Network for Research on Innovation in Construction) has grown to include over 50 researchers and has been hosted by ten different universities in eight different countries. But more importantly, it has established an interdisciplinary critical mass of activity examining the ways that different parts of an international construction sector connect and interact and the implications of these connections on innovation. Indeed, over time, a number of shared principles emerged around which we, the researchers, can organise the multiple and heterogeneous research we all conduct. This edited collection is the result of the network's endeavours to date.

The problem of innovation?

Anyone reading this introduction will no doubt be familiar with the long-standing debates over the innovativeness, or otherwise, of construction. Whether oriented around national policies and strategies for improvement, the value added by the delivery and supply chain or the adoption of techniques and technologies from elsewhere, the need to become more innovative has been a constant theme in construction sector discussions for decades, within and outside academic debate (e.g. Egan, 1998; Bröchner, 2011; Tennant and Fernie, 2014).

It is by no means a simple debate, ranging from claims of a significant lack of innovation through celebrations of various successful technological and process-based advances to criticism of the measures used to evaluate innovation being inappropriate for construction activities (Winch, 2003, 2014). Research on innovation in construction is equally extensive and heterogeneous. It is certainly the case that the topic remains contentious and contested and continues to attract interest (Walker, 2016). There is a significant body of work that identify various barriers to and challenges of innovation. Much of this rehearses well understood features of construction, such as fragmentation and specialisation, competitive tendering, improving project-to-organisation learning, site-based conditions or economic pressures (Latham, 1994; Blayse and Manley, 2004). There are also many studies that deal with single or specific types of innovations, such as new technology use, whether process technologies such as BIM (building information modelling), products such as low-carbon materials or building technologies, or new processes such as integrated project delivery/public private partnerships as innovative contract forms, LEAN construction etc. (Nam and Tatum, 1989; Baxter and Berente, 2010; Rowlinson, 2017). Alongside these are many demonstrator or proof-of-concept studies, such as those into low-carbon homes, IT use and prefabrication processes, which larger-scale implementation and exploitation are left as 'next steps' (Thuesen and Hvam, 2011; Shapira, Filin, Wicnudel, 2014) These are often centred on specific project-level activities. A further category would be research that seeks to explain the specificities of construction and managerial and contextual factors influencing the process of innovation such as case studies and evaluations of specific 'real world use' of new information technologies (Mitropolous and Tatum, 1999; Winch, 2003; Harty and Whyte, 2010; Whyte and Hartmann, 2017). So what might we add here?

One recurring argument that dominates much of the debate is that the fragmentation of the organisation of production has a negative impact on organisational learning and scaling up of successful project-specific solutions (e.g. Dubois and Gadde, 2002; Miozzo and Dewick, 2004; Harty, 2008). Large numbers of specialised firms and organisations come together for time-bound, usually one-off projects, which make learning difficult to apply elsewhere. It also refers to the types of relationships generally applied among construction-related firms and organisations; even when it is not needed, traditional tendering based on lowest price is often practiced. While this research certainly has merit in demonstrating specific types of problems that characterise the inter-organisational practices of the industry, it provides less of an understanding of the fundamental organisational processes that enable learning and innovation to take place in this sector. It might even discourage further studies of these very processes, treating them as given, something we try to address in this volume.

Recently, scholars have sought more in-depth investigation of what construction innovation actually is by drawing on multiple perspectives. One such example is the edited volume by Orstavik, Dainty and Abbot (2015). In their editorial chapter, the authors state that by placing different theoretical perspectives on construction innovation, the common view that surfaces is that of innovation as "a largely emergent, non-linear, multi-level and hence, highly complex phenomenon" and of innovation outcomes as "multidimensional" (Orstavik et al., 2015, p. 11). This suggests that there is no one simple explanation for why organisational learning and innovation appear difficult within this industry, nor is there one simple remedy. This also suggests that there is no one single approach to studying innovation in construction.

Placing the fragmentation of actors and activities at the forefront of what is "wrong" with the industry has led to a number of organisational cures for increasing the industry's overall effectiveness and efficiency. The most prominent proposed methods of doing so are new project delivery forms (e.g. partnering), coordination tools (e.g. VDC/BIM), process thinking (LEAN), standardisation and industrialisation. However, the configuration of the industry has made implementation of these approaches challenging, and thus there appears to be a missing link in our understanding of why such attempts are not as effective in this industry as in others (Sage, Dainty and Brookes, 2012; Dainty, Leiringer, Fernie and Harty, 2017; Rowlinson, 2017).

One response is to designate construction as "a special case" in that construction innovation differs from innovation in other sectors such as manufacturing (e.g. Hobday, 2000; Gann and Salter, 2000; Winch, 2003). However, the specificities of the way construction actors and activities are organised do not mean that decades of empirical research on innovation is not of use also in this context.

Rather, it means that it needs to be applied very carefully and with a meticulous understanding of those specificities. In particular, it can assist in the exploration of what innovation *is* in this industry.

In making such an exploration, in this book we wish to highlight the empirically based contributions of numerous prominent innovation and management scholars that emphasise the interactive nature of innovation processes in terms of being emergent (e.g. van de Ven, 1986; van de Ven, Polley, Garud and Venkataraman, 1999), taking place over long periods of time and involving different (confronting) bodies of knowledge (Utterback and Abernathy, 1975; Utterback, 1994), and therefore being more cumulative than perhaps is realised (Rosenberg, 1994). This has (earlier and later) been expressed in various ways, for instance that innovation indeed is *new combinations* of existing knowledge and/or technologies (e.g. Schumpeter, 1975).

This has several important implications. One is that *the new* arises from *the old*, which means that to understand how and why innovation comes about, there is a temporal and spatial context to consider. It also means that neither its origin nor its process is necessarily easy to trace, capture or "unpack"; what are the various pieces of knowledge and technology that eventually has formed into something that we identify as innovation? A second implication is that innovation appears to arise in the interfaces of different entities, be they knowledge fragments or material solutions/technologies. This implies that what will come out of attempted innovation processes is highly uncertain. It also means that innovation can be the outcome of initially *unintended* innovation attempts; e.g. through problem solving, different bodies of knowledge or material solutions are combined in new ways that may present innovation opportunities. Thus, innovation is unpredictable in several ways (Kline and Rosenberg, 1986; Pinch and Bijker, 1987), and it is the different paths that learning and innovation can take within construction as an innovation context that we wish to explore in this book.

Such an interactive view has also earlier been acknowledged within the construction management literature. For instance, in contesting the role of any single organisation or individual as in control of the innovation process, Harty (2008) introduced the concept of *relative boundedness*:

> [W]hat happens if innovation's effects or repercussions extend beyond the control or sphere of influence of the implementer – if it is relatively unbounded? In such cases, how does implementation play out? [. . .] Considering relative boundedness avoids common assumptions that innovation always takes place within coherent and unilateral landscapes. It also brings more clearly into focus the range of pre-existing conditions and practices into which an innovation is implemented.
>
> (Harty, 2008, p. 1032)

Thus, while acknowledging that the specificities of construction need to be considered in order to learn how and why innovation takes place, the *way* in which these specificities are considered, in terms of setting the temporal and spatial boundaries of innovation work, is crucial for how we are to understand construction as an innovation context.

Process-based studies of innovation in various industries, including construction, suggest that it is not a one-shot event nor can it be controlled or driven by any one actor. Thus, we propose that innovation efforts in construction (deliberate and emergent) need to be viewed across an *inter-organisational landscape* that includes *interaction processes* within and between both permanent (i.e. firms) and temporary organisations (i.e. projects) *over time*. In our view, this stands in contrast to the predominant approach of highlighting the fragmentation and discontinuities of the industry. Instead, in this edited volume we wish to address how innovation processes unfold in terms of the *connectivity* of actors, processes and resources over time. By emphasising connectivity (instead of connections) we acknowledge the dynamic nature of connections, i.e. processes of connecting and disconnecting. Thus, connectivity signifies both the present and the possibility of a different future; connections may break, transform and new ones may arise (Kolb, 2008). We believe that in-depth empirical studies with a processual, inter-project and inter-organisational angle represent an understated and needed perspective in order to grasp the underlying processes and reasons for how construction innovation evolves long term. In such a pursuit, the concept of connectivity can serve as a powerful tool to trace interrelations between process and context.

In this book, we take forward three tenets; a commitment to revealing organisational processes within contexts of innovation in construction, the need to apply multiple perspectives to empirical phenomena, and the recognition of the different temporal and spatial distributions of innovation as processual activities. We therefore identify connectivity as a phenomenon that deserves more attention in efforts of grasping the progress of an industry that is currently experiencing accelerating developments concerning project complexity, internationalisation and digitalisation. More specifically, through a number of empirically grounded chapters representing several different national contexts, various aspects of connectivity in relation to learning and innovation are addressed. The aim is placing an interactive and inter-organisational perspective on how learning and innovation processes unfold in this particular sector. This implies addressing different aspects of how construction actors, resources and processes are connected (as well as disconnected) in relation to single product innovations, policymaking processes, procurement decisions, digital tools, different contractual forms, and supply chain interfaces on project, firm, sector and international levels. This includes a multi-organisational perspective and the perspectives of various types of industry actors (e.g. suppliers, entrepreneurs, clients, end users, policymakers etc.).

In the next and final section of this introduction, we briefly introduce the separate chapters making up the book. As we will see, the chapters illustrate that the empirical scope of how connectivity can be identified and traced ranges from single case studies of projects to sector-level analyses and transnational networks. This also consciously reflects the organisation of the chapters, starting with illustrations of connectivity on the single-firm and project levels, subsequently on multiple projects involving conditions within and between countries, and lastly on sector and transnational network levels. In the concluding editorial chapter, we address the learnings from the chapters by discussing construction organisation and innovation as subjected to both boundaries and connections and the paradoxical tensions this gives rise to. From this, we generate a set of analytical questions concerning the challenges and opportunities of tracing learning and innovation processes as multidimensional phenomena across a connected and disconnected business landscape over time. Based on these challenges and opportunities, we suggest a research agenda for considering connectivity as an inherent part of organisational life in construction.

Introducing the chapter contributions

The first part of the book focuses on case studies on firm and project level and how connectivity appears in individual as well as connected projects. Chapter 2, relates to the emerging literature on innovation that shows the unfolding of socio-technical connections that condition innovation. The study builds upon and complement this research. Using actor-network theory, the authors explore how unfolding socio-technical connections facilitate and hinder innovation in a case of sustainable building construction at Inland Norway University of Applied Sciences. The study contributes to the extant literature and current debates and strategies regarding the transition to a more sustainable society by showing that the unfolding socio-technical connections as *actants* shape the building project and its context in surprising and innovative ways.

Chapter 3 investigates the use of BIM within what has been referred to as the largest hospital construction and BIM project in Europe, the construction of New Karolinska Hospital in Stockholm. The study reveals how the use of BIM affects how actors' (re)connects to other actors, how resources are (re)adapted and change, as well as how activities are (re)organised within and between the organisational borders of firms and projects. It shows how the use of technology in construction to a high degree relies on the interaction patterns between various construction actors and their established and associated resources and activities.

Chapter 4 addresses the process discontinuity as a difficult boundary for innovative ideas to get to the market. The chapter draws on a combination of insight from a transaction cost perspective and business development. The multiple modes of overcoming this problem are explored in the context of new business models, and the empirical work explores new kinds of solution that are emerging in innovation practice. The authors examine a case of an innovative company that has removed process discontinuities and is technologically innovative. The findings show that traditional industry structures and norms do not necessarily encourage technological innovation. In other words, innovative entrepreneurs operate outside traditional market structures.

Chapter 5 illustrates innovation as the reorganising of construction logistics activities. The findings are based on a seven-year case study of a Swedish firm, transforming from a construction materials wholesaler to a specialist in construction logistics. The chapter points to the importance of considering activity interdependencies to address long-term change and how the reorganisation of activities exploits business opportunities to bring about efficiency improvements and innovation. Furthermore, it stresses the importance of involvement in different projects over time and the importance of interaction with several actors to develop solutions that fit with the respective projects' and actors' conditions and requirements.

The subsequent chapter, Chapter 6, illustrates the complex dynamics of innovation processes in terms of the negotiations between a diversity of actors in an innovative hospital construction project in Italy. The chapter highlights how innovation was generated because of the inclusion of different actors, who brought a set of heterogeneous competences and focal concerns into the agenda of the project. Focus is placed on how these actors negotiated and combined their roles during the different phases of the project.

The ensuing chapters focus on displaying multiple case and project illustrations. Using the metaphor of the project as an island, Chapter 7 addresses the dilemma of projects being subject to boundary setting while also being embedded in interdependencies across time and space. Through several (earlier published) empirical studies from Sweden, it is shown that project actors are affected by a number of technological and organisational interdependencies. Emphasis is thus placed on how learning and innovation in construction is determined through different kinds of interdependencies across projects, which construction actors can use in more or less systematic ways. 'Bridging' between project islands is introduced as a way of arguing how actors actively try to use earlier experiences and resources to innovate over time.

The following Chapter 8 explores how construction projects can function as vehicles for innovation within other sectors, in this case the Hungarian health care sector. By investigating the interdependencies of the different networks that the project actors are related to, the authors demonstrate the presence, variability and lack of connectivity between the actors in hospital construction projects and their extensive network, which includes health care professionals and patients. Although the two projects had different outcomes in terms of the more or less successful use of the hospital buildings, it is shown how innovation in health care – patient-centred care – was supported by innovative processes in the construction projects and vice versa.

Chapter 9 investigates the development of the strategic capabilities of Swedish municipalities being involved in the construction process. Through three case studies of construction projects concerning innovative wooden buildings, it is shown that the municipal clients build their capabilities through connecting to suppliers and technical experts, and by assessing the competence at hand and their own involvement for each upcoming construction project. It is indicated that, in spite of these capabilities, there is an increasing importance of connectivity in terms of connecting learnings within and across projects for building strategic capabilities for municipal clients.

The last part of the book is oriented towards illustrations of connectivity on sector and international levels. Chapter 10 addresses the role of communities of practice for learning and innovation. Through two in-depth case studies from the Swedish and French construction sectors, the authors illustrate that such informal and voluntary-based communities can foster learning and innovation in construction by connecting (1) the permanent organisation with the temporary projects, (2) temporary projects with the permanent organisation, and (3) temporary projects with temporary projects. Best developed outside any formal authority or hierarchical control, communities of practice can work as links among projects, firms and their wider network in promoting innovation. As such, the chapter investigates how learning can take place across the different organisational levels of a construction firm (temporary and permanent organisation) and across the organisational boundaries of several firms (inter-firm relationships).

Chapter 11 addresses the supply networks of an input product, windows, to the construction industry. The aim of the chapter is to discuss the role of different domestic and international actors and their connectivity in product innovation based on the example of Polish windows manufacturing, taking the perspective of the domestic windows manufacturer. The analysis contributes to the innovation literature by providing the picture of the domestic and international connectivity of actors who influence product innovation. Based on these findings, the author suggests that managers need to consider a wide spectrum of interactions with different actors when addressing their innovation strategies.

Chapter 12 explores narratives of innovation that address climate change in the construction sectors of the UK and Norway. The authors specifically focus on the ways British and Norwegian construction firms respond to the textual narratives articulated at the industrial policy and government levels. It is demonstrated that they respond to the agenda by formalising their sustainability strategies, creating new job roles with sustainability and innovation in their titles, and creating an environment and culture of sustainability and innovation. Narrative interactions have important implications for policymaking, and constructing identities and images.

The final contribution, Chapter 13, aspires to create a model for innovation in construction by viewing the project organisation as a coalition of activity systems. One reason put forth for why innovation in construction is still not fully understood is that specificities of construction production have been overlooked. In this chapter, these fundamentals are considered. The elemental units of production and innovation in construction are populated nexuses of knowledge, materials, rules and routines. Significant innovation is realised by activity systems, most frequently in the form of product innovations sourced from multinational industries via local intermediaries. Much more challenging innovation depends on changes *across* activity systems. Therefore, it is argued that connectedness between heterogeneous sets of activity systems and their respective corporate or institutional homes is a precondition for innovation success. Trust-based collaborative relationships are a precondition for such innovations to succeed.

References

Baxter, R.J. and Berente, N. (2010) 'The process of embedding new information technology artifacts into innovative design practices', *Information and Organization*, 20(3–4), pp. 133–155.

Blayse, A.M. and Manley, K. (2004) 'Key influences on construction innovation', *Construction Innovation*, 4(3), pp. 143–154.

Bröchner, J. (2011) 'Statlig utredarkritik av svensk byggbransch – det långa perspektivet', in Landin, A. and Lind, H. (eds.), *Hur står det egentligen till med den svenska byggsektorn? Perspektiv från forskarvärlden*. Lenanders Grafiska AB: Kalmar.

Dainty, A., Leiringer, R., Fernie, S. and Harty, C. (2017) 'BIM and the small construction firm: A critical perspective', *Building Research & Information*, 45(6), pp. 696–709.

Dubois, A. and Gadde, L.-E. (2002) 'The construction industry as a loosely coupled system: Implications for productivity and innovation', *Construction Management and Economics*, 20(7), pp. 621–631.

Egan, J. (1998) *Rethinking Construction. Report of the Construction Task Force*. London: DETR.

Gann, D.M. and Salter, A.J. (2000) 'Innovation in project-based, service-enhanced firms: The construction of complex products and systems', *Research Policy*, 29(7–8), pp. 955–972.

Harty, C. (2008) 'Implementing innovation in construction: Contexts, relative boundedness and actor-network theory', *Construction Management and Economics*, 26(10), pp. 1029–1041.

Harty, C. and Whyte, J. (2010) 'Emerging hybrid practices in construction design work: Role of mixed media', *Journal of Construction Engineering and Management*, 136(4), pp. 468–476.

Hobday, M. (2000) 'The project-based organisation: An ideal form for managing complex products and systems?', *Research Policy*, 29(7–8), pp. 871–893.

Kline, S. and Rosenberg, N. (1986) 'An overview of innovation', in Landau, R. and Rosenberg, N. (eds.), *The Positive Sum Strategy. Harnessing Technology for Economic Growth*. Washington, DC: National Academy Press.

Kolb, D.G. (2008) 'Exploring the metaphor of connectivity: Attributes, dimensions and duality', *Organization Studies*, 29(1), pp. 127–144.

Latham, M. (1994) *Constructing the team*. London: HMSO.

Miozzo, M. and Dewick, P. (2004) *Innovation in construction. A European analysis*. Cheltenham: Edward Elgar.

Mitropolous, P. and Tatum, C. (1999) 'Technology adoption decisions in construction organisations', *Journal of Construction Engineering and Management*, 125(5), pp. 330–338.

Nam, C. and Tatum, C. (1989) 'Toward understanding product innovation process in construction', *Journal of Construction Engineering and Management*, 115(4), pp. 517–534.

Orstavik, F., Dainty, A. and Abbott, C. (2015) *Construction innovation*. London: Wiley-Blackwell.

Pinch, T. and Bijker, W. (1987) 'The social construction of facts and artifacts: Or how the sociology of science and the sociology of technology might benefit each other', in Bijker, W., Hughes, T. and Pinch, T. (eds.), *The Social Construction of Technological Systems: New Directions in the Sociology and History of Technology*. Cambridge, MA: MIT Press.

Rosenberg, N. (1994) *Exploring the black box-technology, economics, and history*. Cambridge: Cambridge University Press.

Rowlinson, S. (2017) 'Building information modelling, integrated project delivery and all that', *Construction Innovation*, 17(1), pp. 45–49.

Sage, D., Dainty, A. and Brookes, N. (2012) 'A "Strategy-as-Practice" exploration of lean construction strategizing', *Building Research & Information*, 40(2), pp. 221–230.

Schumpeter, J. (1975) *Capitalism, socialism, and democracy*. New York: Harper.

Shapira, A., Filin, S. and Wicnudel, A. (2014) 'Quantitative analysis of blind tower-crane lifts using laser-scanning information', *Construction Innovation*, 14(39), pp. 383–403.

Tennant, S. and Fernie, S. (2014) 'Theory to practice: A typology of supply chain management in construction', *International Journal of Construction Management*, 14(1), pp. 56–66.

Thuesen, C. and Hvam, L. (2011) 'Efficient on-site construction: Learning points from a German platform for housing', *Construction Innovation*, 11(3), pp. 338–355.

Utterback, J. (1994) *Mastering the dynamics of innovation—How companies can seize opportunities in the face of technological change*. Boston: Harvard Business School Press.

Utterback, J. and Abernathy, W. (1975) 'A dynamic model of product and process innovation', *Omega*, 6(3), pp. 639–656.

Van de Ven, A.H. (1986) 'Central problems in the management of innovation', *Management Science*, 32(5), pp. 590–607.

Van de Ven, A., Polley, D., Garud, R. and Venkataraman, S. (1999) *The innovation journey*. New York: Oxford University Press.

Walker, D.H.T. (2016) 'Reflecting on 10 years of focus on innovation, organisational learning and knowledge management literature in a construction project management context', *Construction Innovation*, 16(2), pp. 114–126,

Whyte, J.K. and Hartmann, T. (2017) 'How digitizing building information transforms the built environment', *Building Research & Information*, 45(6), pp. 591–595.

Winch, G.M. (2003) 'How innovative is construction? Comparing aggregated data on construction innovation and other sectors – A case of apples and pears', *Construction Management and Economics*, 21(6), pp. 651–654.

Winch, G.M. (2014) 'Three domains of project organising', *International Journal of Project Management*, 32(5), pp. 721–731.

2 Forming innovative projects in sustainable construction

How socio-technical connectivity shapes the building project and its context

Mårten Hugosson, Kristin Stevik, Per Søberg and Kjell Tryggestad

Introduction

The aim of this chapter is to explore how socio-technical connections both facilitate and hinder innovation in sustainable building construction. In the literature, as well as in practice, there exist a multitude of approaches and guidelines to sustainability in construction. These include environmental certification standards at the component level or the level of the built facility, supplemented with methods to calculate and assess environmental performance in terms of CO_2/GHG emission and energy consumption. In the most technical complex approaches, performance is not only assessed at a single point in time but also developed to estimate and predict the performance over the whole lifecycle of the built asset – during construction, use and after being decommissioned (for useful overviews, see Ortiz, Castells and Sonnemann, 2009; Pearce and Ahn, 2013). The literature can demonstrate an increase in the technical sophistication and in the number of guidelines it provides. It is also quite evident that sustainability in construction has surfaced as a highly pressing and challenging global topic for policy intervention. The assessments made by the United Nations Environment Programme is an example to the point. "Buildings are responsible for more than 40 percent of global energy use and one third of global greenhouse gas emissions, both in developed and developing countries" (UNEP, 2009, p. 6). The United Nations Environment Programme (UNEP) calls for innovation in sustainable construction. However, when considering the contributions from research, there seems to be relatively more normative research on the technical guidelines on 'how to do' sustainability in construction while research on how innovation in sustainable construction actually unfolds for a building project is still in relative short supply. In particular, there seems to be a lack of empirical research on the building practices and project processes that facilitate and/or hamper innovation in sustainable construction. The normative literature seems to assume a simple causal relation between generic sustainability guidelines and actual performance. By contrast, our research adopts a descriptive and analytic 'socio-technical' approach informed by actor-network theory (ANT, e.g. Akrich, Callon and Latour, 2002).

Due to its socio-technical perspective and symmetrical emphasis on human and non-human actors and their complex interactions, the ANT approach appears to be particularly useful when studying innovation in sustainable building construction. As a practice, building construction is characterised by substantial materiality and the mobilisation of heterogeneous resources; spanning from materials such as concrete, wood, glass and steel, to equipment, money, knowledge and expertise in architectural design and construction (Bresnen and Harty, 2010). Harty (2005) used ANT to consider innovation in construction, and, recently, Georg and Justesen (2017) used ANT to consider sustainability accounting in building construction. In our work, we take inspiration from the preceding ANT contributions to consider if and eventually how innovation in sustainable construction is accomplished for a particular building project.

The remaining part of the paper is organised as follows: the next section engages with the topic of innovation from an actor-network theory (ANT) perspective and positions the study vis-à-vis the normative literatures on sustainability in construction. Next, our empirical case and analysis illustrates the multifaceted design phase and how innovation in construction is accomplished for a building project. The last section concludes with our findings and considers the theoretical and practical implications.

Theory/literature

As noted by Law (2010), ANT is a material semiotic approach, which posits that "everything – people, the natural world, and the social and cultural context – are all shaped in relations" (p. 177). According to ANT, the context does not have an independent existence but is a relational outcome and an effect of unfolding processes of connecting. The connections are heterogeneous and held together by a composite array of humans and textual-material inscription devices. An inscription device such as an architectural drawing represents something, a school building, for example. It is but one among many possible forms of visualizations and inscriptions that can be connected to the emerging building construction. According to ANT, an inscription device such as an architectural drawing matters because it enacts and performs a particular reality. But the drawing cannot do a school building. For the drawing to play such a performative role, it will require a whole array of additional connections – to humans (architects, building engineers, construction workers and management) and non-humans (building materials, construction equipment, engineering and economic calculations). This is also why ANT considers the actor that is doing something a composite and connected entity – and an 'actant' (after semiotics). In brief, then, the school building enacted in the architectural drawing only becomes a real physical building within a specific set material practices and unfolding heterogeneous connections. The existence of a particular reality (such as the school building) is integral to this unfolding network of connections.

In a similar way, when ANT is used to consider how innovation is accomplished, Akrich et al. (2002) propose a 'socio-technical perspective' and conceptualise the innovative 'entrepreneur' accordingly, as a composite actor (or actant) consisting of human and non-human/technical relations. But innovation is an ongoing process and accomplishment; it is never a final accomplishment. The innovation transforms when new socio-technical connections extend the network, for example, through the mobilisation of additional inscription devices and/or when previous connections between humans and non-humans are undone.

Latour (2014) used the ANT approach to address the question of sustainability and the advent of the Anthroposcene, that is, a new geological time in which the earth's natural and geological processes are shaped in fundamental, perhaps even in irreversible ways by unsustainable human activity. The author is urging scholars to pay more attention to what is going on at particular localities on the ground. Construction activities, for example, are very much about breaking new ground and reshaping landscapes. In an ANT perspective, innovation in sustainable construction appears to be a strategic topic and research site. The approach differs from Pearce and Ahn's (2013) normative approach and wish for more 'objective' sustainability ratings. This approach implies the asymmetrical presumption that unbiased scientists and experts, in contrast to biased ordinary or lay people, can and should be trusted with the task of defining what a sustainable building is. The ANT approach is more symmetrical and open by considering that valuable contributions can come from a diverse range of actors, specialists and lay, humans and non-humans. Second, while the normative approach to sustainability is generic and claimed to be relevant across the construction sector, the ANT approach posits that sustainability in construction can be done in many ways and is contingent on specific and unfolding connections. The advantage, then, compared to the generic normative approaches, is that we can inquire into the emergent unfolding connections of innovation in sustainable construction and address new questions about the socio-technical connections. As an example, which is also figuring in our empirical case research, is the concept 'zero-emission building' (ZEB) that scientists at the ZEB Research Centre in Norway define as a "building that produces enough renewable energy to compensate for the building's emissions".[1] A concept like ZEB is technical since it implies complex calculations of energy and emission numbers, counting to zero and accounting, as also noted by Georg and Justesen (2017). Bebbington and Larrinaga (2014) point to the fundamental uncertainties, complexities, ambiguities and political interest groups implicated in the accounting for sustainable development and conclude that there are no formulae for getting the accounting right. The authors call for further empirical research and engagements with practice. To paraphrase Latour (1987), can a technical device such as ZEB accounting become a valuable ally or 'actant' (p. 84) that helps to mobilise and sustain commitment and expectations for innovation in sustainable building construction? Or can it play other, less faithful roles that stop or otherwise undermine innovation? What other or additional human and non-human devices are mobilised in the 'doings' of innovation in sustainable construction? How do these connections unfold and shape, facilitate and/or hamper innovation in sustainable construction for this particular building project? These are all empirical questions in need of further inquiry.

Several contributions have pointed to the important role of representations and visualizations such as architectural drawings on paper, 3D models, budget calculations, time schedules and written project plans (Ewenstein and Whyte, 2009). These inscription devices can be active in generating "matters of concern" (Latour, 2004) about organisational spaces and practices (Kreiner, 2010; Van Marrewijk and Yanow, 2010; Kreiner, Jacobsen and Jensen, 2011; Våland and Georg, 2014; Harty and Tryggestad, 2015), corporate strategy (Skærbæk and Tryggestad, 2010) and sustainability concerns related to animal extinction and care (Tryggestad, Justesen and Mouritsen, 2013; Sage, Justesen, Dainty, Tryggestad and Mouritsen, 2016). Yet, as also noted by Georg (2015) and Georg and Justesen (2017), there is a lack of research on the role of sustainability tools in building practices and, more generally, regarding how sustainable 'green' product qualities are taken into account (Reijonen and Tryggestad, 2012). For a building project to take into account concerns about sustainability, a whole array of technical devices might be required. The present chapter illustrates the unfolding socio-technical connections for a particular construction project the media has labelled "the world's most sustainable building". We use the ANT approach to look into the internal workings of "the world's most sustainable building" before it is accomplished and taken as given as a "matter of fact" (Latour, 2004). We do so by considering how socio-technical entities become connected so that the building materialises and qualifies as sustainable. A basic assumption of ANT is that humans cannot manage innovation alone (Akrich et al., 2002); they do indeed need additional support from non-human technical devices (Callon, 2007), even built infrastructures (Latour, 2008), not least when considering global ecological and economic challenges such as CO_2 emission (Latour,1998, 2014). However, ANT does not assume that those technical devices such as ZEB's zero-emission and energy accountings remain faithful in supporting the sustainability ambition of the building project. Instead, the successful career of any interest or ambition presupposes a mobilisation and enrolment of actors' support. Such support is what strengthens the network in a certain direction, backing up or undermining a specific constellation's credibility, power and influence (Callon and Latour, 1981; Clegg, 1989). Our focus is not on the essential properties that ostensibly define a ZEB building. Instead, our focus is on what the ZEB and other technical devices do to the building project in practice. The ANT distinction between ostensive and performative definitions (Latour, 1986) can be useful in further illuminating the two different approaches. Going along with an ostensive definition, the researcher adopts the position that it is in principle possible to list the properties that define the ZEB building, although in practice these might be difficult to detect. By contrast, adopting a performative definition, the researcher considers that it is impossible in principle to assemble the list of properties that defines the ZEB building, although in practice it is possible to do so. The ANT approach sides with a performative definition and does not assume a fixed list of properties for the ZEB building or a fixed distribution of roles and responsibilities between humans and non-humans. Instead, the ANT-inspired researcher focuses on the project-related practices and keeps it an open empirical question how, for example, technical devices such as environmental accounting support or hinder innovation in sustainable building construction. While the ANT approach acknowledges the possibility that technical devices play a faithful and expected role only in the hands of humans, our focus and interest lie in exploring their more surprising, performative and innovative roles in shaping the context and content of a building project. For example, technical devices can be actively involved in generating new and surprising decision-options regarding alternative building designs and sustainability performances. Thus, when we use the notion of 'context' we take inspiration from ANT by considering how the project context is shaped in interaction between humans and non-humans. It is an open empirical question who or what acts and makes a difference to innovation in sustainable construction. Here it should be noted that the concept of a context has spurred debates across disciplines such as management and organisation studies, sociology, anthropology, science and technology studies and architecture. For example, Goodwin and Duranti (1992) question the kind of contextual explanations that fail to pay attention to the possibility that the context can be negotiated and transformed. In their own words, such "[a]nalysis can then focus on aspects of the larger social system while the cognitive activity of actual actors is treated as either epiphenomenal or defective" (p. 28). The authors draw upon Garfinkel's (1967) notion "judgemental dopes" in order to summarize what they see as a problematic outcome from such a taken-for-granted notion of context. An ANT approach provides a small, yet important supplement to this debate by considering the material practices and unfolding socio-technical connections as actants that can shape the project and its context in surprising and innovative ways.

Method

Our case study approach is inspired by actor-network theory (ANT) and Latour's (1987) methodological rule of thumb: to 'follow the actors' (or actants) and the chain of related events consisting of both humans and non-human technical devices such as written project proposals, sustainable building concepts, accounting calculations and designs. We first account for the historical background of the construction site and then engage with the building project as it evolves during the initial phases of concept development and design, planning, contracting and construction. The case study is processual and longitudinal and is about the massive wood building at Inland Norway University of Applied Sciences (INN),[2] campus Evenstad. It is a recently accomplished building project that media have termed "the world's most sustainable building". The habitants moved in in December 2016, and test and minor adjustments were completed during spring 2017. Figure 2.1 summarizes the key actors and agencies involved in the project network.

For the purpose of this chapter, we focus on the key devices implicated in developing building design concepts (summarized and marked bold in Table 2.1), notably the transition during the years 2010–2012, going from an ordinary functional

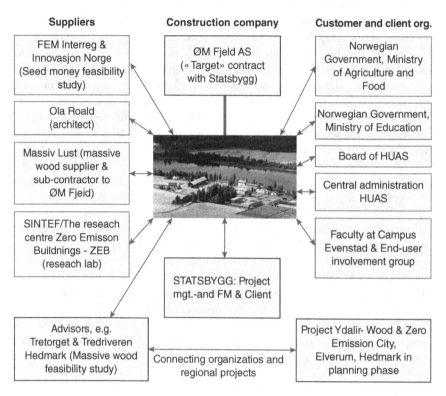

Figure 2.1 Project network

campus building to an innovative sustainability concept based on extensive use of massive wood and natural ventilation (Tredriveren 2012a, 2012b; Tretorget, 2012). Next, we show how this design concept went through further negotiations and transformations to become a zero-emission building (ZEB)-construction, operations, materials (COM). This concept does not take into account recycling/ reuse of wood building materials (except when incinerated), and exclude the CO_2 storage capacity of wood in the definition (Statsbygg, 2017, p. 81). During these years, the project came to evolve and include and, to some extent, exclude different people, organisations and design options.

The study is based on a collection of different empirical materials. The documents we have collected are in digital or paper format. The collection includes architectural drawings that visualise building designs and the site plan; documents that estimate different aspects of sustainability such as greenhouse gas emission and energy use and production; planning documents that provide estimates of project cost and time schedule; decision and meeting protocols from the project; cartoon drawings that narrate and visualise the history of the campus site Evenstad. We have supplemented the document studies with in situ visits at campus

Table 2.1 Project timeline with key devices, design concepts, actors and events

2010	2012 summer	2012 fall–2013 fall	2014	2015	2016–2017
Key device: Written building project proposal from the University to the Ministry	**Key device:** Written feasibility study and calculations for a revised concept and project proposal, with high sustainability ambition (by Tredriveren i Hedmark and Tretorget)	**Key device:** New report and calculations from new client advisors consider sustainability concept too ambitious	**Key device:** Written bids for the contract return early spring	**Key device:** Architectural drawings	**Key device:** CO_2 accounting for construction activities and time schedule Concrete foundation finished early spring 2016
Key design concept: Ordinary specification. Spatial-functional needs are specified but not a sustainability ambition.	**Key design concept:** Ambitions include extensive use of massive wood and natural ventilation to minimize CO_2 emissions and energy use in building. 150-year lifecycle, reuse of wood materials after decommissioning.	**Key design concept:** Ambition unresolved: advisor report, along with the prior feasibility study, are included in the competition brief (Nov. 2013).	**Key design concept:** Client introduces ZEB-COM. Negotiations with prospective contractors regarding the task and target price.	**Key design concept:** ZEB-COM Negotiating design changes, from 1 to 2 floors and new ventilation solution Negotiations finalised Contractor signed late fall. Construction management appointed Dec.	**Key design concept:** ZEB-COM Massive wood frame and wall construction finished late summer Technical installations summer and fall Moving in December 2016 Project report at public celebration of the ZEB-COM building January 27, 2017

Evenstad and the prospective building site and semi-structured interviews with key actors. Interviews include project and construction management, the client and user representative at campus Evenstad, the project owner and facility management at Statsbygg,[3] the management at Tre Torget, a private-public-funded industry research association for the development of knowledge and policies about wood manufacturing and use of wood in the built environment, and a consultant affiliated with Tredriveren i Hedmark, which is part of a national network of regional promotors for the innovative use of wood.

Mobilising measures for the world's most sustainable building

Regionally, campus Evenstad is located in Hedmark County in the heartland of the Norwegian woods and forest industry. The site carries the family name of a large farm that since the mid-seventeenth century included forestry and the extraction of timber among its core activities. The built infrastructure on the campus area has developed in several steps to meet the demands of an expanding and very successful operation of research and education in applied ecology, biodiversity and forestry. During campus development, there has been a focus on connecting the present building projects to the existing buildings to reflect the interest in environmentally friendly solutions. The guiding idea has been to preserve old structures and develop them to fit current needs of students and researchers. As an example, the old barn was completely renovated to create office spaces and a lecture room in 2007, and solar panels were installed on the roof – at the time becoming the largest solar panel plant in Norway. Important to notice here is how the existing wood buildings and bio energy infrastructure, along with local tradition and academic identity of the campus facilitated this new connection and "natural step" towards a campus and built environment with high ambitions regarding sustainable energy performance. Additionally, an idea of having a biomass power plant emerged. This idea had different origins: the Norwegian Research Council supported at the time small-scale supply chains for bio energy, and the idea was facilitated further by the development of educational programs. The energy plant now in place provides energy to the barn and two other campus buildings. For Statsbygg, the formal owner and facility manager of the buildings on-site, the plant also serves as a showcase for how to build for a sustainable future. No doubt, it seems that context matters and that this particular campus site was a perfect fit for 'the world's most sustainable building'. That, however, is not self-evident, and will be explained in this chapter.

The current wood building project at campus Evenstad

The Department of Applied Ecology and Agricultural Sciences at campus Evenstad's good international reputation has led to increase in student intake and faculty. Local concerns about the lack of built space at the campus turned translocal as top management at Hedmark University of Applied Sciences (at present Inland Norway University of Applied Sciences, INN) put the need for more space on its agenda. A board meeting at the HQ in Elverum resulted in a decision in September of 2010 to ask the Ministry of Education and Research to approve a project for a single-story, 800-square-metre building to be finished in 2012 and with an estimated budget of approximately 50 million NOK. The proposal did not put an emphasis on wood as a construction material or what a wood building could do in relation to sustainability. Instead, the emphasis was on the spatial-functional requirements. It was a functional specification for an ordinary building: the proposed building should be able to accommodate 28 offices for staff and PhD students, three rooms for meetings, and two larger rooms that could be merged for teaching with a total capacity of around 160 students or used for larger social gatherings for up to 200 people.

Mobilising through feasibility study

It appears that the Ministry did not reply to the written proposal. At INN, they nevertheless still considered the building project and reminded the Ministry about the previous mail exchanges. They also returned with a revised project proposal, but this time with a new emphasis on massive wood (cross-laminated timber) and what important role this construction material could play for a sustainable building. The revised project proposal was developed about two years after the first attempt, during spring 2012. It was a well timed occasion, since it coincided with the 100-year anniversary of the Evenstad School of Forestry established in 1912, in accordance with the will of Anne Evenstad. Through the focus on the extensive use of wood materials, the revised proposal established a new temporal connection to the history and tradition of the place. Simultaneously, the new emphasis on a novel massive wood material (CLT) forged a stronger connection to the present academic identity of campus Evenstad, while extending it into the future by articulating an innovative sustainability ambition related to the wood materials. The project team conducted a feasibility study in order to develop new knowledge about what 'massive wood' could do for a new building at the campus. The study considered the use of massive wood in construction design and as insulation material in walls and as part of the solution to ventilation and indoor climate. In addition to these performance aspects of the imagined future building, the project would also consider the role of wood in the building process with an eye to innovations and gains in terms of cost and time efficiency in construction. Lastly and related to the product and process aspects of the building construction, the project would inquire into the energy performance of the building as well as the CO_2 emission. All these considerations and inquiries were going to be part of feasibility studies, prior to an eventual final formal approval of the project by the Ministry. At this stage, as a feasibility study, the project only needed approval from Statsbygg.

Enrolling an influential project owner

Statsbygg assumed the role as project owner for the feasibility study, which was formally proposed in writing in March 2012. Prior to this proposal, a consultant with a doctoral degree in wood construction technology and affiliated with the consultant Tredriveren i Hedmark had played an important role. Tredriveren i Hedmark was part of a national network promoted by the national financing body Innovation Norway. The design concept and initiative to build in massive wood with natural ventilation was brought forward to Statsbygg by the consultant who had earlier visited Evenstad and then invited a representative from Evenstad and a representative from Statsbygg to visit existing wood buildings in Hedmark with natural ventilation.

Extending the network: enrolling policy

The emerging project network was extended further during spring 2012. Another representative from Tredriveren i Hedmark assumed responsibility for the feasibility study, which now included one representative from campus Evenstad and four people with expert knowledge about wood materials. When the members in the feasibility study held their first meeting in April 2012, the network also included an architect that was later to become the chief architect for the building project. The architect had a proven record within building designs based on wood. Next, in May that year, a representative from Tretorget assumed responsibility for writing up a project proposal (Tretorget, 2012) with the aim of using campus Evenstad's building as 'pilot project', an occasion for facilitating innovation and sustainability in the region's building and construction industry. The project network was extended still further by this second proposal, since it also enlisted suppliers in the construction and 'wood industry', while noting the strategic significance of a possible breakthrough for wood with regard to Statsbygg's environmental policies and interests.

> There is an interest in using wood as the main material in building solutions with considerable environmental gains. As an integral part of this, Statsbygg wants to do a feasibility study to shed light on central problems and challenges.
> (Tredriveren i Hedmark, 2012a, p. 1, and b, p. 11, authors' translation)

As suggested by the preceding quote, Statsbygg developed their interest in novel use of wood due to this emerging building project and network. This interest further materialised as a representative from Statsbygg, together with the representative from Tredriveren i Hedmark, assembled in Statsbygg's office in Oslo to write a report (Statsbygg, 2012) in July 2012, which benchmarked the massive wood project against alternative designs in terms of sustainability performances. An important finding concerns the environmental accounting of CO_2 emission from alternative materials (depicted in Figure 2.2). Although being an expert in wood construction technologies, the representative from Tredriveren i Hedmark admitted that these calculations were exploring the boundary of what was known. "At least to our knowledge it was the first time that this kind of calculation was done for a massive wood building".

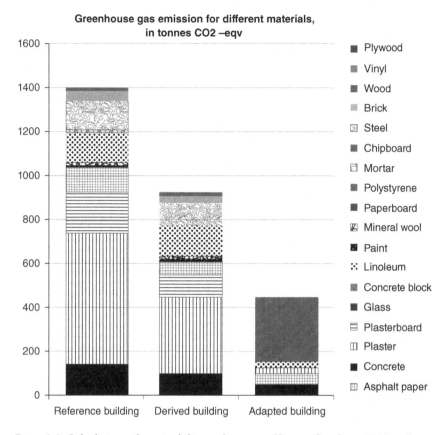

Figure 2.2 Calculations of sustainability performances (Source: Statsbygg, 2012, p.4)

Influencing the innovation process

The concept development and calculations depicted in the feasibility reports help to reinforce Statsbygg's interests and commitment to do projects with innovation in sustainable wood constructions. The interest is now connected in a particular way to massive wood, through the project report, feasibility study and its environmental accountings. These technical-textual devices shape the project and its stakeholders' interests in novel ways. The Evenstad project became different from Statsbygg's many other routine projects. The project owner now defined it as a pilot and innovation project. According to Statsbygg's facility manager in the project, this implied a more open/less structured approach than what they normally used. The project management approach was not linear and planning driven, as in the routine projects, but iterative and based on involvement and dialogue with other stakeholders. For example, the approach taken during contract negotiation with prospective construction firms did not seek to reach a fixed price contract but instead sought to reach agreement on a 'target price' based on incentive contracting. To summarise: while being an ordinary functional building, the emerging project did not materialise beyond the written proposal. It remained in a fragile condition during its first two years. However, when the building project was edited, rewritten and articulated as an innovation in sustainable massive wood construction, it gained new momentum. Good spokespersons with knowledge of wood construction were able to demonstrate its feasibility through visits to existing building constructions, novel calculations of CO_2 emissions and written feasibility studies.

The spokespersons are doing more than talking. They are also writing reports and doing complex CO_2 calculations that are included in the reports. These are inscription devices that enact the future sustainability performance of the building in the present. New connections are forged that render the building project less fragile because it shapes its context, notably the interests of the prospective client, Statsbygg. This sustainable building 'seemed natural' in a place like campus Evenstad, according to the representative from the client. But the connection between the sustainable building and the construction site was not given (or 'natural') in the first project proposal. This connection had to be constructed. To become 'natural', the connection has first to be done through socio-technical means – through good spokespersons equipped with inscriptions devices.

Enrolling alternative accounting devices

Experiences from previous building designs helped to define a benchmark for what the building project could strive for and go beyond in terms of energy efficiency and CO_2 emissions. According to the project members, CO_2 accounting is far less usual than energy accounting, which was also reflected in the use of established concepts and notions such as zero-energy building. Extensive use of wood was not a given property of the building project. Rather massive wood became the preferred construction material as the subsequent reports (Tredriveren i Hedmark, 2012a; Tretorget, 2012) and more elaborated technical accountings (Tredriveren i Hedmark 2012b; Statsbygg, 2012) showed the relative advantage in terms of the low level of CO_2 emission compared to 'cold' constructions in concrete, steel and glass. The aim was to take advantage of wood as a 'warm' organic and renewable construction material, its heat and its carbon storage capacity. It was further an ambition that the project should lead to development of new environmental and cost-effective solutions and, as such, act as a catalyst in the national construction industry for increasing the use of massive wood elements in buildings. The project developed an ambition to set a new sustainability standard for the construction industry. As the client became interested, the project eventually also mobilised further knowledge resources concerning the sustainability performance by linking up SINTEF; a Norwegian research institution with laboratory facilities and specialised knowledge in sustainability standards in building construction. The researchers were actively involved in developing the ambitious theoretical standard –zero-emission building (ZEB) – to include a lifecycle involving

Construction, Operations, Materials (COM): ZEB-COM. Statsbygg now wanted to explore whether the ZEB-COM could be realized in the 'pilot project' at Evenstad. The project members at campus Evenstad were not aware of this additional possibility until Statsbygg suggested this standard at a meeting in August 2014, i.e. about two years after the first CO_2 accountings were conducted as part of the feasibility study during the spring and summer 2012 (see also Figure 2.2). The inclusion of the ZEB-COM emerged as a possibility and addition to the project; it did not precede the project, nor did its principles undermine the key design assumptions about the sustainability of wood. The concept was supposed to be neutral when it came to the selection of materials. The concept is also relative; what matters is that the building compensates for the greenhouse gas emissions by producing a renewable energy surplus. CO_2 equivalents are thus translated into renewable energy equivalents; the higher the emissions, the more renewable energy must be produced to compensate for these. Like its predecessor in the feasibility study from 2012, the ZEB-COM in 2014 came to transform the project by forging new connections that extended the boundaries of the project to consider the whole campus site at Evenstad.

Initially, the project was more about the singular building in use and with a particular emphasis on the massive wood materials, CO_2 and energy performances. When it eventually developed into ZEB-COM also, the boundary of what to take into account changed from a focus on the built facility to its relations to the site context. This implied a careful consideration of how to source the construction materials, including the supply logistics. Wood will be supplied locally, concrete to the foundation will be transported about 200 kilometres from the Gardermoen area because this concrete implied lower CO_2 emissions. The project members decided to abandon solar cells as an option, due to the greenhouse gases generated during their manufacturing (Statsbygg had a few years earlier opted for solar cells on the Barn). The ZEB-COM accounts indicated that the project had to clad the whole campus with solar cells to generate an energy surplus that would compensate for the greenhouse gases. Instead of solar cells, the project members considered three different solar heating options that they pitched against an option based on biomass. The calculations showed the biomass option to be the most sustainable. Since the site was already equipped with a bioplant facility, it would be interesting, thought the project members, to explore the possibility of bio-energy further and eventually develop it into a local biogas plant for the new building *and* the whole campus: "We really do not know if this will work!" Only a few international facilities, one in the UK and one in Finland, could demonstrate a similar solution. The project group, including facility management, thus conducted a visit to Finland in order to learn more about this energy issue. Project members mobilised ZEB-COM along with a Building Information Model (BIM) in calculating and evaluating the energy and emission budget for the building process. An important effect of this was that project members dropped the three different solar heating options and instead opted for the yet to be invented biogas facility. The biomass option is based on wood that must be locally sourced, to save on the transport emissions. The inventive ambition went beyond the boundary of a zero-energy/emission building (ZEB-COM) to also include the whole campus site, as in a 'ZEB-COM Campus Village'. Intervening in this transformation were two newly built wood buildings, student dormitories that require energy and heating. The concept and ambition eventually also extended beyond the campus site because the new innovative biogas facility cannot produce the required renewable energy without local supplies of biomaterials. The project then worked to create interests and as an effect develop an energy market with local producers of the bio-wood materials. Redrawing and extending the boundary of the project in this way helped to invent a larger ambition and concept of a Campus Village community organised as a circular bio-economy based on local sourcing of wood for energy and heating. Redrawing the boundary in this way also helped the ZEB-COM calculation to add up because what matters is that the building compensates for the greenhouse gas emissions by producing a renewable energy surplus. It is these emerging dynamic connections that condition the sustainability of the project and building and make it go beyond current national and global sustainability standards, including ZEB. This is so because ZEB is neutral, it is 'objective', when it comes to the selection of materials for the building construction – it could have been a building in concrete and steel. It appears that choices related to novel wood constructions have no particularly important role to play in a ZEB-COM calculation. Other, more specific concepts and calculations must be mobilised for these design choices to materialise, which is also why this project became interesting for Statsbygg in the first place. Presumably, this is also why the ZEB-COM calculations became an addition, being more decisive in stopping a solar cell solution and in supporting a biomass energy solution for the whole campus but hardly decisive in supporting innovation in novel wood building designs and construction.

Discussion and conclusion

The aim of this chapter was to explore how innovation in sustainable building construction is accomplished. More specifically in our case study, we have focused our exploration on how unfolding socio-technical connections shape an ordinary project and transform it unexpectedly into a project on innovation in construction. Our case analysis shows that opening the 'black box' may reveal more or less active and faithful roles for the technical devices in mobilising interests and the connections that shape the project and its characteristic innovation features. Perhaps most importantly, we have shown that a first important moment in the project's lifecycle occurred early when key stakeholders such as Statsbygg recognised it as an interesting proposal through the early feasibility studies (Tredriveren i Hedmark, 2012a, b; Tretorget, 2012). This points to the importance of connecting with powerful allies in furthering the process (Callon and Latour, 1981; Clegg, 1989). Prior and less interesting proposals had failed to establish this connection to stakeholder recognition. The project gained in existence and momentum due to that written project proposal and the interest its authors and spokespersons at Tredriveren i Hedmark and Tretorget created. The subsequent written feasibility study and CO_2 calculations, co-authored in joint collaboration with Tredriveren i Hedmark and Statsbygg (2012), helped to strengthen the interest and commitment to sustainable innovation in massive wood construction. These technical-textual devices played an active role in shaping the project and concept and in gaining support from the stakeholder environment, in effect shaping the context in favour of innovation in sustainable wood construction.

As the case also illustrates, the project itself can be seen as a more active actant than usually assumed when emphasising the project as driven by clear goals and plans. The goal is not given and stabilised at the outset. It transformed from a clearly specified functional goal about an ordinary building to a building project with a goal and ambition to do innovation in sustainable construction. During these project processes, new socio-technical connections are forged. The spokespersons for the sustainable massive wood building developed and equipped themselves with technical devices that succeeded in convincing and enrolling the support of key stakeholders such as the prospective client. The actant played an active role in helping key stakeholder in developing and attaining their new goals and ambitions for innovation in sustainable construction.

The sustainable wood building project played a role in shaping its context in several ways: it helped Statsbygg to strengthen its leadership role by supplementing its large portfolio of more routine execution projects with innovative projects with the strategic goal of developing a more sustainable built environment. The massive wood building helped to set a 'warmer' strategic agenda for a new building program in both public and private construction work. In effect, it helped to negotiate the much more established and 'cold' construction program in concrete, steel and glass, i.e. a macro actor with 'steely' frames of power (Callon and Latour, 1981; Clegg, 1989). It is a program and practice that sustain global design and construction standards and that generate concerns locally and in international bodies like the United Nations Environment Programme (2009). The innovative pilot project implied a demonstration and experiment with an alternative and more sustainable building program and future (Callon, 2007). The connection between wood constructions and sustainability accounting is not given (or 'natural') but tense and difficult to establish. The zero-energy building account appears to simplify the task and challenge to the single denominator of becoming a net producer of renewable energy, or a zero-energy building. It is an account that is 'neutral' to the selection of different construction materials and designs because energy solutions that produce more and enough become the most visible and important concern. It is a subtle shift in focus, as recently also noted by Georg and Justesen (2017), but one that also foregrounds energy concerns while backgrounding and 'neutralizing' the important decisions regarding material selection and construction design. While Tredriveren i Hedmark (2012a, b) assumed an extensive use of massive wood in the exterior walls, a 150-year lifecycle and reuse of materials, the ZEB-COM calculation assumed the much shorter 60-year lifecycle, less use of massive wood in the exterior walls and no reuse and recycling of wood except by incarnation for energy purposes (Statsbygg, 2017). However, what makes the campus Evenstad case unique is that the innovative massive wood construction concept was already in place before the introduction of the ZEB-COM concept with its stronger emphasis on expert knowledge about renewable energy solutions. The ZEB-COM came too late to actually challenge the massive wood construction concept. However, as an actant, the ZEB-COM building helps to make a stronger case and connection to locally sourced renewable energy by facilitating the incineration of wood. In turn, it spurs the invention of a new local biogas plant along with the invention of a bio-economy and community of local producers of biomass. Due to these unfolding connections, the massive wood building has also become involved in the invention of a local circular bio-economy – a ZEB Campus Village – and not simply the invention of a singular ZEB building. While the wood building still existed in a fragile state, as a 'paper project' on digital drawings and in planning documents and CO_2 calculations, it helped to build a sustainable future for campus Evenstad and strengthen its identity and global reach on sustainability matters. The building also helps the academic institution INN, to strengthen its local, regional and national profile as it supports the development of a sustainable university infrastructure.

Previous research has also noted the importance of the building in strengthening the identity of the university and academic institution, as in the case of London School of Economics (Czarniawska, 2009) and the case of SCANCOR at Stanford (Eriksson-Zetterquist and Georg, 2013). Our research complements these contributions by describing and analysing how the building and project can help to forge new connections and a sustainable identity for the university institution. In addition, the study complements the preceding contributions by paying particular attention to how materials and technical devices such as the project plan help to forge new connections between the past, present and future. The connection to the future is integral to the project plans – as projection devices (Harty, Jacobsen and Tryggestad, 2015), the drawings, feasibility reports and CO_2 calculations are about enacting the future in the present, that is, building in massive wood. The wood materials that are integral to the project plan forge the connection between the project's different time temporalities (Tryggestad et al., 2013). When using wood, there is always a specific organic link to the past. From a sustainable forest management perspective, it will probably take more than the 60-year timeframe of the ZEB-COM calculation for a tree to grow strong enough to hold a campus building *and* contain a significant amount of CO_2[4]. Then there is an industrial time, when the harvested tree is transported and manufactured into massive wood (cross-laminated timber, CLT) and assembled into walls and elements able to construct and carry a two-story house. The connections are simultaneously about the present, materialised in a house that now keeps its students and staff warm and shielded from the cold winter climate. It is also about the future in the present in another way. The project has materialised in a massive wood building in use that marks the beginning of innovation in 'warm' sustainable constructions. For the major public client and owner, it implies a new interest and emphasis in sustainable construction, which is also materialised in a new sustainable strategy for future public construction projects (Statsbygg 2013, 2015). Since the client is a major player on the market for construction, there are potential significant long-term implications for not only public constructions in the nation but for how private construction firms will work. "Matter matters", as Law (2010, p. 173) pointed out. It does matter how our house is constructed because it is the physical-artificial context where we live. As we have shown in the case of 'the world's most sustainable building', this context can be executed in many ways, being warmer or colder and more or less sustainable. Only the future can tell whether it can be extended to many local sites and challenge urban contexts and established building practices dominated by concrete and steel. This kind of sustainable transition in building practices also challenges the industry's short-term linear perspective. In a longer term circular perspective, such as a 150-year lifecycle or more, there is a much stronger emphasis on the reuse of wood materials (beyond mere incineration) and its carbon storage capacity over multiple reuse cycles. As our case analysis suggests: to adopt a circular sustainable perspective is a tall order because construction management in both public and private business needs to reconsider and recalibrate their linear short-term planning tools, concepts and accounting devices.

Acknowledgements

The authors value the suggestions and contributions to earlier versions of this chapter made by several readers and reviewers and especially our conversations with our late colleague Harald Romstad and the comments made by Eric Bjurström. This research is funded and supported by the Bioeconomy grant at the Business school faculty, Inlandet University of Applied Sciences and the interregional project ecoINSIDE2.

Case documentation

Figure 2.3 Design visualization, massive wood building (By architect: Ola Roald Arkitektur)

Figure 2.4 Foreground: newly built bioplant. Background: newly built student dormitories, early spring 2016 (By Kjell Tryggestad)

Figure 2.5 The massive wood building in construction, early summer 2016 (By Kjell Tryggestad)

Notes

1   ZEB, ZEB Definitions, http://zeb.no/index.php/en/about-zeb/zeb-definitions (last accessed January 29, 2018).
2   Previously Hedmark University of Applied Sciences (HUAS).

3 Statsbygg is a public sector administration company and the Norwegian government's key advisor and project management (PM) in public construction and property affairs, building commissioner, facility manager (FM) and property developer: www.statsbygg.no/Om-Statsbygg/About-Statsbygg/ (last accessed September 23, 2018).
4 According to our late collegue Harald Romstad, who also earned an academic degree in forest management in Norway and practiced as such as a forest owner for decades, it takes about 80 years to grow a sprouce for timber construction purposes, somewhat less time in the south and longer time further north.

References

Akrich, M., Callon, M. and Latour, B. (2002) 'The key to success in innovation part I: The art of interessement', *International Journal of Innovation Management*, 6(2), pp. 187–206.

Bebbington, J. and Larrinaga, C. (2014) 'Accounting and sustainable development: An exploration', *Accounting, Organizations and Society*, 39, pp. 395–413.

Bresnen, M. and Harty, C. (2010) 'Editorial: Objects, knowledge sharing and knowledge transformation in projects', *Construction Management and Economics*, 28(6), pp. 549–555.

Callon, M. (2007) 'What does it mean to say that economics is performative?', in Mac-Kenzie, D., Muniesa, F. and Siu, L. (eds.), *Do Economists Make Markets? On the Performativity of Economics*. Princeton, NJ: Princeton University Press, pp. 310–357.

Callon, M. and Latour, B. (1981) 'Unscrewing the big leviathan: How actors macrostructure reality and how sociologists help them to do so', in Cetina, K.K. and Cicourel, A. (eds.), *Advances in Social Theory and Methodology: Toward an Integration of Micro- and Macro-Sociologies*. London: Routledge and Kegan Paul, pp. 277–303.

Clegg, S. (1989) *Frameworks of power*. London: Sage Publications.

Czarniawska, B. (2009) 'Emerging institutions: Pyramids or anthills?', *Organization Studies* (01708406), 30(4), pp. 423–441.

Eriksson-Zetterquist, U. and Georg, S. (2013) 'The sustainability and serendipity of SCANOR', *Nordiske organisasjonsstudier*, 14(4), pp. 23–40.

Ewenstein, B. and Whyte, J. (2009) 'Knowledge practices in design: The role of visual representations as "epistemic objects"', *Organization Studies*, 30(1), pp. 7–30.

Garfinkel, H. (1967) *Studies in ethno-methodology*. Englewood Cliffs, NJ: Prentice- Hall.

Georg, S. (2015) 'Building sustainable cities: Tools for developing new building practices?', *Global Networks*, 15(3), pp. 325–342.

Georg, S. and Justesen, L. (2017) 'Counting to zero–accounting for a green building', *Accounting, Auditing and Accountability Journal*, 30(5), pp. 1065–1081.

Goodwin, C. and Duranti, A. (1992) 'Rethinking context: An introduction', in Goodwin, C. and Duranti, A. (eds.), *Rethinking Context: Language as an Interactive Phenomenon*. Cambridge: Cambridge University Press, pp. 1–42.

Harty, C. (2005) 'Innovation in construction: A sociology of technology approach', *Building Research and Information*, 33(6), pp. 512–522.

Harty, C., Jacobsen, P.H. and Tryggestad, K. (2015) 'Visualizations as projection devices of future perfect spaces: The case of innovation in hospital constructions', *Presented at track 1: Temporary organizing, and organizing by projects: 23rd Nordic Academy of Management Conference*, August 12–14, Copenhagen. https://conference.cbs.dk/index.php/NFF2015/NFF2015/paper/view/2638.

Harty, C. and Tryggestad, K. (2015) 'The hospital building as project and matter of concern: The role of representations in negotiating patient room designs and bodies', *Engineering Project Organization Journal*, 5(2–3), pp. 95–105.

Kreiner, K. (2010) 'Organizational spaces: From "matters of facts" to "matters of concern"', in van Marrewijk, A.Y.D. (ed.), *Organizational Spaces. Rematerializing the Workaday*. Northhampton, MA: Edward Elgar, pp. 200–212.

Kreiner, K., Jacobsen, P.H. and Jensen, D.T. (2011) 'Dialogues and the problems of knowing: Reinventing the architectural competition', *Scandinavian Journal of Management*, 27(1), pp. 160–166.

Latour, B. (1986) 'The powers of association', in Law, J. (ed.), *Power, Action and Belief*. London: Routledge and Kegan Paul, pp. 264–280.

Latour, B. (1987) *Science in action*. Cambridge, MA: Harvard University Press.

Latour, B. (1998) 'Essays on science and society: From the world of science to the world of research.' *Science*, 280(5361), pp. 208–209.

Latour, B. (2004) 'Why has critique run out of steam? From matters of fact to matters of concern', *Critical Inquiry*, 30(2), pp. 225–248.

Latour, B. (2008) 'A cautious Prometheus? A few steps towards a philosophy of design (with special attention to Peter Sloterdijk)', in Glynne, J., Hackney, F. and Minton, V. (eds.), *Networks of Design: Proceedings of the 2008 Annual International Conference of the Design History Society (UK) University College Falmouth, 3–6 September*, pp. 2–10. www.bruno-latour.fr/node/69.

Latour, B. (2014) 'Agency at the time of the Anthroposcene', *New Literary History*, 45, pp. 1–18.

Law, J. (2010) 'The materials of STS', in Hicks, D. and Beaudry, M. (eds.), *The Oxford Handbook of Material Culture Studies*. Oxford: Oxford University Press, pp. 173–183.

Ortiz, O., Castells, F. and Sonnemann, G. (2009) 'Sustainability in the construction industry: A review of recent developments based on LCA', *Construction and Building Materials*, 23(1), pp. 28–39.

Pearce, A. and Ahn, Y.H. (2013) *Sustainable buildings and infrastructure: Paths to the future*. London: Routledge.

Reijonen, S. and Tryggestad, K. (2012) 'The dynamic signification of product qualities: On the possibility of "greening" markets', *Consumption Markets and Culture*, 15(2), pp. 213–234.

Sage, D., Justesen, L., Dainty, A., Tryggestad, K. and Mouritsen, J. (2016) 'Organizing space and time through relational human–animal boundary work: Exclusion, invitation and disturbance', *Organization*, 23(3), pp. 434–450.

Skærbæk, P. and Tryggestad, K. (2010) 'The role of accounting devices in performing corporate strategy', *Accounting, Organizations and Society*, 35(1), pp. 108–124.

Statsbygg. (2012) 'Klimagassberegninger for nybygg ved HiH Evenstad' (Version dated July 1, 2012; adjusted July 19, 2012).

Statsbygg. (2013) 'Tre for bygg og bygg i tre. Kunnskapsgrunnlag for økt bruk av tre i offentlige bygg. Analysedokument fra Strategi- og utviklingsavdelingen'. https://www.regjeringen.no/globalassets/upload/lmd/vedlegg/brosjyrer_veiledere_rapporter/rapport_tre_for_bygg_og_bygg_i_tre_statsbygg.pdf?id=2113691.

Statsbygg. (2015) 'Miljøstrategi 2015–2018'. https://www.statsbygg.no/files/samfunnsansvar/miljo/Miljostrategi2015-2018.pdf

Statsbygg. (2017) 'Campus Evenstad – Statsbyggpilot. Jakten på nullutslippsbygget ZEB-COM'. https://www.statsbygg.no/Nytt-fra-Statsbygg/Nyheter/2017/Presseinvitasjon-Evenstad/Miljogrepene.

Tredriveren i Hedmark. (2012a) 'Bærekraftig byggeri på Evenstad – en mulighetsstudie' (Version dated March 25, 2012). Rapport mulighetsstudiet Statsbygg/Evenstad

Tredriveren i Hedmark. (2012b) '"Treplusshus" – Bærekraftig byggeri på Evenstad – en miljøinnovasjon. Rapport mulighetsstudiet Statsbygg/Evenstad' (Version dated July 21, 2012; adjusted August 6, 2012).

Tretorget. (2012) 'Prosjektbeskrivelse: Nytt bygg på Campus Evenstad som pilot for leverandørutvikling orientert mot energi-og miljøinnovasjoner' (Version dated May 7, 2012).

Tryggestad, K., Justesen, L. and Mouritsen, J. (2013) 'Project temporalities: How frogs can become stakeholders', *International Journal of Managing Projects in Business*, 6(1), pp. 69–87.

United Nations Environment Programme. (2009) 'Buildings and climate change: Summary for decision-makers', *UNEP. Sustainable Buildings and Climate Initiative.* http://www.greeningtheblue.org/sites/default/files/A_summary_buildings_%26_climate_change_summary_for_decision_makers.pdf.

Van Marrewijk, A. and Yanow, D. (2010) 'Introduction: The spatial turn in organization studies', in van Marrewijk, A. and Yanow, D. (eds.), *Organizational Spaces. Rematerializing the Workaday.* Northhampton, MA: Edward Elgar, pp. 1–19.

Våland, M.S. and Georg, S. (2014) 'The socio-materiality of designing organizational change', *Journal of Organizational Change Management*, 27(3), pp. 391–406.

3 The use of technology and its effect on innovation

The case of BIM in the New Karolinska Solna Hospital project

Åse Linné

Introduction

Several government initiatives in European countries have been issued with the aim to push for implementing new digital technologies in the construction industry and thereby enhance productivity, cut costs and facilitate production and facilities management. Building Information Modelling (BIM) is a technology that is put forth as useful for developing, storing and transmitting digital information about a building object throughout various phases of its lifecycle (Bryde, Broquetas and Volm, 2013). It has also been pointed out as an important technology to facilitate information sharing and collaboration in the otherwise fragmented construction sector (Succar, 2009; Bryde, Broquetas and Volm, 2013; Won, Lee, Dossick and Messner, 2013). Existing research on the sector's ability to embed and use new digital technologies is, however, rather disappointing with only minor outbreaks of digital 'epidemics' observed (Brandon, Li and Shen, 2005). Instead, adoption is identified as challenging as it transcends single organisations and individual experiences and preferences and involves technical as well as environment and contextual factors (Peansupap and Walker, 2005). With the broader aim of furthering our understanding of how new technologies are used and developed within construction, this chapter examines how BIM is used and implemented within a large construction project and how this use relates to other projects and related business networks.

Several construction management scholars (Harty, 2005; Davies and Harty, 2013; Linderoth, 2010; Kokkonen and Alin, 2016) have shown the difficulties of implementing and using BIM. They emphasise that use is heavily context dependent as it is directed not only by its technical properties but by how actors are socially organised and adapt to the technology. This means that the use of BIM impacts existing work practices and how individuals organise work as well as how other artefacts are used (Kokkonen and Alin, 2016). Hence the use of BIM can be seen as a change process influencing individuals, organisations and connected artefacts. Harty and Arajou (2009, p. 275) explains this further: "The introduction of new technologies may lead to a series of connected changes, transforming the technology and the context in which it is introduced".

The Industrial Marketing and Purchasing (IMP) approach similarly views the use of technology as dependent on how it is combined with other technologies and physical resources as well as social resources, including organisational relationships and units of various actors (Håkansson and Waluszewski, 2009). Hence any new innovation such as a specific technology "should not be seen as the product of only one actor but as the result of interplay between two or more actors; in other words a product of a 'network' of actors" (Håkansson, 1987, p. 3). Previous IMP studies have shown the importance of users and the user setting when establishing and spreading the use of a new technology (cf. Håkansson and Waluszewski, 2007; Håkansson and Waluszewski, 2009; Ingemansson, 2010, Linné, 2012). These studies demonstrate that interaction is an important aspect of adapting and adjusting new technology to its usage setting, consisting of 'activated' actor, resource and activity structures (Håkansson and Waluszewski, 2007). Based on empirical studies of technology development and innovation during the last 40 years, it is a commonly held view among IMP researchers that long-term and stable relationships among individuals, companies and other organisations set the basic conditions for the possibility to use new technology and engage in innovation and renewal processes (Håkansson and Snehota, 1995; Håkansson, Ford, Gadde, Snehota and Waluszewski, 2009). The construction sector is, however, characterised as a special setting with discontinuities of production activities, which makes the use of new technology challenging. As main activities are performed in separate time-bound projects, tight couplings within the project network exist while the permanent network of organisations has been described as 'loosely coupled' (Dubois and Gadde, 2002). This means that within the single project, it is possible to establish innovative use of a particular technology, while lack of connectivity between projects makes it difficult to capitalise on what has been learnt between and across projects. Several IMP studies have, however, pointed out that long-term relationships imbued by trust and commitment exist in the sector, which can be one way of bridging the discontinuities over time and hence facilitate the use of new technology and work practices across individual projects (Crespin-Mazet, Havenvid and Linné, 2015; Havenvid, Hulthén, Linné and Sundquist, 2016).

This chapter rests on the insights from the IMP approach and the basic notion that actors are related to one another in 'network-like structures' (Håkansson and Snehota, 1995). An actor can, for instance, be an individual in a company, an organisation or a subdivision within an organisation. However, in order to become an actor, you have to be recognised and acknowledged by other actors in the network as an agent of specific resources or activities that other actors need in order to develop their own business. Hence actors become dependent on other actors such as individuals, departments, customers and suppliers etc., which in turn are embedded into existing networks of resources (such as knowledge, methods, tools, money, training etc.) and activities (such as procurement, production, distribution, maintenance, operations etc.) (Håkansson et al., 2009). Over time, this results in an interdependent network of intertwined actors, resources and activities. This means that existing interdependencies between actors, resources and activities within the network will shape the use of new technology. It also means that implementing new technology can create 'network effects', imprints on interdependent actors and their associated resources and activities. These effects could result in what Boland, Lyytinen and Yoo (2007) refer to as 'wakes of innovation', Havenvid et al. (2016) refer to as 'renewal effects', or Harty (2005) refers to as 'unbounded innovation', i.e. significant learning and innovation achieved among involved actors across organisational and project boundaries. In this vein, this chapter aims to investigate *how the use of BIM may drive renewal and innovation processes in construction.* Based on the IMP approach, such change processes are investigated as the reconfiguration of actors, resources and activities across projects, i.e. how organisations relate to one another and how they organise central resources and activities within and across projects.

The empirical case is a study of New Karolinska Solna Hospital (NKS), a project that has been referred to as one of the largest European hospital projects, including 17 housing bodies containing more than 12,000 rooms from simple examination rooms to highly specialised care units. The client required the use of BIM throughout the project due to its long-term commitment to maintain and operate and due to the complexity and uncertainty of the project. As a consequence, it became Sweden's largest BIM project.

The chapter is organised as follows; firstly, the IMP approach is discussed as useful in examining the effects of using new technology in networks. Thereafter, a discussion on the specificities of construction innovation is presented and how this can be viewed from an IMP perspective. Some notes on the method are followed by a presentation of the empirical case of New Karolinska Solna hospital project, the use of BIM on the project and its effects on the organisation of actors, resources and activities. The chapter ends with a discussion of how the use of technology relates to the connectivity of interdependent actors, resources and activities in business networks.

Introducing the IMP perspective

IMP emphasises the notion of interaction as being the core of economic and industrial activity where actors are viewed as both 'incomplete' and 'heterogeneous' (Håkansson, 1987; Håkansson and Snehota, 1995; Håkansson et al., 2009). Hence no single actor can possess all necessary resources and knowledge internally to develop their business or to innovate. As a consequence, actors must interact with other actors to be able to access, combine, adapt and connect resources or activities. Due to the need for interaction, actors become dependent on others' for their development. Interaction is an important way for actors to learn about their counterparts, and over time they may develop interdependent relationships with a number of actors such as customers, suppliers, subcontractors etc. This results in networks of rather stable, yet dynamic relationships (Håkansson et al., 2009). Actors not only become dependent on direct counterparts but also become embedded in network-like structures that are indirectly connected, for instance a customers' supplier or the suppliers' supplier. These established structures of relationships affect not only how actors organise their work internally but also how work is organised in relation to direct counterparts, as well as indirectly to how the whole structure of the network of relationships develops over time.

This has consequences for how new solutions can be implemented; the new must arise from the old (confrontations between and combinations of knowledge), and in its use contexts, it must fit into existing structures and practices (Håkansson and Waluszewski, 2009). As such, established relationships may be a facilitating factor for change to take place but may also mean that friction can arise. As Havenvid, Hulthén, Linné and Sundquist (2016, p. 84) states: "the substance of business relationships, the type of exchange they entail and whether they are connected determine what is possible to achieve in terms of renewal in the network". This means that any new innovation thus needs to confront the already existing structures of relationships between actors and their associated resources and activities in order to be used (Håkansson and Waluszewski, 2007; Håkansson and Waluszewski, 2009). Hence, in order to spread new technology and innovate, it needs to find its place in the existing relationships of interdependencies. It is also concluded that it is only when a new technology is used that features of the specific technology are crystallised and become visible (c.f. Penrose, 1959) as different users have different perceptions on how to use the technology and to connect the technology to other materials, methods or organisations in specific ways. Any new technology will hence cause effects on the already existing structure of how actors relate to one another and their associated resources and activity structures. If the use of a new technology causes too much change on established actors and their associated resources and activities, the actors tend to resist the new technology. On the other hand, when implementing a new technology, it may get unforeseen types of use and features due to how it is combined with existing resources and work practices (Håkansson and Waluszewski, 2007). Consequently, networks of relationships can both inhibit new technology and ultimately innovation, as well as be a source and possibility for new resource combinations. From an IMP perspective, time is also a central aspect affecting what can be changed and how. How companies organise their operations is largely dependent on established and previous interaction processes, which means that past interaction influences future interaction processes. In turn, this will determine how a new technology can be used and diffused in the network (Håkansson et al., 2009).

The construction sector: a specific setting for using new technology and achieving innovation

With the purpose of analysing inter-organisational conditions for innovation in the construction sector, this section reviews the features influencing the industry's ability to innovate as identified by Blayse and Manley (2004). Throughout the section, these features are juxtaposed to an IMP interpretation with the purpose of using the comparison as a framework for analysis. According to Blayse and

Mainley (2004), the main determinants of the construction industry's requisites for renewal should be viewed in the light of (1) key actors, (2) structure of production, (3) relationships and (4) organisational resources.

Blayse and Manley (2004) view *key actors* as playing dominant roles in the sector, where especially clients and manufacturing firms are pointed out as critical in steering innovation. Clients put specific requirements on the building object that can force other project actors to act in a way that fosters innovation (cf. Ivory, 2005), while professional clients may have the competence to "mobilise greater resources to acquire and assimilate innovations" (Hartmann, Gao and Fisher, 2008, p. 440). Manufacturers, on the other hand, can engage in innovation by supplying new solutions and materials to be incorporated into specific building objects as these normally have specific R&D units within their organisations to support new developments (Blayse and Manley, 2004). In considering the issue of key actors and their role in construction innovation from an IMP perspective, the roles of actors in steering innovations and their use are also emphasised. Holmen, Pedersen and Torvatn (2005) conclude that the main innovation initiatives in the construction sector are associated with how actors relate to one another, while Havenvid et al. (2016) conclude that clients' specific requirements can cause unintentional innovative effects across both organisations and projects. However, Blayse and Manley's (2004) insight in how key actors influence innovation relates mainly to the roles of specific actors, i.e. clients and manufacturers. From an IMP perspective, one could argue that it is not necessarily the role of the actors that determine their impact on innovation but rather the position of the actors and how the actors are 'acknowledged by other actors' in the network (Håkansson et al., 2009, p. 156). As actors cannot act in isolation, the use of a new technology or a new innovation is always dependent on a number of other actors in the network. Hence the power of specific actors is related to the possibility of 'mobilising' other actors. This also means that the position in a network is the result of an actor's connections to other actors (Linné and Shih, 2016) and that the power of specific actors in directing innovations is dependent on how they relate to other actors (Harrisson, Holmen and Pedersen, 2010).

The *structure of production* is also put forward by Blayse and Manley (2004) as influencing innovation in construction. One central element here is that main production activities are taking place within time-bound projects (cf. Winch, 2003; Dainty, Briscoe and Millet, 2001). For any project, a new actor constellation needs to be assembled to collectively deliver it, to set up a new actor constellation for every new project can inhibit innovation and learning outside of individual projects – to other projects or to other organisations (Slaughter, 1993; Tennant and Fernie, 2014) – hence the organising of construction in projects can cause discontinuity across projects. Overall, construction management and project management scholars conclude that the project environment in itself is a good base for problem-solving and innovation (Ayas and Zeniuk, 2001; Principe and Tell, 2001; Scarbrough, Swan, Laurent, Bresnen, Edelman and Newell, 2004). The IMP research community also recognise the project context as challenging in achieving innovation, where projects are viewed as temporary resource and activity constellations between tightly coupled actors (Dubois and Gadde, 2002), while the relationships between projects can be characterised as more loosely coupled.

Blayse and Manley (2004) also emphasise the role of *industrial relationships* among actors in the construction sector as a key feature in influencing construction innovation. Blayse and Manley's (2004) interpretation of relationships and their role for innovating in construction lies close to the IMP perspective of as they are crucial to "facilitate knowledge flows" (Blayse and Manley, 2004, p. 147), which is a prerequisite for new inventions and innovations to come about. However, Blayse and Manley (2004) mainly view construction as a difficult sector to enhance more long-term collaboration of knowledge flows, while some IMP studies (Holmen, Pedersen and Torvatn, 2005; Crespin-Mazet, Havenvid and Linné, 2015; Havenvid et al., 2016) have pointed out that construction actors actually want to establish continuity across projects to be able to capitalise on investments across several projects. For instance Havenvid et al. (2016, p. 804) conclude that "relationships in fact 'carry' renewal as they reuse and develop specific resource combinations and activity arrangements". Thus, relationships may be critical in maintaining and facilitating the spread of new technologies or innovations across projects. The IMP approach views industrial relationships as critical in achieving innovation, and some studies have also indicated that 'dormant' or 'sleeping' relationships (Hadjikhani, 1996) can be (re)activated and used as supporting innovations outside of individual projects. During the last two decades, the focus on price and arms-length relationships has been questioned, and new ways of relating to one another have been introduced to the construction sector, such as partnering contracts, project alliances and integrated project delivery (Blayse and Manley, 2004). By engaging in partnership and alliances with counterparts, it is possible to share the risk and engage in cooperation and knowledge exchanges that can stimulate innovation and industrial renewal (Bresnen and Marshall, 2000). The IMP view sees interactivity and cooperation between actors as a way of sharing risk and thereby diminishing the uncertainty of business, for instance related to engagement in innovation and the use of new technologies. A rather recent IMP study showed that while partnering is primarily chosen as a new project mode when the project is functionally challenging, the continued selection of specific partners is not only related to the risk level or functional challenge of the project but dependent on previous interaction and relationship history (Crespin-Mazet, Havenvid and Linné, 2015). When functioning as intended, partnering contracts have shown to intensify collaboration and contribute to enhanced trust and commitment among actors. Thus, potentially this project mode may facilitate the development of new innovations and industrial renewal in a construction setting (Havenvid et al., 2016).

Another key feature identified by Blayse and Manley (2004) as affecting the possibility to innovate in the sector is the *organisational resources* that the various construction actors possess. Blayse and Manley (2004) refer to aspects such as the culture and strategy of innovations as constituting organisational resources that impact whether new solutions and methods are developed and encouraged

within the organisation or not. Also the use of 'innovation champions' can mobilise support for new ideas and solutions in organisations (Nam and Tatum, 1997).
The scholars, however, only view organisational resources as something internal
and internally controlled by the company and refer to learning as the possibility
to 'transfer' knowledge from outside into the organisation. Here, IMP takes a
rather different stance as the assumption is that the resources of a firm are related
to other resources not necessarily controlled by that organisation. In addition,
according to IMP scholars, organisational resources are related to material/tech-
nical resources. The interdependence between internal and external resources of
a firm implies that relationships are a main means of innovating through combining, confronting and adapting resources in new combinations. As explained by
Hartmann (2006, p. 571), "This transformation [the innovation] mostly requires
additional in-house resources to be connected with resources from other organisations in a networking process". As the IMP approach emphasises, the inter-
organisational interactivity of resources means that the individual organisation
cannot be solely in control of innovation processes and the use of new technology: it is related to the resources and actions of other actors. Consequently,
innovation and the use of new technologies are unruly processes (Harty, 2005;
Havenvid et al., 2016). From an IMP perspective, the 'innovation champions'
emphasised by Blayse and Manley (2004) would therefore instead be seen as part
of a larger constellation of interdependent actors within which, for historical
reasons, some changes would be easier or harder to implement than others.

To conclude, the preceding discussion indicates that, while the industry features addressed by Blayse and Manley (2004) are relevant for analysing the construction industry's ability to innovate, an IMP interpretation places them in
the context of an interactive and interdependent business landscape. One main
difference can be found in the interpretation of *key actors*, where IMP does not
consider the role of the actor in particular but instead the *position* of the actors
in a network as influencing the *power* and possibility to *mobilise* for construction
innovation. The *relationships* are viewed – rather similarly between Blayse and
Manley (2004) and IMP, as both emphasise the role of *relationships as connecting
knowledge bodies* – as important in creating possibilities for new combinations
of knowledge that can result in innovation. The structure of production, more
specifically organising production in projects, is handled differently, as Blayse and
Manley (2004) mainly show and conclude that the project organisation hinders
continuity and thus constrains innovation and learning. IMP also highlights the
project as a challenging for innovation and learning to spread beyond the individual project but, compared to Blayse and Manley (2004), IMP sees *long-term
commitment and relationships* as a possible solution to create continuity across projects and thereby enhance learning and innovation. In relation to *organisational
resources*, Blayse and Manley (2004) consider resources as an internal issue that
can be controlled by the individual organisation; hence through strategies and
champions, innovations can be enhanced in the organisation. IMP, on the other
hand, views organisational resources as (*direct or indirectly*) *related to organisational and technical resources of other actors* within the network. Hence the main

difference between Blayse and Manley (2004) and IMP scholars in how they view innovation is the interactivity in the sector, an aspect that IMP scholars always take into consideration, whereas Blayse and Manley (2004) do not. The four key features and the two interpretations of them will be used as an analytical framework when considering the use and development of BIM in the case study. Before presenting the case, the next section will present the method used for the empirical study.

Method and data collection

The study is part of a larger research project investigating the use of BIM in a Swedish construction context with the overarching research aim to understand the drivers for and barriers to the use of BIM among various actor groups in the sector. The main data for the chapter is based on 23 interviews with main construction actors, including technical engineering consultants, architects, developers and contractors. The interviews were performed between 2015 and 2016. The respondents all held managerial positions, usually the position of BIM manager or technical manager. Due to the respondents' position, there is a bias towards having a rather positive attitude towards the use of BIM that cannot be ignored. The selection of companies was based on the notion that main innovative activities are related to large construction firms with extensive internal and external networks (Håkansson and Ingemansson, 2013); hence the largest actors in each actor group were selected for the interviews. The data collection was steered by the need to understand how the various actors used BIM and how it impacted its organisation, how they relate to others within and outside of the organisations, how resources are adapted and changed, as well how activities are adjusted and linked due to the use of BIM within and across projects.

When collecting, reviewing and analysing the data, it became obvious that most interviewees mentioned examples from the New Karolinska Hospital Solna project (NKS); hence it was concluded that NKS has made an impact on several actor groups in the sector. For instance, almost all the technical engineering companies and architecture firms interviewed had been involved in NKS, one way or another. In addition, the NKS project was also referred to as the largest BIM project in Sweden, ever, in regard to number of individuals involved, as well as the cost of the project. When looking into the use of BIM in NKS, it was also possible to identify that BIM did impact the work practices, tools and methods used, some of which could be regarded as innovations. One main effect of the NKS project was, for instance, the development and introduction of a new BIM platform. Thus, to use the NKS project as a way to illustrate change in construction, as well as construction innovation, emerged over time. Because the case emerged over time and the interviews were not aimed at understanding the use of BIM in the NKS project per se, the case study should be seen as a pilot study on the use of BIM in NKS. The case study approach has, however, already been proven suitable when investigating interactions and interdependencies between organisations in networks (Halinen and Törnroos 2005; Dubois and Araujo, 2007). The following case illustration is mainly based on interviews with architect firms and technical engineering consultants involved in the design and planning phase of the project. To complement the interview data, written material was also collected, such as magazine articles on the use of BIM in NKS, marketing materials from involved suppliers and other publicly available materials online. Due to the size and importance of NKS, extensive written materials are available that were instructive in understanding the context of the project.

The case is written to illustrate how various actors engage in the use of BIM as a joint endeavour, especially how the actors relate to one another, how resources are combined, and how activities are adjusted due to the use of BIM. In analysing and discussing the case, the four features of construction innovation presented by Blayse and Manley (2004) – key actors, structure of production, the industrial relationships and organisational resources – are utilised. These features are discussed in relation to the NKS case and how it relates to using new technology in construction and its impact on innovation.

Using BIM in the New Karolinska Hospital Solna (NKS)

Background to the NKS project

The new Karolinska Hospital Solna (NKS) is one of the largest hospital construction projects in Europe. The project includes 320,000 square metres spread among 17 housing bodies consisting of 9–12 floors with a total of 12,000 rooms, stretching a variety of functions such as treatment rooms, examination rooms and recreation areas etc. The total construction cost is estimated at 14.5 billion SEK, not including the health care equipment. Health care projects have extra complexity due to the extensive specialist services required to be installed, and additionally the buildings were required to be LEED (Leadership in Energy and Environmental Design) certificated. In addition, ongoing health care operations could not be disturbed during the construction process. The project was approved by the Stockholm City council in 2008, initiated in 2010 and completed in 2018. The Stockholm City Council appointed the Swedish Hospital Partners (SHP), a partnership between Skanska Infrastructure Development and the UK pension fund Innisfree, for managing its construction and operations until 2040. SHP contracted in turn Skanska Healthcare, a joint venture between Skanska UK and Skanska Sweden, for its design and construction and Coor Service Management for its facility management. The Stockholm City Council is responsible for providing the health care treatment in the new facilities.

BIM a mandatory technology in NKS – resulting in new actor constellations and new work practices

As the main client SHP would be responsible for facility operation and maintenance until 2040, SHP emphasised that design and construction would consider and support management and operations of the future facilities. In doing this,

SHP saw the benefits of using digital information generated in the construction of the facilities more systematically in managing its operations. As a consequence, SHP mandated the use of BIM in the contract, and for the first time in Sweden the entrepreneur, Skanska Healthcare, signed a contract with requirements to deliver all documentation using BIM. This is how NKS became the largest BIM project in Sweden to date. Two of Sweden's largest and well-known architect firms, White and Tengbom, established a joint collaboration company, the White Tengbom Team (WTT), in 2010 to be responsible for design and planning of the challenging NKS-project. This new organisation was formed in response not only to the size and the complexity of the project but also to the new demands of delivering BIM for further operations.

It is estimated that more than 400 individuals were involved in the design and planning of the project, of whom around 150 represented WTT, while the rest belonged to the largest technical engineering consultant firms in Sweden, including Sweco, ÅF, Ramboll and WSP. The individuals involved in design and planning had varied experience using BIM, but it was a requirement that BIM should be used as a main technology in managing information in the project. The BIM manager at White explains this: "The ones doing design and planning for hospital projects such as NKS know there is no idea to even question it [the use of BIM]".

Due to the high demands of digital information and the complexity of the project, a specific actor constellation responsible for the digital information was established within the design and planning organisation, the WTT ICT Board. The board consisted of BIM managers from the main disciplines, all having extensive experience in working with BIM and digital solutions in the construction sector. Also, representatives from the contractor and real estate management were included in the new board. The head of the WTT ICT board explained: "In being able to make BIM work in practice you need the whole chain [of actors] in B-meetings such as the entrepreneur and the facility management. When production and procurement access data where it is produced it can save a lot of time". The experience the board represented included various disciplines as well as experience from the entrepreneur, especially Skanska UK's health care projects (for instance, St Barts in London). This experience was mobilised as input to the WTT ICT board in order to set up the methodology for how to use BIM. Through discussions within the WTT ICT board, it was decided to deliver BIM Level 2 on the project, requiring a new way of organising design and planning in the project. The BIM manager at White expresses this intent:

> If we were going to be able to handle the details, materials, colours, functions, changing conditions and a very large group of people who had to work together [in NKS], then we couldn't do it the usual way. Instead we had to develop BIM to cover new technical solutions as well as management aspects, almost like BIM 2.0.

The quote reflects how the WTT ICT board views BIM – not only as a technical tool but as a management tool that can change people and work practices.

One new way of using BIM compared to previous projects was to use BIM as an integrated function within the design and planning organisation. Prior to NKS, BIM and digital information was usually handled as a separate function in the project, not integrating it within the whole design and planning organisation. The ability to integrate the design and planning with digital information depended on increased interaction and communication among individual actors. A key issue was understanding how each actor influences others and what information actors need at what time and why. Making this visible to all connected actors required co-location, meeting forums and transparency. Through formal and informal interaction with other actors, individuals became dedicated to the task, and a joint consensus of the process of the various actors was established. This collective act is also emphasised by the head of the WTT ICT board manager when saying, "One of the biggest experiences from NKS is the feeling of consensus among the involved planning actors, how interaction among actors could solve each other's problem".

The technical limitation of BIM models creates a possibility for a new BIM platform

Prior to the NKS-project, the use of BIM had been focused on developing and inserting all necessary digital information in a joint BIM model that all disciplines were connected to. Due to the complexity and size of the NKS project, it was, however, impossible to use only one model; instead 17 models were required (one for each building). When inserting all required information into the models, each individual model became impossible to use as it included too much information and required hours to be opened. This became a central challenge for the design and planning organisation and for the WTT ICT board in particular. The advantage of using BIM in storing and structuring information was hindered due to the technical limitation of the BIM models. In establishing a new way to use the BIM models, the WTT ICT board approached the main ICT supplier in the project. The company was one of the first companies worldwide that was contracted by Autodesk as a retailer of their main BIM software, Revit, outside of the United States. Due to this opportunity, the company established a market-leading position in supplying the Nordic market with CAD tools as well as training in CAD methodologies. Hence the company already had established relationships to all larger construction actors, such as technical engineering consultants, architectural firms and construction companies in Sweden, including both White and Tengbom.

In order to solve the technical limitations of the BIM models, a joint discussion between WTT ICT Board and the ICT supplier began. The experiences of the ICT supplier in adjusting BIM software for the Swedish market, as well as insight into BIM methodology and experiences of establishing databases for various construction actors stretching over hundreds of projects, resulted in a suggestion by the supplier to jointly develop a new cloud-based solution together with the WTT ICT board. Here, the main information load would be located in databases, not in the specific models as previously. The WTT ICT board saw the need for a new BIM platform and decided to test and develop the solution together with the supplier. The WTT ICT board developed the requirement specifications and the methodology, while the supplier built the actual system, a cloud-based database solution.

All necessary BIM models, 17 models in total for the whole NKS project, were connected to a room function database, the RTP database. The database was connected not only to the BIM models but also to other information systems. Due to the interconnectedness of the database to the models, changes made in the database resulted in an automatic update of the connected BIM models. The point of departure of the new solution was to focus more on information management and move away from the graphic focus of the BIM models. Having a database system resulted in a possibility to trace changes. The new solution became the first cloud-based BIM platform in Sweden, and it could be seen as an information hub that connects various information sources and information systems. The solution could be used regardless of BIM software tools on the market such as Revit, Tekla, MagiCad etc. During the NKS project the ICT supplier developed the room database for various purposes such as door management, indoor management etc. The database system was later connected to Autodesk BIM Field 360 software, where construction workers and project members could access the BIM models on-site as well as the document management system, Sharepoint.

The new BIM platform facilitated the work with room descriptions – only one individual could manage the room descriptions of all buildings – work that was estimated to have required 10 individuals without the database. The BIM platform also facilitated communication in the project among project actors or as the BIM manager at White expresses it: "The BIM tool [the BIM platform] made it possible to see changes quickly, trace points of conflict and find solutions. In this interactive process, the tools and methods have made it easier to interact, bring about transparency and cooperation". This transparency, easy access to changes and open communication contributed to the high involvement and engagement of the various actors in the project. The head of the WTT ICT board emphasises this: "Here [in NKS] you really see the effects of more developed BIM, not only focusing on 3D model but how to manage the information [more systematically]". This also resulted in new ways of managing digital information compared to prior projects: "We went against the existing BIM norms with the focus on putting information in a CAD or BIM-model. Instead we lifted the information [out of the model] and put it into databases". This is also commented on by the business manager of the ICT supplier when saying:

> The success with BIM has nothing to do with technology but instead it has to do with courage . . . [The WTT ICT board] decided to base the whole design and planning on a database that we built for them. It not only demands courage but trust with those you work with as it is not possible to fail on such a project [like the NKS].

Hence the ICT supplier emphasises the trust and commitment among actors on the project, especially between the WTT ICT board and the ICT supplier.

Spreading the new BIM platform to other projects and organisations

Both during and after the NKS project, there has been increased demand by construction actors for the new BIM-platform. The sales manager of the ICT-supplier describes it as:

> During 2012/2013 we notice an increased interest of our experiences of managing BIM-data. Many knew that we were engaged in the New Karolinska Solna and were interested in our solution to be used in their projects. To meet customers' demands we continued developing our cloud-based solution which resulted in [the BIM-platform] as we know it.

Currently more than 500 users of the BIM platform are spread among 150 customers on the Nordic ACE market. How did the use of the new BIM platform spread outside of the NKS?

The *spread of the new platform* can be illustrated and explained by the mobility of the actors involved in the NKS project. For example the head of the WTT ICT board was, after the NKS project, appointed as head of the BIM department within the public health care real estate organisation managing the health care facilities within Stockholm City Council. He was employed due to his experience working with the design and planning of health care facilities on the NKS project. Prior to the appointment of a new BIM manager, the organisation had already started digitalisation of existing facilities and drawings. With experience using BIM in NKS, it was decided to implement the new BIM platform in the organisation, resulting in the use of the BIM platform for all new health care projects in the Stockholm area. Similar illustrations of spreading the BIM platform to other projects through mobility of design and planning actors can be found in the Slussen project in Stockholm and the ESS facility in Lund where a majority of involved of design and planning actors had experiences from NKS. The spread and use of the BIM platform also reflect the size and impact of the NKS project in relation to BIM where 400 individuals were involved in the design and planning organisation, representing a large share of technical consultancy and architectural firms in Sweden. The mobility of the design and planning actors played an important role in diffusing the use of the BIM platform. But individual actors who already had an established relationship to the ICT supplier also facilitated the use of the new BIM platform on other projects and within other organisations. The BIM manager at White summarises the effects that the use of BIM in NKS had on construction actors in Sweden:

> NKS has been very instructive for the whole sector. New work practices have been developed and together with the collective experiences of many

involved actors spread [new practices] broadly to the sector. . . [W]hen there is interest, ambition and consensus you can come very far.

Analysing the use of BIM in NKS and its' innovative effects

The following analysis of the case concentrates on the four features influencing construction innovation identified by Blayse and Manley (2004) but interpreted from an IMP perspective. The following discussion will analyse the use of BIM and its innovative effects in NKS by discussing key actors, industrial relationships, resources and structure of production (i.e. projects).

Key actors and the use of BIM in NKS

We can identify several key actors involved in the use of BIM in NKS. To begin with, the use of BIM was initiated through the *client* who required delivery of information as BIM models, reflecting the importance of client demands, as emhasised by Blayse and Manley (2004). The client wanted to have the project delivered through BIM to facilitate the operations of the future facilities. The client demands, however, resulted in indirect and unintentional effects that can be considered as renewal effects, much as described by Havenvid et al. (2016). Foremost, the decision to use BIM affected another key actor group, the *design and planning actors*, especially through the establishment of the *WTT group* and the new actor constellation, in particular the *WTT ICT board* – a constellation responsible for managing the digital information of the project. The board consisted of experienced and well known BIM managers representing various disciplines. These individual actors were 'acknowledged' by the network of actors, especially within the design and planning organisation and the WTT group as having the required experience, competence and knowledge to set up BIM methodologies and implementation of BIM in NKS. The individual actors were not selected randomly but as the most experienced individuals. Hence the WTT ICT board became a key actor constellation in steering the use of BIM in NKS. With their experiences and their connections to other actors, they could 'mobilise' and convince other actors within the design and planning organisation to implement BIM as an integrated function within design and planning. This required increased interaction and communication among the project actors. Thus it is evident that the use of BIM as a new technology impacts multiple actors, actors who are not only passive receivers but to a large extent collectively determine how the technology is used, adapted and for what purposes (cf. Harty and Arajou, 2009; Håkansson and Waluszewski, 2009).

The *ICT supplier* also had a large impact on how BIM was used in NKS. The case displayed the supplier's central role in using BIM in Sweden on a general level as the actor already had a significant network position due to connections to all large construction actors prior to the project. Through the established network position, the supplier could 'mobilise' other actors in the network and the project itself (Håkansson et al., 2009). The established network position becomes extra visible in relation to the development of the new digital platform. Trust and commitment already existed between the ICT supplier and main actors in the WTT ICT board, which facilitated the decision to jointly develop a new platform. Engagement in joint new developments facilitated by prior interaction has also been verified by other scholars such as Crespin-Mazet, Havenvid and Linné (2015). It can also be noted that some of the main individual actors in the WTT board had previously worked at the ICT supplier in establishing Revit as a new BIM tool in Sweden ten years prior to NKS. In spreading the use of the new digital platform to other projects and organisations, the involved key actors and their pre-existing network connections, especially the design and planning organisation, the WTT group and the WTT ICT board, played a crucial role. With the extent of individuals involved, the mobilisation of other organisations and subsequent projects assisted the transformation on the platform from an invention (in NKS) to an innovation, i.e. widespread use outside of NKS (cf. Rosenberg, 1982).

The preceding discussion concerning key actors in influencing the use of BIM in NKS clearly reflects that identified key actors in the project did not enter the project as 'blank sheets' but had already established competences, experiences and knowledge from prior interaction processes that was activated in NKS.

Activated relationships and the use of BIM in NKS

Several established relationships are also present in the case influencing the use of BIM and resulting in innovative effects in and 'outside of' NKS. Thus established relationships constitute a possibility for establishing use of new technology, and new solutions in the case. The long-term relationship between the ICT supplier and the design and planning actors, especially the WTT ICT board, was activated in NKS and resulted in the joint development of the new digital platform in the case. The content of the relationship between the ICT supplier and the main project actors in the board acted as a main determinant of even daring to engage in the development and use of the new platform. Without pre-existing trust and commitment, this may not have been possible. To conclude, the pre-existing relationship facilitated initiating new development, but during the project the relationship also developed and changed and resulted in new ways to organise project work and thus create a joint understanding of the use of BIM in NKS.

The preceding discussion reflects that the actions of individual actors and their possibilities to engage in change processes extend beyond the individual project. The industrial relationships in the NKS case can be characterised as tightly coupled within the project, but these tight couplings also play an important role during its sleeping phases, between projects (Hadjikhani, 1996). The relationships become important when reactivated on individual projects that facilitated the use of technology and new work practices. In accordance with Havenvid et al. (2016), relationships become carriers of learning, knowledge and innovation over time and space.

Activated resources and the use of BIM in NKS

The combining of resources across organisations was a prerequisite for the new digital platform to come to life in the NKS project. It was a solution developed with resources such as knowledge, facilities within the ICT supplier, established during a long period. The WTT ICT board, on the other hand, had extensive experience and knowledge in specifying BIM methodologies and in developing requirements in terms of BIM. The actual BIM platform was developed through the joint combination of the technical specification and methodology developed by the WTT ICT board and the technical set-up of the database performed by the ICT supplier. Combining resources from both actors resulted in a solution consisting of 17 different BIM models, connected to a room function database. These were, in turn, connected to other digital resources such as IT systems and existing BIM tools such as Revit, Tekla and MagicCad. The interconnectivity between the BIM platform and other information systems and IT tools was important during the development of the new solution.

The combining of resources reveals that the new digital platform became not only related to the internal resources of the ICT supplier but also connected to resources (both organisational and physical/technical) belonging to the WTT ICT board and IT systems belonging to other organisations and companies.

Structure of production and use of BIM in NKS

The NKS project reflected influences from and interconnections with several previous projects, for instance the St Barts Hospital in London. The project context was special in NKS as the project was extreme in terms of both size and complexity. In order to manage this complex project, other prior projects were used for benchmarking and reference. Moreover, the involved design and planning actors – the WTT group, the WTT ICT board and ICT suppliers – had extensive experience from a whole range of projects prior to NKS. Experience, competencies and resources developed in prior projects were combined and (re) activated in NKS. Without these prior projects, it would have been difficult to establish the extensive use of BIM in NKS and also difficult to develop the new digital platform. The large project budget also facilitated the use of BIM and engagement in innovative activities in NKS. The BIM manager of Tengbom expresses it: "There is no budget in the small projects to learn and develop new work practices as you cannot procure the new work practices [as they do not exist], instead you have to have time to learn and it is in the large projects where you have to opportunity to do that". As a consequence, large BIM projects like NKS constitute a good context for experimenting and learning among the involved actors (cf. Principe and Tell, 2001; Scarbrough et al., 2004). They are also good contexts from which to spread what has been learnt to other subsequent projects due to the large number of actors involved, and this is especially evident in relation to the spread of the new digital platform through subsequent engagement of actors involved in NKS.

The discussion of the project context of NKS and its impact on BIM clearly reveals that NKS is closely connected to past, present and future projects in terms of the actors involved, as well as how they combine and recombine their resources and activities over time.

Concluding remarks: connectivity as a possibility for use of new technology

The aim of the chapter was to understand how the use of new technology, such as BIM, drives renewal and innovation in construction. More specifically, it asks under what circumstances does the use of new technology happen and how is it spread in construction? The case of NKS reflects that use of technology in construction relies to a high degree on the connectivity patterns between various construction actors and their established and associated resources and activities in the network. The possibility to impact and influence the use of the technology along a certain trajectory relates significantly to how actors mobilise other actors through their pre-existing relationships. Key actors are acknowledged and legitimised through connections to others in the network, and, by being acknowledged by others, they can convince those others of the benefits of a new technology and facilitate the use of it (cf. Håkansson and Waluszewski, 2007; Håkansson and Waluszewski, 2009).

The preceding analysis is separated into the four features identified by Blayse and Manley (2004). However it is clear that these features are interconnected through interactivity of the business landscape as implied by the IMP perspective (Håkansson, 1987; Håkansson and Snehota, 1995). The features are thus to a large extent interactive and dependent on one another. Key actors need established relationships to mobilise other actors and create continuity across several projects, which will influence how BIM is used, adjusted and spread in the network. The connectivity between actors and their associated resources and activities relates to past, present and future interaction processes that stretch across both organisations and projects, resulting in inter-organisational and inter-project connections. It is also due to these connections that the use of technology cause "wakes of innovation" (Boland, Lyytinen and Yoo, 2007) and "renewal effects" (Havenvid et al., 2016) that spread beyond NKS.

If BIM and other digital tools can enhance project activities and improve the construction process, it is important to understand the introduction and implementing of new technology as a non-linear process characterised by high complexity and difficulty. For instance, there has to be willingness to implement and use technology, and the technology needs to be adjusted to the specific project context through established connections among actors in the network. This can cause 'unintended', 'uncontrollable' and 'unforeseen' effects, solving some problems but giving rise to others.

References

Ayas, K. and Zeniuk, N. (2001) 'Project-based learning: Building communities of reflective practitioners', *Management Learning*, 32(1), pp. 61–76.

Blayse, A.M. and Manley, K. (2004) 'Key influences on construction innovation', *Construction Innovation*, 4(3), pp. 143–154.

Boland, R.J., Lyytinen, K. and Yoo, Y. (2007) 'Wakes of innovation in project networks: The case of digital 3D representations in architecture, engineering, and construction', *Organization Science*, 18(4), pp. 631–647.

Brady, T. and Davies, A. (2004) 'Building project capabilities, from exploratory to exploitative learning', *Organization Studies*, 25(9), pp. 1601–1621.

Brandon, P., Li, H. and Shen, Q. (2005) 'Construction IT and the "tipping point"', *Automation in Construction*, 14(3), pp. 281–286.

Bresnen, M. and Marshall, N. (2000) 'Building partnerships: Case studies of client–contractor collaboration in the UK construction industry', *Construction Management and Economics*, 18(7), pp. 819–832.

Bryde, D., Broquetas, M. and Volm, J. (2013) 'The project benefits of Building Information Modeling (BIM)', *International Journal of Project Management*, 31, pp. 971–980.

Crespin-Mazet, F., Havenvid, M.I. and Linné, Å. (2015) 'Antecedents of project partnering', *Industrial Marketing Management*, 50(October), pp. 4–15.

Dainty, A., Briscoe, G. and Millet, S. (2001) 'New perspectives on construction supply chain integration', *Supply Chain Management: An International Journal*, 6(4), pp. 163–173.

Davies, R. and Harty, C. (2013) 'Implementing "Site BIM": A case study of ICT innovation on a large hospital project', *Automation in Construction*, 30(1), pp. 15–24.

Dubois, A. and Araujo, L. (2007) 'Case research in purchasing and supply management: Opportunities and challenges', *Journal of Purchasing and Supply Management*, 13(3), pp. 170–181.

Dubois, A. and Gadde, L.-E. (2002) 'The construction industry as a loosely coupled system: Implications for productivity and innovation', *Construction Management and Economics*, 20(7), pp. 621–632.

Gann, D.M. and Salter, A.J. (2000) 'Innovation in project-based, service-enhanced firms: The construction of complex products and systems', *Research Policy*, 29(7–8), pp. 955–972.

Hadjikhani, A. (1996) 'Project marketing and the management of discontinuity', *International Business Review*, 5(3), pp. 319–336.

Håkansson, H. (1987) *Industrial technological development. A network approach*. London: Croom Helm.

Håkansson, H. and Snehota, I. (1995). *Developing relationships in business networks*. London: Routledge.

Håkansson, H., Ford, D., Gadde, L.-E., Snehota, I. and Waluszewski, A. (2009) *Business in networks*. Sussex: John Wiley & Sons.

Håkansson, H. and Ingemansson, M. (2013) 'Industrial renewal within the construction network', *Construction Management and Economics*, 31(1), pp. 40–61.

Håkansson, H. and Waluszewski, A. (eds.) (2007) *Knowledge and innovation in business and industry – The importance of using others*. London: Routledge.

Håkansson, H. and Waluszewski, A (2009) 'Introduction: Use of science and technology in business', in Håkansson, H., Waluszewski, A., Baraldi, E. and Prenkert, F. (eds.), *Use of Science and Technology in Business*. Bingley: Emerald Group.

Halinen, A. and Törnroos, J-Å. (2005) 'Using case methods in the study of contemporary business networks', *Journal of Business Research*, 58(9), pp. 1285–1297.

Harrisson, D., Holmen, A.-C. and Pedersen, E. (2010) 'How companies strategise deliberately in networks using strategic initiatives', *Industrial marketing Management*, 39(6), pp. 947–955.

Hartmann, A. (2006) 'The context of innovation management in construction firms', *Construction Management and Economics*, 24(6), pp. 567–578.

Hartmann, T., Gao, J. and Fisher, M. (2008) 'Areas of application for 3D and 4D models on construction projects', *Journal of Construction Engineering*, 134(10).

Harty, C (2005) 'Innovation in construction: A sociology of technology approach', *Building Research and Information*, 33(6), pp. 512–522.

Harty, C. and Arajou, L. (2009) 'Aligning user practices in innovation: The case of Heathrow's Terminal 5 project', in Håkansson, H., Waluszewski, A., Baraldi, E. and Prenkert, F. (eds.), *Use of Science and Technology in Business*. Bingley: Emerald Group.

Havenvid, M.I., Hulthén, K., Linné, Å. and Sundquist, V. (2016) 'Renewal in construction projects: Tracing effects of client requirements', *Construction Management and Economics*, 34(1), pp. 790–807.

Holmen, E., Pedersen, A.-C. and Torvatn, T. (2005) 'Construction relationships for technological innovation', *Journal of Business Research*, 58(9), pp. 1240–1250.

Ingemansson, M. (2010) 'Success as science but burden for business? – On the difficult relationship between scientific advancement and innovation', doctoral thesis, Uppsala University, Uppsala.

Ivory, C. (2005) 'The cult of customer responsiveness: Is design innovation the price of a client-focused construction industry?' *Construction Management and Economics*, 23(8), pp. 861–870.

Kokkonen, A. and Alin, P. (2016) 'Practioners deconstructing and reconstructuring practives when responding to the implementation of BIM', *Construction Management and Economics*, 34(7), 578–591.

Linderoth, H.C. (2010) 'Understanding adoption and use of BIM as the creation of actor networks', *Automation in Construction*, 19, pp. 66–72.

Linné, Å. (2012) 'China's creation of biopharmaceutical drugs: Combining political steering, militaryresearch, and transnational networking', doctoral thesis, Uppsala University, Uppsala.

Linné, Å. and Shih, T. (2016) 'The coordinating role of Chinese policy actors in developing new biotechnology start-up companies to promote industrial development', in Aaboen, L., La Rocca, A., Lind, F. Perna, A. and Shih, T. (eds.), *Starting Up in Business Networks – Why Relationships Matter in Entrepreneurship*. London: Palgrave.

Nam, C.H. and Tatum, C.B. (1997) 'Leaders and champions for construction innovation', *Construction Management and Economics*, 15(3), pp. 259–270.

Peansupap, V. and Walker, D. (2005) 'Exploratory factors influencing ICT diffusion and adoption within Australian construction organisations: A micro analysis', *Journal of Construction Innovation*, 5(3), pp. 135–157.

Penrose, E.T. (1959) *The theory of the growth of the firm*. Oxford: Basil Blackwell.

Principe, A. and Tell, F. (2001) 'Inter-project learning: Processes and outcomes of knowledge codification in project-based firms', *Research Policy*, 30(9), pp. 1373–1394.

Rosenberg, N. (1982) *Inside the black box: Technology and economics*. Cambridge: Cambridge University Press.

Scarbrough, H., Swan, J., Laurent, S., Bresnen, M., Edelman, L. and Newell, S. (2004), 'Project-based learning and the role of learning boundaries', *Organization Studies*, 25(9), pp. 1579–1600.

Slaughter, S. (1993) 'Builders as sources of construction innovation', *Journal of Construction Engineering and Management*, 119(3), pp. 532–549.

Succar, B. (2009) 'Building information modelling framework: A research and delivery foundation for industry stakeholders', *Automation in Construction*, 18(3), pp. 357–375.

Tennant, S. and Fernie, S. (2014) 'Theory to practice: A typology of supply chain management in construction', *International Journal of Construction Management*, 14(1), pp. 72–87.

Winch, G.M. (2003) 'Models of manufacturing and the construction process: The genesis of re-engineering construction', *Building Research and Information*, 31(2), pp. 107–118.

Won, J., Lee, G., Dossick, C. and Messner, J. (2013) 'Where to focus for successful adoption of building information modeling within organization', *Journal of Construction Engineering and Management*, 139(11).

4 Entrepreneurial innovation in the construction sector

Will Hughes and Lars Stehn

Introduction

The design and construction processes create a complex supply chain in the construction sector. Because of the complex, inter-firm networks, the supply chain is fragmented. This results in process discontinuities horizontally, as the project passes through stages of work from one group of actors to another. In addition, it involves process discontinuities vertically, as work of all kinds is subcontracted, often in multiple layers (Hughes, Gray and Murdoch, 1997). This complex network of contracts is significant. It occurs not only because of the way that the process is usually organized but also because of the high level of risk attached to much of the work. Regardless of the type of contract, horizontal process discontinuities, accentuated by contractual obligations, are an inherent part of this network. These discontinuities have an impact on communications among stakeholders, specifically communications that enable or inhibit innovation. Our focus is primarily on how these process discontinuities help or hinder the development and use of technological innovations in building, both as a process and as a product. There are several simultaneous reasons for the occurrence of these significant discontinuities in the process, making it a seriously difficult problem to resolve.

With a focus on technological innovations in the building process and the building product, the key innovators are contractors and specialist subcontractors. To bring an innovative product to market in the construction sector, the innovator must overcome these discontinuities, especially in the horizontal dimension where different organizations are responsible for only part of a project. The discontinuities between demand for the building, specification of the building and installation of materials, components or equipment seem to be of specific importance as inhibitors to getting innovative technology to the market. The general contractor plays a pivotal role in coordinating the construction tasks and realizing a building. However, the practice of subcontracting most of the work results in construction firms with little need of capital assets; this results in a "hollowed-out firm" that does not own the means of production for the construction process (Green, Newcombe, Fernie and Weller, 2004). They are paid for work in progress and pay their subcontractors for work in progress, result-ing in a cash-flow business with few assets of its own. Indeed, Chiang and Cheng (2010) show that this leads to low barriers to entry for highly competitive firms with little access to finance, posing a major barrier to innovation. They conclude that this holds back industry development. These conventional structures result in tasks that are typically split into different firms through a network of contracts. The institutional infrastructure of professional roles, standard-form contracts and traditional business models creates a lot of inertia and conservatism in the sector. The logic of contractors as hollowed-out firms is that actors operate only within a specific task or within a specific phase of the project. The business model depends on the suppliers of technology being subcontractors to cash-flow businesses with little in the way of assets, especially by comparison to the projects they build. The route to getting materials and components into a project involves contracts being set up with specifications of what is required before a supplier of technology is identified. This is both a horizontal and a vertical discontinuity. It is horizontal because the specification is drafted at one stage and the installer identified at a later stage. It is vertical because the installer is (frequently) a subcontractor to a contractor who was not involved in writing the specification. It might be said that it is difficult to conceive of a more effective way of *preventing* entrepreneurs with technological innovations from introducing their ideas into the buildings they are contracted to contribute to. This phenomenon of the hollowed-out firm is an unintended consequence of the contemporary approach to construction contracting. It is the first obstruction to innovation.

The major horizontal discontinuity between design decisions and construction decisions has long been recognized in reports on the UK construction industry (Emmerson, 1962; Banwell, 1964; Latham, 1994; Egan, 1998), which all com-mented on the discontinuity between the design and construction process. Less obvious and perhaps more impactful are the discontinuities at all the other stages in the overall process. The process runs from the need for development through to the operation of the completed facility. There may be discontinuities at every stage in this process, which could account for many of the issues that plague the construction sector and make it distinctly different from other industry sectors. For example, Hughes (1989), in four detailed case studies of the organization of UK public sector building projects, found that it was quite normal for a project to be in the capital planning stage for years until it becomes approved for expendi-ture, at which point, the entire project becomes the responsibility of others, with no further involvement from the capital planning team (and little access to all of the associated information and history about the funding decisions). These organizational characteristics of how projects progress from one stage to another form the second obstruction to innovation.

Discontinuities in the process may be further understood through the theo-retical framing of transaction cost economics (TCE) (Williamson, 1979), i.e. the 'make-or-buy' decision. TCE holds that such decisions will tend to be influenced by the differential costs of making vs. buying, all other things being equal. We argue that, while this may lead to a more economical decision for the buyer, when the result is to contract out, a supplier then takes on the responsibility for procuring the goods or services, and they, too, face a similar decision. In the construction sector, this often leads to the establishment of a series of contracting-out decisions, each of which is a rational and economic decision for the buyer of the subtransaction. The rationale is that specific resources cannot be retained in-house since the need for them varies a lot between one project and the next. In combination, these result in vertical discontinuities through multiple layers of subcontracting and horizontal discontinuities through handing responsibility from one organization to another at successive stages. This combination of vertical and horizontal discontinuities is suboptimal for the end user, who is far removed from the initiators of innovative and even speculative technologies. The successive, contracting-out decisions make it almost impossible for innovation to take place, if innovative entrepreneurs with ideas for new technological solutions are at the end of a long chain of subcontracts. The need for suppliers of construction goods and services to maintain continuity of use for their resources is a third obstruction to innovation.

One reason for the success and longevity of this discontinuous process is that construction often involves major decisions about capital development, where the price of land is the larger part of the equation, compared to the price of construction. Some developers of real estate lease their property and, in common with end users, often engage with long-term revenue and operational issues. However, many developers seek to sell the asset on completion. Thus, in many cases, the major decisions in development are driven by the optimization of transactions around capital acquisition. This favours a market structure that prevents optimization of transactions around operational acquisition through revenue. These two aspects of capital and revenue are familiar to anyone who is knowledgeable about construction. TCE alone does not account for the economic issues that prevent the construction industry from improving productivity and technological innovation. A business model focus provides specific questions that help to expose how the different business models required for the success of companies at each stage and layer of the process are fundamentally incongruent. It is this incongruence of business models that explains a widespread lack of construction industry development (see, for example, Pan and Goodier, 2012, addressing off-site construction take-up in relation to business models) and offers potential agendas for modernizing the industry. The role of construction in the development of real estate is a fourth obstruction to innovation.

The aim is to investigate how an innovative technology gets to the market and to examine how the multiple obstructions to innovation may be overcome in practice. Two theoretical bases are adopted: transaction cost economics (TCE) explains make-or-buy decisions at multiple tiers and business development (BD) explains how different companies in the process respond to the way that demand is put to them and how markets for products are developed. TCE provides the basis for modelling the contractual relationships that can be observed in and between a variety of construction firms. BD provides the empirical basis for interviewing one actor in Sweden, whose business is developed around the emergence of innovations and productivity improvements. We explore some key questions such as how the construction firm positions itself in the market, how clients put demand to the market, how markets are altered by innovators, and what entry points into the market are used by the innovator. These two theoretical framings help to deal with all four obstructions to technological innovation in construction.

Horizontal discontinuity in the process

While vertical discontinuity through subcontracting is well known and virtually indispensable in construction contracting (see, for example, Hughes, Hillebrandt, Greenwood and Kwawu, 2006); less is written about horizontal discontinuity. Essentially, horizontal discontinuity is about the specific stages through which all projects must progress, involving handoffs from one organization (or one part of an organization) to another, sometimes with overlaps and not always in the same sequence. These main stages approximate to:

- *Developing*: Someone with some real estate to develop or acquire
- *Funding*: Needed to pay for the development, perhaps also for the land
- *Designing*: Figuring out, defining and documenting what is needed
- *Managing construction*: Coordinating the construction work
- *Installing*: Installing equipment and carrying out construction work by specialists
- *Servicing*: Heating, lighting, ventilation, etc.
- *Operating*: Facility operation, not usually the remit of construction sector

The idea of horizontal discontinuity is that a different organization may be responsible for a part of a project at each of these stages. Some stages may be done in-house by certain types of organization, but even then sometimes different parts of the organization are responsible for carrying out the work. And, within this sequence of stages, there will, inevitably, be contracting-out, i.e. vertical discontinuity, as the mix of specialized resources required is different in each project, and, as stated earlier, it is uneconomic to keep them all in-house as they cannot be kept continuously busy due to the variety and variance in the building projects.

At each stage, work is subcontracted, and suppliers are enrolled into a project through a variety of contracting techniques. It is common to subcontract, and values up to 70% of the contract sum are not uncommon in housebuilding (Johnsson, 2013); moreover, it makes sense to do so because of the continuity of work. However, this involves putting the demand to the market such that parties may negotiate the terms of their contract (usually via competitive tendering) on assumptions about the kind of technology that will be eventually installed. This dominant approach to construction procurement is based on economic, organizational and business practices that unintentionally conspire to prevent innovative technologies getting to the market. Of course, in the construction management literature, these issues have long been recognized as significant. Because of this recognition, a variety of techniques have been developed in many countries for overcoming various kinds of discontinuity:

- Direct relationships with suppliers as in construction management procurement (see Hughes, Champion and Murdoch, 2015, pp. 69–79)
- Integrated project delivery (Fischer, Ashcraft, Read and Khanzode, 2017)
- Integrated supply chains (Cox and Ireland, 2002)
- Early contractor involvement (Gil, Tommelein and Ballard, 2004; Song, Mohamed and AbouRizk, 2009)
- Nominated subcontracting (Hughes et al., 1997; Hughes et al., 2015, pp. 81–92)
- Partnering (extra-contractual) and strategic alliances (Black, Akintoye and Fitzgerald, 2000)

One message that comes out clearly from the research cited in the list is that the most effective means of overcoming discontinuity is in creating a direct relationship between the client and the producer. Alternatively, it is about overcoming the problem caused by the lack of such a direct relationship through one or more of the preceding integrating techniques, some of which require resource and effort to bring them about. Something that is often not emphasized in the literature is that the client is not always the employer of contractor and the contractor is not always the producer of the technology. Thus, there will often be horizontal discontinuity between the end user and the supplier of a specific technology.

In many cases, the specification of the work to be done is contracted out to a design team. Typically, they are not part of the same organization as the contractor or subcontractor. The client of the process may be an end user, unknown at the time of designing and producing the building. Even if the end user is in direct contract with the contractor, the work tends to be mostly subcontracted to others, who subcontract again and buy their materials and components from a network of builders' merchants. The merchants compete on selling catalogue items where the competitive advantage is price. The range of items is limited to reduce overheads and remain competitive. The sub-subcontractor is not motivated or incentivized to buy anything but the cheapest product for installation, unless their contract specifies precisely what they are to install, through one of the contractual techniques for overcoming the process discontinuity.

In some cases, particularly in sectors other than construction, rather than contracting out the labour, a customer may just buy something in an instantaneous transaction. This transaction involves the supplier in all aspects of design, labour, manufacture and production. For this transaction to happen, the supplier must have been engaged in product development in the expectation of finding a customer, perhaps with this specific customer. A question that arises is how could the seller maximize the benefits of using innovative product development before the event of establishing a contractual relationship? Let us illustrate this with an imaginary example. This example concerns the plight of an imaginary, specialist engineering design company who has a new product that they wish to bring to market. To develop such a product, investment is needed. Finding customers requires contact with those responsible for making decisions in a project. If the designers and contractor are contracted to a client, the situation is difficult. The client has delegated to the design team decisions about what to build. The designers have professional indemnity insurance that precludes them from specifying untried technologies; the contractor makes decisions about whom to buy from based on their own supply chain and tendering processes. This leaves the innovative product designer with no route to market. So how do innovative technologies in construction find their way to market in the light of the process discontinuities described so far?

The problem we confront is that the specification of specialist technical work often takes place at a point that is either too early or too late, caused by the horizontal discontinuities present in all projects and exacerbated by vertical discontinuities in the supply chain. This seems to preclude the technology provider from influencing the choices that are made about what to incorporate into a building. Technology providers are brought into a project via a contract, and technology procurers must decide whether to make or buy each kind of technology that is to be incorporated. Thus, the opportunities for introducing innovative technology into buildings are compromised by both kinds of discontinuities in many or most projects. A key question is, therefore, how an innovative technology gets to market.

Conceptual framework

Transaction cost economics

The ideas for this research are, essentially, rooted in transaction cost economics (TCE). While this is not an analytical basis of the research reported here, it provides a useful context for some of the key issues. A series of ideas are brought together in TCE.

- TCE analysis involves considering the cost of tendering vs. costs of employment. All things being equal (ceteris paribus) the balance between these costs will dictate the choice that is made. In the construction sector, the difference between making and buying results in a serious inequality in the extent to which resources are kept fully occupied. Due to the diverse nature of buildings, the requirements for skills and materials are not consistent across projects. This makes production very inefficient for a main contractor who seeks to keep the resources in-house. Thus, they can successfully keep one trade in-house, such as concrete or steel, but no more than that. The flow of work must be regulated to keep that in-house resource fully occupied and the other resources are subcontracted. The practice is so widespread at all stages and levels of construction that the result is a complex contractual network, or a "nexus of contracts" (Reve and Levitt, 1984). The involvement of different participants through contracts between businesses rather than contracts of employment only serves to exacerbate the discontinuities between organizational units.

- It is not claimed that firms make TCE calculations but that "the invisible hand of the market" (as discussed in Thornton, 2009) means that common business practices emerge because of natural self-interest and the market mechanisms of profits and prices (among other things). For example, firms who choose unwisely will be uncompetitive and inevitably go bankrupt. This is a compelling argument, but what if practices have become so entrenched, there is no competitive opposition to customary practices in the organization of projects?
- TCE analysis involves considering costs under a range of headings. Hughes et al. (2006) listed these as market costs (buyers and sellers searching for information about each other); contract preparation costs (specifying requirements, choosing suppliers, fixing a price); monitoring and supervision costs (ensuring that what is being produced matches the specification); and dispute resolution costs (dealing with nonconformances). These costs are extremely variable, difficult to capture and *very small in relation to production costs*. Therefore, it is not the costs of transactions that are significant but the specificity of assets that creates the economic difference between make-or-buy decisions.
- The narrative around TCE also involves ideas of bounded rationality, opportunism, hold-ups and information asymmetry. It is held that these ideas may also account for why the make-or-buy decision is sometimes problematic, but, for our purposes, they do not define the discontinuities; in the process, they merely compound them.

The construction sector seems to be characterized by a series of regular problems such as change orders, claims for extensions of time and for loss and/or expense. It may be misleading to characterize them as problems, since they are often a solution to a more profound problem, which, in its simplest sense, is the impossibility of predicting the future or creating certainty of information. Moreover, frequent problems are brought about because of the discontinuities introduced into the construction process through subcontracting. One key problem is that there is a time lag between creating the specification for construction work to be put to the market (tendering with general contractors) and carrying out the work of installation by subcontractors. Worse, the subcontractors who are installing complex equipment that requires detailed design and specification are faced with the difficulty of coordinating this information with the design team. Third, the responsibilities for deciding the specification of the building require the decisions about what to build to be taken by a design team, the decisions about who is to install the equipment to be taken by the main contractor and the decisions about how to install it to be taken by the subcontractor. Fourth, construction planning and cost planning are surely instrumental in managing projects to a predictable conclusion. However, the traditional focus in contracting requires a focus on time, cost and quality, apparently to the exclusion of overarching agendas, such as stakeholder management, health and safety law, environmental impact and intermittent supply of resources. These other agendas often lead to the basic scope requirements being missed, since they impose inescapable obligations on contractors and other suppliers. Importantly, the responsibility for the means of production does not lie with the actors who are taking the decisions about design specification or subcontractor selection. Given this, TCE provides some insights into how and why construction work is organized the way it is. Essentially, the problems caused by the necessary separation of work into different organizational units are heightened when each organizational unit is a different firm enrolled through a transaction. This sets up the complex nexus of contracts scoped on a small subset of the governance issues in projects. Ultimately, it is this that presents the major coordination and control issues. A contractual, transaction-based focus alone does not provide a sufficiently rich picture for overcoming the lack of innovation and low productivity that we often see in construction. A fuller picture requires a broader focus, such as that offered by the business development literature.

Business development in construction

Parts of a business development framework provide additional insights for this work by offering a business model lens. The aspects of how business models explain the operation of the kind of firms considered in this work are as follows:

- A business model conceptualization considers how actors define the market they operate in. At the centre of market position is value creation for customers and customer satisfaction but also the ability to be a legitimate actor in the business and institutional networks in the market. Following Brege, Stehn and Nord (2014), market positions are related to customers but also to the business network and the surrounding institutional network. Indicators for how market position is attained are the customer and market segmentation/specialization and the role in the building process (or, in generic terms, supply chain). From a client point of view, the business model notion of 'offering' boils down to how clients present demand to the construction market.
- Salient business model literature (e.g. Zott and Amit, 2007), following Mintzberg's (1983) notations about fit and congruence, view the business model as the moneymaking logic and the 'blueprint' of how companies operate. Firms that do not consider the internal and external fit between the business model and the business environment (congruence) and between the business model elements and connections between the offering and market position to the source of funding for their work ultimately become uncompetitive.
- The contingency idea of a fit business model may also help to explain how firms define and organize their supply chains.

Construction businesses tend not to provide entire buildings to their customers, except in certain markets, such as housebuilding and commercial developments.

There are many examples of so-called turnkey projects where the idea is that a buyer finds a seller who will indeed provide everything (Lessing, Stehn and Ekholm, 2015). Most construction projects are not provided on a turnkey basis. The client has a make-or-buy decision that may be made at any point in the process, not simply at the first point of contact with the construction sector. Some clients carry out their own design, some coordinate their own construction sites, some provide and install their own specialist equipment, and some provide their own building services and operational aspects of the finished building. Some take on the responsibility for procuring stages of the process themselves rather than asking a firm to take control of the whole process. Generally, large portions of the work are procured from the market, using suppliers who have developed an expertise in the relevant area. It is for the supply companies to consider what stages of the process they are providing and how they identify clients, secure contracts and set prices. This is what their business development activities entail. The point here is that it is difficult to make assumptions about how a project is being procured, even after a construction client has taken the procurement decision. Further, different types of firms in the process have distinct and different business models.

In summary, the TCE framework helps us to understand why the complex contract network occurs, and the business model framework helps us to understand how each business operates within the contract network.

Research question

There is an empirical question that arises from this discussion. Multiple contractual interfaces exacerbate the discontinuities throughout the stages and layers of the process. These interfaces create a focus on contractual deliverables rather than fulfilling client and end-user needs with the best possible solution. In this context, how does an innovative construction technology get to market? To put this more simply, what would the construction process look like if those discontinuities were removed? Would innovation become a regular part of such a process, as the discussion implies? Does horizontal and vertical integration involve different business models? Following contingency reasoning, there is no one best way to organize (Woodward, 1965), so what happens in different forms of organization? Under what circumstances can an innovative product be introduced into the design and construction processes? What kind of processes exist, and are they amenable to the introduction of new products?

Again, TCE provides an interesting insight into the operation of markets when work is contracted out, as discussed in Hughes et al. (2006, pp. 16–20). To recap: for a buyer to approach the market, they need to carry out the work of ascertaining what is available to buy in the market. On the other hand, the seller needs to put information out into the market for buyers to discover. Second, there are costs associated with the task of negotiating the deal, specifying the work, choosing the supplier (perhaps through competition) and settling the terms of the contract. Third, the work must be monitored by the buyer to ensure that it conforms with the specifications. Finally, there are dispute resolution costs. The latter are not relevant in this paper. The point of the TCE argument is that it helps in identifying how the market operates. It raises interesting questions about how buyers find sellers, and sellers find buyers. In many markets, this is straightforward, but, in the construction supply chain, there are added complexities. The processes that are described in TCE provide the context for the business models of those firms operating in the construction sector. TCE is about the transactional interfaces in the market; business models are about how a firm within the market operates.

Much of the literature on TCE focuses on interfaces around a single organization (e.g. Williamson, 1979). Similarly, much of the literature on business models focuses on how a single business organizes itself in relation to a market (Osterwalder, Pigneur and Tucci, 2005; Zott and Amit, 2007). From a production point of view, what defines construction is the project-based type of production where the key points about construction work are that:

- Construction tends to be a production factor for its customers;
- The organization of construction is about the relationships between temporary and complex network of firms (the temporary multiorganization discussed by Cherns and Bryant, 1984), held together with a network of contracts (Hughes et al., 2015), that creates complex interdependencies between organizations often lacking a single authoritative actor putting demands for or allowing for innovations (Harty, 2008, p. 1032);
- The process occupies significant periods of time, which makes it difficult to predict the outcome;
- The inputs and outputs of construction represent significant proportions of the annual turnover of buyers and sellers. This means, potentially, that every project, every transaction for some parties, has the possibility of threatening the business survival of every participant.

To investigate the questions effectively, it is useful to reduce the variables. The empirical work for this research will focus on discovering and describing the business model and innovative tendencies for one case study company in a specific market. As an example, we focus on a Swedish housebuilding firm with an unconventional form of organization. Using the three-element business model construct of Brege et al. (2014), we sought empirical data on:

- *The offering*: Market into which they are selling, price determination and revenue/capital mix;
- *Market position*: Supply chain relationships and contractual interfaces;
- *Operational platform*: Forms of organization.

These elements are interconnected in the business model approach. The empirical questions are around whether certain combinations of these business model elements are associated with the emergence of innovations in the case study firm.

Empirical questions

Leaning on the TCE and BD frameworks leads to a series of practical questions. In examining the activities of a firm in the construction sector, these questions evolve into an analytical framework. The purpose is to examine the way that this construction firm defines its market(s). We want to understand how they position themselves and what kind of supply chains they set up. By investigating a range of projects in the firm, the aim is to identify the points at which the client approaches the construction firm. Thus, the questions that provided direction for the case study were:

1   How does the construction firm strategize and position itself in the market?

- For each market, how do they find buyers?
- To what extent does each market involve subcontracting?
- How does the firm introduce its own productivity-enhancing innovations in the supply chain, in each market it operates in?

2   How do clients present demand in this specific construction market?
3   What are the processes of market making, marketing and business development?

Empirical case

The selection of the case study company involved identifying a firm in Sweden whose business is developed around improved productivity and technological innovation. Data collection is a combination of secondary data published by the company in relation to how they see their own market position and interviews with directors of the firms to clarify and augment this information and ascertaining the details of specific innovation introduction incidents. Transcribed interview data was examined for specific innovations that result from how the firm positions itself in the market, especially in relation to entry points for innovative solutions.

The focus of the interviews has, therefore, more to do with barriers and enablers in the organization of the process (horizontal discontinuity) and the supply-chain fragmentation (vertical discontinuity) than with the definition of the innovation per se. We argue that, to bring an innovative product to the market, the innovator must overcome these discontinuities. Successive contracting-out decisions may make it almost impossible for innovation to take place, such that innovation and productivity rely on a series of interconnected (and potentially incompatible) business models, potentially different for each firm in the supply chain. By selecting a firm that seems to operate without these discontinuities, the arguments in this paper would lead us to expect to see easier paths for innovation.

The case of Lindbäcks Bygg

Lindbäcks Bygg is a family-owned business. The original business, in the first generation (from 1924) of Lindbäcks, was a small sawmill. The emerging contracting business was separated from the sawmilling business in 1948, and in 1964 Lindbäcks Bygg was formed and worked as a local construction company. In 1982, they developed a planar-wooden-elements method of construction. In 1992, during in the Swedish Big Recession, Lindbäcks Bygg decided to move most of their on-site work inside a factory and then transport completed units to the building site. Lindbäcks Bygg constructs multistorey dwellings in timber, and the first project was built in 1994. About 11,000 units have been built to date. A substantial part of the engineering work and assembly work on-site are made by their own personnel. Depending on the geographical market, Lindbäcks' own personnel do all the assembly work on-site; in other geographical markets, about 70% of the assembly work may be subcontracted. However, the proportion of their own work (assembly and design/engineering) is steadily increasing, but exact figures are not known. In 1994, everything was built for their own real estate company. Nowadays, about 70% of the production output is sold as projects, preferably under long-term partnerships and as a main contractor, and about 30% to their own real estate company, where the real estate company deals directly with the end users.

Lindbäcks Bygg concentrates its total business around a series of technological and process innovations collected into their building system platform. At the centre of the technology and productivity-driven platform are the volumetric elements. The volumetric elements consist of wall, floor and ceiling elements assembled into a closed three-dimensional structure and various support systems. The volumetric elements are as complete as possible, including interior finishing, before being transported to the construction site. Every house is unique for each developer/contractor, but the platform is always the same. Substantial improvements to refine the platform in both specific methods employed as component and technical developments have taken place over the years. Based on a working method for experience feedback, the gradual refinement of the platform has been concentrated on supporting IT systems, investments in automation of the production lines and business development, i.e. forming subsidiary specialized product companies (for bathroom pods, balconies etc.).

The market-restraining factor is the need to convince real estate owners (other than themselves) to buy houses in this way. The traditional house in Sweden still tends to be a concrete house based on the developer/contractor specifications. Lindbäcks has to get into contract with a developer/contractor very early in the development processes, so that their requirements (thermal performance, balconies, height of building etc.) can be met by Lindbäcks' platform requirements. The game changer, or key selling point (much dependent on the developer/contractor's choice of facade), is the payment method. The customer pays 90% of the settled price when Lindbäcks starts the assembly process on the building site. The remaining 10% is paid when tenants start moving in. The customer needs only a very short-term building loan to finance the construction part of the project, usually only four or five months (the time on-site is dependent on the choice of the type of facade). Since most of the work (about 75%) includes all resources put into the pre-work (winning projects, pre-design and the substantial part of pre-manufacturing in the factory), Lindbäcks has a bank guarantee to protect themselves against non-payment in case of the customer, for example, becoming insolvent.

Analysis of Lindbäcks Bygg

Lindbäcks Bygg has all but eliminated the horizontal and vertical discontinuities between stages and layers of the process of work that typifies the construction process, especially when they are suppliers to their own real estate business.
This means that finding a customer and securing funding for a development is in
their own hands. Thus, they control the demand for the products. By developing
the off-site, volumetric-wooden-elements method of construction, they bring the
fundamentals of the design and specification process in-house, removing the traditional horizontal discontinuity between responsibility for design and responsibility for construction. By making fully finished volumetric units in their factory,
they have complete control over the installation of the technological equipment
in the completed buildings. This control of the means of production has also
removed barriers for innovative product development, whether by themselves or
by other suppliers/installers. By subcontracting specialist products to subsidiary
specialized companies (for example, for whole bathroom pods), they control the
specification and quality of the more complex technological aspects of the house.
And by operating as a landlord, they are dealing directly with the final consumer
of the product, i.e. the tenant. This provides them with direct feedback on the
performance of their buildings. This results in an integrated process with very
few contractual interfaces, limited to interfaces with subsidiary companies. It is
a single integrated company that owns, and takes responsibility for, its entire
supply chain, one way or another, dealing directly with end users, Lindbäcks
Bygg represents an archetype for the idea of completely removing discontinuities
in the processes that surround construction and development. Thus, they have
opportunities for technological innovation that are more far-reaching than those
available to most construction companies, particularly in the area of production
engineering.

Discussion

The case displays interesting empirical evidence of the effects of short-circuiting
the omnipresent discontinuities in construction. The case shows that innovative solutions and developments of productivity improvements could be brought
to the market. The off-site volumetric and development of complete building
solutions was developed through a long-term series of entrepreneurial product
and process innovations that created a direct link between the client and the
producer. Through an integrated business model, Lindbäcks is acting as the client, technology provider and contractor. Lindbäcks Bygg clearly has a strategy to
not only remove horizontal discontinuities between stages in the work but also
the vertical discontinuities by removing most layers of subcontracting. With the
business development lens, we can clearly see how Lindbäcks Bygg defined the
market they operate in. They have created a business model that includes control
of the stages and layers in the process, thereby putting themselves in control of
the demand for the product through their control of the means of production.

Control of the means of production, in this housebuilding sense, implies not only control of the stages of developing, funding, designing, managing construction and installing but also implementing technology innovations per se, e.g. the volumetric construction method or the building system platform. In other words, the Lindbäcks entrepreneurial innovation is their success at removing the horizontal and vertical discontinuities by creating an integrated supply chain, becoming suppliers to their own real estate business and making the decisions regarding design specifications and installations. In this way, they have used integration of the process as a purposeful integrating mechanism.

Taking responsibility for all of the processes involved in a construction project, including the competing priorities between management control systems. One way to achieve a single point of governance and responsibility is the way that Lindbäcks Bygg has achieved it, but it is not the only way. Indeed, there are many construction sub-sectors where this could not work. But in those sectors, some of the other techniques for actively overcoming the process discontinuities are needed. It is not sufficiently clear from the research literature that the need for these techniques is more than just a slight increase in productivity or the continuation of long-term business relationships for their own sake. Indeed, it is the most imperative problem in the modern construction sector; someone has to have a role of governance and be in command of the decision-making processes, especially in relation to management control systems. It is this governance that is the key to the successful completion of projects, whether innovative or not, and whether in-house, like Lindbäcks Bygg, or not.

Conclusions

Specifications required for contracts are often written before the technology installer is known. They focus on a limited range of criteria for success, which limits the opportunity for contracted suppliers to innovate in their process or their product. The technology installer is often restricted to providing something that has already been specified. The economics of construction tend to make subcontracting inevitable. The independence of the design function prevents specifiers from engaging in dialogue with those who own the means of production. Because of this, contractors are generally not adding value, or they are disabling innovation, or they are preventing improvements in productivity.

The case study shows a different approach for overcoming the conventional contractual boundaries in the development and supply of buildings. They are bringing highly innovative solutions to market and claim to be making great productivity improvements. Full-scale off-site fabrication offers an opportunity to make this more like a manufacturing business than a traditional construction business. Vertical and horizontal integration opens the option of focusing on satisfying customer needs and requirements with every resource of the organization rather than focusing on fulfilling narrowly defined contractual obligations.

Our example shows how the perennial construction problems have been overcome in practice. Indeed, several techniques have emerged to overcome discontinuities in the process. This shows one route to enabling more effective dialogue between producers and buyers. But this requires much more sophistication than a mere contract. While much of this is self-evident to practitioners, we hope that this chapter provides a useful rationale about why their instincts for collaborative working practices seem to be effective.

References

Banwell, H. (Chmn) (1964) *The placing and management of contracts for building and civil engineering work*. London: HMSO.

Black, C., Akintoye, A. and Fitzgerald, E. (2000) 'An analysis of success factors and benefits of partnering in construction', *International Journal of Project Management*, 18(6), pp. 423–434.

Brege, S., Stehn, L. and Nord, T. (2014) 'Business models in industrialized building of multi-story houses', *Construction Management and Economics*, 32(1–2), pp. 208–226.

Cherns, A.B. and Bryant, D.T. (1984) 'Studying the client's role in construction management', *Construction Management and Economics*, 2(2), pp. 177–184.

Chiang, Y.-H. and Cheng, E.W.L. (2010) 'Construction loans and industry development: The case of Hong Kong', *Construction Management and Economics*, 28(9), pp. 959–969.

Cox, A. and Ireland, P. (2002) 'Managing construction supply chains: The common-sense approach', *Engineering, Construction and Architectural Management*, 9(5/6), pp. 409–418.

Egan, J. (1998) *Rethinking construction: The report of the Construction Task Force to the Deputy Prime Minister, John Prescott, on the scope for improving the quality and efficiency of UK construction*. London: Department of the Environment, Transport and the Regions Construction Task Force.

Emmerson, H. (1962) *Studies of problems before the construction industries*. London: HMSO.

Fischer, M., Ashcraft, H.W., Read, D. and Khanzode, A. (2017) *Integrating project delivery*. Hoboken, NJ: Wiley-Blackwell.

Gil, N., Tommelein, I.D. and Ballard, G. (2004) 'Theoretical comparison of alternative delivery systems for projects in unpredictable environments', *Construction Management and Economics*, 22(5), pp. 495–508.

Green, S.D., Newcombe, R., Fernie, S. and Weller, S. (2004) *Learning across business sectors: Knowledge sharing between aerospace and construction*. Reading: University of Reading.

Harty, C. (2008) 'Implementing innovation in construction: Contexts, relative boundedness and actor-network theory', *Construction Management and Economics*, 26(10), pp. 1029–1041.

Hughes, W.P. (1989) *Organizational analysis of building projects*, unpublished PhD thesis. Liverpool: Department of Surveying, Liverpool Polytechnic.

Hughes, W.P., Champion, R. and Murdoch, J.R. (2015) *Construction contracts: Law and management*, 5th ed. London: Taylor & Francis.

Hughes, W.P., Gray, C. and Murdoch, J.R. (1997) *Specialist trade contracting: Report*. London: CIRIA Publications.

Hughes, W.P., Hillebrandt, P.M., Greenwood, D.G. and Kwawu, W.E.K. (2006) *Procurement in the construction industry: The impact and cost of alternative market and supply processes*. London: Taylor & Francis.

Johnsson, H. (2013) 'Production strategies for pre-engineering in house-building: Exploring product development platforms', *Construction Management and Economics*, 31(09), pp. 941–958.

Latham, M. (1994) *Constructing the team: Final report of the government/industry review of procurement and contractual arrangements in the UK construction industry.* London: HMSO.

Lessing, J., Stehn, L. and Ekholm, A. (2015) 'Industrialised house-building: Development and conceptual orientation of the field', *Construction Innovation*, 15(3), pp. 378–399.

Mintzberg, H. (1983) *Structure in fives: Designing effective organizations.* Englewood Cliffs, NJ: Prentice Hall.

Osterwalder, A., Pigneur, Y. and Tucci, C.L. (2005) 'Clarifying business models: Origins, present, and future of the concept', *Communications of the Association for Information Systems*, 16(1), pp. 1–25.

Pan, W. and Goodier, C. (2012) 'House-building business models and off-site construction take-up', *Journal of Architectural Engineering*, 18(2), pp. 84–93.

Reve, T. and Levitt, R.E. (1984) 'Organization and governance in construction', *International Journal of Project Management*, 2(1), pp. 17–25.

Song, L., Mohamed, Y. and AbouRizk, S.M. (2009) 'Early contractor involvement in design and its impact on construction schedule performance', *Journal of Management in Engineering*, 25(1), pp. 12–20.

Thornton, M. (2009) 'Cantillon and the invisible hand', *The Quarterly Journal of Austrian Economics*, 12(2), pp. 27–46.

Williamson, O.E. (1979) 'Transaction cost economics: The governance of contractual relations', *Journal of Law and Economics*, 22, pp. 233–261.

Woodward, J. (1965) *Industrial organization: Theory and practice.* London: Oxford University Press.

Zott, C. and Amit, R. (2007) 'Business model design and the performance of entrepreneurial firms', *Organization Science*, 18(2), pp. 181–199.

5 Construction logistics innovation

Tracing connectivity from activity interdependencies

Kajsa Hulthén and Viktoria Sundquist

Introduction

In the construction industry, the outcomes of projects such as buildings, roads or bridges, for example, are conditional on temporary factory set-ups at the construction site. This requires materials, equipment, tools and workers to be transferred to the site to enable production, which makes logistics a central activity in construction and an important contributor to project success. The construction industry is characterized by a fragmented pattern of numerous activities carried out by several actors that come together in a temporary project setting. The activities in each project are interlinked in order to accomplish various tasks, in accordance with the project phase and project progress. Each single activity is interdependent with other activities in two ways: (1) with previous and subsequent activities sequentially as activities have to be undertaken in a certain order; (2) with other activities conducted simultaneously. These interdependencies must somehow be handled to allow the relevant activities to function together to create outputs in line with project goals. Thus, each project requires extensive planning and organization to enable the coordination of activities. This coordination of activities applies both within and across the firm's boundaries and therefore requires joint boundary-spanning efforts with other companies (Håkansson, Ford, Gadde, Snehota and Waluszewski, 2009). Therefore, the way that activities are interlinked and coordinated within and across projects is related to the aforementioned activity interdependencies. It can be argued that, because of these interdependencies among tasks, parts and firms, the construction industry is, in many ways, more complex than other industries (Bankvall, Bygballe, Dubois and Jahre, 2010).

In this chapter, we focus on construction logistics activities to illustrate recent construction industry efficiency improvements due to innovation. Logistics activities are embedded in a broader range of activities, and the changes promoted by these complex patterns have consequences on other parts of the project activity. Engwall (2003, p. 789) points to the importance of considering projects as connected, based on the interdependencies across projects since "the structure and procedures employed in a project have to be understood in relation to previous and simultaneous courses of activity, to future plans, and to standard procedures, traditions and the norms of its surroundings". This embeddedness of project activities has implications for how an activity, such as logistics, is organized within and across projects. Accordingly, scrutinizing activity interdependencies requires an analytical scope that goes beyond the individual project.

Innovation implies significant change and improvement to a process, which renders it new to the actor initiating and developing the change (Freeman, 1989). Much of the innovation literature focuses on the development of new technologies (see e.g. Von Hippel, 1988; Fagerberg, Mowery and Nelson, 2004) and how firms develop and commercialize new products (Pavitt, 2002). Therefore, what innovation is in terms of product or technological change has been well researched. However, innovation in the form of changes to processes/activities to reflect changes in the way products and service are being created and delivered has been less well explored (Adams, Bessant and Phelps, 2006; Piening and Salge, 2014). Furthermore, when the process aspects of innovation in construction are scrutinized, the actors are in focus: the actors involved in these processes; the relationships among them; their capabilities; and clients and/or suppliers as key sources and drivers of innovation (Reichstein, Salter and Gann, 2008). Coordination and integration are vital to eliminate fragmentation in project-based industries and are key to successful development and implementation of innovation (Xue, Zhang, Yang and Dai, 2014), and several studies highlight the need for more in-depth insights into the actual activities involved in process innovation (Woiceshyn and Daellenbach, 2005; Keupp, Palmié and Gassman, 2012). In this context, a focus on the content of processes, as sequences of interdependent and interlinked activities, complements the focus on actors and their capabilities in relation to construction innovation. Gann and Salter (2000, p. 962) state that new approaches require suppliers to deliver bundles of products and services aimed at problem-solving:

> The cocktail of drivers for innovation in construction is leading to the emergence of new forms of production, which centre on the delivery of products and services. There appears to be a growing need for suppliers to provide more than basic physical products.

This means that, in the delivery of these services, various activities become central, and this centrality helps to explain construction innovation. The research described in this chapter investigates activity interdependencies and their implications for how activities are organized within and across projects as part of construction innovation processes.

The following two sections discuss the great potential for improvements to construction logistics and explore innovation as changes to activity interdependencies. We propose a framework to analyse construction logistics innovation. The third main section discusses some methodological issues and describes the underlying study. The empirical section describes the case of ConSite Logistics (CSL) and other initiatives exemplifying construction logistics innovation. The penultimate section analyses construction logistics innovation in terms of the reorganizing of activities, and the chapter ends with an identification of connectivity in the form of interdependencies among activities, resources and actors, across projects, and their importance for innovation: their connectivity allows change to develop and diffuse.

Logistics in construction: great potential for improvement

Construction logistics activities involve many types of off-site actors, such as materials manufacturers, distributors and transport and logistics firms, as well as on-site actors such as contractors and subcontractors. Materials are produced by materials manufacturers, and off-site logistics activities include packaging, labelling and storing. These activities are carried out by the manufacturers and/or distributors, who also provide transport activities if these are not undertaken by external transport or third-party logistics (3PL) providers. On-site logistics activities include logistics planning and coordination and materials handling to support production on-site. Materials handling comprises delivery control, inbound transport, movement of materials around the site, intermediate storage, sorting of materials, moving materials to installation areas and waste management procedures. Figure 5.1 illustrates the supply chain including off-site and on-site logistics. All these off-site and on-site activities are interlinked and need to be coordinated to achieve a satisfactory end result.

Construction logistics is gaining increased attention among both practitioners and academics (Janné, 2018; Sundquist, Gadde and Hulthén, 2018). Logistics performance is generally perceived to be low (Segerstedt and Olofsson, 2010) and to involve problems related to the supply of materials, equipment and tools hampering efficient production (Almohsen and Ruwanpura, 2011), which causes project delivery delays and increases costs (Josephson and Saukkoriipi, 2005; Strandberg and Josephson, 2005). Logistics account for a substantial share of total construction project costs. Wegelius-Lehtonen (2001) analysed logistics costs for eight Finnish building materials supply chains involved in a specific construction project and found that, in seven cases, logistics costs accounted for

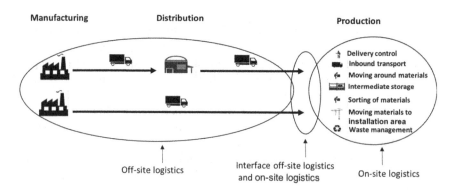

Figure 5.1 The construction supply chain involving off-site logistics and on-site logistics

more than 10% of the materials purchase price. In one case, the figure exceeded 60%, and in two others, the share was between 25% and 30%. Thus, construction logistics hold huge potential for cost reductions. For example, Thunberg and Persson (2014) investigated site deliveries and found that less than 40% of the total supply to a Swedish site was delivered in the right volume, at the right time and to the right location, was undamaged and was appropriately documented. This shows that quality improvements can be achieved through improvements in construction logistics.

The quantities of materials and equipment and the amount of transport involved are also substantial. Among the 79,000 heavy vehicles in Sweden, a third of them serve construction sites daily (Sveriges Byggindustrier, 2010). In addition, the construction sector accounts for 20% of total CO_2 emissions in Sweden, a substantial part of which comes from transport (Boverket, 2011). Therefore, there are environmental reasons to reduce the number of journeys to and from construction sites and to create more efficient transport solutions.

The purchasing behaviour of contractors and subcontractors affects transport and logistics activities. Both types of actors tend to have contracts with distributors that include 'free' transport to sites, that is, the cost of transport is included in the price of the product. This leads to an ordering process featured by delivery at very short notice, commonly the day after the date of the order. Although several orders may be placed by the same actor and be destined for the same site, lack of coordination can result in several individual deliveries and lorries only partly filled (Dubois, Hulthén and Sundquist, 2016).

In other cases, deliveries are organized to maximize vehicle load capacity; in some cases, the customer is offered a discount for ordering a full truck load or for combining several deliveries for the same construction site. This reduces the number of transport vehicles but results in huge amounts of materials arriving at the construction site before they are needed for installation, which can reduce the efficiency of on-site logistics. Storing large quantities of materials on construction sites over a long period can result in their being lost, stolen, or damaged by the weather or by being moved around on-site (Lindén and Josephson, 2013). Thus, activities, such as purchasing and ordering, affect the organization of construction logistics activities.

These examples highlight various issues related to construction logistics. There is huge potential for innovation and improvements in how construction logistics activities are performed and coordinated. In Sweden, the industry acknowledges that implementation of more efficient logistics and transport solutions could reduce overall project costs by 20% (Sveriges Byggindustrier, 2010). A study by Boverket (2009) shows that well planned logistics throughout the various phases of an inner city project reduced the total cost per rentable square metre by 23% compared to an equivalent project in the same area. Similar benefits of improved supply and delivery of materials have been shown in the Danish case by Agapiou, Clausen, Flanagan, Norman and Notman (1998), in the U.S. case by Jang, Russell and Yi (2003) and in the UK case by Fadiya, Georgakis, Chinyio and Nwagboso (2015). Logistics specialists are important actors in the construction industry;

they are responsible for reorganizing activities and materials flows among supply chain actors in order to increase construction site operations efficiency and to handle the logistical challenges related to the supply of materials and equipment.

Most industry efforts and studies of performance gains focus on on-site logistics activities. However, there are indications that many of the potentially positive effects of improved logistics relate to the coordination of on-site and off-site logistics (Ying, Tookey and Roberti, 2014; Fadiya et al., 2015; Sundquist, Gadde and Hulthén, 2018). It is important, therefore, to include off-site logistics activities, on-site logistics activities and the coordination of them in investigations of how activities are organized within and across projects as part of the construction innovation process.

Innovation as a change to activity interdependencies

The first part of this section describes the need for a network perspective to investigate the complexity of innovation in construction. The second part proposes a framework for the investigation of logistics reorganization.

Complexity of innovation in construction calls for a network perspective

The previous section highlighted the many challenges faced by the construction industry in the area of logistics, which, in this sector, often result in poor performance. Several studies discuss attempts to improve logistics, often addressing on-site logistics in a particular project (see, e.g., Lindén and Josephson, 2013). Other studies include the coordination of on-site and off-site logistics, although still focused on an individual project (see, e.g., Ekeskär and Rudberg, 2016). A few works examine off-site as well as on-site logistics and thus consider the whole supply chain. For example, Vrijhoef and Koskela (2000) discuss four roles of supply chain management and logistics in construction, including four areas for potential change: (1) on the supply chain–construction site interface, (2) the supply chain (ending at the construction site), (3) transfer of activities from the construction site to the supply chain, and (4) integrated management of the supply chain and the construction site. Efforts related to these four areas may involve project-specific solutions but might also be directed to improvements that would benefit several projects. Conflicting logics make it difficult to achieve efficient organization of activities. The main contractor defines its supply chain in relation to its subcontractors and suppliers and the needs of the individual project. Efforts to coordinate this supply chain efficiently from a project perspective may clash with subcontractors' and suppliers' arrangements. What might be beneficial from the main contractor's perspective might interfere with 'the best' solution developed by a particular subcontractor with its materials suppliers. This can cause tensions among the actors, resulting in each actor following its own 'best' logic. Since the industry is project based and projects can extend over long time periods and involve many actors that need to interact, in this setting, it can be difficult to make changes and to innovate (Slaughter, 1998; Dubois and Gadde, 2002). Due to the fragmentation of actors and activities across space and time, the construction industry has been described as a 'special case' (Bresnen and Marshall, 2001; Harty, 2008).

Projects are important sources of innovation as they connect actors that need to interact to solve problems (Slaughter, 1993; Winch, 1998). These interactions among actors can result in the emergence of new ideas and innovations (Havenvid, Hulthén, Linné and Sundquist, 2016). The innovation process is not straightforward and involves negotiation over ideas from the perspectives of the various actors (Winch, 1998), whose supply chain management logics might differ depending on their roles and positions in the supply chain and their connections to other actors.

A logistics innovation is any logistics service that is seen as new or helpful to a particular audience in a logistics setting (Flint, Larsson, Gammelgaard and Mentzer, 2005). In line with work on construction logistics, the focus in the literature on construction innovation is mostly a single project or organization (Dulaimi, Ling and Bajracharya, 2003; Harty, 2008). Also, these studies generally adopt a product or technical perspective on innovation in construction (Ivory, 2005; Clegg and Kreiner, 2014). However, it has been argued that, innovation in construction needs to be studied and understood in the context of the industry's organizational complexity (Slaughter, 1998, 2000). Slaughter (2000, p. 2) argues that innovation is "a nontrivial improvement in a product, process, or system that is actually used and which is novel to the company developing or using it".

Due to the specific organizational character of construction projects, Harty (2008, p. 1029) calls for a new approach to innovation in construction: "trace and unpack the interactions occurring around implementation of these artefacts [human and material related to the innovation process]". Based on these interactions, Harty (2008, p. 1038) describes innovation as resulting in "unexpected outcomes". This means that construction innovation entails both dynamic and ambiguous characteristics of social and technical artefacts combined through the innovation process. The interactive aspect of innovation and its socio-technical character, that is, resources such as individuals, organizations and technologies, are identified as an important cornerstone of innovation (ibid.). Similarly, Boland, Lyytinen and Yoo (2007, p. 633) call for an 'ecological' perspective to understand innovation in construction: "When innovation is viewed as a distributed phenomenon, it is characterized by network effects, messiness, ambiguity, and combinability". This suggests that construction is a difficult setting in which to achieve innovation. Innovation in construction also can be considered unpredictable and unexpected due to the complex interaction patterns across organizational borders (Boland, Lyytinen and Yoo, 2007; Harty, 2008).

It can be argued that the exploration of innovation in construction requires tracing interactions in space and time and extending the analysis beyond a focus on individual actors. Such analysis would include several actors in the network and identification of what is done, how it is coordinated and how the various actors interact to cope with project-specific conditions and the simultaneous need for coordination among projects. These efforts enable innovation, which can benefit various projects. Innovations in construction logistics can be captured by tracing activity interdependencies within and across projects, including how the activities are carried out and by which actor. The level of analysis is the network level, beyond the scope of the individual project, and instead a focus on the connectedness among projects. Therefore, a network perspective is an appropriate way to capture the complexity of innovation in construction.

Framework to capture logistics reorganizing as innovation in construction

To capture the complexity of innovation in construction, we draw on industrial network theory, which identifies the most important source of innovation as the relationships among both buyers and sellers, how these relationships are activated and how they increase efficiency and innovation (see, e.g. Håkansson et al., 2009; Gadde, Håkansson and Persson, 2010). In this perspective, companies are embedded in networks that consist of constellations of different actors, resources and activities (Håkansson and Snehota, 1995). To investigate how this embeddedness affects the development, implementation and diffusion of innovation, we rely on the ARA (Actors, Resources, Activities) model (ibid.). The ARA model relies on these three distinct but interconnected network layers. Actors perform activities and control resources, and actors make use of resources in their activities. The ARA model captures the complexity inherent in construction logistics since numerous activities need to be performed simultaneously, in temporary project settings, and are interlinked with parallel ongoing, previous and future projects. The interconnections among the three network layers means we need also to consider the actors that perform the activities and the resources that are activated by these activities.

Activity interdependencies occur at many levels. In the area of construction logistics: (1) activities need to be performed in a certain order, for example, logistics to enable installation of insulation before application of plaster boards; (2) some activities make use of the same resources; for example, many construction site activities make use of a tower crane; (3) firms need to coordinate activities among each other; for example, deliveries to construction sites (off-site logistics) need to be coordinated with materials-handling activities on-site (on-site logistics); and (4) activities performed in one project are connected to what is happening in parallel projects, what was done in previous projects and what is being planned for new projects. For example, firms that try out a new way of managing delivery to a construction site in one project might use the same approach in their next project. These examples are illustrations of the interdependencies among activities.

How activities are coordinated depends on their interrelation based on activity interdependencies. Logistics activities are subject to two types of interdependencies: sequential and parallel. Sequential interdependence relates to activities that are complementary or closely complementary (Richardson, 1972).

Complementary activities represent "different phases of a process of production and require in some way or another to be coordinated" (ibid., p. 889). When activities are not only sequential but also need to be matched to specific plans or directed to specific counterparts, they are referred to as closely complementary. This means that firms need to exchange information and coordinate activities among one another so that the output from activities performed by one actor match the input of activities from another actor. Accordingly, complementarity and close complementarity require different levels of coordination of serial interdependencies.

Parallel interdependence relates to activities that are similar, that is, "when they require the same capability for their undertaking" (Richardson, 1972, p. 888). Hence, if two or more activities make use of the same resource, they are similar, and this similarity captures parallel interdependence, including the need for coordination of such similar activities. Coordination of interdependent logistics activities in construction is complex. For the actors involved in construction logistics, it is important to coordinate activities to capture similarities, that is, to achieve economies of scale in resources use and, at the same time, to manage activities that are closely complementary. This can become especially problematic since each firm might be involved in simultaneous ongoing projects that require different coordination of interdependent activities.

At each point in time, there is a certain division of labour in the activity structure, describing who does what, that is, what activities are performed by which actor. Each actor may perform particular activities, but each actor needs also to relate its activities to the activities performed by others. Such a structure is never 'stable', but different kinds of efforts to reorganize the current activity structure are ongoing. Actors constantly try to reorganize construction logistics to improve efficiency or value creation by, for example, changing the way logistics activities are performed, coordinating logistics activities in new ways, changing the nature of logistics services or expanding their scope. This implies that when firms try to reorganize logistics and change the coordination of activities, this impacts on the activities undertaken by other firms and in other projects. This is due to the existing interdependencies among activities.

Each actor has a role in connecting and coordinating construction logistics activities, both within and across firm and project boundaries. These roles are related also to the roles of other actors as the activities of each individual actor are interrelated to various extents. Actor roles change over time along two dimensions (Gadde et al., 2010): (1) the space dimension refers to the coordinating role played by a focal actor in connecting its own activities to the activities of other actors in the network; and (2) the time dimension refers to how this 'connecting' changes over time based on previous experiences and future expectations (see Figure 5.2). Hence, at any point in time, the firm's current role can be described in terms of how its activities are related to and coordinated with the activities of other actors, as well as the resources required to perform these activities (see actors A–F in Figure 5.2). This role and activities are related to previous experience and previous roles and to expectations about future roles and activity

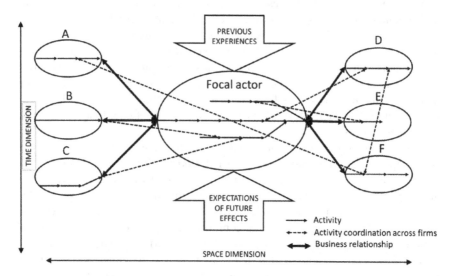

Figure 5.2 The role of the focal actor regarding activity coordination at a specific point in
time (Inspired by Gadde et al. [2010])

coordination. Important, here, is how the focal actor manages the connectedness
among projects and how experience gained in one project is brought to the next
project. This is an important aspect of innovation.

The framework proposed to capture logistics reorganizing as innovation in
construction, including the coordination of activities within and across projects,
centres around two issues. First, investigation of activity interdependencies enables analysis of efficiency and resources use by considering complementarities and
similarities among activities. Second, as depicted in Figure 5.2, actor roles are
analysed by addressing the division of labour and coordination of activities across
space and time. This framework is used for the analysis.

Methodological issues

This empirical study in this chapter involves an investigation of Swedish construction logistics conducted between 2011 and mid-2018. It involved collecting
information on the firm ConSite Logistics's (CSL's) development from its foundation in 1997 up to 2018. A case study approach is used to capture the changes
that have taken place in the firm's role both in construction logistics and in the
larger construction network. We studied how CSL operated with different kinds
of customers, suppliers and projects over time to obtain an in-depth understanding of how its role had developed. We were interested in both CSL's perspective
and those of other actors, such as materials suppliers, distributors, transport service providers, clients, main contractors and subcontractors. Taken together, this
information shows how CSL transformed its business through a reorganization

of construction logistics and how, in turn, that had effects both on-site and off site. The study of construction logistics also includes information about three other actors' initiatives to organize and reorganize construction logistics as part of their business. We identified three examples: (1) a main contractor's initiative to increase on-site logistics collaboration; (2) a distributor's expansion to provide customer-adapted logistics services; and (3) a third-party logistics service provider's offering of new on-site logistics services.

Both primary and secondary data were important inputs to the study. Primary sources of data were interviews and site visits. The study relies on 32 interviews (see Table 5.1).

Six site visits were conducted, which provided information on various on-site activities, such as unloading, transport, delivery control and delivery planning. Two visits were made to distributors and their storage facilities, and we also visited one materials manufacturer. Secondary data include requests for tenders, tenders and site disposition plans, CSL's materials-handling directives and CSL delivery planning system information. The secondary data were important to complement the primary data in order to understand the complexity of activity coordination and CSL's role in the construction network.

A focus on how logistics activities relate to other activities, within and across projects, allowed us to trace activity interdependencies and their implications in relation not only to the activities but also to how these activities connected to various resources and actors. By focusing on single activities and tracing their links to other activities, we were able to identify serial interdependencies. In the case of resources, for example, we were able to identify parallel interdependence

Table 5.1 Summary of interviews

Companies/ type of company	Number of interviews	Function and number of interviewees
CSL	14	2 logistics managers, 2 logistics coordinators, 1 material delivery planner, 1 work manager, 1 arrival controller, 1 quality manager, 2 business developers, 2 logistics consultants, 2 materials handling managers
Main contractor	4	3 site managers, 1 work manager
Subcontractor	2	2 work managers
Materials manufacturer	3	1 production manager, 1 logistics manager, 1 sales manager
Distributor	5	2 logistics manager, 2 store manager, 1 sales manager
Transportation firm	2	1 transport leader, 1 chauffeur
Management consultancy firm	1	1 sales manager
Project management firm	1	1 project manager

and similarities among activities. In addition, interpreting actor roles as the focal actor's connections to other actors, within and across project boundaries, helped our understanding of the effects of logistics reorganization.

ConSite Logistics (CSL) and reorganizing construction logistics

This section describes how a Swedish actor, ConSite Logistics, developed its business by changing how it performed logistics activities and how this promoted the reorganization of construction industry activities. This development was enabled by interaction with other actors, in various projects, over time. The section starts by describing how the type and scope of activities undertaken by CSL changed over time. Following that, we describe in detail CSL's current operations and its focus on on-site logistics and outline the effects of CSL's reorganizing activities. These effects are visible both on-site and off site and have consequences for several actors. The section ends with examples of other initiatives related to the reorganization of logistics activities in the construction network.

The changing role of CSL: changing the type and scope of logistics activities

Currently, CSL specializes in on-site logistics. However, some 20 years ago, CSL was a materials merchant, selling building materials to contractors and subcontractors. Its offer included delivery of these materials to various construction projects; thus, CSL was involved in the delivery of building materials from the warehouse to construction sites. On one occasion, a customer asked for materials to be delivered to the exact installation area on the construction site rather than unloading in a large storage area on-site. CSL recognized this request as representing a potential business opportunity and reorganized the firm to focus on 'inbound transport of building materials'. More precise deliveries, in terms of on-clock deliveries to designated installation areas, became an extra service, which more and more customers perceived as beneficial and were willing to pay extra for.

The next transformation, was delivering deliver building materials outside regular working hours, which substantially reduced disturbances to production activities at sites. These arrangements attracted considerable interest from contractors, and CSL became increasingly focused on on-site logistics and materials handling rather than just selling building materials and delivering them to construction sites. The demand for these extended logistics services grew rapidly to become the firm's main business. After some years, CSL decided to focus its business solely on on-site materials handling. On-site materials handling required CSL personnel being stationed at construction sites to be responsible for unloading vehicles, carrying out quality control and the transport of materials from unloading to installation areas. Consequently, the building merchants and the transport service business were disposed of. Over time, there were calls for more and more sophisticated logistics solutions, and CSL's operations evolved to encompass logistics analysis of site conditions and development of a web portal for delivery planning. Currently, CSL acts as a construction logistics consultant, offering planning and logistics analysis prior to project start, management of on-site logistics including delivery planning and physical execution of materials handling including unloading and transport of materials from incoming vehicles to installation areas on-site.

CSL's role in the construction network has changed over the years. It began as a traditional building merchant but then began to deliver materials to construction sites in a more structured logistical manner than other distributors. Its focus turned to on-site materials handling, and it currently operates as a construction logistics specialist, performing on-site logistics operations and logistics analysis. The story of CSL's logistics activities reorganization shows how the actor's role changed over time to a construction logistics specialist, within a network of other actors. The interactions between CSL and these other actors, in various projects, changed how logistics activities were undertaken, when and by whom.

CSL's logistics activities

CSL performs logistics analysis prior to project start and/or undertakes on-site logistics operations during the project production phase. Thus, CSL is responsible for logistics coordination, but CSL's level of logistics involvement differs among projects. CSL is not involved in any off-site supply chain logistics operations.

Logistics analysis, undertaken by CSL prior to the project building phase, includes planning how logistics at the construction site should be undertaken and coordinated, taking account of the conditions unique to each project. For instance, projects located in dense cities present difficulties related to confined on-site space, which reduces the possibility of storing materials, while traffic restrictions around the construction site pose problems for delivery vehicles related to when they can enter the area and/or their size and weight. If the project is located in a hospital, this can be problematic: the hospital must remain fully operational during construction activity, and incoming and outgoing project-related traffic must be coordinated with ambulance and other hospital-related traffic. Logistics analysis allows decisions about the location of resources such as cranes and elevators, and routes for project traffic.

Typically, CSL is hired by contractors to organize the logistics related to house-building and public building projects, or building refurbishment projects. In some cases, CSL may be hired by the client. The hirer pays CSL for logistics services, including the personnel responsible for locating resources such as cranes and elevators on the construction site. CSL's on-site logistics services during building activity comprise: (1) planning the site layout for cranes, elevators, transport routes and storage areas; (2) coordination of physical deliveries of vehicles to and from the site; and (3) materials-handling operations on-site. The various phases of the building process involve different aspects. In the initial phase, logistics organizing involves coordination of shuttle traffic to move demolition materials, transport of shaft and detonation bulk from the site and delivering materials to the site. This involves heavy vehicles but minimal personnel at the site. The next phase involves organizing inbound deliveries of – often – fragile and weather-sensitive materials to the contractor and subcontractors involved in the building operations. CSL may also be involved in organizing the removal from the site of elevators and cranes after the premises have been occupied.

CSL provides a dedicated construction site team, which includes a logistics manager, a logistics coordinator, a delivery planner, someone responsible for arrivals, and one or several gate guards. This team is responsible, collectively, for logistics planning and management of logistics operations on-site. CSL also provides materials handlers who are hired people by the hour to unload vehicles as they arrive at the site, inspect the goods and direct internal transport to the relevant installation area. Materials are delivered to the installation area according to a system of coordinates, which indicate the relevant right building, floor and location on the floor, for example, building X, floor Y, coordinates WZ. As far as possible, materials handling takes place outside of regular site working hours to minimize disruption to construction operations.

CSL charges contractors and subcontractors for materials handling according to the size and volume of the goods and whether they are palleted or need to be stacked on trestles. CSL has developed a web-based delivery planning system, and all contractors and subcontractors must book materials deliveries to sites using this system, at least five days in advance. The CSL delivery planner assigns appropriate resources, such as elevators and cranes, for the materials handling required for these deliveries.

Efficient materials handling is achieved through strict regulations regarding their packaging. Contractors and subcontractors are responsible for forwarding these instructions to their suppliers. They include instructions about the use of pallets as much as possible, as well as pallet sizes and weights to allow them to be lifted, two at a time, by an elevator. CSL prefers construction elevators to cranes because they are faster and more efficient for materials handling. Only especially long and large items are moved by cranes. Each material requires appropriate packaging to avoid damage or losses of loose parts such as handles. The packages must include clear details to enable delivery to the relevant installation area without involvement of the contractor or subcontractor, but as they later on will install the materials they must know what each pallet contains.

Effects of CSL's reorganizing of logistics activities

The way CSL undertakes and coordinates logistics operations has several effects. Since delivery and materials handling take place on-site outside of regular site working hours, construction operations are not disrupted. Also, since construction workers are not involved in any materials handling, they can focus solely on production activities, with no need to search for, collect or inspect materials. However, this requires managers to forward-plan and place orders for materials at the appropriate time to avoid expensive last-minute deliveries. Thus, construction workers, work managers and the site manager need to interact intensively regarding the progress of production to ensure that the right materials are available at the right time. This requires, also, that work managers and other responsible personnel interact closely with suppliers. In some cases, depending on the contract with the supplier, contractors or subcontractors may have to pay extra for delivery of materials outside of regular working hours rather than free delivery during normal site working hours. Since materials are not being stored on-site but are delivered directly from the vehicle to the installation area, waste due to bad weather and loss or theft is greatly reduced.

Some actors consider a logistics specialist to be beneficial because it allows them to focus on production activities, such as assembly and installation; however, some find it difficult to meet logistics requirements, which differ from their 'traditional way of working'. For example, some contractor construction workers consider materials handling as constituting a 'nice break' from their construction work, and this is lost if CSL undertakes materials handling. Some actors have managed to reduce their hours on-site because they are no longer involved in materials handling, which, in turn, reduces costs. However, if contractors fail to reduce man-hours on-site, their costs will increase; they will be paying their site staff and also paying the extra materials-handling costs.

Suppliers must adapt their off-site operations to allow deliveries outside of regular site working hours and to comply with CSL delivery times. There are stricter requirements regarding packaging of goods, which may also deviate from suppliers' standard procedures. Deviations from these rules could reduce the efficiency of logistics related to storage, packaging and transport. One project required a supplier to establish a temporary, intermediate storage facility near the construction site in order to meet the customer's delivery needs. Although the contractors and subcontractors paid a small extra fee for materials storage, for the supplier the arrangement was costly.

For all projects, CSL has a standardized logistics operations procedure, which has evolved over time based on CSL's experience in different projects and on its interactions with various actors and specific project logistics conditions. For instance, from its involvement in materials handling, CSL learnt about the problems related to logistics coordination on-sites, and, over time, this knowledge allowed its specializing in complex project logistics coordination and management.

Other initiatives of reorganizing construction logistics

Our study of construction logistics reveals that it was not just CSL that was involved in reorganizing construction logistics; other actors exploited business opportunities related to the new construction logistics conditions. Such initiatives are examples of innovation and change in how activities are interlinked and coordinated and of changes to actors' roles. We distinguished three recent initiatives that emerged from various actors' reorganizing (Hulthén, Sundquist, Gadde and Eriksson, 2016): (1) a main contractor that increased its collaboration to address on-site logistics; (2) a distributor that expanded its off-site and on-site logistics services; and (3) a 3PL provider that began to develop construction logistics solutions on-site to complement its off-site logistics services.

The main contractor's increase in on-site logistics collaboration

To cope with the logistical challenges involved in a project in a dense city area, the main contractor takes responsibility for closer collaboration among the actors working with production on-site. The refurbishment and building of new office premises allow little space for materials, equipment and personnel at the construction site, and narrow city streets make it difficult to deliver and unload materials at the construction site. The main contractor makes demands on subcontractors at the tender phase, regarding, for example, more precise delivery times and the packaging of materials to facilitate unloading and materials handling, reduced materials storage on-site and less waste. A site disposition plan allows visualization of logistics conditions including transport routes, areas for unloading and placement of cranes and elevators. The plan is updated as the project progresses.

From a total 25 subcontractors, the most important ones are those providing electricity, heating, plumbing and sprinklers. They are required to collaborate closely in the planning and production phases. Planning involves close cooperation over tender instructions, meetings with the main contactor's project planner and joint planning meetings. This allows the subcontractors' knowledge and experience to be exploited to allow the most efficient logistics and production. The main contractor assigns a logistics coordinator to coordinate deliveries of materials to the site and the resources required for materials handling. In the production phase, there is intense interaction between the logistics coordinator and the other actors on-site, to manage deliveries and materials handling. Planned deliveries are published on a planning board. The increased collaboration involves meeting to manage coordination and to report project progress including deviations from the production time plan and morning meetings to provide regular updates about what to expect that day.

The initiative regarding the logistics coordinator and closer collaboration was successful and resulted in better coordination of deliveries, materials handling and storage, which, in turn, enabled good quality in the production process and fewer deviations from plans. However, coping with changes to the production time plan, often at short notice, made it difficult to adjust logistics activities and required materials to be moved around on-site, which increased the risk of damage to and loss of materials. There was a lack of transparency and information exchange among actors about when to place orders for materials, lead times and types of materials related to a particular production stage. This disrupted the integration between off-site and on-site logistics. Inadequate drawings and materials specifications added to these problems, and materials were delivered to the site in the wrong quantities or at the wrong time. However, the benefits of these logistics efforts outweighed the drawbacks, and the main contractor decided that a logistics coordinator would be included in all future projects.

The distributor's expansion of logistics services

The distributor involved maintain stocks of over 40,000 different items in its central storage, which supplies 70 stores. Delivery precision reaches over 99%, but the high service level requires excess storage, which increases costs. The distributor's role changed from being solely a 'supplier of goods' to becoming a service provider with logistics services that enable customer-adapted logistics solutions. The logistics services provided include on-clock delivery, packaging/labelling, intermediate storage near the site, unloading and transport of materials directly to a specific area of the construction site. These services fulfilled the materials manufacturers' need for standardization and the construction sites' need for local adaptations. The distributor also has developed customer-adapted prefabricated solutions that involve the assembly of materials, thus taking on a large share of the assembly activities previously conducted at the construction site. It now delivers a system solution to the site, and a complete rebuilding of wet floor spaces, including plumbing, can be completed in less than ten days.

In terms of both customer-adapted logistics solutions and delivery of prefabricated solutions, the distributor's changed role increased efficiency at the construction site. In both cases, the time needed for materials handling on-site was reduced significantly and, in the case of prefabricated solutions, production times at sites were also reduced. Quality was also improved when the packaging of the goods was adapted to suit the on-site conditions and the goods were handled by fewer actors before assembly.

The 3PL provider's offering of logistics services

The 3PL provider had many years of experience with off-site logistics, including planning and coordination and physical resources for transport and storage, and it operated in other industries than construction. The 3PL provider's customers include both upstream and downstream actors: materials manufacturers, distributors, contractors and subcontractors. The main challenge for the construction industry is coping with a process where unplanned changes require greater flexibility than in many other industries.

The 3PL provider's new role includes full responsibility for logistics flows including materials supply both to the site and at the site. Thus, its role has expanded to include on-site logistics. It is crucial to utilize on-site resources efficiently to enhance productivity and link off-site and on-site logistics. Transport activities can be reduced by increased coordination and co-loading of goods aimed for the same site or for sites in the same geographical area. These efforts reduce costs and provide for more sustainable logistics. The logistics terminals and the vehicles owned by the 3PL provider are vital in this regard. The 3PL provider realized that the potential advantages from increased logistics planning and coordination were achievable only if logistics were included in the tendering phase of new projects. This required that the individuals responsible for preparing the calls for tenders should have logistics competences to allow them to specify what was needed in the projects. The 3PL provider has this competence, but it is crucial that it is involved early in the process to allow it to implement the appropriate logistics solution.

An important aspect of logistics coordination both off site and on-site is the use of a common information technology (IT) system among supply chain actors. A system that was developed by an IT firm was purchased by the 3PL provider and incorporated into its offering of construction logistics services to contractors and project managers. The IT system connects all actors in the supply chain, from materials manufacturers to contractors and subcontractors, and enables information sharing and transparency regarding materials supply. It requires standardized labelling of materials to allow goods to be tracked throughout the materials flow. The contractors are generally positive about the system and the effects of standardization, but the materials manufacturers and distributors are less convinced. A major advantage allowed by the IT system is that all information regarding materials supply is saved in the system and is available to future projects. The IT system improves delivery precision and optimizes transport, resulting in reduced waiting times for unloading at sites and an ability to co-load order for the same site. However, although the IT system is not that expensive in itself, the use of the system is costly as it requires all actors to adopt standardized labelling of goods. The investment can be justified only if it is used for several projects.

Analysis of the reorganizing of construction logistics

To capture activity interdependencies and actor roles across time and space and how they impact on logistics innovation, we exploited the framework proposed earlier in the chapter. The analysis shows that the reorganization of logistics activities initiated by CSL included interactions with various actors and had various consequences. CSL's role changed, with the result that the roles of other actors' have been redefined as CSL has taken on more logistic activities and reorganized the coordination of logistics. In the analysis that follows, we compare two situations illustrating two different divisions of labour and roles at CSL. Situation 1 considers CSL acting purely as a wholesaler of construction materials, with materials handling performed by contractors and subcontractors on-site. Situation 2 refers to CSL's role as a logistics specialist, responsible for materials handling. The analysis includes (1) differences in activity interdependencies, efficiency and resources use; (2) differences in the division of labour and roles; and (3) changes to interactions and mobilization of actors. Table 5.2 summarizes Situations 1 and 2.

Activity interdependencies, efficiency and resources use

In Situation 1, materials deliveries to sites and materials-handling activities on-site are complementary but not closely complementary. Hence, deliveries and materials handling activities can be regarded as decoupled by intermediate storage on-site. In this scenario, large quantities of materials are ordered by the

Table 5.2 Summary of characteristics of Situations 1 and 2

Characteristics	Situation 1	Situation 2
Activity interdependencies		
Interdependencies between deliveries of materials to site and materials handling on-site	Complementary activities: low degree of coordination as intermediate storage of materials on-site act as buffer	Closely complementary activities: high degree of coordination due to JIT solution
Interdependencies between materials-handling and production activities on-site	Parallel interdependence due to common resources use	No parallel interdependence as separated activities in time
Interdependencies across supply chains	No coordination: each supplier delivers according to its own logic in respective supply chain.	Coordination required: deliveries need to be synchronized across supply chains.
Efficiency and resources use		
Efficiency and resources use in materials handling and production on-site	Low efficiency due to low similarity among activities. Resources shared among the two types of activities: low level of exploiting economies of scale.	High efficiency when exploiting similarity in both activities, and specialization among actors. Resources use: high level of exploiting economies of scale
Efficiency for off-site actors (distributors and materials manufacturers)	High efficiency due to standard procedures	Low efficiency as adaptions of deliveries and packaging are needed
Division of labour and roles		
The role of CSL	'Wholesaler': performing traditional wholesale activities	'Logistics specialist': focusing on materials handling and logistics
The role of the contractor	'Contractor': Focusing on materials handling and construction operations	'Construction operations specialist': Focusing on construction operations
Interaction and mobilization		
Level of interaction between (sub) contractors and CSL	Low: due to decoupled activities between (sub)contractors and CSL	High: need to coordinate materials-handling and construction operations
Level of interaction between (sub) contractors and materials suppliers	Low: due to decoupled activities between sub(contractors) and materials suppliers	High: need of information exchange regarding details about deliveries and packaging

contractor and subcontractors, independently, in accordance with their respective project production activities and progress. In Situation 2, these activities are closely complementary, with each delivery directed not just to a specific site but to a specific installation area and at a specific time. This is a JIT (just-in-time) system where deliveries are closely coordinated and matched to sites. The coordination of these activities is enabled by use of an advanced logistics planning system, a vital resource for the management of serial interdependencies among delivery, materials handling and production. These planning and coordination of deliveries requirements demand the supply chain to be coordinated, as well as more advance planning compared to Situation 1 where these activities are more loosely coupled. Also, in Situation 2, since not all goods deliveries can be planned 'in isolation' from other deliveries, there are interdependencies across supply chains. Finally, exploitation of the interdependencies among off-site and on-site activities increases the need in Situation 2 for the coordination of activities.

The specific packaging of goods and batch size requirements to enable materials-handling activities on-site, call for off-site adaptations by suppliers in Situation 2 compared to Situation 1. The customer-specific adaptations required by suppliers and materials manufacturers reduce the possibilities to exploit similarities and to benefit from economies of scale. For example, windows suppliers may need to stack their windows on pallets differently for different customers or to deliver windows with the handles already attached. Also, to adapt to out-of-hours delivery might require the supplier to set up an intermediate storage near the construction site. To reduce costs by increasing use of intermediate storage, three subcontractors cooperated and shared the storage to exploit similarities and obtain some economies of scale. This is another example of how Situation 2 creates interdependencies not only within supply chains but also across supply chains. This interdependence explains the increased need for activity coordination.

In Situation 1, materials-handling and production activities make use of the same resources, such as the crane, and the contractor's and subcontractors' workers alternate between the two activities. Hence, these activities are similar in that they involve the same personnel. However, they differ in nature, which means that despite involving the same resources, this is unrelated to efficiency and a specialization logic, as the different activities cannot be undertaken at the same time. Resources use is instead based on alteration among materials handling and production, which hampers efficiency. In Situation 2, the materials-handling activities and the production activities are separate, with each activity performed by specialized resources (CSL staff and construction workers respectively). This means that efficiency in both production activities and materials handling is greater in Situation 2 compared to Situation 1 due to more efficient resources use based on specialization.

Division of labour and roles

As just highlighted, the main difference in the division of labour in Situations 1 and 2 is that the materials handling in the latter is transferred from contractors and subcontractors to a logistics specialist (CSL in our case). This affects the roles of the actors in this construction network. The new role of 'logistics specialist' is introduced in Situation 2. It involves specializing in on-site materials handling and on-site logistics management, including the interface between on-site and off-site logistics. The analysis of CSL shows that this role is the outcome of historical connections across projects across time and space. This role has been developed and fine-tuned over time, based on experience and learning in various projects, and interactions with other actors in the construction network. The requirement for different services from various contractors played a crucial role in CSL's evolvement as a logistics specialist.

The introduction of this new logistics specialist role redefined the roles of other actors. For example, in Situation 2, contractors and subcontractors are no longer involved in materials handling and assume a 'construction operations specialist' role. The reorganization of the division of labour was not friction free. Some contractor and subcontractor workers saw it as reducing their autonomy and the possibility of taking 'a break' from regular construction activities.

Also, management of the interface between on-site and off-site logistics was transferred to CSL from contractors and subcontractors and their suppliers. It meant that contractors and subcontractors could no longer 'bring in' materials on-site at will; advance planning was required. This approach was new to and was found difficult by many contractors and subcontractors. However, over time they developed procedures to cope with CSL's requirements and were less reluctant to assume a new role.

So, the new division of labour in Situation 2, established new roles and new connections. However, not all effects could be foreseen or controlled by a single actor. The case of CSL shows clearly that innovations in the form of new processes occur in contexts where reactions to these initiatives and other development processes initiated by other actors take place in parallel. In the next subsection, we discuss the importance of interaction and mobilization among actors to achieve innovation.

Interaction and mobilization of actors

As just discussed, the change from Situation 1 to Situation 2 involved a new role for CSL as logistics specialist and also affected other actors in the network. A new role changed the content of existing connections, created new connections and dispensed with some other connections. For example, our case illustrates that new connections were needed between CSL and the contractors and subcontractors in order to organize the planning and coordination of deliveries, materials-handling and construction operations. A new type of more extensive interaction, involving the exchange of production and delivery information, was required. Also, the connection between contractors and subcontractors and their materials suppliers changed and required the exchange of more detailed information on deliveries and packaging requirements, etc. It rendered the interactions between contractors and subcontractors and their materials suppliers to be more extensive. This provoked changes to the interactions between materials suppliers (e.g. distributors/wholesalers) and materials manufacturers, since packaging demands were transferred upstream in the supply chain to all actors affected by the new requirements.

The case also illustrates the frictions generated by the change to Situation 2. They emerged as a result of changes to 'established ways of working'. Introducing new ways of working challenges established structures and the inherent connections that have evolved over the years. It involved adaptation and investment in the interaction process. When introducing a new division of labour that changes actors' roles, it is necessary to (1) clarify the effects of the various actors' roles and (2) ensure that actors understand the changes and buy into (or at least accept) the new situation.

Overall, reorganizing activities and changing the division of labour affect the pattern of interaction in a network. In our case, it required closer interaction between on-site and off-site actors to enable CSL's logistics specialist role. Innovations that change activity interdependencies result in increased efficiency alongside more extensive interaction. The effects of the change spread throughout the wider network. It should be noted that, some actors will benefit while others will find it difficult to adapt to the change and make it fit their own business logic. (See Table 5.2 for a summary of the analysis of Situations 1 and 2.)

Conclusions

The story of CSL presents innovation as significant change and improvement to a process that was new to the actor initiating and developing the change (Freeman, 1989). The reorganizing of activities and processes was new to CSL as well as to the other actors in the network, although the individual construction logistics activities were not new per se. On-site activities, such as logistics planning and materials handling, always occur in a temporary project setting to enable production. Similarly, packaging, labelling, storing and transport are part of all off-site logistics operations. The difference (change) lay in their different performance when CSL becomes a logistics specialist. For example, inbound transport to the site utilized elevators as much as possible. However, the change to this particular activity would have been impossible without activity interdependencies being exploited in a different way. Thus, activities were reorganized to be differently interlinked and coordinated. This reorganization included several adaptations, for example, packaging and labelling of materials delivered to the construction site to allow CSL to use elevators and to track goods and deliver them to the appropriate installation area on-site. The reorganization of logistics activities enabled more efficient materials handling. It provided benefits related to CSL's specialization in on-site logistics and construction workers' production specialization. Activity interdependencies are enablers of innovation to achieve a new construction logistics process. The activity is embedded in a context of other activities, where activity interdependencies are managed to produce a comprehensive and workable solution.

Therefore, logistics as an 'innovation activity' cannot be studied in isolation; exploration of innovation requires integrated investigation of a bundle of activities (Teece, Pisano and Shuen, 1997; Peng, Schroeder and Shah, 2008). What was identified as new in our exploration of construction logistics innovation was not 'a new activity' but a new way of interlinking and organizing activities. In this innovation process, efficiency increased as a result of changed activity interdependencies and adaptations among activities and resources alongside more extensive interaction. Thus, efficiency improvements depend on the existence of and increase in connectivity in the form of more intense interaction and stronger interdependencies among not only activities but also resources and actors. Interdependencies are an enabler of innovation since changes to them emerge in construction projects. Our study shows that projects are important for innovation since it is within project settings that construction actors come together, and it is through the interaction among various actors that learning takes place. This allowed CSL to develop its offering and allowed other actors access to the knowledge provided by CSL with regard to construction logistics. The connectivity among interdependencies promoted the innovation and efficiency gains that emerged. Thus, innovation is not produced by an individual company but rather is "the result of an interplay between two or more actors" (Håkansson, 1987, p. 3). The core to innovation, in terms of knowledge sharing and interactive learning processes, is the existence of connectivity. Exploiting connectivity to induce change results in stronger interdependencies, which form the basis for further development. Hence, innovation builds on and also promotes connectivity. The innovation process is complex and is the result of the interactions among many actors over an extended period of time (De Martino, Errichiello, Marasco and Morvillo, 2013). This highlights the importance of understanding interdependencies, interaction and connectivity, across space and time, and in the context of innovation.

This chapter has depicted innovation in processes based on the exploitation of interdependencies among activities. It focused on logistics to show that innovation takes the form of changes and improvements to an activity, the reorganization of activities to create new patterns, and the interplay among activities, actors and resources over time. Reorganizing activities is one example of construction innovation. Connectivity among the various actors and their activities is central for these innovation processes since change takes place via the interlinked activities within and across projects. Examining innovation in construction by considering activity interdependencies addresses the complexity of introducing long-term change and how the reorganization of activities exploits business opportunities to bring about efficiency improvements and innovation.

An actor's ability to develop and implement process innovation is embedded in various interrelated activities (Zollo and Winter, 2002; Teece, 2007). Its development cannot be explained as a simple progression based on 'internal business innovation' such as the invention of something 'new', introduced to a passive audience of potential customers. The analysis of CSL points to the importance of the interactions among different actors in various projects, with diverse demand for changes and improvements to logistics operation processes, which require the reorganization of activities. This is in line with previous studies showing that "innovation requires the creation of different forms of inter-organizational relationships among network actors" (De Martino et al., 2013, p. 131). The CSL example stresses the importance of the involvement in different projects over time, and the importance of experience gained from interactions with several actors to develop solutions that fit the project conditions and customer requirements. Inter-organizational and inter-project aspects of innovation complement the focus in previous research on single projects or organizations (Dulaimi et al., 2003; Harty, 2008). In the context of construction logistics, in particular, our tracing of activity interdependencies involved the broader supply network to examine the nature of logistics services (De Martino et al., 2013) and a scope beyond the individual project as the unit of analysis (Lindén and Josephson, 2013; Ekeskär and Rudberg, 2016).

The changes introduced by CSL were not welcomed by all the actors. Some adapted easily to the new conditions on-site and perceived CSL's service as beneficial; others found it difficult to cope with the new logistical arrangements and experienced drawbacks. Changing roles among interacting actors can introduce tensions and potential conflict and may decide whether or not the innovation is implemented. Along these lines, Bygballe and Ingemansson (2014, p. 516) state that "The adoption of new ideas and thus innovation in construction will depend on how well physical and organizational solutions fit with each other, as well as on the acceptance by various actors in the construction network". The interaction among actors is crucial for coping with resistance to the innovation, and the perception of change as negative by some network actors is inevitable.

The innovations introduced by CSL were examined in the context of the construction network, in which prerequisites for and opportunities to exploit new alternatives are in constant flux. Previous studies suggest that innovation in construction is both unpredictable and unexpected, due to complex patterns of interactions across organizational borders (Boland et al., 2007; Harty, 2008). The actions that occur in networks bring about 'counteractions', and, at each point in time, the actors are involved in several ongoing initiatives. The reorganization at CSL took place simultaneously with other changes to construction logistics. Changes to construction logistics are not coincidental but rather reflect (new) needs and requirements to cope with changing conditions. In turn, new solutions affect the surrounding network and introduce new conditions, which explain the dynamics of change processes, improvements and innovation. Logistics are central to construction to provide input to 'the factories' on-sites in the temporary construction projects. Most current major constructions are in large cities, providing new challenges for construction logistics and promoting new logistics solutions from various actors that recognize a business opportunity. This applies to CSL, 'the main contractor', 'the distributor' and 'the 3PL provider'. Previous experience, the skills developed and expectations about future outcomes are the basis for new ideas and new solutions.

Connectivity among activities (and actors and resources), in the form of interdependencies, both promotes and hinders innovation. Activity interdependencies (and how resources and actors relate) enable innovation by creating opportunities for change, and the reorganization of activities and interdependencies 'carry this change' in space and time, across project boundaries and throughout the construction network. At the same time, interdependencies restrict innovation by locking in activities to settings in complex patterns. This chapter points to the complexity involved in introducing change in projects (and the need for high levels of coordination) and what this means for actors trying to achieve increased efficiency (innovation) over time. Actors need to change their roles in relation to one another as part of any reorganization; this is shown by how the construction actors in the case in this chapter attempted (and were successful) in reorganizing their logistics activities.

References

Adams, R., Bessant, J. and Phelps, R. (2006) 'Innovation management and measurement: A review', *International Journal of Management Reviews*, 8(1), pp. 21–47.

Agapiou, A., Clausen, L.E., Flanagan, R., Norman, G. and Notman, D. (1998) 'The role of logistics in the materials flow control process', *Construction Management and Economics*, 16(2), pp. 131–137.

Almohsen, A. and Ruwanpura, J. (2011) 'Logistics management in the construction industry'. *Proceedings of the CIB W78-W102 2011, 26–28 October*, Sophia Antipolis.

Bankvall, L., Bygballe, L., Dubois, A. and Jahre, M. (2010) 'Interdependence in supply chains and projects in construction', *Supply Chain Management: An International Journal*, 15(5), pp. 385–393.

Boland, R.J., Lyytinen, K. and Yoo, Y. (2007) 'Wakes of innovation in project networks: The case of digital 3-D representations in architecture, engineering, and construction', *Organization Science*, 18(4), pp. 631–647.

Boverket (2009) *Effektiv logistik i innerstadsprojekt*, Boverket mars 2009.

Boverket (2011) *Miljöindikatorer för bygg och fastighetssektorn 1993–2007*, Rapport 2011:2.

Bresnen, M. and Marshall, N. (2001) 'Understanding the diffusion and application of new management ideas in construction', *Engineering Construction and Architectural Management*, 8(5–6), pp. 335–345.

Bygballe, L. and Ingemansson, M. (2014) 'The logic of innovation in construction', *Industrial Marketing Management*, 43, pp. 512–524.

Clegg, S. and Kreiner, K. (2014) 'Fixing concrete: Inquiries, responsibility, power and innovation', *Construction Management and Economics*, 32(3), pp. 262–278.

De Martino, M., Errichiello, L., Marasco, A. and Morvillo, A. (2013) 'Logistics in innovation in seaports: An inter-organizational perspective', *Research in Transportation Business and Management*, 8, pp. 123–133.

Dubois, A. and Gadde, L.-E. (2002) 'The construction industry as a loosely coupled system: Implications for productivity and innovation', *Construction Management and Economics*, 20(7), pp. 621–632.

Dubois, A., Hulthén, K. and Sundquist, V. (2016) 'Configuring transport and logistics activities in construction', *Nationella transportforskningskonferensen, 18–19 October*, Lund, Sweden.

Dulaimi, M., Ling, F. and Bajracharya, A. (2003) 'Organizational motivation and inter-organizational interaction in construction innovation in Singapore', *Construction Management and Economics*, 21(3), pp. 307–318.

Ekeskär, A. and Rudberg, M. (2016) 'Third-party logistics in construction: The case of a large hospital project', *Construction Management and Economics*, 34(3), pp. 174–191.

Engwall, M. (2003) 'No project is an island: Linking projects to history and context', *Research Policy*, 32, pp. 789–808.

Fadiya, O., Georgakis, P., Chinyio, E. and Nwagboso, C. (2015) 'Decision-making framework for selecting ICT-based construction logistics systems', *Journal of Engineering, Design and Technology*, 13(2), pp. 260–281.

Fagerberg, J., Mowery, D. and Nelson, R.R. (eds.) (2004) *The handbook of innovation*. Oxford: Oxford University Press.

Flint, D.J., Larsson, E., Gammelgaard, B. and Mentzer, J.T. (2005) 'Logistics innovation: A customer-value-oriented social process', *Journal of Business Logistics*, 26(1), pp. 113–147.

Freeman, C. (1989) *The economics of industrial innovation*. Cambridge, MA: MIT Press.

Gadde, L-E., Håkansson, H. and Persson, G. (2010) *Supply network strategies*. Chichester: John Wiley & Sons.

Gann, D.M. and Salter, A.J. (2000) 'Innovation in project-based, service-enhanced firms: The construction of complex products and systems', *Research Policy*, 29, pp. 955–972.

Håkansson, H. (ed.) (1987) *Industrial technological development – A network approach*. London: Croom Helm.

Håkansson, H., Ford, D., Gadde, L.-E., Snehota, I. and Waluszewski, A. (2009) *Business in networks*. Chichester: Wiley.

Håkansson, H. and Snehota, I. (1995) *Developing relationships in business networks*. London: Routledge.

Harty, C.F. (2008) 'Implementing innovation in construction: Contexts, relative boundedness and actor-network theory', *Construction Management and Economics*, 26(10), pp. 1029–1041.

Havenvid, M.I., Hulthén, K., Linné, Å. and Sundquist, V. (2016) 'Renewal in construction projects: Tracing effects of client requirements', *Construction Management and Economics*, 34(11), pp. 790–807.

Hulthén, K., Sundquist, V., Gadde, L.-E. and Eriksson, V. (2016) *Logistikens roll i effektiva byggprocesser*. Research report. Sveriges Byggindustrier.

Ivory, C. (2005) 'The cult of customer responsiveness: Is design innovation the price of a client-focused construction industry?', *Construction Management and Economics*, 23(8), pp. 861–870.

Jang, H., Russell, J.S. and Yi, J.S. (2003) 'A project manager's level of satisfaction in construction logistics', *Canadian Journal of Civil Engineering*, 30, pp. 1133–1141.

Janné, M. (2018) *Construction logistics in urban areas*. Thesis no. 1806 Licentiate thesis, Linköping University.

Josephson, P.-E. and Saukkoriipi, L. (2005) *Slöseri i byggprojekt. Behov av förändrat synsätt*. Göteborg: FoU-Väst.

Keupp, M.M., Palmié, M. and Gassman, O. (2012) 'The strategic management of innovation: A systematic review and paths for future research', *International Journal of Management Reviews*, 14(4), pp. 367–390.

Lindén, S. and Josephson, P.-E. (2013) 'In-housing or outsourcing on-site materials handling in housing', *Journal of Engineering, Design and Technology*, 11(1), pp. 90–106.

Pavitt, K. (2002) 'Innovating routines in the business firm: What corporate tasks should they be accomplishing?', *Industrial and Corporate Change*, 11(1), pp. 117–133.

Peng, D.X., Schroeder, R.G. and Shah, R. (2008) 'Linking routines to operations capabilities: A new perspective', *Journal of Operations Management*, 26(6), pp. 730–748.

Piening, E.P. and Salge, T.O. (2014) 'Understanding the antecedents, contingencies, and performance implications of process innovation: A dynamic capabilities perspective', *Journal of Product Innovation Management*, 32(1), pp. 80–97.

Reichstein, T., Salter, A.J. and Gann, D.M. (2008) 'Break on through: Sources and determinants of product and process innovation among UK construction firms', *Industry and Innovation*, 15(6), pp. 601–625.

Richardson, G.B. (1972) 'The organisation of industry', *The Economic Journal*, 82(327), pp. 883–896.

Segerstedt, A. and Olofsson, T. (2010) 'Supply chains in the construction industry', *Supply Chain Management: An International Journal*, 15(5), pp. 347–353.

Slaughter, S. (1993) 'Builders as sources of construction innovation', *Journal of Construction Engineering and Management*, 119(3), pp. 532–549.

Slaughter, S.E. (1998) 'Models of construction innovation', *Journal of Construction Engineering and Management*, 124(3), pp. 226–231.

Slaughter, S. (2000), 'Implementation of construction innovation', *Building Research and Information*, 28(1), pp. 1–17.

Strandberg, J. and Josephson, P.-E. (2005) 'What do construction workers do? Observations in housing projects', in *Proceedings of the 11th Joint CIB International Symposium Combining Forces*, Helsinki, June 13–16, pp. 184–193.

Sundquist, V., Gadde, L.-E. and Hulthén, K. (2018) 'Reorganising construction logistics for improved performance', *Construction Management and Economics*, 36(1), pp. 49–65.

Sveriges Byggindustrier. (2010) *Effektiva byggtransporter*, Sveriges Byggindustrier, Stockholm. www.bygg.org. Accessed 3 September 2014.

Teece, D.J. (2007) 'Explicating dynamic capabilities: The nature and microfoundations of (sustainable) enterprise performance', *Strategic Management Journal*, 28(13), pp. 1319–1150.

Teece, D.J., Pisano, G. and Shuen, A. (1997) 'Dynamic capabilities and strategic management', *Strategic Management Journal*, 18(7), pp. 509–533.

Thunberg, M. and Persson, F. (2014) 'Using the SCOR model's performance measurements to improve construction logistics', *Production Planning and Control*, 25(13–14), pp. 1065–1078.

Von Hippel, E. (1988) *The sources of innovation*. New York: Oxford University Press.

Vrijhoef, R. and Koskela, L. (2000) 'The four roles of supply chain management in construction', *Journal of Purchasing and Supply Management*, 6(3–4), pp. 169–178.

Wegelius-Lehtonen, T. (2001) 'Performance measurement in construction logistics', *International Journal of Production Economics*, 69(1), pp. 107–116.

Winch, G. (1998) 'Zephyrs of creative destruction: Understanding the management of innovation in construction', *Building Research and Information*, 26(5), pp. 268–279.

Woiceshyn, J. and Daellenbachm, U. (2005) 'Integrative capability and technology adoption: Evidence from oil firms', *Industrial and Corporate Change*, 14(2), pp. 307–342.

Xue, X., Zhang, R., Yang, R. and Dai, J. (2014) 'Innovation in construction: A critical review and future research', *International Journal of Innovation Science*, 6(2), pp. 111–126.

Ying, F., Tookey, J. and Roberti, J. (2014) 'Addressing effective construction logistics through the lens of vehicle movements', *Engineering, Construction and Architectural Management*, 21(3), pp. 261–275.

Zollo, M. and Winter, S.G. (2002) 'Deliberate learning and the evolution of dynamic capabilities', *Organization Science*, 13(3), pp. 339–351.

6 Cross-fertilization between construction and clinical actors

The dynamics of health care construction projects

Alessandra Tzannis, Silvia Biraghi and Rossella C. Gambetti

Introduction

In the framework of the construction industry, health care represents a vibrant nexus that connects a complex network of private and public actors, political and societal issues, technical/technological and organizational requirements, developers, and customers' expectations and needs.

Taking into consideration the Italian health care landscape, we can see that it has profoundly changed in recent years. There is a need for a new scenario that contributes to change and develops a new hospital model, the so named hospital for intensive care. The hospital for the intensity of care is a model focused on becoming increasingly characterized as a place fully dedicated to acute care and one that solidly relies on the territorial activities that promote this continuity of care. The resulting organizational model brings with it an important change both in the mentality and in the modus operandi of all professionals who work there.

The main pillars on which this new model is based are manifold. The philosophy that guides the structure is a service optimization program, the main objective of which is to increase the quality of the services provided using the same resources. In terms of this intensity of care, the main protagonist is the patient, unlike the traditional hospital, which is organized by discipline and where patients are hospitalized in different units according to their pathology. In the new model, patients are admitted on the basis of their clinical instability and the complexity of their needed care, and it is the duty of these several professionals to provide satisfactory care.

Any hospital's prerequisites is to guarantee high-quality services through a close integration of all the actors (clinical and technical) thanks to key integration tools (briefing, clinical health records, data sharing, etc.). However, these assumptions cannot be feasible without a total rethinking of the health facility in a more modern way. This rethinking starts with the physical spaces and a new architecture of the spaces themselves, so that service innovation (the new hospital model for intensity of care), as proposed by the new instances of such care, is made possible. Thus, the key research questions that inspired the work presented in this chapter are the following:

R1: How can innovation in a hospital context be generated?
R2: How can the construction industry contribute to generating this innovation?
R3: What role does the interaction among heterogeneous project actors play in innovative construction projects?

In terms of contributions, this chapter provides insights into how multiple and diverse actors (related to the construction industry, the clinical and technical field) interact, interface, and negotiate their perspectives, priorities, and solutions to accomplish complex construction projects. The final aim of our work is to understand how these interactions and negotiations affect the way in which the processes develop the specific aims and solutions of a project.

For analysing the interactional patterns within an innovative construction project, and more specifically, analyzing a health care construction project, we adopted the Actors, Resources. Activities (ARA) model (Håkansson and Snehota, 1995; Harrison and Prenkert, 2009) that was developed within the IMP research approach (Industrial Marketing and Purchasing). The ARA model is a framework that conceptualizes firms embedded in the network-like constellations of business relationships. A number of empirical studies over the last 40 years have shown that building relationships is an opportunity for firms to access strategic resources in an innovative and dynamic way. This framework was developed with the intention of empirically tracing the variety of perceptions regarding relationships (Corsaro, Ramos, Henneberg and Naudé, 2012; Laari-Salmela, Mainela and Puhakka, 2015) that underline the characteristics of the contexts (Henneberg, Rohrmus and Ramos, 2006), the surroundings, and the interactions (Ramos, Roseira, Brito, Henneberg and Naudé, 2013) that are held by a multiplicity of interrelated, cooperating, and sometimes even competing actors.

The remainder of this chapter is organized as follows: Section 1 presents the theoretical perspective grounded in the IMP approach and the ARA model. Section 2 outlines the research setting and the case study, which is then followed by the objectives of the chapter, the research methodology, and framework for data analysis in section 3. Section 4 presents the results and a discussion of the major findings. Finally, Section 5 reports concluding remarks indicating that the heterogeneity of the actors' operating in innovative health care construction projects works both as a facilitator and as a developer of friction in the renewal processes. On the one hand, a range of specific competences is needed to re-conceive the relationship between the physical design and the construction of a hospital and its delivery of health services. On the other hand, the hospital requires a re-conception of the project organization and how it should operate across the different phases of the project. Thus, in the actual execution of such innovative and complex projects, which actors are involved and how they should interact during the course of the project are key issues for the successful innovativeness of each project.

Theoretical perspective: using the ARA model to analyse innovation in construction projects

When companies perform new or existing activities in a new way, that action is often considered to be innovation. In other words, innovation involves a "change in routine" (Nelson and Winter, 1982, p. 128) and the "carrying out of new combinations" (Schumpeter, 1934, p. 65). How innovation is achieved and what drives and impedes innovation processes are processes heavily related to industry-specific features and the evolution of industries (Abernathy and Utterback, 1978; Malerba, 2004). The construction industry is constantly accused of being non-innovative and too conservative. The discussion indicates the need for a deeper understanding of what innovation actually is within construction, how it happens, and the impact of the construction industry's specific features on innovation processes (Bygballe and Ingemansson, 2014).

The industry has several specific features that are likely to affect how innovation is or can be achieved. Earlier studies have shown that contextual features, such as the regulatory environment, have a strong effect on how innovation is either fostered or hindered (Blayse and Manley, 2004; Bygballe and Ingemansson, 2014). Organizational features also have an impact. Project organization is arguably both a driver and an innovation hindrance (Slaughter, 2000; Winch, 2000), and a lack of long-term relationships (Dubois and Gadde, 2000, 2002) and integration in the supply chain (Akintoye, McIntosh and Fitzgerald, 2000) are often pointed to as an inhibiting innovation. The complexity of the construction process itself is yet another complicating factor (Gidado, 1996; Miozzo and Dewick, 2004). The industry involves many actors and interactions at multiple levels, which means that the innovation process needs to engage a set of different actors who have different logics (Bygballe and Jahre, 2009; Bygballe and Ingemansson, 2014).

Particularly, construction companies must interact with other actors in order to develop and implement new solutions. According to Blayse and Manley (2004), clients are often the recipients of new solutions; yet without the knowledge about what fits into the use context, it is difficult to implement new solutions and create benefits (Bygballe and Ingemansson, 2014). Companies are interlaced by continuous interaction processes wherein they undergo reciprocal adaptation (Håkansson and Snehota, 1995). In such interactions, companies have access to and exchange activities and resources with other actors. In this regard, the ARA model (Håkansson and Snehota, 1989) conceptualizes the links that exist among actors, activities, and resources in both dyadic and multiple inter-organizational relationships, which can then be considered a suitable lens through which innovation in the construction industry can be analysed well.

The ARA model (Håkansson and Johanson, 2001) represents a conceptual framework of the processes and outcomes of interaction. This model is based on three variables: actors, resources, and activities. The application of this model allows, as stated by Håkansson and Snehota (1995), an integrated analysis of the stability and development of an industrial system. De facto, this model implies that the result of a business relationship can be described in terms of three layers: Actor Bonds, which are created between actors who create and transfer resources of various natures (Resource Ties) through activities (Activity Links). Moreover, the model implies that all three layers are interconnected. Each influences and is influenced by the constellation of resources, the pattern of activities, and the actual actors in the wider network (Ford, Gadde, Håkansson and Snehota, 2003).

- *The actor layer*: This layer refers to interpersonal relationships and the links developed between individuals through interaction. As discussed by Huemer (1998; 2014), the stability of this layer depends on the degree to which the actors see, know, and feel close to one another; how they trust, appreciate, and influence one another; and how they become mutually committed. The strength of the bonds of this relationship will influence the actors' perception of the future of that specific interaction. As emerged in the research of Dahlquist (1998) and Håkansson and Johanson (2001), actor bonds are fundamental for the 'learning' and 'teaching' of counterparts of solutions and opportunities.
- *The activity layer*: This layer considers the more or less large integration and coordination of activities that may grow among the actors. De facto, it is possible to have more or less integrated activities together, such as production, logistics, or deliveries. Through this layer, the activity structures of two companies may become more or less systematically and firmly linked (Richardson, 1972; Torvatn, 1996; Dubois, 1998). Activity links will also have economic effects on the actors who are involved.
- *The resource layer*: This layer relates to the degree of adaptation or connection between two actors' resources, as their interaction develops. In this layer, both tangible and intangible resources are considered. Resource ties occur as the two actors in the relationship confront and jointly adapt their resources over time (Hallen, Johanson and Seyed-Mohamed, 1991). The process of adapting resources can make their use more efficient. However, the most important aspect is that the continuous confrontation of resources highlights the development of new joint resource combinations in the process of innovation (Håkansson, 1987; Biemans, 1992; Lundgren, 1995; Laage-Hellman, 1997; Holmen, 2001; Håkansson and Waluszewski, 2002, 2007).

The interconnection of these three elements (Ford et al., 2003) results in a network of different business relationships (Håkansson and Johanson, 1992). Therefore, from this perspective, business interactions are analysed as part of a wider network of relationships and take place over time (Axelsson and Easton, 1992), also including certain interdependencies among the organizational, the relational, and the network levels of that analysis. Thus, the interactions will occur among:

- The perceived organizational structure, the actor bond, and the network of actors;

- The perceived resource collection, the resource ties, and the resource constellations;
- The perceived activity structure, the activity links, and the activity patterns.

As Håkansson and Ingemansson (2013) and Havenvid et al. (2016) contend, studying the dynamics of connections among activities, resources, and the actors in inter-firm relationships is a way to investigate innovation from the perspective of renewal being made possible in three different dimensions; how the actors relate to one another over time (changes in the actor bonds), how they interrelate the activities (changes in activity links), and how they combine their resources (changes in resource ties) in new ways. Drawing on the IMP research tradition (see Håkansson, Ford, Gadde, Snehota and Waluszewski, 2009), the construction industry is seen by these authors as an industrial network. This perspective is adopted because any big change that is introduced, such as a new construction project, certainly does not affect only the firm that oversees the construction project but also many other organizations involved in the architectural, operational and management work related to the specific project. In line with Slaughter's definition, innovations in a construction industry are related to "the carrying out of new combinations" (Schumpeter, 1934, p. 65; Bygballe and Ingemansson, 2014) for interconnected activities, resources, and actors (Håkansson and Waluszewski, 2007) that then lead to "a non-trivial improvement in a product, process, or system that is actually used and which is novel to the company developing it" (Slaughter, 2000, p. 3). From an industrial network perspective, therefore, there is a certain correspondence between the type of inter-organizational interface and the likelihood of innovation occurring.

The construction industry involves many actors and interactions at multiple levels, which means that the innovation process must engage a set of different actors with different economic logics (Bygballe and Jahre, 2009). Building on Havenvid, Hulthén, Linné and Sundquist (2016), we argue here that any form of innovation will involve changes from a network perspective in how the actors relate to one another, and how resources are combined and activities are coordinated with one another.

Construction companies are increasingly working more systematically to turn project-level ideas into company-wide knowledge. This scenario indicates an innovation logic that is oriented towards the exploitation of new combinations through an internal network. The companies are also increasingly concerned with establishing closer connections to those customers and users that have traditionally been weak. However, this consideration requires that not only the customer relationships must change but also the relationships on the supply side. Companies in the construction industry should be conscious about their innovation logic in terms of whether they base their innovation behaviour on a biased orientation towards exploitation or exploration and towards the internal or external network (Bygballe and Ingemansson, 2014).

Innovation in the construction industry can take many forms based on whether that innovation is "incremental" (small, and based on existing experience and knowledge) "radical" (a breakthrough in science or technology), "modular" (a change in concept within a component only), "architectural" (a change in links to other components or systems), or "systematic" (multiple, integrated innovations) (Slaughter, 1998).

Construction innovation encompasses a wide range of participants within a "product system" (Marceau et al., 1999). As Blayse and Manley contend (2004, p. 144), this broad view includes such actors as governments, building materials suppliers, designers, general contractors, specialist contractors, the labour workforce, owners, professional associations, private capital providers, end users of public infrastructure, vendors and distributors, testing service companies, educational institutions, certification bodies, and others.

Going further in depth, not considering a generic construction project or innovation process but a contextualized setting – that is to say the health care environment – the concept of innovation and its generation process may assume certain unique characteristics in terms of the links among actors, resources, and activities. This specific health care context emerges as a prototypical context within which to examine in depth how the innovation is developed in the links among the three layers of the ARA model. Following Havenvid et al. (2016, p. 794), the health care sector emerges as a notable empirical setting to analyse for how the whole network of firms involved in such a project can influence innovation in construction. Health care projects are highly demanding in terms of their design and architectural function as well as their construction process. Hence, they place high expectations on the construction actors, which are then urged to strive for new and efficient solutions while relying on unprecedented combinations of activities and resources. This is why this chapter will focus on this setting.

In the next sections, we empirically illustrate this networked view on innovation that leverages the ARA model by offering a case study set in the health care context, which elucidates how interactions and collaborations between diverse actors have actually represented key enabling factors for the negotiation and definition of innovation.

The research setting: the health care sector

Health care is one of the areas where the rate of progress of science and technology over the last century has been most remarkable, both in terms of medical procedures and technologies and innovations in the construction dynamics and solutions developed. However, many questions associated with innovation in the health care context remain unanswered, and the level of knowledge about the critical factors that drive innovation are yet to be explored. Particularly, very little is known about the contribution to innovation that originates in the construction process. Little effort has been made to clear up the mechanisms through which progress in medicine takes place and the general properties of health care innovation processes proceed (Gelijns and Rosenberg, 1994; Gelijns et al., 2001).

In Italy, 60% of hospitals are over 40 years old. To date, the state of health of these Italian hospitals is not the best. Here are some data (Mauri, 2017, www. cneto.it): 60% of these facilities are over 40 years old, and half of all the hospitals are too small. It follows, then, that in the first case we are dealing with buildings that are not always safe; in the second case, inefficiency dominates. A good hospital, on the other hand, must be designed and built specifically, from the roof to the cellar. Old historical buildings, no matter how evocative, can certainly not be adapted to the medical care being delivered in the third millennium.

Furthermore, the future is increasingly moving towards the so-called day hospital. If until recently facilities were designed largely to accommodate sick patients – 80% of these spaces were in fact dedicated to hospitalization. However, now the trend is the opposite. Thanks to the evolution of technology, increasingly large spaces in hospitals are occupied by machines dedicated to diagnostics, therapies, and operating theatres. Optimizing care processes, shortening expectations, reducing the length of diagnostic and therapeutic pathways and the hospitalization – giving more space to the day hospital – means improving the yield of the 'hospital machine' and also the quality of life of the patient. Yet to achieve this result of fundamental importance, it is the architecture with which this hospital is designed that needs to be further innovated.

From a structural point of view, and thus a construction perspective, hospitals need to be lower and developed horizontally. For years, these facilities were built following a vertical model. Today, we know that this logic is highly inefficient. Hospitality, efficiency, and flexibility are realized only when a building is developed horizontally. Reducing height development means, for example, reducing vertical transport, often a source of disruption and construction hitches. That is why it is preferable that a modern hospital is no higher than three floors and that the patient in his or her different paths – from the operating room to the hospital – should not be forced into vertical transfers or be 'transported' for more than 100 metres. All this detail means better conditions for the patient – today in some hospitals the transition from one department to another is even done in an ambulance – and fewer resources needed for use.

Another element is the rethinking of the location of surgery units and first aid. A crucial issue in the organization of the facility is the separation of the different paths for those who go to the hospital. The outermost part must be dedicated to outpatient clinics, then to hospitalization, and finally to surgery units. On the alternative side, however, access to the emergency room should be immediately connected to the latter in case of extreme urgency. All thus falls into a 'village' that is quite similar to a small city, wherein there is a great variety of services, from laundries to gyms, from restaurants to various businesses, just as occurs in the 'mall' of the metropolis.

No longer departments but instead areas divided according to the severity of the clinical situation will create a hospital conceived for intensity of care. This is another innovation represented by the absence of departments divided by specialty. If until now, the inpatient units have always been divided by specialty and gender, today it is more important than ever to organize these departments in different kinds of groups, graduated by intensity, type, complexity, and duration of care based on the needs of patients. Medical ambulatories will be placed immediately next to these areas and will be aggregated to facilitate this exchange of knowledge and opinions.

Furthermore, having single rooms to reduce nosocomial infections, a further innovation, is even more visible to those who enter the hospital and see the organization of beds. Single rooms with private bathrooms, with the possibility of hosting a relative, and a series of services, starting with room temperature and adjustable lights, will become more and more widespread. The data in this regard are clear. When there are single rooms, the well-being of the patient is greater, and the possibility of nosocomial infections – a real scourge for hospitals – is thus reduced to a minimum.

Nevertheless, the structure and dynamics of innovation in health care are often assumed instead of being analysed. They tend to be considered in isolation from the broader framework of socio-economic systems, or they are rather narrowly seen as being disconnected from the system through which health services are delivered. Scholars seem to have neglected the systemic and dynamic aspect of the innovation processes in health care (Consoli and Mina, 2009). So far, the studies have adopted specific perspectives on innovation. That has resulted in privileging technological aspects (Gelijns and Rosenberg, 1994; Gelijns, Zivin and Nelson, 2001), economic issues (Pammolli et al., 2005; Wagrell and Waluszewski, 2009), or organizational mechanisms (Coombs and Metcalfe, 2000; Foss et al., 2011) as alternative drivers of the innovation promoted by lead users (Greer, 1988; Von Hippel, 2005; Ketley and Woods, 1993) or via cross-fertilization processes (Rogers, 1983; Gelijns and Rosenberg, 1994; Rosenberg, 1994).

Despite that circumstance, innovation in health care is an emergent non-deterministic process. Building new hospitals not only allows savings for the health system, but today several facilities are already beginning to resemble the hospital of the future, places where patients go, just as when you go to the airport for check-in. Patients will no longer be forced to 'run' to different departments but can be served in a single clinic where all the various specialists will be available. No longer will a hospital be built based only on the needs of the doctor but instead based on the needs of the patient.

As such, this hospital model relies on interconnected relationships (Tzannis, 2013) and is generated via complex interactions across heterogeneous knowledge bases (Blume, 1992; Coombs et al., 2003; Metcalfe et al., 2005) that belong to heterogeneous actors (Corsaro et al., 2012). These interactions, in order to be possible for this innovative hospital model, strongly rely on developing partnership relationships with all the project actors along the entire construction process. Construction is indeed the key process that has been variously documented to clearly affect project innovation. Such partnering in construction has been described as "the most significant development to date as a means of improving project performance" (Wood and Ellis, 2005, p. 317). Indeed, it represents a fundamental shift from the traditional adversarial relationships in construction. Different approaches and applications of this concept have been developed, and they have captured a wide range of behaviours, attitudes, values, practices, tools, and techniques' (Bresnen and Marshall, 2000, p. 231). Still, as Bygballe and colleagues (Bygballe, Jahre and Swärd, 2010, pp. 239–240) have noticed, despite a serious interest, efforts to implement the partnering concept in the construction industry have yet to yield the positive effects that have occurred in other industrial contexts (Winch, 2000). This perceived underperformance is explained by the tendency to focus on the dyadic relationships between clients and main contractors while neglecting the importance of further involving subcontractors and suppliers (Dainty, Briscoe and Millett, 2001; Bresnen and Marshall, 2002; Miller, Packham and Thomas, 2002).

Inside the health care sector, the hospital represents a complex service structure that acts as a privileged melting pot wherein the perspectives, needs, experiences, and expectations of all the actors working in health care meet. Therefore, understanding how the development of partnership relationships throughout the construction process can help liberate the innovation potential of any project is particularly relevant, from both a conceptual and a pragmatic standpoint. In addition, the hospital in its operational logic is a uniquely innovative context in which value co-creation can be achieved only by understanding how the actors negotiate and manage the institutions along the whole construction process (rules, procedures, meanings, standardized or replicable). In addition, it is a context where knowledge is crystallized and shared in the network to support the different project management phases.

The case study presentation: the Vimercate Hospital

In the last ten years, Italy has carried out numerous structural and technological innovations in health care construction. Examples are 496 yards of new or renewed hospital surface for a total investment of around €3 billion by the Lombardy Region; construction of several new structures (i.e. Varese and Broni-Stradella, Niguarda, Bergamo, Como, Vimercate, and Legnano); and innovative forms of contracts (Project Financing and Concession).

Our study is specifically set in the context of the Vimercate Hospital (Figure 6.1), which:

> represents a change project in the relationship between illness and health and an effective hospital built on collaborative work: each actor must understand and triangulate developers', adopters', and users' expectations (clinicians, patients, caregivers, hosts, etc.).
>
> (Vimercate Hospital, General Director)

Here we specifically focus on the Vimercate project because in its construction, three main aspects stand out that characterize its innovative contribution to how the construction industry operates when improving health care facilities. Those aspects are the following:

- *Renewal*: Moves from traditional and old hospitals made of multi-buildings often added at different times to a unique structure with connected areas that follow an organizational model based on an 'intensity of care' hospital

Figure 6.1 Vimercate Hospital's new shape: the top view rendering

(115.588 square metres of total area); each project is guided to suitably meet the staff (clinical) and the host (care) needs; a structured work flow and different competences are involved; the rationalization of pathways from external users/patients, to operators and suppliers; the new structure lends itself to future adaptations without major costs thanks to planar floors and plasterboard walls, plants that go into a suspended ceiling; a pneumatic tube that connects all departments (for transport tests and drugs); heavy transport for catering, materials, and linen via robots with a wireless monitoring; the entire hospital is connected via a computer network; a dedicated heliport for transporting patients from the Vimercate Hospital to other specialized hospitals; a rationalization of the number of beds (from 700–800 in the old hospital organization to 538 in the new one);

- *Internationalization*: Is an international architectural project in terms of the actors involved at the different stages of the construction management process; the idea of 'petals' or buildings for the hospitalization area derives from the cross-fertilization perspective (buildings not necessarily pertaining to the health care sector, coming from an international comparison/inspiration); international suppliers for technical/medical equipment and the PVC floors; the idea of dedicated parking areas (1,350 car parking spaces) comes from the observation of international construction industry projects; the same model for a hospital that is based on intensity of care is a concept that pertains to European guidelines;
- *Sustainability*: Construction materials for the building are locally supplied; large amounts of green spaces (the ground on which the new hospital is built was ex-farm land) all around with a park in front of the "petals" area; a cogeneration plant feeds on energy to the entire building; the horizontal structure of the building reduces the energy loss and reduces the environmental impact;

large amounts of glass surfaces are able to provide natural light; thanks to its peripheral location, traffic is reduced in Vimercate City, allowing lower noise generated by cars/ambulances; thanks to infrastructural rethinking, greater accessibility is guaranteed for those coming from outside; a recovery project for the old hospital makes space available for both residential areas and citizen services.

From its temporal development, the Vimercate Hospital began in 2002 and was completed in 2009 (Table 6.1 presents details about the different phases of the project development and the activities carried out in each phase).

In particular, after a zero phase that was dedicated to the feasibility study and a first phase for the preliminary project settings, the building construction work started in December 2006 and lasted until August 2009; the excavation work started in December 2006 and lasted until March 2007; the facilities construction work started in December 2006 and lasted until March 2008; the finishing work, utility systems, and equipment installation started in November 2007 and lasted to August 2009. The end of the overall project work was October 2009.

Research methodology and the framework for data analysis

From a methodological point of view, this section applies a qualitative approach (Dubois and Gadde, 2002; Dubois and Araujo, 2004) to develop the Vimercate case study fully (Harrison and Easton, 2004; Beverland and Lindgreen, 2010; Barrat et al., 2011). This methodological approach is particularly suitable to analyse, understand, and map the network designed for this large construction project so as to support the understanding of how partnership relationships along the construction process helped its innovation to develop. A case-study approach is particularly relevant when the research aims are the following:

- Exploring a thematic area that is currently under-researched (namely, innovation through interconnectedness among actors, resources, and activities);

Table 6.1 The macro phases of the longitudinal project development

Project macro-processes	Scheduling
Feasibility study (2002)	Choice of location, volumes and space definition, financial and economical settings
Preliminary project (2002–2004)	Project and health care settings
Project financing (2005)	Concession contract, concession grantor organization
Signature of grant (2006)	Signature of grant
Work schedule (2006–2009)	Building construction work, excavation work, facilities construction work, finishing work, utility systems and equipment installation, completion and commissioning of co-generation plant

- Reconstructing and giving more sense to complex situations, multi-site and contextual data, and the mutable phenomena that characterize big project development;
- Gaining a deep and specific understanding of innovation dynamics of a big project to identify the key concepts, the central themes, and the situations (contexts and praxis) that are ideally typical for innovation;
- Inductively building a conceptual frame capable of depicting the phenomenon under study, starting with the context-intensive data (Eisenhardt and Graebner, 2007; Richards and Morse, 2009).

The data collection for this current case study was based on in-depth interviews and discussions that were directly collected during interactions with the actors involved in the project, archival sources and editorial materials (i.e. websites, business portals, research reports, and specialized publications), and also an analysis of the online conversations generated by the project and participant observation. Interviews were based on an ethnographic guide and were conducted face to face in the actual hospital/business setting.

The actors engaged in the research were selected according to the following criteria: all should be both internal actors and external actors with regard to the focal company (the Vimercate Hospital); they should represent different roles in the project development phases (technical, decisional and managerial, financial, clinical, etc.); and they should be actively part of the construction project to be able to provide precisely related insights.

Applying these criteria, the study collected 11 interviews that lasted from 60 to 120 minutes each and engaged the main players involved in the project, that is to say, the following participants:

- *Vimercate Hospital external actors*: one architect from Studio Redaelli, and one consultant from Studio Sinesis (a consultancy company offering effective solutions for accounting, management, organizational, and information needs);
- *Vimercate Hospital internal actors*: The General Director, one engineer from the internal technical office, the Risk Manager, the Medical Director, two clinicians, the Nursery Director, and two nurses.

Further, we visited the facility (the new Vimercate Hospital) and conducted sessions on focused observations to appreciate the innovative services actually at play. The interviews were structured to allow all participants to address the following research questions:

R1: How can innovation in a hospital context be generated?
R2: How can the construction industry contribute to generate this innovation?
R3: What role does the interaction among heterogeneous project actors play in innovative construction projects?

Table 6.2 Framework of analysis

Phase – Stages under consideration for naming the different phases			
Actor type	*Actor name*	*Activities*	*Resources*
Label of the actor according to role in the project	Specific identification of the actor under investigation and its positioning in terms of being local or international	Details about the activities carried out by the specific actor in the specific phase under consideration	Details about the resources, competences, and contributions in general provided by the specific actors in the specific phase under consideration that fostered the project development

In terms of our own data analysis, the approach was informed by the IMP Actors, Resources, Activities (ARA) model as a framework for that analysis (Hakansson and Snehota, 1995; Harrison and Prenkert, 2009). This framework was selected in order to capture the variety of perceptions that were gathered (Henneberg et al., 2006), the network pictures[1] (meaning the mental representations of the contexts) (Corsaro et al., 2012; Laari-Salmela et al., 2015), the surroundings, and the interactions (Ramos and Ford, 2011) held by a multiplicity of interrelated, cooperating, and even competing actors. Further still, a temporal dimension lens (Henneberg et al., 2013; Tzannis, 2013) was included in the framework to capture the evolution of the relationships during the different phases, the kinds of actors entering into the project development at each stage and their contributions in terms of the resources they brought to the project step by step (Table 6.2).

Results: interpreting the Vimercate Hospital project by applying the ARA model

The Vimercate Hospital was completed in 2009. The whole project involved a multiplicity of actors who brought to the project heterogeneous goals, expectations, approaches, competences, and resources across the different realization phases. In order to understand this complexity, the multi-actors' engagement, and the partnership relationships linking the heterogeneous actors, Figure 6.2 presents the overall network picture configuration of the Vimercate Hospital construction.

As the network picture indicates, four main categories of actors were strongly intertwined and revolved around the focal firm:

- *Institutional financial actors*: Such as the Lombardy Region and Infrastrutture Lombarde, specifically selected in order to grant the presence of actors' focus and the attention paid to the Regional Level development;

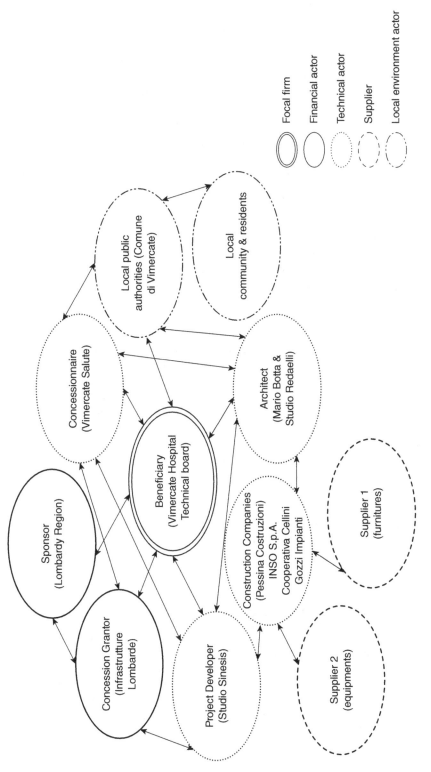

Focal firm

Financial actor

Technical actor

Supplier

Local environment actor

Figure 6.2 Vimercate Hospital network configuration

- *Technical actors (pertaining to different areas of support)*: Consultants specialized in construction industry projects management (such as Studio Sinesis), selected to grant expertise in this kind of project complexity; experts in big projects in the health care sector (such as Vimercate Salute) to grant a specific focus on industry constraints; the construction companies (such as Pessina Costruzioni, INSO S.p.A., Cooperativa Cellini, and Gozzi Impianti) selected to grant a local reward, all of them being regional realities; and architects (such as Studio Redaelli and Mario Botta, recognized at an international level) to grant overall project management not only in terms of costs, conflict management, timing and constraints but also for design, materials selection, and effective hospital health care service design;
- *Suppliers*: Specifically, selected to grant sustainability as a key value for the entire project development with all being locally located;
- *Local actors*: Such as Comune di Vimercate and the local community of residents, selected to grant their agreement and engagement in the sharing of the result for a project affecting the local environment (new infrastructure requirements, conversion of the old hospital into something for the community, new services diffusion, visibility, etc.).

As observed by the consultants from Studio Sines, these actors collaboratively institutionalized the hospital project management practices by designing, negotiating, and sharing rules, norms, meanings, and procedures in order to impact the degree to which the innovation was embedded and enacted throughout the project development phases. This aspect also brought to a new internal facility a reshaping, considering the relationships between the different internal actors (clinical ones) that strongly interacted with the external actors (technical and those related to the construction domain).

Starting with the research questions noted here in the methodological section, the main contributions that emerged from the case study are ascribable to interconnections and cross-fertilization among heterogeneous actors from both construction and health care as characterized by different core activities and different competences that contributed to develop innovative construction solutions. In the next section, we elaborate and offer critical analysis to highlight how innovation did emerge, thanks to the engagement of a multiplicity of actors during the construction project of the focal hospital.

How innovation emerged for the Vimercate Hospital

Currently, unlike in other European countries, the modification program in Italy is taking place within a quite underdeveloped context in terms of infrastructure. Examining the data of the Ministry of Health, we learn that 70% of public hospitals (approximately 800 facilities) are older than 30 years, while approximately 20% of them were built before 1900 and 30% are facilities that have fewer than 120 beds. Similar deficiencies are being found in long-term care units. On average, the equipment rate per 1,000 inhabitants is equal to 0.5% versus the 1% required by regulations.

Therefore, the infrastructure situation in Italian health care, as mentioned in the research setting sections herein, requires the system to be updated through the building of new facilities and conversion of the more obsolete ones. Public resources are not sufficient for rationalizing this necessary but costly program. Therefore, it is essential to resort to private capital or find other financial instruments than the typically traditional ones, as these will be more suitable for supporting the investment needed, for example in this case, the project financing instrument Vimercate Hospital Administration used to realize their new hospital.

Project financing is the instrument selected by the Vimercate Hospital Administration and supported by Infrastrutture Lombarde S.p.A. for the realization of the Vimercate's new hospital complex. This choice can be considered one of the aspects of innovation in this case study that was strongly made possible by collaboration. Project financing is an effective method that can provide private capital in addition to allocated public resources, at the same time enhancing the crucial role that even private organizations can play in the national health sector. The investment necessary for the realization of a new health care facility is partly guaranteed by the regional government and partly by the hospital building contractor, who became also its manager. Through a tender procedure managed by Infrastrutture Lombarde, in our case, the Lombardy Region entrusted the construction and management of the hospital to a temporary consortium affiliated with Pessina Costruzioni, which then established a special-purpose vehicle called Vimercate Salute S.p.A. upon contract awarding.

Vimercate Salute, as concessionaire, took care of drawing up the financial execution plan for the new hospital and the construction work and its management. Infrastrutture Lombarde supervised the quality of the procedures and work, acting as the body in charge of the high surveillance procedure. By virtue of the concession agreement that was signed, Vimercate Salute, whose investment was also remunerated through the collection of an availability payment for the use of the facility, was also entrusted with the management of the so-called non-core services (cleaning, food service, security), then entered into the management of the hospital services by necessarily interacting and avoiding conflicts with the internal board.

A hospital facility is a particularly complex structure, and this complexity affects both the construction phases and the management of the facility, namely, the hospital lifecycle. Project financing that covers both the stage of facility construction and that of its management seems to be the most appropriate instrument for this type of large enterprise. Attracting private capital, it ensures the great availability of funds that a health care infrastructure needs. On the other hand, this method implies having a precise assessment by the different parties, both private and public, technical and clinical, and, in this case, internal and external. All the parties involved needed to collaborate and share to make the mechanism fruitful, but how did they do this?

What background existed and conditioned the construction project?

The excellence of health care is measured based on the degree of humanization it offers. The Lombardy Region understands the humanization of services as the accommodation of patients in state-of-the-art facilities that are no longer conceived to meet only the needs of the medical staff but rather to also meet those of its patients.

> Patients have to feel at their ease, welcomed, and the plans for the building of new healthcare facilities, like the new Vimercate Hospital project, should be understood in this sense. What this project tries to achieve is to create spaces in which the culture of life and wellbeing is promoted, and in which doctors are motivated to constantly improve their performances.
>
> (Vimercate Hospital, General Director, Medical Director)

The Vimercate Hospital project offers certain considerations regarding the development of the urban area on the outskirts of towns, applying a perspective that takes into account and respects overall urban growth. Giving sense to the development of the area was the responsibility of the architects who were involved and entrusted with redesigning and healing the urban fabric of areas that were losing their significance and meaning due to urban sprawl. This project, in particular, represented downright 'surgery' because the building, given its considerable size (about 25,000–square-metre gross area), was meant to act as a benchmark for the future urban development of the neighbouring land. The choice of an orthogonal square mesh outlining the area that was meant to be taken up by the new hospital structure extended the built-up portion beyond its boundaries, including outdoors spaces (car parks and trees), which could become, without interruption, the natural extension of the indoor functions of the hospital.

> This way, the project wishes to take care of the whole extended area, protecting the dignity of the place its users, who enter the new structure after having left the major arterial route (tangenziale est) while still driving their cars. Visitors are tactfully received and introduced along this driveway into a place whose main aim is that of taking care of people's health.
>
> (Studio Redaelli, Architect)

Thus, we can say that the projects related to the new hospital of Vimercate could be understood as the:

> architectural expression of physical and psychological health care, and at the same time a symbol of respect of the environment and of the human beings through the progressive scale reduction of a building marked by an extraordinary size in physical terms, and an exceptional significance in relation to its intellectual, psychological and technological content.
>
> (Vimercate Hospital, Risk Manager)

The choice of a horizontal building structure contributes to creating a warm and friendly atmosphere, a mark of civility inserted between urban and natural environments, between town and park.

(Vimercate Hospital, Technical Office Engineer)

The urban morphology of Vimercate would certainly be badly affected by edifices that upset a typology that has, with very few exceptions, built a human scale environment over the course of time. This is the reason why the 'petals' of the inpatient units would take on the shape of large leaves, thereby harmonically blending into a park.

Building a hospital means building a home, a shelter for the difficult moments in life. That is why the project builds new spaces offering exceptional new properties that can take care of patient lives. The building's structure was divided into three sectors: the reception, the surgery block, and the inpatient units.

The overall look contributes to mark the complex as a little town which, experienced from within, becomes a central part of the actual town and no longer a peripheral place, providing a strong and comforting sense of belonging to this area.

(Studio Redaelli, Architect)

The subdivision of the three main functions into three separate and yet connected building blocks facilitated the understanding of structures the layout of which is often hard to grasp but that still ensures easy orientation for the users of this new compound as a whole.

The perception of the 3 main units of the hospital is also supported by the layout on inner spaces, where visitors – thanks to open courtyards – easily realize their position within the complex thanks to a rhythmical relationship with outdoor spaces. The courtyards also ensure that the inner spaces are sufficiently lit with natural light and properly aired. Everywhere the presence of plants characterizes nature's taking part in the life of the persons that have to spend some time in this place. Nature becomes a meditation element as well as an indicator that helps patients be aware of the time of the day and the passing of seasons.

(Vimercate Hospital, General Director)

A main street leads from the reception-admission area through the operating theatres and as far as to the petals of the inpatient units, which is exactly like a little village, where all shops look onto the main street. The inner spaces follow the principle of continuous scale reduction too, from the spacious car park dotted with vegetation to the two-floor-high reception/admission area, to the microcosm of the inpatient rooms, whose wide windows overlook the peaceful park.

The way the compound is structured enables a neat separation of its functions thus avoiding any crossing of activities that are mutually incompatible.

This is something new compared to the previous facility. This is not only an architectural innovation, it has an impact also in the service supply, generating more efficient space allocation, more effective healthcare services. This effectiveness relies not only on the service supplied to the patients, but also in the way in which the staff can work together thanks to the new space possibilities.

(Vimercate Hospital, Nurse Director and clinicians)

The reception block is connected to the town's fabric and acts as a link that marks the public function of the edifice, thanks to the presence of shops, cafeterias, etc. The inpatient units, marked by a more intimate atmosphere, face the park; the surgery block is placed between the two former units, almost as though to protect its delicate and precious technology content, whereas noisier areas like the accident and emergency department and the supplies unit are located on the sides of the facility. For the surgery block as well as the inpatient unit, the project provides spacious modular inner courtyards that are meant to supply natural lighting to most of the rooms and at the same time ensure sufficient flexibility to a facility that is ready to evolve and transform further so as to meet the continuous progress in the field of health care.

The prevailing material of the new building was brick and glass, a modern use of the traditional materials that are still typical of the Lombardy's Region known architecture.

The contributions of a 'technical board' to innovation

This aspect may be the most innovative aspect of the specific Vimercate project, as it provides an innovative insight into the construction industry sector.

The Vimercate Hospital was the first project in the Italian construction industry created by a so-called technical board made by clinicians (at different levels and pertaining to different health competences) and the internal directors of the operational activities (the technical office or the internal unit dedicated to the management of the project from an engineering point of view). Both were immediately engaged in the shaping of the future hospital and closely worked with the external actors involved. It was a real opportunity and an innovative way of managing this project in such a way as to engage its different health care management directions starting from the beginning. The idea was to involve representatives of all categories of internal users of the future hospital. Clinicians, nurses, administrative, technicians, logistics, etc., offered their ideas on daily operations to avoid creating project-related guidelines that rely only on technical aspects and that instead looked also at the health care service for its effectiveness and efficiency and considered both the strengths and weaknesses of the old hospital in order to improve, renew, and in some cases innovate the new hospital. The creation of this technical board, made up of mixed professions, had the goal of running smoothly and facilitating communications and interaction among the different actors (both inside and outside the hospital). Particularly, its contribution was to collect, monitor, and constantly guide the actions of all the different actors (internal and external), with the precise aim of maintaining a holistic view of the final result desired and thus obtained.

Indeed, it was necessary to construct a new hospital not only from a physical point of view (a new building compared to the previous one) but also a new concept of a hospital that could be more adherent to the guidelines and requests of the National Health System. It had to be a hospital for intensity of care. A new model of care based on collaboration, aggregation, and integration among the various clinical professionals had to be able to put patients and their health needs at the centre of the services supplied. Thus, the new hospital had to be designed differently from previous ones and had to have new types of spaces that were no longer linked to the traditional departmental health care approach. Thus, a so-named technical board was introduced: the internal technical office (particularly the engineer responsible for this hospital office) was called on to participate in the project design, as well as the clinical directors (doctors, nurses, laboratory responsible, etc.) and other responsible specialists (administration, logistics, procurement, etc.) (Figure 6.3). This technical board had to be a collegial body made up by the different actors' pertaining to different areas of the new care centre and in this way have a 360° vision and thus guide the management of the new internal service planning. As with any company board, all the members had a role inside, but someone was needed to represent this board outside, with the external actors bringing the board's requests to all the other actors involved; this role was assumed by the engineer of the technical office who became the representative of this board, similar to a gatekeeper.

Guided by the engineer of the technical office who represented the leading actor of this complex net of relationships, everyone was asked to imagine the ideal hospital, expressing the desired and trying to find alignments between these desired and the project ideas as carried out by the technical management of the project. The idea was to create a heterogeneous team of actors who were able to share specifics and visions about the final result to meet the defined needs and to correct any defects in the totally new hospital compared to the previous one (both in terms of dimensions, physical spaces, and service architecture).

According to Table 6.1, which relates to the scheduling of the construction project, five phases of development were identified: the *feasibility study*, the *preliminary project phase*, the *project financing*, the *signature of the grant*, and the *work schedule phase*. In a very interesting way, the contribution of the technical board can be seen in all of them, but it was particularly relevant in the first two, the phase in which the projects were settled, even as in each phase, the technical board contributed, new actors emerged, and specific activities and resources were shared. According to the framework of analysis noted in the methodological section, the ARA model was applied to identify the contributions of the technical board during the first and second phases of the construction project development.

The ARA model applied to the first contribution of the technical board: the feasibility study

The first contribution of the technical board to the project development can be called the feasibility study. This was the very first phase dedicated to the

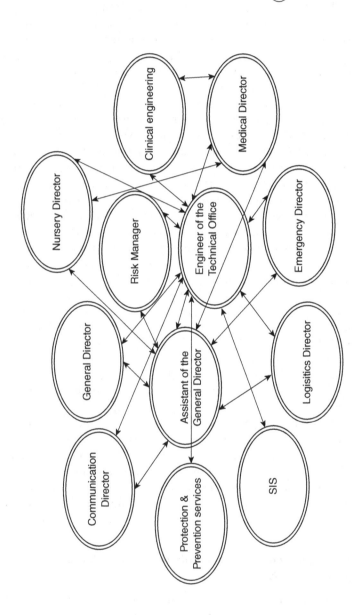

Figure 6.3 The network picture of the so-called Vimercate Hospital technical board

Table 6.3 The ARA model applied to the first contribution of the technical board

The feasibility study contribution

Actor type	Actor name	Activities	Resources
Technical board	Technical board	Owner of the feasibility study on volumes and financial requirements	Technical competencies (project management)
Local public administration	Comune di Vimercate	Area identification and urban variance	Network competencies Network relationships
Concession grantor	Lombardy Region with Infrastrutture Lombarde SpA	Sponsorship of the project for renewal and concessionaire and also the Final Inspection Authority	Financial resources Quality control competencies

relationship building among the parties and in which the technical board, thanks to its competencies (technical resources related to project management), was confronted with the local public administration and especially the Lombardy Region in order to evaluate the proposed construction of the new hospital and identify the possible area where to build. In that regard, phone calls, joint inspections, discussions took place on the project planimetry, necessary areas for the new facility development, discussions on the volumes to be dedicated to each future service or space, etc.

The aim of this relationship was to internally assess the technical board's skills and idea sharing with the territory, evaluate their feasibility, and prepare the steps of project development from bureaucratic planning and, above all, an economic point of view. Further, the Lombardy Region provided in this phase both contacts and relationships to allow the project to start (contact people for bureaucracy, for solvency evaluation, and for territorial authorizations, as well as urban planning experts, municipal authorities, etc.). At this moment, the Lombardy Region gave its approval to the financing (financial resources) (Table 6.3).

The ARA model applied to the second contribution of the technical board: the preliminary project phase

The second contribution of the technical board to the project development can be called the preliminary project phase. Here the technical bases of the project were laid out from both an operational and a financial point of view. It was a moment wherein all the main actors came into play. The contribution of the technical board, following a call for tenders, was supported by an external actor:

the professionals from the Studio Sinesis[2]. Thanks to these professionals the area identification, from a hospital location point of view, could be set up; Studio Sinesis also assisted the new hospital management in figuring out how to finance the project.

From a clinical needs point of view, a further specialized external actor (Vimercate Salute[3]) started working side by side with the designers and architects (Architetto Botta and Studio Redaelli) to support about space analysis and allocation for all the areas, i.e. the volumes and spaces to allow them to be interconnected in the best way possible.

In terms of the economic aspect, the Lombardy Region also decided to create a new ad hoc actor for the project (Infrastrutture Lombarde[4]), to which was assigned the role of concession grantor, as sponsor and controller of the project, thanks to its competencies in quality control and project management.

Then came the moment when construction experts and health experts entered. The local community during this moment thus loses its relevance. It is precisely from this moment that the technical board acquires its leading role over the other actors involved. Its responsibility from now going forward is to set up the better planning of health care services and attempt to realize certain innovations not ever possible in the old hospital facility (Table 6.4).

The third, fourth, and fifth contributions of the technical board: project financing, signature of the grant, and work schedule

In these moments, the concession contract, the organization of the grant, and the technical construction started on the building construction works, the excavations, the facilities construction, the single block units building, the equipment

Table 6.4 The ARA model applied to the second contribution of the technical board

The preliminary project contributions

Actor type	Actor name	Activities	Resources
Concession grantor	Lombardy Region with Infrastrutture Lombarde SpA	Sponsorship of the project for renewal and concessionaire	Financial resources Quality control competencies
Concessionnaire	Vimercate Salute	Working plans, construction, and management of the structure	Technical competencies (project management and engineering)
Project development	Studio Sinesis	Professionals in construction industry and owners of the engineering and systems planning	Technical competencies (project management and engineering)

The preliminary project contributions

Actor type	Actor name	Activities	Resources
Technical board	Technical board	Supervision of the entire project and responsible for health care needs (An internal committee guided the connection between the external and the internal needs of the project.)	Medical competencies Services competencies Quality control competencies Communication and marketing competencies Public sector competencies ITC competences and resources Technical competencies (project management competencies) Architectural and design competencies Logistic competencies
Architects	Arch. Mario Botta and Studio Redaelli Associati	Design projects and master plans that represent renewal in spaces and building concepts, shapes, layout, materials and components.	Architectural and design competencies Technical and material competencies

installations, and the collateral services development. These phases can be considered together. Having decided on the project financing contingencies, this is the moment in which the technical board, together with all the actors of the project, needed to interact to manage the construction and its different activities. It is a complex moment in which the heterogeneous actors need to contribute according to their roles and work to overcome conflicts. Conflicts, for example, can be due to the different objectives related to the different roles in the project (clinical objective compared to technical ones) in terms of time management, the priorities settings for the project development process, the resource allocation, project financing sources, conflicts generated by dysfunctional communications ambiguity in designated responsibilities, etc. Examples of the ways in which these conflicts can be solved is related to the ability of the gatekeeper actor (the board) to maintain the connection with all the interlocutors for meetings, reports creation, engaging representatives of the different roles in decision making, and asking for contributions.

Further, new actors enter those last phases that relate to the construction companies and the local suppliers being engaged. The local community and the residents in this phase become active once again in terms of interlocutors who are able to support the reshaping of the surroundings, the diffusion of the project, and the visibility provided to any new services.

Conclusions and insights from the Vimercate Hospital case study

Based on our analysis, a first result that emerged was that, in this specific project, the Vimercate Hospital, innovation *was developed, thanks to the productive interactions among the multiple actors involved*. This manner of creating innovation by adopting a network approach seems particularly interesting in the construction industry whose value chain interconnects local and global actors who can bring to projects their specialized knowledge, skills, and solutions, as well as their agendas and expectation of the final outcomes. The interrelations among these actors generated a cross-fertilization among construction and related clinical actors, pushing them towards interdependencies and also interplay, ultimately affecting how innovation manifested. That process represents a critical issue that the construction industry must confront to enhance its innovation capabilities (Miozzo and Dewick, 2004) and to face tomorrow's challenges and demands and overcome the traditional pitfalls found in knowledge transfer between individual projects and actors (Håkansson and Ingemansson, 2013).

Additionally, and still related to these first results, we believe this case study provides interesting insights that can concurrently enrich the ongong literature debate on both innovation in construction and IMP business relationships by unpacking the connectivity logic that characterizes each phase of the implementation process of any complex construction project, such as that of a hospital. As stated earlier, the health care sector lacks any thorough investigation of how innovation can occur by interconnecting a plethora of heterogeneous actors in each phase of the construction process. In this case, our study, although not generalizable and needing some consolidation, offers a holistic and contextualized perspective for how the management of multiple actors as a network of interconnected agents, activities, and resources during construction process can release innovation potential, especially at both architectural and system levels (Slaughter, 1998). According to these considerations, as a second result of the Vimercate Hospital, we could see emerge *a construction process that introduced changes in the construction system of health care projects by adopting a collaborative partnership orientation, thanks to the contributions of a gatekeeper actor*.

The main actor involved in this instance, the hospital technical board itself, outlined the clinical needs and the service gap and was the gatekeeper actor. A new idea of hospital, by considering the National Health System requirements, and a new configuration of patient services were the necessities leading the project and guiding the relationship with all other technical actors involved and the eventual integration of the different perspectives as to create a step-by-step managed process orientation.

The cooperation seen within the health and technical organizations here called for other partners' selection and alignment for the project construction idea: The financial actors, the local authorities, the project developers, the architect, the construction companies, and the different technical departments and suppliers. Thanks to the interaction between the different actors involved in the project, the Vimercate Hospital sustained and proposed its organization as a new, innovative, local service within the Regional Health System. On the one side (business relationships), members of both the clinical and technical sectors (pertaining to the broad construction industry) could develop and deepen new skills, while the members of the industrial sector could find new perspectives for the creation of new applications in the health care context. On the other side (social ties) the presence of the internal technical board represented an occasion for competencies, needs, and perspective sharing that otherwise would not have been possible. Technicians and health care professionals were seated at the same table, working together at the same project and contributed to it by offering their different perspectives according to the roles covered in their daily activities. In this way, the new hospital design thus emerged as systemic: a bundle of different and mixed exigencies, not concentrated on a unique perspective (the technical or the clinical one in an exclusive way).

On the other side (social ties), the final customers, the patients, can benefit from new types of intervention and treatment, thereby benefiting from a simplified and more 'human–oriented' clinical path. In fact, the way in which this hospital was conceived was completely different from any other facility in the health care sector: its architectural shape, materials selected, the space allocation, the technologies introduced, the internal pathways, and close attention to sustainability. This aspect, of course, is related to the innovation in the construction industry, but it affects in a very deep way the very services being delivered.

Applying these considerations, as a third result of the Vimercate Hospital, we can note that *networking improves the effectiveness of health services overall.* One insight related to the contribution of heterogeneous actors is highlighted in the ARA model. In a complex health care project, certain key actors can be highlighted (Tzannis, 2013): *technicians* who are represented by those actors who bring into the project the specialized technical know-how required to design, plan, execute, and construct the hospital and its related technologies and services; *managers* or anybody involved in the project who must deal with budget issues, administration, or regulation; *clinicians* who are the personnel working in the hospital under study; the *public* including patients, their caregivers, and public opinion in general, including people from the local community, the media, and more broadly any commentators on the project. All these actors are characterized by their different focal concerns and different degree of involvement in the development and accomplishment of the actual project (Ibarra, 1993) through future actions (Lenney and Easton, 2009) and to the degree of influence they do exert in driving codifying and institutionalizing innovation development (Vargo et al., 2015).

In particular, this consideration divides the results herein into two subsets: mono for the actors who were involved mainly in one phase of the big project, for example, the design, project development, construction, etc.; and multi for those actors who became key players in more than one phase of the full project. This consideration can lead to the underlying finding and conclusion that different types of actors do bring into big projects different priorities, issues, and expectations. Since each of these categories can have different agendas, it becomes valuable here to say that any actor provides specific contributions and influences the final outcome of any project and the codifying practices that link to further development of positive innovation based on a network approach.

According to these considerations, as a fourth result of the Vimercate Hospital, it became evident that *the networking promoted by the project allowed changes in health care relationships*. Two different professional actors, the clinicians from the one side and the industrial actors pertaining to project management and the construction industry from another side, previously worked separately and at a different step of the service supply chain. They were professionals working in separate worlds with no connections or points of common activities. In the new hospital generation, however, they needed to shift and above all decide to share their approaches. A common technical board composed of mixed actors was able to look at the same picture (the implementation plan of the hospital) and work together to foresee and preview the activities and provide unique and needed insights for how to shape the facility. All actors required and needed the sharing of common data, common languages, and a holistic approach towards the entire project development. The conflicts arising from the different perspectives on the service supply and the priorities were overcome, thanks to the common goal of the project, which was a unique facility with connected areas that was built according to an innovative and more functional model of a hospital based on patient-centred intensity of care.

In line with that focus, our case study depicts how the management of different kinds of partnership relationships makes possible such an output, the main final objective of which is related not only to needed innovation in construction industry but also to creating (thanks to the output of this construction project) a new hospital facility, increased value, and enhancing the overall quality of services both for the internal (personnel) and the external interlocutors (local community, patients, institutions, etc.).

In conclusion, therefore, innovative services are best generated through the development of relationships that enable the exchange and sharing of resources among all heterogeneous actors whose innovative outputs are made up of new interactions (new ways of interacting and new kinds of actors who are involved in such interaction), of new solutions being proposed, and of new ways of doing business that integrate the activities of different professionals. The development of innovative health care services requires that all involved parties overcome their individual barriers and single/unilateral-view approach and work to adopt a collaborative approach that works to achieve the end goal of a planned project.

Notes

1 The network pictures presented here are the result of the alignment effort among the different mental representations of the actors that were interviewed. Therefore, the result shown in this chapter is not something created by the authors autonomously, but rather it is an agreed network picture coming from a shared discussion among all the actors mentioned in the bullet points in this methodological section. The actors were called on to reconstruct the actors and the relationships drawing them together for a unique discussion. The authors mediated the conflicts and guided the finding of the shared solution.

2 Sinesis Consulting is an organization founded with the intention of offering concrete and effective solutions for the accounting, management, organizational, and information needs of the medium-sized and small business. Its specific competencies pertain to accounting consulting; budget analysis and economic-financial simulations; group accounting and control; business planning; bookkeeping; report preparation; information systems for high direction; management and reporting control systems; project management and benchmarking.

3 Vimercate Salute is a company that operates in the oil, industrial, and civil sectors in the design of projects and plants. It provides private clients and public administrations with engineering and architectural services related to feasibility studies, supervision of the construction of buildings and infrastructures in the fields of oil and gas, large-scale distribution, hospital and residential construction. The group, strong and cohesive, is oriented towards a global type of design research and offers modern and effective design solutions in terms of time, cost, and quality to meet the needs of the client fully. The company, with its experience and technical professionals, has worked in various fields of civil engineering, plant engineering, and management with dozens of achievements noted in various sectors. Thanks to these competencies, in this specific project, it is responsible for developing the initial project and then, going forward, for the project management until there is complete realization and testing.

4 Infrastrutture Lombarde S.p.A. is a company wholly owned by the Lombardy Region and established to coordinate the construction of new infrastructure projects and operating according to the 'in-house providing' module. It carries out contracting services for the contracting authorities and operates as a central purchasing body, implementing the strategic guidelines established by the Lombardy Region. The main activities in which Infrastrutture Lombarde exercises the skills it has acquired over the years are construction of new infrastructures, as a granting authority or as a technical-administrative support to the Companies of the Regional System; offering assistance activities during the design and construction phase of these works; enhancing existing infrastructures, with asset, property and facility management services; the development and coordination of strategic projects, thereby contributing to the realization of the most important infrastructural works of Lombardy; and the development and implementation of regional policies.

References

Abernathy, W.J. and Utterback, J.M. (1978) 'Patterns of industrial innovation', *Technology Review*, 80(7), pp. 1–9.

Akintoye, A., McIntosh, G. and Fitzgerald, E. (2000) 'A survey of supply chain collaboration and management in the UK construction industry', *European Journal of Purchasing and Supply Management*, 6, pp. 159–168.

Axelsson, B. and Easton, G. (1992) *Industrial networks: A new view of the reality*. London: Routledge.

Barratt, M., Choi, T.Y. and Li, M. (2011) 'Qualitative case studies in operations management: Trends and future research implications (1992-2007)', *Journal of Operations Management*, 29(4), pp. 329–342.

Beverland, M. and Lindgreen, A. (2010) 'What makes a good case study? A positivist review of qualitative case research published', *Industrial Marketing Management*, 39(1), pp. 56–63.

Biemans, W.G. (1992) *Managing innovation within networks*. London: Routledge.

Blayse, A.M. and Manley, K. (2004) 'Key influences on construction innovation', *Construction Innovation*, 4(3), pp. 143–154.

Blume, S. (1992) *Insight and industry: On the dynamics of technological change in medicine*. Boston: MIT Press.

Bresnen, M. and Marshall, N. (2000) 'Partnering in construction: A critical review of issues, problems and dilemmas', *Construction Management and Economics*, 18(2), pp. 229–237.

Bresnen, M. and Marshall, N. (2002) 'The engineering or evolution of co-operation? A tale of two partnering projects', *International Journal of Project Management*, 20(7), pp. 497–505.

Bygballe, L.E. and Ingemansson, M. (2014) 'The logic of innovation in construction', *Industrial Marketing Management*, 43(3), pp. 512–524.

Bygballe, L.E. and Jahre, M. (2009) 'Balancing value creating logics in construction', *Construction Management and Economics*, 27(7), pp. 695–704.

Bygballe, L.E., Jahre, M. and Swärd, A. (2010) 'Partnering relationships in construction: A literature review', *Journal of Purchasing and Supply Management*, 16(4), pp. 239–253.

Consoli, D. and Mina, A. (2009) 'An evolutionary perspective on health innovation systems', *Journal of Evolutionary Economics*, 19(2).

Coombs, R., Harvey, M. and Tether, B.S. (2003) 'Analysing distributed processes of provision and innovation', *Industrial and Corporate Change*, 12(6), pp. 1125–1155.

Coombs, R. and Metcalfe, J.S. (2000) 'Organizing for innovation: Coordinating distributed innovation capabilities', in J.F. Nicolai & V. Mahnke (eds.), *Competence, governance, and entrepreneurship*. Oxford: Oxford University Press.

Corsaro, D., Ramos, C., Henneberg, S.C. and Naudé, P. (2012) 'The impact of network configurations on value constellations in business markets – The case of an innovation network', *Industrial Marketing Management*, 41(1), pp. 54–67.

Dainty, A.R., Briscoe, G.H. and Millett, S.J. (2001) 'Subcontractor perspectives on supply chain alliances', *Construction Management and Economics*, 19(8), pp. 841–848.

Dahlquist, J. (1998) 'Knowledge use in business exchange, acting and thinking business actors', Doctoral thesis no 74, Department of Business Studies, Uppsala University.

Dubois, A. (1998) *Organising industrial activities across firm boundaries*. London: Routledge.

Dubois, A. and Gadde, L. (2000) 'Supply strategy and network effects – purchasing behavior in the construction industry', *European Journal of Purchasing and Supply Management*, 6, pp. 207–215.

Dubois, A. and Gadde, L. (2002) 'Systematic combining: An abductive approach to case research', *Journal of Business Research*, 55(7), pp. 553–560.

Dubois, A. and Araujo, L. (2004) 'Research methods in industrial marketing studies', in H. Håkansson, D. Harrison and A. Waluszewski (eds.), *Rethinking marketing: Developing a new understanding of markets* (pp. 207–227). Chichester: John Wiley & Sons.

Ford, I.D., Gadde, L.E., Hakansson, H., Lundgren, A., Snehota, I., Turnbull, P., et al. (2003) *Managing business relationships*. Chichester: Wiley.

Foss, N.J., Laursen, K. and Pedersen, T. (2011) 'Linking customer interaction and innovation: The mediating role of new organizational practices', *Organization Science*, 22(4), pp. 980–999.

Gelijns, A. and Rosenberg, N. (1994) 'The dynamics of technological change in medicine', *Health Affairs*, 13(3), pp. 28–46.

Gelijns, A.C., Zivin, J. and Nelson, R.R. (2001) 'Uncertainty and technological change in medicine', *Journal of Health Politics, Policy and Law*, XXVI(5), pp. 913–924.

Gidado, K. (1996) 'Project complexity: The focal point of construction production planning', *Construction Management and Economics*, 14(3), pp. 213–225.

Greer, A. (1988) 'The state of the art versus the state of the science: The diffusion of new medical technologies into practice', *International Journal of Technology Assessment in Health Care*, 4(1), pp. 5–26.

Håkansson, H. (1987) *Industrial technological development: A network approach*. London: Croom Helm.

Håkansson, H., Ford, D., Gadde, L.E., Snehota, I. and Waluszewski, A. (2009) *Business in networks*. New York: John Wiley & Sons.

Håkansson, H. and Ingemansson, M. (2013) 'Industrial renewal within the construction network', *Construction Management and Economics*, 31(1), pp. 40–61.

Håkansson, H. and Johanson, J. (2001) *Business network learning*. Netherlands: Pergamon.

Håkansson, H. and Johanson, J. (1992). 'A model of industrial networks', in B. Axelsson & G. Easton (eds.), *Industrial networks, A new view of reality* (pp. 28–34). London: Routledge.

Håkansson, H. and Snehota, I. (1989) 'No business is an island: The network concept of business strategy', *Scandinavian Journal of Management*, 5(3), pp. 187–200.

Håkansson, H. and Snehota, I. (1995) *Developing relationships in business networks*. London: Routledge.

Håkansson, H. and Waluszewski, A. (2002) *Managing technological development. IKEA, the environment and technology*. London: Routledge.

Håkansson, H. and Waluszewski, A. (eds.) (2007) *Knowledge and innovation in business and industry: The importance of using others*. London: Routledge.

Hallen, L., Johanson, J. and Seyed-Mohamed, N. (1991) 'Interfirm adaptation in business relationships', *Journal of Marketing*, 55(2), pp. 29–37.

Harrison, D. and Easton, G. (2004) 'Temporally embedded case comparison in industrial marketing research', in Steve Fleetwood and Stephen Ackroyd *Critical realist applications in organisation and management studies* (pp. 194–210). London and New York: Routledge.

Harrison, D. and Prenkert, F. (2009) Network strategising trajectories within a planned strategy process, *Industrial Marketing Management*, 38(6), pp. 662–670.

Havenvid, M.I., Hulthén, K., Linné, Å. and Sundquist, V. (2016) 'Renewal in construction projects: Tracing effects of client requirements', *Construction Management and Economics*, 34(11), pp. 790–807.

Henneberg, S., Gruber, T. and Naudé, P. (2013). 'Services networks: Concept and research agenda'. *Industrial Marketing Management*, 42, pp. 3–8.

Henneberg, S., Rohrmus, D. and Ramos, C. (2006) 'Sensemaking and cognition in business networks: Conceptualization and propositional development', *2nd IMP Journal Seminar Chalmers*, Gothenburg, Sweden.

Holmen, E. (2001) 'Notes on a conceptualisation of resource-related embeddedness of interorganizational product development', PhD dissertation, Institute for Marketing, University of Southern Denmark.

Huemer, L. (1998) *Trust in business relations. Economic logic or social interaction*. Borea: Umeå.

Huemer, L. (2014) 'Creating cooperative advantage: The roles of identification, trust, and time', *Industrial Marketing Management*, 43(4), pp. 564–572.

Ibarra, H. (1993) 'Network centrality, power, and innovation involvement: Determinants of technical and administrative roles', *Academy of Management Journal*, 36(3), pp. 471–501.

Ketley, D. and Woods, K.L. (1993) 'Impact of clinical trials on clinical practice: example of thrombolysis for acute myocardial infarction', *Lancet*, 342, pp. 891–894.

Laage-Hellman, J. (1997) *Business networks in Japan, supplier–customer interaction in product development*. London: Routledge.

Laari-Salmela, S., Mainela, T. and Puhakka, V. (2015) 'Beyond network pictures: Situational strategizing in network context', *Industrial Marketing Management*, 45, pp. 117–127.

Lenney, P. and Easton, G. (2009) 'Actors, resources, activities and commitments', *Industrial Marketing Management*, 38(5), pp. 553–561.

Lundgren, A. (1995) *Technological innovation and network evolution*. London: Routledge.

Malerba, F. (2004) *Sectoral systems of innovation: Concepts, issues and analyses of six major sectors in Europe*. Cambridge: Cambridge University Press.

Marceau, J., Houghton, J., Toner, P., Manley, K., Gerasimou, E. and Cook, N. (1999) 'Mapping the building and construction product system in Australia', *Sydney: Commonwealth Department of Industry, Science and Resources*, a White Paper.

Mauri. (2017) https://www.youtube.com/watch?v=s3RYpNaywps&feature=youtu.be

Metcalfe, J.S., James, A. and Mina A. (2005) 'Emergent innovation systems and the delivery of clinical services: the case of intra-ocular lenses', *Research Policy*, XXXIV(9), pp. 283–1304.

Miller, C.J., Packham, G.A. and Thomas, B.C. (2002) 'Harmonization between main contractors and subcontractors: A prerequisite for lean construction?', *Journal of Construction Research*, 3(01), pp. 67–82.

Miozzo, M. and Dewick, P. (2004) 'Networks and innovation in European construction: Benefits from inter-organisational cooperation in a fragmented industry', *International Journal of Technology Management*, 27(1), pp. 68–92.

Nelson, R.R. and Winter, S.G. (1982) *An evolutionary theory of economic change*. Cambridge: Belknap Press/Harvard University Press.

Pammolli, F., Riccaboni, M., Oglialoro, C., Magazzini, L., Salerno, N., and e Baio, G. (2005) 'Medical devices competitiveness and impact on public health expenditure'. Enterprise Directorate-General, European Commission, Brussels.

Ramos, C. and Ford, I.D. (2011) 'Network pictures as a research device: Developing a tool to capture actors' perceptions in organizational networks', *Industrial Marketing Management*, 40(3), pp. 447–464.

Ramos, C., Roseira, C., Brito, C., Henneberg, S. and Naudé, P. (2013) 'Business service networks and their process of emergence: The case of the health cluster Portugal', *Industrial Marketing Management*, 42(6), pp. 950–968.

Richards, L. and Morse, J.M. (2009) *Fare ricerca qualitativa: prima guida*. Milano: Franco Angeli.

Richardson, G.B. (1972) 'The organisation of industry', *Economic Journal*, 82, pp. 883–896.

Rogers, E.M. (1983) *Diffusion of innovations* (3rd ed.). New York: The Free Press.

Rosenberg, C. (1994) *Exploring the black box*. Great Britain: Cambridge University Press.

Schumpeter, J.A. (1934) *The theory of economic development*. London: Routledge.

Slaughter, E.S. (1998) 'Models of construction innovation', *Journal of Construction Engineering and Management*, 124(3), pp. 226–231.

Slaughter, E.S. (2000) 'Implementation of construction innovations, *Building Research and Information*', 28(1), pp. 2–17.

Torvatn, T. (1996) 'Productivity in industrial networks – A case study of the purchasing function', PhD dissertation, Department of Industrial Economics and Technology Management, Norwegian University of Science and Technology.

Tzannis, A. (2013) 'Chronic disease management in the Lombardy region: An evolutionary service network perspective', *Industrial Marketing Management*, 42(7), pp. 1042–1056.

Vargo, S.L., Wieland, H. and Akaka, M.A. (2015), 'Innovation through institutionalization: A service ecosystems perspective', *Industrial Marketing Management*, 44, pp. 63–72.

Von Hippel, E. (2005) *Democratizing innovation*. Cambridge: MIT Press.

Wagrell, S. and Waluszewski A. (2009) 'The innovation process and its organizational setting – fit or misfit?', *IMP Journal*, III(2), pp. 57–85.

Winch, G.M. (2000) 'Institutional reform in British construction: Partnering and private finance', *Building Research and Information*, 28(2), pp. 141–155.

Wood, G.D. and Ellis, R.C.T. (2005) 'Main contractor experiences of partnering relationships on UK construction projects', *Construction Management and Economics*, 23(3), pp. 317–332.

7 Innovation among project islands

A question of handling interdependencies through bridging

Malena Ingemansson Havenvid, Lena E. Bygballe and Håkan Håkansson

Introduction

It has long been argued among Industrial Marketing and Purchasing (IMP) scholars that the existence of interdependencies is a key feature of the business landscape (Freytag, Gadde and Harrison, 2017) and that business relationships are important for dealing with these interdependencies (Håkansson and Snehota, 2017). Relationships connect actors to their activities and resources, which is particularly important for developing and implementing innovations (Håkansson, Ford, Gadde, Snehota and Waluszewski, 2009). Through interaction processes, firms can have a direct influence on one another, and there is the potential to learn from making mutual adaptations (Bygballe, 2006). In this way, relationships provide opportunities for inventing new processes and products by connecting the resources of each party in the development process. Furthermore, relationships between two actors, such as producers and users, help to ensure that these new inventions are actually used and become innovations (Håkansson and Waluszewski, 2007). Thus, relationships are important for innovation through the connectivity they incur.

When looking at the construction business landscape, however, another picture emerges. Contrary to the preceding arguments, actors in the construction industry seem overly concerned about *avoiding* interdependencies, and relations among actors are largely confined to individual projects (Dubois and Gadde, 2000). This short-term orientation has profoundly negative effects on the productivity and innovation capacity of the industry (Dubois and Gadde, 2002). There are, of course, examples of long-term relationships among construction actors, as well as evidence of the benefits such relationships provide (Håkansson, Havila and Pedersen, 1999; Holmen, Pedersen and Torvatn, 2005; Crespin-Mazet, Havenvid and Linné, 2015; Havenvid, Hulthén, Linné and Sundquist, 2016; Havenvid, Håkansson and Linné, 2016). However, it is typical for the construction industry to organise its core business activities in projects that are made up of collectives of interdependent actors, "designed to disintegrate within a predetermined time frame" (Bakker, DeFillippi, Schwab and Sydow, 2016, p. 1705). The key argument underpinning project-based organisation is to protect the project from the constraints of the permanent organisation and ensure the flexibility needed to perform unique tasks and grasp new business opportunities. Thus, there may be good reasons for setting clear boundaries around an individual project. However, the traditional focus on treating the project as an 'island' has been called into question since Engwall's (2003) classic 'no project is an island' article, in which he argued that, to understand projects, we need to take into consideration their organisational and historical contexts.

In this chapter, we address this apparent dilemma, namely that projects are, by their nature, subject to boundary setting while also being embedded and subject to interdependencies across time and space (Brookes, Sage, Dainty, Locatelli, Whyte, 2017). We believe that this offers several interesting issues in relation to innovation that deserve further investigation. The first question in such an investigation is simply *what does a project actually look like?* How do boundaries work, and how may we understand the embedded nature of projects? Next, *how does this dual nature of projects influence the innovation processes in the industry?* We are particularly interested in investigating interdependencies (embeddedness and connectivity) between project 'islands' (boundaries) and how these interdependencies are handled.

In the following parts of this chapter, we look into the literature on boundaries and interdependencies, which provides a basis for revisiting examples of innovation in construction from our previous research. We use these examples to identify and discuss various bridging initiatives between the project islands. Bridging, here, refers to initiatives that deliberately aim to deal with interdependencies and create benefits from their existence – in other words, *activated* interdependencies. Following the presentation of the empirical examples, we discuss what bridging means in this particular setting. We argue that it can be considered a basic mechanism for importing and exporting valuable resources and activities between projects and thus for utilising and activating interdependencies. We also discuss two types of bridging: bridging across *time* and bridging across *space*. Finally, we conclude the chapter by proposing a set of conditions that characterise the dual nature of projects in terms of the inevitable existence of interdependencies and also a set of conditions for how such interdependencies influence learning and innovation in construction.

The nature of projects and innovation in construction

The creation of a project necessitates the introduction of boundaries, demarcating the project from its environment (Lundin and Söderholm, 1995). In general, boundaries are intrinsic to the process of organising, and organisations evolve through the process of boundary setting (Hernes, 2004). Thus, the issue of boundaries is central to any theory of organisation, as well as to theories of temporary organising and projects. Boundaries take multiple forms, ranging from tangible structures to social and cognitive processes (Hernes, 2004). Similarly, in project settings, there are different kinds of boundaries as well as boundary work, i.e. the negotiating, establishing, managing, challenging or removing of demarcations, through which boundaries come to life (Stjerne and Svejenova, 2016). Boundaries exist between the temporary project organisation and the permanent organisation – particularly in an economic sense. In multi-actor project settings, such as construction projects, boundaries reflect the organisationally separated processes of commissioning, design and construction, as well as the contractual boundaries among the partners involved (Bresnen, 2010). Furthermore, boundaries exist between the organisations involved because of the different contextual interpretations of the participants they bring in, and these participants possess different experiences, perspectives and knowledge (Pemsel and Widén, 2011).

In the traditional project management literature and from an economic point of view, projects and their boundaries resemble isolated 'islands', being decoupled from history and context (Engwall, 2003). However, as Engwall (2003) clearly shows, projects are embedded in the social and historical context. Following this notion, the embedded nature of projects (Manning, 2008) and the relationship between the temporary and permanent nature of projects (Bakker et al., 2016) have attracted much interest from project scholars. For example, Brady and Davies (2004) show how project-based organisations learn from projects and develop capabilities through recurrent flows of experiences between the organisation and its projects. Similarly, Stjerne and Svejenova (2016) show how these types of organisations balance innovation and persistence through boundary work with roles that create connections between the past, present and future 'shadows' of projects. The project management and construction literature has primarily discussed the embedded nature of projects in relation to their intra-organisational contexts – a notable exception being Pemsel and Widén (2011). IMP-based construction research, on the other hand, has looked into the interdependencies between actors and the (non-)existence of business relationships in this setting. For example, Dubois and Gadde (2002) take as their starting point the notion of tight and loose couplings to discuss interdependencies in the construction industry and the patterns of adaptation and adjustments among the actors. They argue that there are tight couplings within an individual project, but because the economic boundaries around the project are also tight, the couplings do not transcend the project. Thus, there are only loose couplings between the actors and their activities and resources in the permanent network, with few long-term relationships. This lack of potential network effects hinders long-term productivity gains and innovation (Dubois and Gadde, 2002). Other IMP-based construction research reports examples of relationships (Håkansson and Ingemansson, 2013) and discusses their effects on renewal in the industry (Bygballe, Håkansson and Ingemansson, 2015). For example, Crespin-Mazet et al. (2015) demonstrate in their study of partnering that the initiation and continuation of using partnering as a project mode across several projects is related not only to the perceived risk or functionality of the individual projects but also to the relationship history between the partners. The study shows that the choice of contractor has to do with the project owner's experiences of particular partners in past projects. In other words, earlier positive experiences and the potential of using previous mutual learning are key reasons for continued collaboration across projects.

Despite the examples from the preceding IMP-based research and the extensive 'partnering in construction' research stream (e.g. Bresnen and Marshall, 2000), the evidence of more long-term business relationships in the construction industry seems rather anecdotal. As the review of the literature shows, boundary setting is the key organising principle that defines projects. At the same time, however, the embedded nature of construction projects is well recognised. In the following section, we address this dual nature of construction and seek to explore its implications for innovation. To do so, we draw on insights from case studies of learning and innovation in relation to the existence and handling of interdependencies across actors and projects in some earlier published work (Håkansson et al., 1999; Bengtsson and Håkansson, 2008; Crespin-Mazet et al., 2015; Havenvid et al., 2016b). We use the terms *learning* and *innovation* interchangeably, as we consider learning as a key process underpinning the invention and implementation of new products and processes (Bygballe and Ingemansson, 2014).

The existence of interdependencies and the need for continuity

Learning through exploitation of interdependencies across projects

In a study of learning in a construction project, Håkansson et al. (1999) showed how long-term relationships between the main contractor and its suppliers were a key driver for learning to take place in the project. The study showed that variation in learning and what the respondents perceived they had learnt during the project were highly related to the parties' previous experiences with one another. More specifically, it had to do with the characteristics of (a) the respective parties, (b) their relationship, and (c) the context of the relationships, that is to say, the network of relationships affecting their relationship. The most distinct finding was that the suppliers who had relationships with both the main contractor and some other supplier(s) reported that they gained the most substantial learning from the project. In other words, the suppliers who perceived that they had learnt most from the project worked within a 'network context'. Almost all the involved suppliers had substantial earlier experience of working together with the main contractor as well as other suppliers. The authors concluded that operating from the standpoint of several connected relationships, where a number of company interfaces are related to each other, created learning opportunities: "by being connected, the relationship becomes a part of a larger organizing and development process" (Håkansson et al., 1999, p. 450).

As will be further discussed, the study showed how relationships among actors spanning several projects can be part of creating more stable conditions for learning over time. This illustrates the need for interactive factors in terms of joint learning in order to utilise the existing interdependencies between activities and/or resources.

Interdependencies affecting opportunities for innovations

While this example demonstrates the role of stability in facilitating joint learning more generally, the way that relationships connect actors, their activities and resources over time has several other consequences for innovation. In a longitudinal case study, Bengtsson and Håkansson (2008) demonstrated how such connections create efficiency and therefore affect innovation in several ways. They investigated the difficulties of reintroducing timber as a frame material in houses higher than two stories in Sweden. A long-standing ban on using timber as frame material in the Nordic countries was overturned when an EU regulation changed this in 1990. As comparisons with the United States indicated important cost savings potential compared to the use of concrete, this started a process where some companies wanted to go back to timber as a frame material. However, changing to timber frames turned out to be a challenge.

In the studied projects, the main contractor initially ran into a whole set of unexpected problems. A number of other products and processes in the building, as well as in the building process itself, had over the years been adapted to the use of concrete. The change of the frame material in this way caused a number of problems regarding related products and processes; it was not just about changing the supplier of the frame material – it meant changing a number of work processes and other materials. The design of the building was affected, which in turn affected architects and their work. The change also affected technical consultants and their way of calculating how sound travels in the buildings and consequently how different technical systems should be designed. The way the contractor had to plan and execute the building process was also affected, as was the design of related components. Therefore, despite extensive knowledge and experience of wood as a general construction material, the first projects became both costly and complicated because a number of related products and processes had to be adapted. In other words, a number of interdependencies were connected to the use of concrete, which, once it was to be replaced with timber, affected a wide array of actors, resources, and activities within the individual projects. There had been a long process of increasing efficiency by adapting processes and products to the specific use of concrete as frame material.

This study shows how a number of interdependencies made it difficult to implement new solutions within projects. Thus, for any change or innovation to take place, these interdependencies need to be handled actively by the involved actors, and we will discuss this in the following section.

The variety of interdependencies and how they are handled

Projects are organised as temporary organisations from an economic point of view. At the same time, they use resources and activities that have been used in earlier projects and that will be used later in new projects. Looking more closely into the content of these connections and the interdependencies they create, we will use two studies as examples: one is a case study of a large-scale hospital construction project by Crespin-Mazet et al. (2015), and the other is a study including seven overlapping housing projects by Havenvid et al. (2016b).

By studying a construction project concerning a specialised health care facility for proton radiation therapy – the Skandion Clinic – Crespin-Mazet et al. (2015) came across a number of interesting aspects related to the context of the specific project. Due to the project's demanding character (involving requirements for radiation safety, a large energy supply, advanced cooling systems, and specialised medical treatment), it placed high demands on those involved. The property developer decided to establish a partnering agreement with the main contractor, which was the first formal partnering project between the parties. However, they had worked together for more than 20 years, so had jointly identified cost-saving solutions. The partnering agreement implied that the relationship had evolved into an even more transparent and collaborative type of relationship. It included an 'open book policy' regarding economic decision making and joint procurement of subcontractors and material suppliers. While costly and demanding, a number of mutual benefits were achieved in the joint development of new solutions, so the two parties decided to engage in the same type of partnering agreement in a subsequent project.

Another interesting aspect revealed in this study was that the relationship proved to be part of a network of relationships that developed across several projects, including two subcontractors, a consultancy firm/planning coordinator, and a frame supplier. With the knowledge of how to work together gained from the two preceding projects, the partnering agreement in the Skandion project allowed for the main contractor and property developer to engage the network more in the planning phase of the project. This also brought forth a number of new solutions that were reused in the subsequent project, including joint procurement, new meeting forums, and a standardised manual for Building Information Modelling (BIM). Thus, a central aspect of the project context in this case was the evolving partnership involving a network of relationships over time.

Finally, the study revealed how the parties consistently used other projects across Scandinavia and Europe to gain knowledge, experience, and relevant material solutions. For instance, projects that were based on the same radiation technology provided valuable insights for the parties in the Skandion project in relation to important safety and building requirements. These other projects also provided important insight for the project owner into how to manage the building and the end users. Other projects provided insight into specific solutions such as lighting and how to construct the concrete foundation of the building.

The second study, by Havenvid et al. (2016b), concerns the construction of a two-storey housing complex. By tracing the renewal in terms of learning and innovation among the main construction parties, the authors found that they had worked together on seven interrelated housing projects spanning 15 years. Five projects prior to the focal one, as well as one subsequent project, involved the same key parties: the public housing developer, the main contractor, several subcontractors, and the frame supplier. The projects were deliberately planned to overlap with one another, with the planning phase of one project commencing before the preceding project had been delivered. Not only was this a way for the parties to keep their resources in constant use (such as the same managers and staff) across a multitude of projects, it also turned out to be an efficient way to develop specific products and production technology over time.

The study revealed several examples of learning and developing new solutions through collaboration between the parties. For example, a prefabricated bathroom wall was developed through joint R&D between the concrete supplier and the main contractor, which was used across different projects. A wall containing only non-organic material was requested by the main contractor in one of the earlier projects, which initiated a further development of an existing wall by the frame supplier. So, while the materials for the wall were developed for one of the projects, a further development in a subsequent project allowed for a full prefabrication of the wall, eliminating the need for on-site production. In turn, this development triggered new ways for several of the parties to operate on-site in subsequent projects. By overlapping projects, the owner could secure specific business partners and key individuals across a number of projects and actively use their experience to develop both material and immaterial solutions.

Both cases show that interdependencies can vary and build on the use and development of organisational solutions (e.g. joint purchasing activities), physical/technical items (e.g. manuals) or individuals (e.g. managers and staff). In the following section, we will further address how specific connections built on such interdependencies can be formed across projects and how they can be part of learning and innovation processes. In other words, we will address how the utilisation and reshaping of different types of interdependency over time have a clear relation to how learning and innovation can take place both within and across projects. We refer to this as *bridging*.

Bridging as a way of handling interdependencies across project islands

The preceding examples all indicate that, while boundaries were set up around construction projects to demarcate them from 'outside' conditions in a temporal, organisational and economic way, the projects were related through a variety of interdependencies. Many of the resources – people and their experience, products, technologies, facilities and equipment – had been used in earlier projects and would be used in later projects. These connections created a large number of interdependencies between the projects, which the actors could take advantage of in terms of learning and innovation. The previous section illustrates several examples of this and what we call *bridging* between the project islands. Bridging has been used in previous construction research as a way for construction parties to overcome communication barriers and differences in perception (Pemsel and Widén, 2011). In our setting, bridging involves the ways in which a project reuses organisational and technological solutions that have proven useful in the past, in a way that is economically beneficial for the project at hand. In other words, it can be seen as a number of deliberate efforts to activate and utilise existing interdependencies to make the project more efficient and effective.

One way to think about bridging between projects is as a basic mechanism for *importing* and *exporting* knowledge and solutions across projects. According to Engwall (2003), acknowledging the embedded nature of projects allows for capturing how knowledge, procedures, structures, and ideas are imported from and exported to the organisational context by the projects. As was shown in the first example of learning in projects (Håkansson et al., 1999), the interdependencies that had formed between some of the actors because of interaction in earlier projects allowed them to apply their learning in a collective sense to past and future projects. In contrast to the actors moving into and out of the project in an unconnected sense, these interconnected actors could relate their learning to conditions 'outside' of the particular project.

Some connections between projects are utilised in a more or less automatic way and therefore do not require any conscious effort – the importing and exporting happen automatically through the reuse of particular solutions and individuals. For instance, project participants bring their experiences from earlier projects into a new project. Products and equipment, in the same way, bring earlier developments into subsequent projects. Thus, these types of connection bring with them quite a lot of earlier experiences and learning, but no specific interdependencies are utilised. However, as the studies showed, actors can also consciously choose to engage in bridging to utilise interdependencies that these connections create across projects. The empirical examples allow us to identify a number of different interdependencies in the execution of projects, different types of connectivity and a whole set of ways of bridging between projects. Firstly, there are clear interdependencies between technical and organisational solutions, which in turn depend on a set of other organisational and technical structures. For example, the use of particular products depends on specific technologies, and, in the same way, there are interdependencies between individuals and organisational units within and between projects that influence the use of the product; this was clearly illustrated in the timber frame example (Bengtsson and Håkansson, 2008). Secondly, some of the interdependencies are incorporated within the boundary of the project and can be handled by the managers directly. Other interdependencies have to be handled across the boundary of the project by the companies bridging to other projects, such as in the bathroom wall example (Havenvid et al., 2016b).

Thus, every project will be a unit within the web of interdependencies, where some are internalised and others handled through bridges to other projects. Finally, some will be handled as day-to-day problems when they appear in the process. Through bridging, the project 'imports' a set of indirect means to handle the external interdependencies, which will then be integrated with the internal ones. Every project will also export such means. Both the importing and exporting will be more or less systematic and performed by the involved actors. In princonual, there are two types of bridging: bridging in *time* and bridging in *space*.

Bridging in time and space

Time is a key dimension in all construction work and the planning of a construction project, and its different phases is usually very detailed. All larger construction companies have various planning models, where key activities within the project are specified and scheduled. Both the starting and ending points are clearly determined in relation to suppliers and customers/end users. Timing in relation to all the external involved business units is important and is based on a different type of bridging. The example in Havenvid et al. (2016b) is a good illustration of how parties engage in conscious, detailed, joint planning across projects and time.

The most obvious way of bridging in time is how companies deliberately utilise the experience of single managers – something that can be observed in all four of the above examples. One way to take advantage of this experience is to use managers who have been involved in earlier and similar projects, which was the case in the study by Havenvid et al. (2016b). Using individuals who have specific experiences systematically across earlier or current projects is thus one way to create project connections. Another way is through different organisational routines or planning tools that have been adapted to include the existence of different types of interdependency. For example, routines can be reflected in the way a construction project is planned in time, as illustrated across the seven projects reported in the Havenvid et al. (2016b) study. Here, the idea was to get project activities to overlap in order to make more efficient use of both actors and resources when moving them from one place to another. In doing so, each project was also consistently related to several earlier or planned projects. These multiple bridging efforts allowed for both a reutilisation of actors and resources from earlier projects and planning for how to use them in the future, beyond the time boundaries of the individual project.

The timber frame example (Bengtson and Håkansson, 2008) is particularly interesting in relation to the importance of bridging in time. It shows how technical design or technical solutions that have been tried and that are related to sets of activities and resources can inhibit attempts to introduce innovative solutions – even when the 'new' solution is actually well known to the parties involved. In these circumstances, bridging means to break up existing interdependencies and adapt and reconnect the new product to other activity and resource constellations. This case also shows that bridging in time is highly related to exploiting dynamic opportunities, for example in terms of taking advantage of the testing process of new opportunities – of new materials/products or the development of new production processes. The involved actors need to adapt their processes and products to other products and processes, thereby taking part in cumulative learning processes. Learning from earlier projects and from one another is, therefore, a way of bridging material interdependencies so that they can be reutilised and developed over time. While the example of learning in projects (Håkansson et al., 1999) stresses backward bridging to earlier projects, it also illustrates attempts to build bridges forward in time – to future projects. The use of the 'new' material was expected to bridge to an increased efficiency and reduced cost for a number of future projects. The timber frame study also illustrates that, because of bridging and the embedding of interdependencies into the resources and activities being used systematically across project islands, change is difficult. For change or innovation to be possible, bridging is part of a constant act of handling existing technological and organisational interdependencies and actively trying to find new ways of using them. As such, knowledge and learning are not just related to people but are built into products and production methods. This in turn influences how they are used in relation to others.

Bridging in space requires the active participation of several actors; the development of a new technology is done in one place (one project) where a certain number of actors have to be involved. Again, this place becomes important to bridge to when the development continues in other places (projects). The construction industry is both local and global – a combination that accentuates the need to take the space dimension into consideration. Some projects are confined to a certain area and utilise primarily local suppliers and personnel, which is illustrated in the example in Havenvid et al. (2016b), where seven interrelated housing projects were executed in the same region. Others are more specialised and have international suppliers, such as the Skandion project, which was based on a radiation technology from an international supplier (Crespin-Mazet et al., 2015). The project was defined by this particular radiation technology, which determined what needed to be built and how. This project had a number of interdependencies that needed to be handled by the project actors, which led to connections being made between a set of international projects connected to the same technology and other indirectly related projects.

Every project creates a set of flows of products, services and other activities that have an important geographical dimension. Considering that there are always a certain number of ongoing projects of which each creates a number of flows, including knowledge, these projects can also be related to differing degrees. They can be related by being started, transformed or handled in the same facilities (e.g. the prefabrication of bathroom walls) or designed and handled by the same managers or business units that have certain competence or skills. If these flows can be bridged, there is certainly potential to reduce costs or increase revenues. In every flow there is the use of certain facilities – production plants, transportation vehicles, cranes and so on – that, through bridging, can be used more effectively. Another way of bridging between projects in the space dimension is through framework or exclusive agreements, where certain actors are preferred and/or partners are chosen for all projects within a specified region or country. This was the situation in the cases featured in the Havenvid et al. (2016b) study, where the partnerships transcended projects and included several actors.

Bridging in *space* can also be combined with bridging in *time* by planning projects in such a way that they overlap chronologically, which permits the use of the same personnel and counterparts, as shown in the study by Havenvid et al. (2016b). Thus, when planning and executing a project, it has to be done in a way that is adapted to earlier and other current projects. This has to do with the utilisation, and thereby the localisation, of resources. Some resources are by nature local, such as manufacturing facilities, while others can be situated almost anywhere, such as prefabricated materials. The geographical spread of company-owned resources is therefore a crucial issue for all project-related companies. Another interesting example of combining bridging in space and time is the Skandion project (Crespin-Mazet et al., 2015). Here, a number of finished or ongoing projects situated across Europe were used as learning arenas for the different project actors in terms of how to execute the project and manage and operate in the building. As such, this project created bridges to several other projects across time and space, which strongly affected the particular solutions chosen for the building and which solutions were carried on to subsequent projects.

Discussion

In this chapter, we set out to investigate the nature of construction projects and its implications for innovation. From the literature, we learnt that there is a dual nature of construction projects in that they are subject to both boundary setting and embeddedness. In this section, we will further discuss our combined insights from the literature and revisit of our previous studies of learning and innovation in construction and what we identified as bridging initiatives. In so doing, we draw in particular on the IMP perspective, where boundary setting and boundary moving have long been essential issues (Gadde, 2014).

From the IMP perspective, using the island metaphor (Engwall, 2003) means that project actors and their activities and resources are organised on the island, while other actors, activities and resources float around in the surrounding 'sea' in a quite independent way. There is thus a distinct boundary separating the use of two different types of economic coordinating mechanisms. On the island, there is planning and hierarchical coordination of activities and resources for which the project manager is accountable, while, in relation to the sea, the project can use the market mechanism, i.e. ad hoc and short-term solutions in relation to suppliers. This can be seen in the traditional practices of selecting suppliers based on tendering processes and using lowest price as the determining factor (Dubois and Gadde, 2000; Eriksson, 2008). In order for this form of organisation to work, there is a need to draw a boundary line – to find a way to decide what should be done on the island and be handled by its managers and what should be imported from the sea (i.e. the market). Thus, from an economic point of view, the island metaphor implies that the shore of the island is the critical boundary. Our return to the previous studies of learning and innovation in construction indicates, however, that the economic outcome of the project will always be affected by the wide array of interdependencies that exists between activities, resources and actors in the broader economic landscape, i.e. between the islands. When constructing a project, these interdependencies have to be considered. They exist between activities and resources, as well as actors (Håkansson and Snehota, 1995), and blur the otherwise traditionally assumed organisational boundary of the firm by providing a more distributed way of gaining capabilities (Araujo, Dubois and Gadde, 2003), and hence innovation.

The traditionally adversarial relationships among construction actors focus on independence and the lack of a long-term orientation and have been seen as root causes of the challenges facing the industry in terms of low productivity and innovativeness (e.g. Dubois and Gadde, 2002; Holmen et al., 2005). Consequently, many scholars, both within the IMP community and more generally in construction management, have called for a shift in how construction actors relate to one another. A key reason underpinning this focus is that learning in construction projects is a collective effort; without the participation of (at least some of) the same actors over time, what has been learnt becomes difficult to reapply or to develop further (Slaughter, 1993; Lundin and Söderholm, 1995; Winch, 1998; Havenvid et al., 2016a). As phrased by Van de Ven (1986, p. 604), a new solution is not an innovation until it has become "an implemented reality and is incorporated into the taken-for-granted assumptions and thought structure of organizational practice". In addition, as pointed out by Harty (2008), due to their dynamic nature, such processes often result in unexpected outcomes. Consequently, the interactive nature of innovation processes presupposes not only the involvement of several actors but also repetition and learning experiences from trying to implement what is being developed or tried out in several contexts (Håkansson and Waluszewski, 2007). These contexts, such as they appear in different types of construction projects, consist of specific collections of actors, resources and activities, which any new solution needs in order to be successfully implemented. Thus, to innovate, several actors have to be involved at the same time (Winch, 1998), and a more long-term orientation towards relationship management is a key means in this respect (Gadde and Dubois, 2010).

While most of the previous IMP-based construction research has focused on relationships between construction actors and their activities and resources, in this chapter we turn our attention towards the relationships between projects, i.e. the 'islands'. We believe that this offers interesting and new avenues for understanding innovation processes in the construction industry. In line with Engwall's (2003) suggestion to extend the temporal and organisational scope of how projects are studied, we focus on the interdependencies between actors and their resources and activities that are adapted to conditions outside of any particular island and that in many ways dictate what happens on the different islands and how it happens. For example, one important reason temporality is a problem in construction is that, for efficiency reasons, construction actors need to make sure that their company resources are in more or less constant use, i.e. that they are part of value-creating processes within projects. Furthermore, for learning and innovation to take place, construction actors need to have a systematic approach to how they take part in activities on the different islands rather than just float around in the sea. This implies that they have to handle these interdependencies in a systematic way if they wish to introduce and develop changes as well as organisational and technological innovations – this is what we refer to as bridging.

Bridging in various forms has always taken place in and across projects – even if boundaries have been set. These can be both structural efforts and strategies for communicating and translating knowledge across boundaries (Pemsel and Widén, 2011). Over time, project actors learn a number of ways to handle external interdependencies by bridging between projects. One type of bridging is to embed the interdependencies into technical and organisational resources or the way activities are performed. One important source for finding ways to handle these external interdependencies is through experience gained in earlier or current projects. As stated by Engwall (2003, p. 793): "the success or failure of an individual project might be more dependent on the experience of the key project team members than on specific project management skills and techniques". If the actors are doing their job, for efficiency purposes all major construction activities resources are already being used on other islands. Thus, there are not a lot of activities or resources floating around independently in the sea or, put differently, that are idle in the marketplace. Therefore, when a new project has to be initiated, it is done not by selecting activities and resources from the sea but by identifying which of the activities and resources on these other islands to activate or bridge to. The project must be adapted to the design of the already existing and new projects. In order to use existing resources in an economic way or to design efficient activities, the new project has to be bridged to the existing structure of activities and resources (Engwall, 2003). These bridges give a set of restrictions and/or possibilities. If the project is designed without creating these bridges, it will become both costly and problematic to finalise. The more the design of the bridges is considered, the better the final results. Thus, all the actors involved take part in several projects, which means that the activities performed and resources used in the focal project should be designed in a related way.

While placing an economic boundary of construction activities around separate projects is deemed efficient for an individual project, it evidently creates problems for innovation and learning from a long-term perspective. Acting mostly as project coordinators for the operations of other specialised firms, construction companies are highly dependent on others to carry out individual projects. Thus, acting like a 'connected company' (Gadde, 2014), construction companies are involved in intense interaction processes between separate projects. These tight couplings in the project (Dubois and Gadde, 2002) provide opportunities for learning and problem solving and often result in inventive solutions within the specific project (e.g. Slaughter, 1998; Winch, 2003, 2014). However, by applying the other type of boundary-setting principle between projects, i.e. acting like an 'integrated hierarchy' (Gadde, 2014) with little recognition of dependence on others, the joint learning and new solutions are easily lost (e.g. Havenvid et al., 2016a). Thus, the learning that construction companies obtain in interaction with others risks becoming trapped on different islands, as it requires the participation of these others, or it may be able to be used only in a fragmented way by separate actors.

This different way of handling boundaries within and between projects creates problems for traditionally assumed ways of inducing innovation. As noted by Winch

(2014), organising centralised R&D efforts within separate firms is an inefficient tool for absorbing learning from separate projects and injecting new knowledge in projects as, in this setting, firms need to work collectively to learn and develop new knowledge. Rather, creating new solutions that 'stick' and that can be turned into 'good currency' (Winch, 1998) seems to rely on how construction actors make use of specific interdependencies and develop different bridges between projects.

To import or export solutions to and from projects, actors will probably need to have had a positive and considerable impact on the actors involved for them to consider it worth the effort to change their practices. This is related to the collective nature of learning in construction, as previously noted (Winch, 1998). In other cases, actors may not have a choice but to handle the various interdependencies involved in trying to do something new. In addition, for such bridging to take place from one project to another, the solutions need to be or need to be *made* 'transferrable'. Either they have made an organisational impact on the actors in terms of their already having implemented internal changes, or they are related to important counterparts that are reused over time, or they are embedded in physical solutions that can be communicated and create interfaces with others. This, in turn, is likely to depend on bridging activities related to communicating the new knowledge (Pemsel and Widén, 2011). As such, while relationships among actors is one way in which interdependencies can be handled, bridging is related not to any one actor or relationship between actors but to several conditions within and across projects that determine which interdependencies need to be handled and by whom, as well as how they can be changed. We now turn to some concluding remarks on the dual nature of projects and the implications of bridging for innovation in construction.

Concluding remarks

While Engwall's (2003) seminal article informed project research into the significance of the wider organisational and historical contexts of projects, in this chapter we set out to consider more specifically, from an innovation viewpoint, the ways in which projects are analogous to embedded islands in a surrounding sea of other project islands. Furthermore, we set out to explore how construction actors actively try to create bridges between such islands in an effort to promote more efficient and effective use of learning and development. Some bridges are built to overcome time differences. Backward bridges are built in order to use earlier experiences, product developments and developments in organisational routines. In order to make the development cumulative in these dimensions, a key issue is to take advantage of these earlier experiences and advancements. Forward bridges are built to take advantage of contemporary investments. In the same way, there are reasons to build bridges in the space dimension. Any individual project is dependent on which other projects are being executed and on the environment in terms of the possibilities to share human or technical resources. These bridges across time and space are important from an economic point of view and determine how much experience and investment will be utilised, as well as how efficient the use of contemporary resources will be. As such, bridges between projects are central to the dynamic development of the companies involved and are therefore a key mechanism for innovation; they are needed to bring experience, learning and the use of new solutions across projects over time and across space.

Based on the insight provided in this chapter, we propose two key conditions for how projects are subject to boundary setting and, at the same time, are embedded and subject to interdependencies across time and space:

> *Proposition 1. A construction project has a set of economic and contractual boundaries, not least in relation to the involved permanent organisations. As most of the resources and activities being used within the project have been used earlier and will continue to be used in the future, a variety of interdependencies affect the project and how it can be executed. These interdependencies may transcend the economic and contractual boundaries.*
>
> *Proposition 2. Many of the interdependencies that affect and that are being affected by a project are made use of (automatically) through the experience of individuals and the reuse of products and equipment across projects.*

Furthermore, we propose the following conditions for how interdependencies are likely to affect learning and innovation and how they can be used actively and deliberately for innovation purposes:

> *Proposition 3. The more interdependencies can be systematically used within and across projects, the higher a project's efficiency will be.*
>
> *Proposition 4. Interdependencies create specific challenges for introducing change (i.e. innovation), however, as they interrelate actors, resources and activities to specific solutions (e.g. products and equipment) that therefore become hard to alter.*
>
> *Proposition 5. To overcome the Janus-faced nature of interdependencies – being both a source to and barrier to change and innovation – actors might engage in bridging efforts and create bridges between projects. Bridging means exploiting and sometimes changing interdependencies among project islands in time and space.*

In sum, we have in this chapter demonstrated how relationships between projects and what we consider as 'bridges' play a major role in developing knowledge and new solutions across space and time. As has been illustrated, in spite of there being a project boundary in an economic and/or contractual sense, interdependencies cannot be separated from the project in a perfect way, and not every important interdependence can be included within the boundary. One solution used by construction actors is to build bridges to other projects to specifically include or handle some of those other interdependencies. This bridging enables connectivity and therefore innovation as well as efficiency.

References

Araujo, L., Dubois, A. and Gadde, L.-E. (2003) 'The multiple boundaries of the firm', *Journal of Management Studies*, 40(5), pp. 1255–1277.

Bakker, R.M., DeFillippi, R.J., Schwab, A. and Sydow, J. (2016) 'Temporary organizing: Promises, processes, problems', *Organization Studies*, 3(12), pp. 1703–1719.

Bengtson, A. and Håkansson, H. (2008) 'An interactive view of innovations: Adopting a new timber solution in an old concrete context', *The IMP Journal*, 2(3), pp. 19–35.

Brady, T. and Davies, A. (2004) 'Building project capabilities: From exploratory to exploitative learning', *Organization Studies*, 25(9), pp. 1601–1621.

Bresnen, M. (2010) 'Keeping it real? Constituting partnering through boundary objects', *Construction Management and Economics*, 28(6), pp. 615–628.

Bresnen, M. and Marshall, N. (2000) 'Partnering in construction: A critical review of issues, problems and dilemmas', *Construction Management and Economics*, 18(2), pp. 229–237.

Brookes, N., Sage, D., Dainty, A., Locatelli, G., Whyte, J. (2017) 'An island of constancy in a sea of change: Rethinking project temporalities with long-term megaprojects', *International Journal of Project Management*, 35(7), pp. 1213–1224.

Bygballe, L.E. (2006) *Learning across firm boundaries: The role of organizational routines.* Oslo: PhD dissertation, BI, Norwegian School of Management.

Bygballe, L., Håkansson, H. and Ingemansson, M. (2015) 'An industrial network perspective on innovation in construction', in Orstavik, F., Dainty, A.R.J. and Abbott, C. (eds.), *Construction Innovation.* London: Wiley Blackwell, pp. 89–101.

Bygballe, L.E. and Ingemansson, M. (2014) 'The logic of innovation in construction', *Industrial Marketing Management*, 43(3), pp. 512–524.

Crespin-Mazet, F., Havenvid, M.I. and Linné, Å. (2015) 'Antecedents of project partnering in the construction industry: The impact of relationship history', *Industrial Marketing Management*, 50(October), pp. 4–15.

Dubois, A. and Gadde, L-E. (2000) 'Supply strategy and network effects – purchasing behaviour in the construction industry', *European Journal of Purchasing and Supply Chain Management*, 6(3/4), pp. 207–215.

Dubois, A. and Gadde, L-E. (2002) 'The construction industry as a loosely coupled system: Implications for productivity and innovation', *Construction Management and Economics*, 20(7), pp. 621–631.

Engwall, M. (2003) 'No project is an island: Linking projects to history and context', *Research Policy*, 32(5), pp. 789–808.

Eriksson, P-E. (2008) 'Procurement effects on coopetition in client-contractor relationships', *Journal of Construction Engineering and Management*, 134(2), pp. 103–111.

Freytag, P.V., Gadde, L-E. and Harrison, D. (2017) 'Interdependencies – blessings and curses', in Håkansson, H. and Snehota, I. (eds.) *No business is an island: Making sense of the interactive business world.* UK: Emerald Publishing.

Gadde, L-E. (2014) 'Strategizing at the boundaries of firms', *The IMP Journal*, 8(2), pp. 51–63.

Gadde, L-E. and Dubois, A. (2010) 'Partnering in the construction industry – problems and opportunities', *Journal of Purchasing and Supply Management*, 16(4), pp. 254–263.

Håkansson, H., Ford, D., Gadde, L-E., Snehota, I. and Waluszewski, A. (2009) *Business in networks.* Chichester: Wiley.

Håkansson, H., Havila, V. and Pedersen, A-C. (1999) 'Learning in networks', *Industrial Marketing Management*, 28(5), pp. 443–452.

Håkansson, H. and Ingemansson, M. (2013) 'Industrial renewal within the construction network', *Construction Management and Economics* 31(1), pp. 40–61.

Håkansson, H. and Snehota, I. (1995) *Developing relationships in business networks.* London: Routledge.

Håkansson, H. and Snehota, I. (eds.) (2017) *No business is an island: Making sense of the interactive business world.* UK: Emerald Publishing.

Håkansson, H. and Waluszewski, A. (eds.) (2007) *Knowledge and innovation in business and industry: The importance of using others.* London: Routledge.

Harty, C. (2008) 'Implementing innovation in construction: Contexts, relative boundedness and actor-network theory', *Construction Management and Economics*, 26(10), pp. 1029–1041.

Havenvid, M.I., Håkansson, H. and Linné, Å. (2016b) 'Managing renewal in fragmented business networks', *The IMP Journal*, 10(1), pp. 81–106.

Havenvid, M.I., Hulthén, K., Linné, Å. and Sundquist, V. (2016a) 'Renewal in construction projects: Tracing effects of client requirements', *Construction Management and Economics*, 34(11), pp. 790–807.

Hernes, T. (2004) 'Studying composite boundaries: A framework of analysis', *Human Relations*, 57(1), pp. 9–29.

Holmen, E., Pedersen, A.-C. and Torvatn, T. (2005) 'Building relationships for technological innovation', *Journal of Business Research*, 58(9), pp. 1240–1250.

Lundin, R.A. and Söderholm, A. (1995) 'A theory of the temporary organization', *Scandinavian Journal of Management*, 11(4), pp. 437–455.

Manning, S. (2008) 'Embedding projects in multiple contexts – a structuration perspective', *International Journal of Project Management*, 26(1), pp. 30–37.

Pemsel, S. and Widén, K. (2011) 'Bridging boundaries between organizations in construction', *Construction Management and Economics*, 29(5), pp. 495–506.

Slaughter, S. (1993) 'Builders as sources of construction innovation', *Journal of Construction Engineering and Management*, 119(3), pp. 532–549.

Slaughter, E.S. (1998) 'Models of construction innovation', *Journal of Construction Engineering & Management*, 124(3), pp. 226–231.

Stjerne, I.S. and Svejenova, S. (2016) 'Connecting temporary and permanent organizing: Tensions and boundary work in sequential firm projects', *Organization Studies*. 37(2), pp. 1771–1792.

Van de Ven, A (1986) 'Central problems in the management of innovation', *Management Science*, 32(5), pp. 590–607.

Winch, G. (1998) 'Zephyrs of creative destruction: Understanding the management of innovation in construction', *Building Research and Information*, 26(4), pp. 268–279.

Winch, G.M. (2003) 'Models of manufacturing and the construction process: The genesis of re-engineering construction', *Building Research and Information*, 31(2), pp. 107–118.

Winch, G.M. (2014) 'Three domains of project organizing', *The International Journal of Project Management*, 32(5), pp. 721–731.

8 Construction projects as vehicles for health care innovation?

Judit Simon, Balázs Révész, Tibor Mandják,
Zsuzsanna Szalkai and Erzsébet Hetesi

Introduction

This chapter deals with how the construction industry can become a vehicle for innovative solutions in other sectors. More specifically, through two case studies of construction projects involving the creation of patient-centred hospitals in Hungary, the chapter investigates the complexities of making construction projects the driving force behind new approaches to health care provision and organisation within this national context. By using Hungary as an example – where the transition to a patient-centred approach to health care can be considered quite radical – we take advantage of the opportunity to investigate what role the construction industry plays as a 'deliverer' of new and innovative user approaches through the buildings it supplies, as well as how its project organisation affects this process in detail. As the cases both involve large-scale projects that benefited from EU-level funding, they also provide the opportunity to investigate and discuss the role of the different types of actors that are involved throughout the course of such large-scale construction projects, not least in terms of financing, the role of public actors and understanding which actors are awarded the legitimacy to intervene during different phases of projects, which in turn affects the outcome of these attempts at innovation. In both projects, a number of different conflicts arose between the project actors, making the project process quite turbulent and in turn affecting the project outcomes. Therefore, identifying these conflicts and the role they played in the innovation processes is a central part of the analysis.

Construction projects are well known for involving a great number of specialised actors that need to interact in different ways over the duration of a project (e.g. Dubois and Gadde, 2002; Bygballe, Jahre and Swärd, 2010; Gadde and Dubois, 2010). Depending on the project delivery format (i.e. the way it is financed, who the project owner is, etc.), these actors will need to relate to one another in particular ways throughout the project. This makes *actor interfaces* central to understanding how and if innovation can be implemented. The essence of innovation is that it involves a novelty diffused into markets or society (Garcia and Calantone, 2002). In the case of a construction project, the innovation process thus includes all the project phases and beyond, including initiation, implementation and use or operation.

Further, following the concept of innovation by Garcia and Calantone (2002), health care innovation is interpreted as a new health service or process that is implemented in a society. In the case of Hungary, one such example is the implementation of patient-centred services, which can be considered a radically new way of delivering health care. The present examination of health care projects provides a good basis for exploring the role of connectedness between different sectors and the consequences for attempts at innovation, not least because health care is part of a complex socio-economic system that, by its nature, involves both economic and non-economic actors and generally also public and private actors.

Complex construction projects, such as hospital construction in the present case, even when they are large or very valuable construction projects in their own right, include the physical content of health care innovation. The hospital building projects we investigate are linked to a large and diverse non-business (health care) network outside the construction business network. One such linkage in this extensive network is the professional network of health care. Members of this professional network include physicians, medical practitioners, those who deal with health-related administrative issues and health care workers. The other part of the network, not at all related to the construction industry, is represented by patients. Patients are the end users of hospitals and the health services provided at hospitals.

This situation leads us to our specific research question, which is the following: *How can construction projects function as vehicles for innovation?* We investigate this question by looking into the different networks that the project actors are related to and the necessary consequences of negotiating new solutions based on the requirements of those different networks. In this sense, identifying conflicts – i.e. specifying why they arise –and their consequences for the innovation processes is a central part of the analysis. *How did the conflicts that are identified in the construction projects support or hinder innovation in health care?*

We investigate the connectedness that needs to exist between a project organisation and the related user environment to which it is supposed to deliver innovative solutions. Our two cases demonstrate the presence, variability and lack of connectedness between the actors in hospital construction projects and their extensive networks (health care professionals and patients). The extensive network represents the clients to whom the construction projects must be finally delivered. In the two cases, a health care innovation that involved the implementation of a patient-centred approach and a fitting innovative hospital design requires a construction innovation involving the modification of a pavilion-style hospital to a single-building one (see later details). In fact, the construction innovation was created to support innovation in health care and is thus linked to both levels.

In the following section, we discuss the connection between construction projects and health care innovation. First, a brief overview of the Hungarian health care system is provided. Then, architectural and health care innovation is discussed from a network – or, more precisely, an extensive network – approach.

These sections lead us to our analytical focus, as illustrated in Figure 8.1. In the following sections, two case studies are introduced and analysed based on the three phases of the construction projects. In the discussion, the conflicts between the actors and the networks will be analysed from the viewpoint of whether they supported or hindered the project, according to the networks. The chapter ends with a concluding section that presents the outcomes of the interdependencies of the public and private networks that we have found in our research.

The connection between construction projects and health care innovation

With regard to health care construction projects, the academic literature mostly focuses on the architectural and design aspects of hospital construction (Bresnen and Marshall, 2000; Dainty, Briscoe and Millet, 2001). However, hospital construction projects and the buildings themselves involve multidimensional levels of complexity. The projects are complex in the sense that a number of different stakeholder rights should be guaranteed. In turn, these rights or requirements might be complex in themselves, such as the need to be able to provide efficient health care services. In addition to adhering to building norms and standards, sticking to budgets and delivering work on time, the medical-professional aims related to the building involve creating the appropriate environmental conditions for meeting health- (i.e. recovery)-related targets. In addition, the resulting buildings (hospitals) are complex systems of interacting environments, ranging in scale from the micro spaces of treatment rooms and wards to the wider 'civic' settings in which the hospitals are located. Though often implicit, a key idea here is that each of these situations needs to 'work' to promote patient recovery and healing: in effect, each site may be imagined as a 'therapeutic environment'. As a result of the health care innovation, this therapeutic environment means that the patients get all the medical services that are necessary for their recovery in the same hospital building. In fact, this is the fundamental goal of a patient-centred health care service.

Hospital construction concepts have changed over the years, from multi-pavilion hospitals to single-building hospitals, while the matrix layout is currently regarded to be the most advanced format (Hungarian report, 2008). Concepts are usually framed in national health care policies to serve as guidelines for hospital construction for a defined period of time.

The patient-centred concept is based upon research findings that have revealed that

> a better patient environment [. . .] improve[s] recovery times and the way that patients perceive [. . .] their hospital experience. However, this notion of producing well-being also extends to staff, for whom morale is seen as a key issue
>
> (Francis and Glanville, 2001, pp. 62–63)

The efficiency of patient-centred health care is also confirmed by financial calculations, primarily in terms of reduced cost (a shortened patient journey leads to cost savings, thus care efficiency is considered to be enhanced).

Luxford, Safran and Delbanco (2011) investigated eight hospitals in terms of the implementation and outcomes of organisational innovation and the restructuring of patient journeys. The main conclusions of the case studies regarding organisational innovation were that a strong, committed senior leadership and the communication of a strategic vision were crucial facilitators. The research also revealed that the lack of a positive attitude of service providers towards change was a major barrier. Another important finding was that institutional management played a decisive role in changing the organisational culture concerning how to provide health care, such as patient-centred services. The main finding of the study is that the entire organisation should be involved in the change process; otherwise its success is at risk (Luxford et al., 2011).

A brief overview of the Hungarian health care system

The Hungarian health care system has been applying more or less the same model since World War II, representing the market minimisation end of the Anderson model. The Anderson (1972) model describes a continuum ranging from market minimisation to market maximisation. With market maximisation, private health insurance and even for-profit insurance play a significant role, whereas with the market minimisation type, the health care system is owned and financed by the state, and salaries are paid from social security revenues and from general state tax revenues.

After the change of regime (i.e. the transition from a socialist system to a capitalist one), one major change was that private health care grew in importance alongside state-financed health care delivery, although the two systems have not been integrated yet. As the majority of the health care system and the entire system of hospital care belong to the sphere of state-funded health care delivery, our study only deals with this system.

There is only one insurer in the Hungarian health care system to which employers pay a health premium, and shortcomings in the health insurance budget are regularly financed from the national budget. The right to health care was universal under the earlier socialist system (i.e. it was a civic right), but after regime change in 1989, this entitlement ceased to exist, and care was provided only to the insured. Although many people theoretically became ineligible for health care services, such services continued to be provided because people were used to a system in which every citizen was entitled to health care. Today, an insurer can issue an invoice after treatment, but in most cases patients fail to pay because they cannot afford it. Thus, the earlier practice fundamentally continues: every citizen is entitled to health care, while other elements of the system have also remained unchanged, including the hospital buildings and the territorial organisation of the health care system.

In general, hospital buildings in Hungary are almost 100 years old and were built according to a so-called pavilion system. These hospitals operate in separate buildings, and although they met the medical and hygienic requirements of the time, both the system and the buildings have since become obsolete. The main advantage of the pavilion system was that it created an environment that could satisfy hygiene-related requirements, that is, ensure that the risk of infection was reduced.

Due to the system of separately located buildings, health care delivery faced – and still faces – various difficulties, and efficiency is hindered. Patients, staff members and test samples have to travel long distances between buildings, and due to duplication and decentralised diagnostic and treatment units, multiple instruments and medical staff have to be employed. Surgical wards have been built and diagnostic tools installed separately in a variety of buildings, thus their inefficient utilisation raises questions about economic efficiency. Furthermore, the maintenance and operation of the buildings involves significant cost. In addition, the pavilion system hinders interdisciplinary collaboration because different disciplines are housed in a variety of buildings and over various sites, making collaboration cumbersome and time-consuming and increasing patient dissatisfaction.

This system has become outdated both in technical and economic terms. Furthermore, there are now more advanced technologies for maintaining hygienic conditions; therefore there is no need to maintain buildings separately. Under these circumstances, it has become increasingly urgent to improve the efficiency of care delivery both in economic and medical terms, to rationalise patient journeys, and thereby to enhance patient satisfaction: namely, to build new hospital facilities such as single-building hospitals in which advanced care can be provided for the population and that are in line with European and Hungarian recommendations.

The health care program of 2011 is the government's strategic development concept about health policy for the period 2010–2014. In this vast document, political intentions concerning development are stated, with strong emphasis being given to infrastructure development mainly based on EU development resources and to organisational restructuring aimed at improving health care delivery. The plan identifies patient-centred care as one of the main priorities for the development of Hungarian health care services for the period and has served as the basis for the financial constructs that were created to support hospital development.

Over the past 20 years, use of the matrix system has started to spread, in opposition to traditional close-structured departmental systems. In this matrix system, organisational units are arranged by function, not by specialisation. Instead of traditional inpatient departments (usually physically divided off), entire inpatient units are operated as one department and may have separated sections at most, while in these sections patients are accommodated in line with their needs. As a result of the use of this type of system, waiting times have been significantly reduced, it is easier for patients to make appointments and for patients to be referred to hospitals as the provision of beds can be flexibly reorganised on a daily basis in line with patients' needs. The equipment, premises and human resources that are available are jointly used by various professions in line with their needs; consequently, the level of utilisation is improved, and entire hospitals operate more efficiently. However, the joint utilisation of physical and human resources requires a higher level of organisation and improved compliance with hygiene-related regulations (Hanna, 2010).

Today, the matrix system sometimes encounters unjustified resistance in Hungary, probably based on subjective opinions. It is largely believed that the system has the potential to fundamentally change the currently no longer optimal system of relationships that were developed and firmly established over the past 100 years (Hungarian report, 2008). The need to structure patient journeys in line with this approach is usually included in official health policy at the level of wishes and slogans, without a trace of investigation of its feasibility; the concept is typically recognised in the Hungarian health care system as well. However, the existence of a real patient-centred patient journey would be a genuine innovation – an organisational innovation in health care delivery.

The public health system from a network perspective

To analyse the complexity of health care construction projects, we apply the network approach of the Industrial Marketing and Purchasing (IMP) Group. The basic finding of IMP research is that the business landscape (Håkansson, Ford, Gadde, Snehota and Waluszewski, 2009) is composed of business networks (Axelsson and Easton, 1992; Håkansson and Snehota, 1995; Håkansson, 2006), which are the results of direct and indirect interactive relationships between companies (Håkansson, 1982). Connectedness is considered the substance of business relationships (Ford, Gadde, Håkansson, Snehota and Waluszewski, 2010). The existence of bonds between actors is a prerequisite for them to actively and consciously develop strong activity links and resource ties. Activity links make it likely that bonds will develop (Håkansson and Snehota, 1995). Actors, resources and activities are mutually related and influence one another. Actor bonds refer to the way in which the parties involved in a business relationship perceive and identify with one another. Resource ties refer to the way in which the tangible and intangible resources that support the activities of two firms in a relationship become oriented towards and integrated with each other. Activity links refer to the way in which the various activities undertaken by two firms in a relationship are coordinated and adapted to each other (Håkansson and Snehota, 1995).

A health care system may be defined as a complex network of individuals and organisations that includes government agencies, health care delivery systems, business, media, non-profit organisations, private health practitioners and academia (Gibbons, 2007). Individuals (more precisely, patients and potential patients) are the focus of this complex network, as all the very different activities of the actors are aimed at curing illnesses or preventing individuals from suffering from illness. We may say that the public health system network encompasses the actors involved in the socio-economic processes who convert resources to services for consumption by end users (the patients, or more generally, the public: i.e. tangible members of society).

Complex interconnectedness is another characteristic of health care network. Connectedness refers to the notion that relations between organisations in a health care network do not exist in isolation and are clearly affected by other organisational relations. Relations in health care networks are connected to each other and are therefore embedded in their environment (Salmi, 2000).

Embeddedness refers to the interdependence among health care actors and the connections between their relations (Håkansson et al., 2009). Actors in a health care network will adjust their behaviours according to the changes in relations they perceive (Corsaro and Snehota, 2011). Therefore, any change in one actor or one relation in the network will result in changes of other actors or relations that are interconnected.

Health care construction projects as embedded in extensive networks

Perhaps even more than in other construction projects, a set of diverse actors must collaborate with one another when planning and implementing health care construction projects. Therefore, constructing a hospital is a typical example of a complex project. A fundamental feature of a project is multiple dependent inter-actions between many stakeholders over time (Caldwell, Roehrich and Davies, 2009). In the case of hospital construction, this complexity is further deepened by the fact that while a project vendor is a company or a group of companies, the project client (i.e. the future operator of the hospital) is typically a non-business actor. This is a particularly important fact when it comes to disseminating inno-vation. Hartmann Reymen and Oosterom (2008) point out that the openness of non-business actors to innovation essentially depends on the extent to which new novelties are expected to contribute to their social commitments more than the conventional solutions already known to them. Therefore, a newly built mod-ern hospital building, for instance, would be accepted by doctors and health care professionals, who are typically non-business actors, if they are convinced that in this new building they can fulfil their social commitments better than before (i.e. cure their patients). If they are not convinced by this, they will not accept the novelty created by the newer hospital. This means that the behaviour of non-business actors is influenced by their own values, not just by business logic.

In trying to execute an innovative type of project, there are both advantages and disadvantages with the involvement of a multitude of different actors. An advantage of involving diverse actors in the innovation process is increasing access to a wide range of resources and the opportunity for multi-sectoral col-laboration among participants (Biemans, 1991). However, as projects rely heav-ily on negotiation processes, different perspectives and economic logics may also complicate matters. As an example, particular sources of financing for hospital construction projects can further complicate the implementation of innovation. From an examination of a hospital construction program in the UK, Barlow and

Köberle-Gaiser (2008) found that the involvement of private financial resources further increased the complexity of the interface between project delivery and hospital operational functions because of the multiplication of the actors and the increasing diversity of their interests.

With regard to hospital construction projects, there is also a general tendency to involve more and more stakeholders in the process of innovation (Aarikka-Stenroosa, Jaakkola, Harrison and Mäkitalo-Keinonen, 2017), both in terms of the implementation of projects and in the use of buildings. The extensive network approach (Aarikka-Stenroosa, Sandberg and Lehtimäki, 2014; Aarikka-Stenroosa et al., 2017; Aarikka-Stenroosa and Ritala, 2017) expands business network theory (Håkansson et al., 2009) by thoroughly examining the role of non-business actors. This approach may allow a deeper understanding of the innovation implementation process. Aarikka-Stenroosa et al. (2017, p. 89) define an extensive network as

> a network setting which comprises a wide range of different actors and stakeholders (with regard to organisational logics, goals, discourses and cultures, along with technologies and industry sectors). It can therefore include firms, public organisations, regulators and policymakers, experts, universities, research organisations, user communities and associations.

The project that should be carried out in collaboration with various actors can be regarded as an investment but, at the same time, an innovation implemented in an extensive network if the resulting solution is used. As with every project, there are tightly and loosely involved actors as well. What is even more interesting is that the level of involvement of the actors can change during the evolution of the project.

Based on the extensive network approach, the realisation of a hospital construction project is fundamentally influenced by the relationship between construction and health care networks and by the mechanisms of interconnection between these networks. The essential element of the relationship of these two networks is their interdependency. This interdependency means that they have to at least partly coordinate their activities and resources to be able to achieve their desired outcomes (Ford, Gadde, Håkansson and Snehota, 2011). The possibility of completing a hospital construction project depends on the demand and investment capacity of the health care network. On the other hand, the possibility of increasing the level of health care service is influenced by the state and equipment in hospital buildings.

However, the two networks are fundamentally different in terms of their values and operational mechanisms (Cova Ghauri and Salle, 2002). A construction network is a business network in which the goal of all the actors is to achieve their own business targets, which is why they enter into (business) relationships with one another. Problem solving and business performance play a central role. Interactive business relationships (Håkansson, 1982; Håkansson, 2006) are the main mechanisms of the interconnection of actors. However, a health care system is a non-business network that has the provision of health-related services (cure and prevention) as its basic activity. The main goal of a health care system is to improve the quality of health care for individual patients, communities and populations (Saha, Beach and Cooper, 2008). Horizontal professional relationships as well as strong hierarchical and administrative ones are the main mechanism of interconnection. Horizontal relationships typically occur between complementary medical activities, while hierarchical relations are generally inside hospitals and health care administrations.

In the present Hungarian situation, this means that the realisation of construction innovation depends on the relationship between two networks that are different according to their values and operating mechanisms. One such network is the health care system, which in Hungary is a public service system based on non-business principles that is heavily centralised and governed by strict power relations and administrative rules. Bearing this in mind, the hospital building (and, broadly, the construction sector) network can be seen as a basically business-oriented, though fragmented (Havenvid, Håkansson and Linné, 2016) business network.

From the point of view of the implementation and the use of innovation, one of the problems with extensive networks is the interaction of many actors with many different values, strategies and organisational cultures (Bresnen and Marshall, 2000; Caldwell et al., 2009) who do not necessarily have the same goals. These actors can simultaneously help or hinder the achievement of each other's and their own goals (Ford et al., 2011; Yang, Hi and Chou, 2012). Closely related to this is a further feature of extensive networks; namely, they are difficult to understand (Holmen, Pedersen and Torvatn, 2005) and thus, in some very complex situations, do not benefit from the use of inter-organisational management governance techniques aimed at facilitating innovation flow. Harty (2008, p. 1029) introduced the concept of 'relative boundedness', according to which "relatively unbounded innovation is characterised by a lack of a coherent central driving force or mediator with the ability to reconcile potential conflicts and overcome resistance to implementation". In addressing such problems, negotiations and translation implementation are proposed to take account of versatile and different expectations.

Given the difficulty and complexity of the interaction process (Ford et al., 2010), interfaces are very difficult to study. However, a business interaction is not only an economic phenomenon but in every case a special form of social relations (Mandják and Szántó, 2010). In addition, social relationships, by their very nature, link different actors (Weber, 1964) and often involve conflicts or the potential for these. Thus, examining conflicts in relationships gives us the opportunity to study the interfaces and to see whether the conflicts involved in any particular interface help or hinder the spread of innovation.

Buying-and-selling companies have shared but also opposing goals that are natural sources of conflict (Ellegaard and Andersen, 2015). During project implementation, conflicts arise naturally between the project vendor and the project buyer (Cova et al., 2002). These are often complicated by conflict between the

project seller companies, which can sometimes jeopardise the successful implementation of projects (i.e. the sale of the projects) (Cova and Hoskins, 1997).
However, conflicts may arise between the various functions and units within
organisations' internal networks (Winch, 1998).

Using a study of the customer relationships of companies that sell complex
projects, Vaaland and Håkansson (2003) explain that two approaches have been
developed to assess the role of conflicts. One is that conflict is a clearly negative
phenomenon that endangers business operations and is therefore essentially to
be avoided. The other view is that conflicts can be a threat but also represent an
opportunity to discuss and resolve disagreements. Thus, conflict and its proper
management can contribute to the further development and improvement of
existing relationships. As a result of the analysis, it is stated that "conflict events
should be related to formal and informal governance mechanisms in order to
understand how conflict can be used to strengthen the business relationship
between the parties" (Vaaland and Håkansson, 2003, p. 127).

In the extensive network that exists in the process of hospital building and
the related innovation implementation, conflicts may arise at different points of
connectedness. Of course, there may be a conflict between the buyer and seller of
the hospital building project. Here, it is worth pointing out that the source of the
conflict may be due not only to the complexity of the construction project (Gann
and Salter, 2000) but because different business (seller) and non-business (buyer)
actors are working together (Vaaland and Håkansson, 2003). There may be further conflicts within the health care network between the buyer and the health
care administration and between the buyer and the political sphere (Ingram,
Scutchfield, Mays and Michelyn, 2012).

Overall, the key to the implementation of innovation in an extensive network seems to be the management of connectedness within the network. These
interconnections can help or hinder the acceptance and implementation of
innovation. Figure 8.1 shows the focus of our analysis based on insights from the
literature. In the centre of the figure is the individual project with the sellers and
buyers from the two networks. The project is embedded in the networks through
not only buyers and sellers but other actors, organisations from the two networks.
In other words, the two networks have interfaces not only in the project but
beside the project as well. The lines between the actors represent the connections between the actors inside the project and outside the project. Regarding
the boundaries of the project, we accept the concept of Engwall (2003) that the
project has a past and future (temporal scope) and also a dynamic organisational
scope. The connections are affected by the existing interdependencies of the networks and the influence of interdependencies stretches across the boundaries of
the individual project. The interdependencies of the public and private networks
raise conflicts between the actors no matter the actor is in the project or outside
the project. In this chapter, we focus on how the project actors are affected by
these interdependencies throughout the stages of the project.

In this chapter, we introduce and explore two case studies in which health
care innovations were implemented in extensive networks, with the purpose of

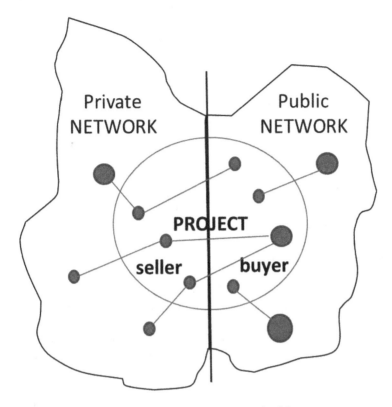

Figure 8.1 Interdependencies in constructions projects in health care

investigating the implementation process and barriers to it from the user's point of view. The rationale for this study lies in the high importance of the services associated with the successful implementation of the related infrastructure. We give an overview of the project process, the actors in the extensive network of projects and their roles.

Through the case studies, the analysis in this chapter explores how such projects can both drive and hinder new approaches to health care provision and organisation within the national context. Both projects were aimed at shortening the patient journey and improving health care delivery through the structure and the operation of the organisational units that were to move into the buildings. These collaborative efforts and newly organised patient journeys involve substantial organisational innovation, not only in the specific hospital blocks but also throughout the entire Hungarian health care system.

Throughout the research, we investigate whether the construction of a new hospital building can increase the success of health care innovation. However, there appear to be numerous obstacles (at both the personal and institutional levels) to accepting and utilising this new form of health care innovation. In other words, we ask whether a construction project can really leverage health care innovation. It drives the following research questions: How can construction projects function as vehicles for innovation? How do the identified conflicts in the construction projects support or hinder innovation in health care?

Research methodology

Our study uses multiple case study methodology. We chose to examine two cases because multiple cases provide stronger evidence and the opportunity to compare and contrast two different projects with similar goals. We used a retrospective lens in our research; a longitudinal, process-based approach was pursued to study the effect of the construction projects on the success of health care innovation in an extensive network. The research was inspired by the logic of network process theory (Bizzi-Langley, 2012; Halinen, Medlin and Törnroos, 2012) that suggested integrating time and process into business network research. We applied the sequential mapping method; we studied in real time and in retrospect as well (Halinen, Medlin and Törnroos, 2012).

The primary data sources include interviews, project documentation, publication and media data. The main data source is primary qualitative research involving 18 expert interviews (Table 8.1) with participants of the project. The personal interview "allows the researcher to interpret the respondents' implied application of diverse time concepts and to compare them across and between different actors within interaction processes" (Halinen, Medlin and Törnroos, 2012, p. 220).

Interviews lasting on average about one hour were conducted with project leaders and professionals (representatives of the project owners and general contractors, architects, project management and government representatives) who

Table 8.1 List of interviews

Type of actor	Number of informants	Informants
Health care network, university actors	13	Head of Finance and Engineering, President of the University Health Centre, senior physician (working in the new building), Procurement Manager Head of Finances, Rector's Commissionaire, head of project management team until 2014, head of project management team 2014-, vice head of project management team, Head of Engineering, mechanical engineer, engineer, project manager
Health care network, political actors	2	Undersecretary at Ministry of Finance, architect consultant at Ministry of Health Care
Construction network	3	Site manager at general contractor, design architect, construction supervisor

were involved in the design and implementation of the projects. We also analysed the documents related to the processes (feasibility studies, contracts, founding documents) when they were available. Some of the documents we analysed were publicly accessible, while others were only partially accessible to the public. After analysis of the documents and interviews, we presented our findings and experience to the project managers during a workshop, which provided an opportunity partly to verify our results during discussions and partly to continue information gathering. The workshops and interviews were often combined with on-site visits typically undertaken not during the time of construction but in the last period of implementation when the buildings were ready or almost ready (when we could examine the structure of the building and the availability – or lack – of equipment).

Introduction of the cases

Two Hungarian university hospital construction projects were selected for analysis. These projects were among the largest health care investments of the last decades in Hungary. As worn-out equipment and buildings are one of the major obstacles to improving health care, hospital construction and renovation constitute an essential step in the development process. As the cases both represent large-scale projects that involve EU-level funding, they also provided the opportunity to investigate and discuss the roles of the different types of actors who are involved throughout the course of such large-scale construction projects.

The Budapest Project involved the construction of a new building in the garden of the hospital block of a university and started in 2006. The construction of a new hospital within this block of buildings, relocating departments from other outdated and poorly equipped buildings and housing the lacking therapeutic departments appeared to be a stopgap solution in itself. The hospital construction project finished in 2015. Most departments started operating, but a part of the building remained empty, lacking equipment and departments to use it. Therefore, we conclude that this project was only partly able to meet its objectives. The building was made ready and the construction work finished, but the innovative approach to providing health care services was only partly successful.

The Szeged Project involved the construction of a new hospital building in Szeged (a university town in Hungary) in the early 2000s. The management of the University Health Centre initially intended to resolve health care–related difficulties by establishing a new hospital. The goal was to create an up-to-date inpatient and outpatient health care centre that could meet modern European standards in terms of its operation, equipment and services and was able to integrate the fragmented and obsolete health care structure of the city and also meet regional needs. The Szeged Project started in 2003 and finished in 2015. The hospital building is now finished and functioning; all the departments that were intended to have moved in and are now operational in the new and well equipped building. We therefore conclude that the project was successfully finished.

The objective of both hospital construction projects was to enable and facilitate medical professional innovation, implement a patient-centred approach, make patient journeys shorter and ensure that care is organised around patients (i.e. it is not patients who are required to move but medical service providers who visit patients).

Case analysis

In the analysis, we follow the three phases of the construction projects. Thus, the initiation phase is presented first, followed by the implementation phase, and then the phase of use of the two hospital building projects. In the case of use, we concentrate on the operation of the new hospitals.

In this section, following the approach shown in Figure 8.1, we illustrate some conflicts during the project phases. There are conflicts between the project sellers, i.e. the construction companies and the project buyers, i.e. the universities. Conflicts during the phases of initiation, implementation, operation and use are illustrated in Table 8.2.

A conflict (and sometimes its management) may support or hinder innovation. The examples in Table 8.2 show hindering conflicts mainly among the participants of the construction process, like the conflict between the university and the architect or between the participants of the construction consortium. We can find examples of organisational conflicts both hindering and supporting; the

Table 8.2 Examples for types of conflicts according to project phase

Type of conflict (from the innovation process perspective)	Project phase		
	Initiation	Implementation	Operation and use
Supporting conflict	Conflicts related to the involvement of the health care departments during the preparation of the project proposal (Szeged Project)	Dual management system (project management team and rector's commissioner) conflicts (both projects) Ventilation system design failure solved by the project owner (Budapest Project)	Conflicts of reorganisation involving provision of new patient-centred health care services (Szeged Project)
Hindering conflict	Conflicts between the university and architect because of cancellation of tenders for designs (Budapest Project)	Conflict as a result of the break-up of the construction consortium (Budapest Project)	Power-related conflict between senior clinic managers who did not want to relocate to new building (Budapest Project)

supporting feature is related frequently to a successful solution of a conflict. In our case description, we will analyse not all the conflicts mentioned in the table, only some examples of conflicts in light of whether they supported or hindered the construction innovation process.

Initiation phase

Budapest Project

The idea of the Budapest Project was generated partly by the need for investment into the Hungarian health care system and partly by an opportunity to apply for EU grants. Governmental bodies whose task is to announce and manage tenders tend to talk to stakeholders and make suggestions before they decide on which large investment projects to take on.

Political will, government bodies and regulations played a decisive role in the initiation of the project. University actors started to think about the project, and project planning commenced. Since the university (the project-owning institution) needed financial support from the government, a sequence of usually very time-consuming interactions between the representatives of the university and the government took place during this phase. Because of this, the ongoing planning process sometimes slowed down or even stopped and then restarted with somewhat different project content. The procedure that originally started in 2006 went through many such interruptions, and in 2011, when the tender was approved, it was the sixth version of the project that was finally accepted.

The initial aim of the Budapest Project was to develop the basic infrastructure of the university to such a level that it would improve its economic potential, cost-effective operation, and the efficient organisation of the care delivery system too.

The basic idea of the project was centralisation, involving the housing of departments in one building, which is also the goal of every European and Hungarian action plan. Recognition of the need for this first dawned on the university when the management structures were reorganised: administrators found that worn-out buildings and the parallel operation of a mixture of units in various clinics were barriers to improving the efficiency of management:

> The key aspect of the plan was to achieve a high level of complexity of blocks and the highest possible level of resource concentration. It was clear that, without infrastructure development, operations would be costly, health care delivery within the constraints of old buildings could not be cost-effective, and would not be competitive either on a Hungarian or Central-European basis, which was one of the strategic goals of the project.
>
> (Feasibility Study, 2015)

The plan, developed between 2006 and 2011 in different formats, was to create a building with five floors, in harmony with the needs of the university clinics, first of all with a central diagnostics unit and central laboratory. The final phase of preparation was influenced by the new health care program of the government, published in 2011. The goals of this program were established as political intentions, one of which included the implementation of the here-introduced Budapest Project. Within the program, the goal of improving the efficiency of care delivery within the framework of the Budapest Project primarily focused on emergency care.

The decision about the enlarged Budapest Project involving the original plans had to be extended to include a building with seven floors and new departments. This required a very rapid elaboration of final plans with extended content (the final plans had to be completed to submit a successful application for EU funds).

In preparation, the university, as the buyer of the project, cooperated with the supplier (the designer himself and the design company). The process of tendering was not based on open business competition: instead, the public procurement procedure for the design of the building was completed without open competition because the original designer who was involved in the reconstruction of one of the university clinics proved that the new building was so close to the pre-existing clinic that it could be seen as part of the original clinic, thus he had the right to design the building. This fact is of great relevance to the mixed success of the project because, although the designer was the same as for the original clinic, the architectural company was different. For the earlier design processes, the designer had been employed by a large company, which was later broken up into several smaller firms during the change of political regime, with the designer becoming the managing director of one of the firms. This situation is specifically connected to the political-historical circumstances of the country, whereby the system change caused changes in many big state-owned companies that were later split into more small, privately owned ones. This example shows the interrelationship between changes in the political-economic scene and the business changes that influenced the outcome of the aforementioned case. Although the designer was able to support his claim of having a right to design the building, the legal regulation did not take into account the fact that the relationships of the designer had changed; it was simply presumed that the designer could complete the work. Thus, the Budapest Project was designed by the managing director of a smaller private company, and many subcontractors were employed in the planning process as a consequence. This change, together with the discontinuity involved in the procedure, resulted in shortened periods of planning. After many restarts of the planning process, the time was too short to prepare a final application that was in harmony with other plans made by the design team. However, this lack of control and harmonisation was also connected to the project preparation phase and influenced by the discontinuity of the project due mainly to external influences. Consequently, there were many design failures in the document that was finally approved.

Szeged Project

Very similarly to the Budapest Project, planning of the Szeged Project restarted several times between 2003 and 2008. The university (project owner) lacked the resources to devote to the development program aimed at renewing delivery of care; thus they requested support from the government. Negotiations were conducted in several stages to acquire financial resources, and the university attempted to include Hungarian state financing, EU funds, and even private equity, but the Hungarian government refused to support the project in its original form. The size of the project decreased with each proposal (originally starting as a 2,000-bed Euro-regional hospital but finally ending up with 256 beds). The then Undersecretary of the Ministry of Finance explained that "seriously, nobody believed that a copy of the [Swedish] Karolinska University Hospital could be built in Hungary".

The complexity of such hospital construction activities can be depicted and examined in the different motivation of the actors who were involved. In the initiation phase, government bodies played an important role since the hospital was designed to be part of the larger, national health care system. The Ministry of Health Care was motivated to develop the level of service of Hungarian health care but had no clearly stated strategy before 2011, when the health care program was introduced. The second governmental actor was the Ministry of Finance. Their objective was to balance resources between the different areas of the national economy. In this particular case, this meant that the Ministry of Finance was responsible for dividing up the national and EU funds that were available between economic priorities and projects.

> In the planning period 2007–2013 [for EU funds] the size of the available monetary resources was clearer, we knew that the budget limit for a health care investment in one location was set at about 13 Billion HUF by the government. Then we understood that this was the maximum amount of financial resources that we could obtain. We had to rethink our plans accordingly.
>
> (Head of Finance and Engineering at the university)

In parallel with the negotiations between the government and the university, the project proposal was further developed based on requirements and opportunities. Units and departments of the university had regular meetings to shape the functional plans for health care and the infrastructural requirements that served as a basis for the subsequent project proposal and the construction planning.

During the redesign procedure, the university put together a proposal for a smaller project involving health care development aimed at enhancing efficiency and shortening the patient journey. A patient-centred, flexible design and single-building construction was defined as the main requirement in the call for tenders. As a result of the development, seven of the oldest regional hospital buildings (86 years old) were to be closed down and withdrawn from care provision, and one new building was to be opened to host the medical functions that were previously located in those buildings.

The local government supported the project by financing the new public road and utility-related infrastructure for the building.

Implementation phase

Budapest Project

A university, with its extensive internal institutions, comprises a complex system of relations in the form of a network of interdependent departments and offices. The decision-making procedures of a university are often bureaucratic; they typically lack flexibility and the dynamism and vigour of for-profit organisations. Public universities (with their hierarchical, rigid and inflexible decision-making structures) are not apt to make quick, flexible decisions within the short time required by the business character of the project. This issue led to many conflicts between the buyer, the university and the supplier, and construction firms. These conflicts not only extended the implementation period but hindered the successful implementation process. To overcome this problem, the university in Budapest set up a project management unit with dedicated decision-making rights whose task was to manage the relations between the university itself – an organisation with bureaucratic decision-making mechanisms – and the business sector.

The operational teams were connected to the operational and decision systems of the university and were thus aware of the rules of this system, just as any other organisational unit at the university. However, their status was different in an organisational sense because the operational team operated as a business-like unit within the university structure. They were supported by the top management of the university and managed to implement the projects in a different way to the normal procedures at the university. "If it was necessary and urgent, we could get all the signatures of the financial and administrative responsible persons within half a day because of the priority of the project. This procedure takes usually at least two weeks" – claimed the manager of the operational team in Budapest.

Through this organisational solution, many problems and conflicts were solved or avoided during the implementation of the project. Here we analyse only one case: the ventilation system problem that occurred in the Budapest project.

During the implementation phase, it turned out that the specifications of the ventilation system has been improperly calculated, meaning it had to be redesigned and some new lamps purchased. However, neither the designer nor the general contractor wanted to take responsibility for this and to do the repair work, but the problem had to be solved. In this case, the conflict occurred between the business actors, but they were not able to solve it, so the solution came from the buyer side. The rector's commissioner and the operational team had two choices: to look for an independent, competent expert and to commission them with this task or to find such an expert but involve them in the network by hiring them as part of the hospital managerial team. By opting for the second opportunity, the problem was solved in a very effective way because the problem became an embedded part of larger tasks and was solved more efficiently by using the network contacts of the involved expert.

During this phase of the project, the university's main task was to monitor and support the work of the architect and later the constructor organisations.

The implementation phase started in 2011 after the bid was accepted and a decision was made about both EU funding and the amount of financial support from within Hungary.

The consortium of two companies (one with good references from health care construction projects and another with extensive experience in implementing large projects) was selected through a public procurement process. The implementation of the construction project was awarded to a consortium that included a multinational company and a smaller company that was able to provide references that included health care construction projects.

Interviews conducted with university actors, the project management team, and the rector's commissionaire revealed that the project represented too much of a challenge for the smaller company, which had completed several large projects of this nature but none as large as that which was planned.

During the implementation phase, it was the task of the project management team and the contractor to maintain operational contact. There was a change in the consortium in 2013, as a result of which the smaller company left the project (and allegedly went into liquidation), while the large company remained part of the project. During the implementation phase, problems typically stemmed from strained relations with the designer and underestimated prices (more precisely, the cost of items). Conflicts between the designer and construction consortium were mainly hindering ones during the implementation phase in the sense that it took time to clarify the responsibility for failures and to find solutions to them during project implementation. These conflicts had no feasible solution in the implementation phase of the project: the designer who was required to be present and to participate in the implementation as an overseer left the project after many conflicts during this initial phase.

Szeged Project

Following the preparation and implementation of the relevant public procurement procedures, the organisations that took part in the construction were commissioned from 2009 onwards. The architect started working in 2009, while the general contractor and the subcontractors started the project in 2011. As with the Budapest project, the construction was undertaken by a consortium of two organisations: a relatively small firm and a general contractor company. The general contractor company had extensive experience and references from projects in the construction industry. Although they had worked with higher education projects in Szeged on several occasions, they had no experience with a health care project of the size of the new project. During construction, the university entered into agreement with about 40 different organisations, although several other subcontractors were also involved, thus the number of directly involved constructors or suppliers (general contractors and subcontractors) amounted to 200.

During the phase of architectural planning, the representatives of the design group and the university met frequently. The architect consortium created a design concept based on the information that the university provided about the intended future functions of the building, and, during regular meetings, the representatives of the project management team and the health care departments of the university had the opportunity to discuss the concept and request changes and modifications. "This was a long process, with multiple rounds. Every head of department wrote down their needs, and sometimes their dreams too" (a senior physician who later worked in the new building). The final construction drawing was created within one year. The most significant conflict occurred during this phase, when the engineering office of the university received the final plans and realised that they had been left out of earlier discussions, meaning that several changes had to be made to the final version due to the university rules and procedures (for example, the university was committed to using renewable energy so the basement level of the building had to be redesigned to make it suitable for hosting geothermal energy infrastructure). This step could have been avoided by involving the engineering office much earlier in the planning process.

While construction was ongoing, discussion continued among the representatives of project management, the engineering office of the university, the architect, the general contractor, the independent engineer, and the technical supervisor, as well as the subcontractors who were involved. These occasions provided an opportunity to discuss and remedy occasional problems and carry out the needed modifications. During this phase of implementation, the previously involved health care professionals and health care departments were not directly involved. The management of the University Health Centre made the decision to decrease the number of people involved in the discussions to avoid any changes arising in relation to new needs and the ideas of health care departments. These departments had the opportunity to state their needs and discuss them with the architect in the initiation phase, but during the stage of implementation their ongoing participation at meetings was not considered necessary.

As an example of supporting conflicts, we can mention the organisational and operational solutions in both projects that improved the flexible nature of project implementation.

This prioritising of the project was significantly supported by the nomination of a competent, responsible project head, as the case of both universities shows. In the Budapest case, it was the rector's commissionaire, a health care expert and the head of a neighbouring clinic with a good reputation. In the Szeged case, the person nominated was the head of the health care centre at the university.

Operation and use

Budapest Project

The project was completed in 2015, or more precisely was declared complete. This meant that the building was completed and some equipment was installed, allowing several departments and clinics to move into the building. All the elements that were included in (and thus eligible for funding from) the EU application were completed to make the whole project eligible for funding. This situation has significantly affected the medical functionality of the building, since – for example – 12 operating rooms were built on the operating floor in line with the goals of the matrix system, but only four of them are now equipped and ready for operation.

The implications of this situation for the internal actors have been investigated, and it can be stated, surprisingly, that no major trouble has been caused. The reason is that not every actor is moving into the building who, according to the initial or subsequent plans, should have moved in. Among these actors are clinical departments that operate in old buildings with outdated infrastructure, while an emergency department has not moved in either. One head of a clinical department that operates in poor conditions refused to move in because under the matrix system their operations would have become more transparent and could have been brought under stricter control. The clinical department is part of the university, thus the rector could have ordered the head of the department to move in, but the former put forward professional arguments against the move that were difficult to invalidate; thus the rector did not have the competence to enforce a move. A similar situation arose with the emergency department. When decision makers came up with the title 'emergency ward', they failed to define who the users of this part of the building would be. Meanwhile, the idea emerged that some parts of the not-so-distant Traumatology Hospital could be relocated, but the affected departments refused to move and had every right to do so. The latest news since the completion of the project is that the university has started to establish an emergency department so as not to leave the relevant part of the building and the infrastructure (for example, the helicopter landing pad) underutilised. The reason why the incomplete parts of the project are not missed is that not all users are housed in the building yet.

The health care innovation that is partly supported by the building in its current form cannot be regarded as entirely complete either. A central diagnostic unit has been installed, and the related service units have also moved into and now operate in the building. A once distant clinic has been relocated; thus one outdated building has been replaced. But the fact remains that implementation is incomplete, and the process of relocation has been accidental, meaning that those who do not want to move in can find ways to avoid doing so.

Szeged Project

The construction of the new hospital building (of 21,500-square-metre total floor area) was completed in the summer of 2015. Following the relocation of the departments, the new hospital building was inaugurated in December 2015. The newly built building provides a modern environment and equipment for departments operating in the field of cardiovascular care (the prevention, diagnosis and treatment of the full spectrum of cardiovascular diseases). The ten departments that moved in were earlier located in seven different buildings. The current situation increases the speed that health care services are provided, since there is no longer a need for transportation between buildings.

> The patient journey has definitely changed. Our connection to diagnostics is much better. The CT, MRI and more [procedures] are located in the same building now. Speaking about logistics, it is much easier to transport a patient between floors than between distant buildings. . . . What is more, the possibility of consultation with other physicians has become easier too.
> (A senior physician who now works in the new building)

Both employees and patients enjoy the modern environment (building and equipment), and the change has affected patient and the employee satisfaction as well. "Nurses have said to me: 'Mr. Professor, this is a totally different world now'; they feel good, are happy to work, and, as a result, the quality of hospitalisation is better" (senior physician, op. cit.).

The ten departments have had to learn how to work under one roof. Many of them were formerly located in separate buildings and had to learn how to use shared facilities successfully. "After one year of work in the new building we finally started to understand how we can help each other and what we can ask (and we can't) from other departments. The operation [of the hospital] is without problems at the moment" (senior physician, op cit.).

As the senior physician from the Szeged project stated, "this was not only a construction project. This was a professional health care project in which a new building was built, and the departments received the infrastructural and technological help that was needed to renew their professional work".

The Szeged project is now complete and, from an architectural perspective, the construction of the 265-bed clinic in Szeged has achieved its goal: the building is possessed of the appropriate functionality and has been put into use.

Finally, both hospital projects were finished. The buildings and the equipment were installed, although in the Budapest project only partly. In this sense, the construction processes were successful and similar in the two cases.

Discussion

In the theoretical section, we declared that we sought to examine connectedness by observing the conflicts that are created in the interfaces between actors. In this section, we analyse our cases according to the supporting and hindering features of conflicts, how conflicts and interdependencies between actors can affect the outcome of innovative health care construction projects. We introduce the conflicts with interdependencies of the two networks -health care and construction – respectively.

Innovation can be realised in both important areas of the projects we describe: in construction (hospital construction) or in health care (patient-centred care), but in our cases they are interrelated, the innovation in health care can be

Table 8.3 Examples of types of conflicts according to network relations

Type of conflict (from the innovation process perspective)	Network relation		Between (actors in) networks
	Within network		
	Health care network	Construction network	
Supporting conflict	Conflict between politicians and universities about health care system/hospital development (both projects)	Conflicts solved by experienced construction consortium (both projects)	Conflict between constructor and university about hygienic surface treatment (Szeged Project)
Hindering conflict	Conflict as a result of political changes and redesign needs (both projects)	Conflict between the architect and the constructor about design failures (Budapest Project)	Conflict between the architect, the constructor and the university (Budapest Project)

realised through the construction project. For example, the resolution of conflicts between a project vendor and a project buyer may support the implementation of both innovations. More specifically, in the present cases these conflicts directly supported the construction of the hospital building (that is, the construction project). However, they only indirectly supported the implementation of health care innovation because the hospital building itself represents only the physical capacity for patient-centred care, that is, health care innovation. This is well illustrated in the Budapest case where the completed building is now only partially used for the implementation of innovative patient care practices. Table 8.3 illustrates the categorisation of conflicts based on two features: the role of the conflict (either supporting or hindering the innovation) and the type of actors that were involved in the conflict (within network, or between network).

Some examples of conflicts are analysed to illustrate the categories that appear in the table.

Conflicts within the health care network

Within this category, two major types of conflicts can be identified. Conflicts that occur between the project owner and politicians (decision makers in the national health care system) and conflicts between the units of the project-owning university. We can identify both supportive and hindering conflicts in these categories.

Supporting conflict: health care politics and institutions set the goal

From the very beginning of the project, the university was a main actor in the process that was embedded in the health care network. It was the institution that could fulfil the goal of improving the health care service, which was the goal of a medical university with university hospitals. If the government defines a health care–related innovation goal, it is obvious that they will cooperate with a medical university. The national government, supported by an initiative of the European Union, and the medical university seem to have had the same health care–related targets; this is relevant in both cases presented here. They also had the same construction-related goals too: the building of a new hospital. The goal of health care policy is to facilitate cooperation between actors in the health care network. But these relationships are interconnected: health care actors need the contacts and support of health care policy, mainly financial support. If a university wishes to implement such a large project, funding from the government and from the European Union is required. This relationship is an interconnected relationship, but in this case this relationship is also hierarchical.

Hindering conflict: changes of the health care initiatives

This relationship in our case involved not only supporting but hindering elements and conflicts because of the frequent changes in the health care initiatives of the government. Because of the hierarchical relationship, the government could request adjustments of the university plans: the consequences of this process were the long preparation time of the project and the discontinuity of this process.

Hindering conflict: organisational challenges

Within the health care network, there were conflicts among the units of the university. The health care objectives and infrastructure developments were defined based on the professional requirements of health care departments. This process was not without conflict. The most significant of these arose when the health care departments had to decide who would move into the new building and what infrastructural development would support their operation in the new building (in other words, what equipment could be bought and installed for how much money?). During this phase, a decision had to be made about who could or should move in; in the phase of use, this situation changed.

The actors in the health care network have the main task of defining and implementing health care goals, the health care innovations in the project. It was an organisational challenge to involve the units of the university in the project and to maintain their participation in the project. The supporting participation of the units could have turned into a hindering conflict because the participation of many units could have obstructed the effectiveness of the regular coordination meetings during the project. Therefore, the representatives of many units of the university were not invited to the regular operative meetings that were designed to promote the efficiency of the decision-making processes in case they hindered the commitment of health care professionals towards the project.

While the construction project was successfully completed in both cases, the health care targets could not be achieved in both cases. As mentioned, for the Budapest Project the health care–related aims were only partly fulfilled: a central diagnostic unit has been installed, and the related service units have also moved into and now operate in the building. However, not all the units that were expected to move into the building have actually done so. This is not the case in the Szeged Project: here, the goals of the health care project were also achieved. Several factors explain the incomplete success of the Budapest Project, one of which is the two different individuals nominated as responsible persons by the rector of the universities. In the Szeged case, the responsible individual was the head of the clinical centre, who was at the top of the hierarchy and had the power to realise the desires and initial structure of the health care participants during the final phase and in the use of the building. In the Budapest case, the rector's commissionaire was the head of a clinic who had no hierarchical relationship with the other directors and thus lacked the power to define the initial structure of departments at the final phase. As a top manager of the Budapest project said, "the rector of the university should have ordered the heads of the clinics to move in to the building as planned. . . . But the organisational culture does not support this mechanism".

Conflicts within the construction network: hindering and supporting conflicts

These conflicts, mainly the hindering ones within the construction networks, have been analysed more from the perspective of project realisation. The conflicts of the consortium partners has a rather hindering feature in the Budapest Project and a rather supportive feature in the Szeged Project. In both projects, the construction consortium was very similar: a large contractor company (multinational or national) with appropriate experience with large-scale construction projects, partnered with a smaller company that had multiple references in the field of hospital construction. The difference between the two consortia is significant: in the Budapest case, the partners cooperated for the first time, while in the Szeged case, the general contractor had been working for the project owner on similarly large-scale projects before the hospital construction project. This earlier cooperation between the buyer and the seller generated a higher level of trust in both actors and resulted in smoother cooperation between them. The expertise of the consortium partners in both projects helped to overcome smaller conflicts and misunderstandings that occurred during the project (as with most construction projects, conflicts related to deadlines, communication, tendering and unrealistic expectations occurred during project execution).

Conflicts between health care and construction networks

Supportive elements of conflicts between public and private networks

Conflicts between construction and health care networks are conflicts between private and public actors as well. The major actors (the university from the public side and the designer and the construction companies on the other) had to cooperate during all the phases of work but especially in the phases of preparation and implementation. The decisions of the major actors are influenced by whether they belong to public or private networks. This usually leads to many conflicts between public and private actors, but in the present case, there were distinct factors that caused unique conflicts.

A good example of this was a decision about the provision of hygienic, easy-to-handle surfaces for the hospital involved in the Szeged Project. Cleaning and disinfection processes are highly important components of hospital operations. In the Szeged Project, the decision about the methodology and the product that should be used was influenced by the fact that the nanotechnology research centre of the project-owner university had developed a new nanotechnology-based product (a gel) during the construction period. Since the product had all the necessary licences and the project owner expressed their willingness to use the product, the constructor consortium accepted their request and utilised the nano-gel, resulting in better sterilisation in the new building.

The best example of conflicts and solutions between public and private actors are conflicts between different operating and decision systems. The institutional solution for this problem in this case was the setting up of an operative team and a responsible manager at both universities. Although the operational team and the managers were embedded in the public health care network, they were able to act as the business project required. They built up business-like competences partly through hiring personnel from business or from other units of the university and demanded a flexible and problem-solving attitude from employees. This operational solution significantly supported the successful completion of the construction project in both cases.

Conclusion

In this chapter we have dealt with the connection between the construction industry and health care innovation. In analysing two health care-related construction projects in Hungary, we attempted to reveal how construction projects can become a vehicle for health care innovation. Health care innovation in this case refers to patient-centred, single-building hospitals. We consider this form of innovation to be successful if the innovation is put to use.

Several networks and several types of connectedness characterised the hospital construction projects and the processes of innovation that was to be implemented. In each case, the first was the hospital construction project itself, which created the connectedness between the internal network of the sales company and the internal network of the buyer who was the future owner and operator of the hospital that will be built.

Connectedness for the buyer involves connectedness in the health care network through which the customer can implement health care innovation (in our case, patient orientation) and the need for the necessary physical resources (the hospital project). These health care interfaces are partially created through health care administration and the associated policy leadership and in part in the individual forms of project organisation that are created within the buyer's organisation.

To analyse the connectedness between the construction industry and health care through hospital building projects, we used the extensive network approach of Aarikka-Stenroosa et al. (2017), where the construction industry represents the private network and health care and governmental or EU policies represent the public network. Both private and public networks include many different organisations and individuals.

Connectedness in extensive networks refers to the interdependencies of the different networks. Interdependency means that networks have to combine their activities and resources at least partly in order to be able to achieve their desired outcomes (Ford et al., 2011). One possible way of identifying interdependencies is to reveal the conflicts between actors within one network and between networks (see Figure 8.1). In other words, the source of conflict is located in the interdependencies between networks. That is what we analysed in our chapter.

Based on the distinction between conflicts made by Vaaland and Håkansson (2003), we introduced examples of supporting and hindering types of conflicts in each phase of the projects within one network and between networks. These examples illustrate well how the conflicts could be identified as supporting or hindering in relation to innovation in health care. We conclude that most of the conflicts we identified were hindering types of conflict.

Conflicts can be analysed based on the temporal and organisational scope of projects. Organisational scope means here the different networks (public and private) that represent the space of the project.

About conflicts in space, we may conclude the following:

> One of the major types of conflict between two networks can occur because of the different decision-making systems of public and private actors. This type of conflict can be solved if the head of an operative team in the public network can build up managerial skills.
> We found that conflicts between public and private networks can be more easily handled than conflicts within the public network (e.g. doctors did not want to move into the new building in the Budapest Project). This type of conflict is actually independent of the project.

About the temporal scope of conflict, we conclude the following:

> We found that the temporal boundaries of the projects we analysed are not relevant regarding the conflicts that originated in interdependencies between networks. Conflicts may arise at different stages of the project and even before the project starts (i.e. independently from the project).
> We saw that, within the construction network, the historical relationship of partners within the consortia resulted in fewer and smaller conflicts within the project (as is true of the Szeged Project).

Conflicts play a role in supporting and hindering innovation. From our case analysis, we found that some conflicts directly supported the construction of the hospital building (that is, the construction project), but they only indirectly supported the implementation of health care innovation because the hospital building itself represented only the physical capacity for the novel patient-centred care. This is well illustrated in the Budapest case, where the completed building is now only partially used for the implementation of innovative patient care practices, mainly due to the unsolved conflicts within the public network.

We can conclude, that the goal setting of health care policy to achieve organisational innovation in health care, that supports the patient-centred delivery of health care services and a better organised patient journey, cannot be successfully performed only with investments into construction projects. We showed examples of how organisational solutions within the public health care network solved some conflicts within the construction network, resulting in the successful implementation of the project. However, ultitmately, the successful implementation of new hospital buildings is a matter not just of production (i.e. the performance of the time-bound construction project) but of interaction between production and the subsequent use of those buildings.

Acknowledgement

The authors thank the EU-funded Hungarian grant EFOP-3.6.1-16-2016-00008 for the financial support of the research on the Szeged Project.

References

Aarikka-Stenroosa, L., Jaakkola, E., Harrison, D. and Mäkitalo-Keinonen, T. (2017) 'How to manage innovation processes in extensive networks: A longitudinal study', *Industrial Marketing Management*, 67 (November 2017), pp. 88–105.

Aarikka-Stenroosa, L. and Ritala, P. (2017) 'Network management in the era of ecosystems: Systematic review and management framework', *Industrial Marketing Management*, 67(November 2017), pp. 23–36.

Aarikka-Stenroosa, L., Sandberg, B. and Lehtimäki, T. (2014) 'Networks for the commercialization of innovations: A review of how divergent network actors contribute', *Industrial Marketing Management*, 43(3), pp. 365–381.

Anderson, O.W. (1972) *Health care: Can there be equity?* New York: John Wiley & Sons.

Axelsson, B. and Easton, G. (eds.) (1992) *Industrial networks, A new view of reality*. London and New York: Routledge.

Barlow, J and Köberle-Gaiser, M. (2008) 'The private finance initiative, project form and design innovation. The UK's hospitals programme', *Research Policy*, 37(8), pp. 1392–1402.

Biemans, W.G. (1991) 'User and third-party involvement in developing medical equipment innovations', *Technovation*, 11(3), pp. 163–182.

Bizzi, L. and Langley, A. (2012): 'Studying processes in and around networks', *Industrial Marketing Management*, 41(2), pp. 224–234.

Bresnen, M. and Marshall, N. (2000) 'Partnering in construction: A critical review of issues, problems and dilemmas', *Construction Management and Economics*, 18(2), pp. 229–237.

Bygballe, L.E., Jahre, M. and Swärd, A. (2010) 'Partnering relationships in construction: A literature review', *Journal of Purchasing and Supply Management*, 16(4), pp. 239–253.

Caldwell, N.D., Roehrich, J.K. and Davies, A.C. (2009) 'Procuring complex performance in construction: London Heathrow Terminal 5 and a Private Finance Initiative hospital', *Journal of Purchasing and Supply Management*, 15(3), pp. 178–186.

Corsaro, D. and Snehota, I. (2011) 'Alignment and misalignment in business relationships', *Industrial Marketing Management*, 40(6), pp. 1042–1054.

Cova, B., Ghauri, P. and Salle, R. (2002) *Marketing project, Beyond competitive bidding*. Chichester: John Wiley & Sons.

Cova, B. and Hoskins, S. (1997) 'A twin-track approach to project marketing', *European Management Journal*, 15(5), pp. 546–556.

Dainty, A., Briscoe, G. and Millet, S. (2001) 'New perspectives on construction supply chain integration', *Supply Chain Management: An International Journal*, 6(4), pp. 163–173.

Dubois, A. and Gadde, L.-E. (2002) 'The construction industry as a loosely coupled system: Implications for productivity and innovation', *Construction Management and Economics*, 20(7), pp. 621–631.

Ellegaard, C. and Andersen, P.H. (2015) 'The process of resolving severe conflict in buyer–supplier relationships', *Scandinavian Journal of Management*, 31(4), pp. 457–470.

Engwall, M. (2003) 'No project is an island: Linking projects to history and context', *Research Policy*, 32(5), pp. 789–808.

Ford, D., Gadde, L-E., Håkansson, H. and Snehota, I. (2011) *Managing business relationships*. 3rd edn. Chichester: John Wiley & Sons.

Ford, D., Gadde, L-E., Håkansson, H., Snehota, I. and Waluszewski, A. (2010) 'Analysing business interaction', *The IMP Journal*, 4(1), pp. 82–106.

Francis, S. and Glanville, R. (2001) *Building a 2020 Vision: Future health care environments*. (Medical Architecture Research Unit, South Bank University). London: Nuffield Trust.

Gadde, L-E. and Dubois, A. (2010) 'Partnering in the construction industry – problems and opportunities', *Journal of Purchasing and Supply Management*, 16(4), pp. 254–263.

Gann, D.M. and Salter, A.J. (2000) 'Innovation in project-based, service-enhanced firms: The construction of complex products and systems', *Research Policy*, 29(7/8), pp. 955–972.

Garcia, R. and Calantone, R. (2002) 'A critical look at technological innovation typology and innovativeness terminology: A literature review', *Journal of Product Innovation Management*, 19(2), pp. 110–132.

Gibbons, D.E. (2007) 'Interorganisational network structures and diffusion of information through a health system', *American Journal of Public Health*, 97(9), pp. 1684–1692.

Håkansson, H. (ed.) (1982) *International marketing and purchasing of industrial goods: An interaction approach*. Chichester: John Wiley & Sons.

Håkansson, H. (2006) 'Business relationships and networks: Consequences for economic policy', *The Antitrust Bulletin*, 51(1), pp. 143–163.

Håkansson, H., Ford, D., Gadde, L.-E., Snehota, I. and Waluszewski, A. (2009) *Business in networks*. Chichester: John Wiley & Sons.

Håkansson, H. and Snehota, I. (eds.) (1995) *Developing relationships in business networks*. London: Routledge.

Halinen, A., Medlin, C.J., Törnroos, J.A. (2012): 'Time and process in business network research', *Industrial Marketing Management*, 41(2), pp. 215–223.

Hanna, A. (2010): 'Patient-centred care' Policy paper, *Ontario Medical Review*, June 2010, pp. 34–49.

Hartmann, A.A., Reymen, I.M.M.J. and Oosterom, van, G. (2008) 'Factors constituting the innovation adoption environment of public clients', *Building Research and Information*, 36(5), pp. 436–449.

Harty, C.F. (2008) 'Implementing innovation in construction: Contexts, relative boundedness and actor-network theory', *Construction Management and Economics*, 26(10), pp. 1029–1041.

Havenvid, M.I., Håkansson, H. and Linné, Å. (2016) 'Managing renewal in fragmented business networks', *The IMP Journal*, 10(1), pp. 81–106.

Holmen, E., Pedersen, A.-C. and Torvatn, T. (2005) 'Construction relationships for technological innovation', *Journal of Business Research*, 58(9), pp. 1240–1250.

Hungarian report (2008) *A kórház mint műszaki létesítmény* (Hospital as Technical Project), Egészségügyi Minisztérium (Ministry of Health Care), p. 40.

Ingram, R.C., Scutchfield, F.D., Mays, G.P. and Michelyn, W.B. (2012) 'The economic, institutional, and political determinants of public health delivery system structures', *Public Health Reports*, 127(2), pp. 208–215.

Luxford, K., Safran, D.G. and Delbanco, T. (2011) 'Promoting patient-centered care: A qualitative study of facilitators and barriers in health care organisations with a reputation for improving the patient experience', *International Journal for Quality in Health Care*, 23(5), pp. 510–515.

Mandják, T. and Szántó, Z. (2010) 'How can economic sociology help business relationship management?' *Journal of Business and Industrial Marketing*, 25(3), pp. 202–208.

Saha, S., Beach, M.C. and Cooper, L. (2008) 'Patient centeredness, cultural competence and healthcare quality', *Journal of the National Medical Association*, 100(11), pp. 1275–1285.

Salmi, A. (2000) 'Entry into turbulent business networks', *European Journal of Marketing*, 34(11/12), pp. 1374–1390.

Vaaland, T.I and Håkansson, H. (2003) 'Exploring interorganisational conflict in complex projects', *Industrial Marketing Management*, 32(2), pp. 127–138.

Weber, M. (1964) *The theory of social and economic organisation.* New York: Free Press.

Winch, G. (1998) 'Zephyrs of creative destruction: Understanding the management of innovation in construction', *Building Research and Information*, 26(5), pp. 268–279.

Yang, W-H., Hi, J-S and Chou, Y-Y (2012) 'Analysis of network type exchange in the health care system: A stakeholder approach', *Journal of Medical Systems*, 36(3), pp. 1569–1581.

9 Innovation in strategic capabilities of municipal clients

Some evidence from a Swedish case study

Mårten Hugosson and Tomas Nord

Introduction

Public purchases and general sourcing of buildings are very important activities: good sourcing enables the various public operations to be sustainable and of good quality. Together with wage costs, real estate economics is crucial for good public finances, where the premises created in and through buildings and construction projects contribute to the creation of meaningful, productive, and creative environments. In practice, however, the obtained qualities for these factors vary and the importance of high-quality purchases cannot be underestimated, which, in turn, sheds light on the existing specific skills and strategic capabilities available for that high-quality procurement and specifically on the organisational availability of specific knowledge that is constitutive of such strategic skills. As to capabilities and public procurement of construction, little knowledge is available in the formal literature (Winch and Leiringer, 2016), but there is an increasing interest in studying these aspects of construction. The general perception is that (e.g., Sporrong and Kadefors, 2014; Dewulf and Kadefors, 2012; Hartmann et al., 2010) there is among public clients who procure single buildings and large infrastructure projects a lack of involvement in the procurement and building processes.

According to these authors, there has been a development that in general has made it so that the public clients in construction projects settle with being able to define functional specifications and are thus generally going for procurement using a design-and-build contracting approach. In the Swedish context, this development has been seen as a general problem, reducing the strategic capability of public clients and normally making the procurement process less innovative and long term oriented (SOU, 2013). Similar tendencies can also be seen internationally as expressed by the EU directives from 2014 and by studying large-scale infrastructure projects in a European context (Winch and Leiringer, 2016; Arrowsmith, 2012). The declining capability is seen to create risks and affect more aspects of construction processes so that unacceptable cost levels become accepted and the long-term performance of the buildings is compromised.

Enforcing the common tendency of reduced client capability, Sporrong and Kadefors (2014) point out that progressively more of the pre-design of public construction projects is procured externally and that in municipal Swedish organisations, there is no emphasis on the fact that formal internal construction process–qualified professionals are not sufficiently involved in these processes; there is a lack of connection between the clients and these actors.

Hartmann et al. (2010) reinforce this image further and argue that the private sector (suppliers and construction companies in general) and its resources through networks and contacts are gaining too significant a responsibility for tasks related to the construction process, including suggesting profound single projects/proposals for entire infrastructure solutions, erecting these buildings/structures, and even arranging financing, which means that the client is increasingly placed in the position of a spectator.

Winch and Leiringer (2016) also stress that the public client involvement is low. The authors' theoretical and empirical study of major infrastructural projects shows that they often involve major problems for the public client and for the taxpayers in the long run. As a result, excessive and rising costs are common, and buildings do not perform as expected from an operational and sustainable point of view (Adukpo and Leiringer, 2016; Arnek et al., 2015). A reason is arguably that many public client organisations have become "thin" (Adukpo and Leiringer, 2016; Terry, 2005), making these organisations devoid of strategic capabilities, i.e. both of the operational and dynamic kind. This means they are unable to be heavily involved in the day-to-day design and construction processes because of a lack of *operational* capabilities. Thus, they can to a lesser degree foresee the risk of arising problems à priori. They also have problems because of a lack of *dynamic* capabilities that would enable the organisations to change their operational capabilities by taking on new strategically relevant knowledge on construction.

Moreover, as argued by the literature, there has been a shift in responsibility for procurement of buildings to general departments for procurement, which has led to some lack of coherence and uncertainty (Sporrong and Kadefors, 2014). This situation also reduces the concentration of construction competence in the organisation, giving more room for professional procurers, i.e. of generalists rather than of experts in construction and construction management.

The outsourcing tendencies contribute thus to that the latter experts are decreasingly connected to suppliers. This renders clients' strategic capabilities problematic when assessing suppliers' capabilities to deliver high-quality products and services and contribute to innovative solutions. It seems particularly problematic since intensified contacts have recently been allowed by new EU legislation on public procurement. The legislators have proposed that dialogues should mutually foster more long-term behaviour, which contributes to increasing connectivity on local and/or regional markets for construction through the dialogues strategically relevant knowledge and, importantly, informed dialogues between buyers and sellers are enabled, similar to what is possible and common between private companies and in that context enabling a "co-opting", i.e. contributing to mutual value creation for the parties involved (e.g. Prahalad and Ramaswamy, 2000).

Although some researchers stress partnering as a solution to problems of connectivity (e.g. Lahdenpereä, 2012), it is plausible that many projects are not suitable for partnering: for instance, other types of involvement might be more appropriate for normal municipal buildings (e.g. schools and day care centres). This point actualises the results of the preceding research and puts in question whether there is as yet an effect of the new legislation and, more importantly, if there are any necessary capabilities among public clients to engage in such dialogues as implied by the new legislation. From our pre-study in the Vinnova BioInnovation project (bioinnovation.se) on public procurement, we see indications, though, that strategic capabilities might not be that depleted as just indicated. Indications are that, among Swedish municipalities, connections with external actors – suppliers, consultants, and internal and external professional networks – are quite intensive, and the clients seem also to be able to be directly involved and even erecting typical municipal buildings in-house.

From these contradicting images arises the question: What is the actual status of capabilities and expertise in public clients? The question arises in actuality when considering the rapid change in environmental properties sought by many public clients, e.g. as regards buildings such as schools and day care centres. A number of innovative solutions are being developed, including wood as the main material in load-bearing constructions to enable long-term performance as regards the environment and economy.

To address the question of actual strategic capabilities, we focus on analysing three cases of municipal actors and their involvement in three projects that represent innovative solutions. The approach intends to assess both the operational and dynamic capabilities of the clients; innovation and change generally require a change of operational capabilities of the involved actors, i.e. they have to be able to have or develop dynamic strategic capabilities.

The projects are chosen on the basis that they show a varying degree of involvement by the public clients. These cases use both design-and-build contracting as well as contracting/organisation that involves the procurer more; an object procured through a type of general contracting; and case that is an in-house build. The public clients in these cases could also be seen as innovative in the sense that they strive to increase the number of "green buildings" (also known as green constructions or sustainable buildings) within a national initiative (trastadsverige. se), with the aim to produce improved results in terms of being resource efficient throughout the building's lifecycle.

We aim to contribute to the research on public client capabilities by studying the three case vignettes and thereby the municipal client organisations that primarily act as procurers of buildings. The studied cases concern the municipalities of Falun, Skellefteå, and Växjö. In these municipalities, three building projects have been studied: a school, a day care centre, and student housing.

Generally, we have been mostly interested in the strategic knowledge formation and learning processes underlying the decisions on the degree of involvement by the clients, i.e. how the decisions relate to the clients' self-assessment on their need for increased strategic knowledge. Knowledge and knowledge formation are constitutive of strategic operational and dynamic capabilities (Teece, Pisano and Shuen, 1997; Zollo and Winter, 2002; Green et al., 2008; Hartmann et al., 2010) and are thus the main signs of the capabilities available to the clients. Formally, operational capabilities are the ones needed to be able to run daily operations, and dynamic capabilities are these required for altering operational capabilities.

Our main focus for the case analysis was accordingly:

1   How do the clients perceive the main features of their strategic knowledge as clients?
2   How do the clients store this knowledge?
3   What are the sources of their strategic learning?

We also aim to contribute categories to a model for municipal operational and dynamic capabilities in terms of the procurement of common municipal buildings, i.e. based on knowledge obtained from this research and from current theory. This is particularly relevant in a context that involves a rapid change of technology towards new sustainable construction methods.

In the rest of this chapter, we will briefly present the classical definitions of strategic operational and dynamic capabilities and clarify knowledge and learning processes as the key components in these formal concepts. We will also introduce the model around client-specific capabilities as proposed by Winch and Leiringer (2016). Then we present a model that dynamically reflects on the knowledge that clients need to relate to when it comes to varying degrees of involvement in a production process. The latter model represents a possible complement to the model of Winch and Leiringer (2016). Finally, we present the three case vignettes followed by a theoretical analysis, discussion, and some concluding remarks.

Strategic capabilities

Over 30 years ago, Kraljic (1983) argued that purchasing is an important strategic feature that must be addressed by acting proactively and in depth: "Purchasing must become Supply management". This is especially true in cases in which there is complexity and where risks must be dealt with, as well as when there are long-term implications of individual projects. In particular, it is emphasised that in such a context, the client must, among other things, carefully consider "make-or-buy decisions" (i.e. choosing between manufacturing a product in-house or purchasing it from an external supplier) or, rather, vary the degree of involvement according to what is situationally implied. From this perspective, one must be prepared to add new strategic knowledge to the organisation and be able to act dynamically as a response to changes in the world, including the acquisition or redistribution of organisational resources. The organisation thus needs operational and dynamic strategic capabilities to be effective.

An operational capability is defined as the knowledge that has become incorporated into the routines of the organisation, and it works to integrate and activate the strategic resource base of the organisation (Zollo and Winter, 2002; Hartmann et al., 2010). The dynamic capabilities concern the modification of what has become manifest in the organisation as operational capabilities and the point of having such capabilities is well expressed by Teece et al.: "the firm's ability to integrate, build, and reconfigure internal and external competences to address rapidly changing environments" (Teece et al., 1997, p. 516; Chen, Paulraj and Lado, 2004). The dynamic capabilities are particularly important to possess when "technological, regulatory, and competitive conditions are subject to rapid change [then] . . . systematic change efforts are needed [through learning]" (Zollo and Winter, 2002, p. 341). In practice, this may mean that other strategic resources are acquired or eliminated as the pattern of action needs to change.

Zollo and Winter (2002) argue that strategic learning processes are always ongoing in organisations and that these process are characterised by conscious, semi-conscious, or unconscious processes involving deliberate cognitive learning and/or learning by doing, incorporating both explicit and tacit knowledge to the strategic knowledge base. These learning processes contribute either to the operational capabilities and the corresponding organisational routines or to the dynamic capabilities of the organisation.

In sum, strategic operational and dynamic capabilities can be seen as "invisible, knowledge-based phenomena", enabling firms to "acquire, develop, and deploy resources, [and] convert these resources into [valuable assets]" (Chen, Paulraj and Lado, 2004, p. 506, after Itami, 1987). Strategic capability (operational and dynamic) is thus constituted by being strategically relevant accumulated knowledge residing in and building the operating routines of the organisation. Zollo and Winter (2002) reason that it is of interest for students to study the learning processes underlying the creation of operational and dynamic capabilities (Figure 9.1). Thus, according to the model, dynamic capabilities are the

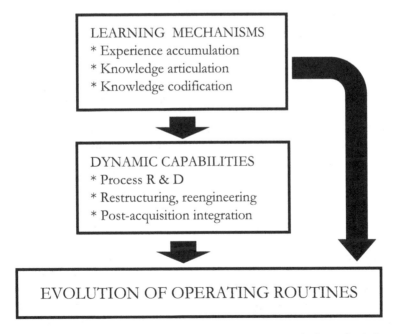

Figure 9.1 Learning, dynamic capabilities, and operating routines (After Zollo & Winter, 2002)

second-order capabilities that transform the operational capabilities, which is strikingly similar to Argyris and Schön's model (1996) of single- and double-loop learning, constituting the core of the discourse of organisational learning. The difference is that, in the discourse of strategic capabilities, the major resources and patterns of behaviour are of concern for assessment and analysis. The theory of organisation and learning (e.g., Argyris and Schön, 1996; Lant and Mezias, 1992) also emphasises that, apart from ideas of the fundamental organisational knowledge as being transforming or adaptive, to become organisational knowledge, it has to be *acknowledged* as knowledge and *spread*, i.e. "engraved" or stored within the organisation. Davenport and Prusak (1998) suggest that this "storage" makes knowledge embedded not only in formal documents or other repositories but also in organisational routines, processes, practices, and norms; i.e. knowledge is transferred by the actors in their actions and interactions.

Capabilities and clients in the construction sector

Effective strategic capabilities depend on the industry and position in the processing chain. It is also important to emphasise that there are significant differences depending on whether you act primarily as a customer or as a supplier in a specific industry. Although there have been several studies on capabilities of suppliers in the construction sector (e.g. Pathirage et al., 2007; Carrillo et al., 2000), there is little research directly addressing the client perspective.

To contribute to knowledge about clients and their capabilities, Winch and Leiringer (2016), with their interest in infrastructure projects, have created a tentative model of desirable capabilities for major public clients. As regards clients' practises, they believe that there is reason to promote the idea that "strong owners" (i.e. involved, knowledgeable, and driving clients) make a difference in providing beneficial results (e.g. economic and other gains) for the clients. Research should therefore study the strategic capabilities that strong owners need to possess. They accuse the traditional literature on project management of failing to address the importance of the client in achieving a good project outcome. The traditional literature assumes that the supplying company/the main contractor and the network it has contact with determine the outcome despite the fact that there are many practical examples indicating that the client's competencies and capabilities are crucial.

As a response, Winch and Leiringer (2016) performed a study to explore infrastructure projects. The study points out the client roles and desired strategic capabilities beyond the individual projects.

Winch and Leiringer (2016) propose and identify three main categories of capabilities: "Strategic Capabilities", "Commercial Capabilities", and "Governance Capabilities", which are divided into 11 subcategories (see Figure 9.2). Although the authors call the concept "Owner Project Capabilities", it is obviously a concept that goes beyond the individual project: all capabilities that constitute the "strategic" main category combine projects and activities over time. For municipal and non-infrastructural projects, not all proposed categories seem

Strategic capabilities	Commercial capabilities	Governance capabilities
Project selection	Packaging	Assurance
Project mission definition	Contracting	Project coordination
Capital raising	Relational	Asset integration
Stakeholder managing		
Project portfolio managing		

Figure 9.2 Owner Project Capabilities (After Winch & Leiringer, 2016)

equally relevant, and a general theoretical assessment is that all of the capabilities under Commercial Capabilities and Governance Capabilities should be considered as strategic from a municipal client perspective.

Winch and Leiringer (2016) also play down the difference between operational and dynamic capabilities without convincing arguments. We believe that there is reason to first focus on the operational capabilities to legitimately address the question on how such capabilities can be altered, i.e. which dynamic capabilities that can be in play.

For our general analysis and our interest in addressing capabilities regarding medium-sized municipalities and common types of municipal buildings, we see the categories "Packaging", "Contracting", and "Project coordination" as important, which is indicated by our pre-study. Because of the new EU legislation about contacts between buyers and sellers, the "Relational" category also becomes of interest.

The category "Packaging" is described as the way in which work breakdown structures are packaged into workable units and who is doing what to ensure that the packages are workable entities. In a smaller municipal context, this might resemble the set-up of the pre-design work and the degree of outsourcing. Concerning the category "Contracting", it is of interest to see that it, according to Winch and Leiringer, encompasses the abilities to assess the capabilities of the market and the supply chains at hand, as well as the ability to make up contracts and sign them.

The idea behind the "Relational" category is that the client should connect on a regular basis with potential suppliers and supply chains to collect ideas for solutions and assess the capabilities of suppliers (and perhaps to enter into formal cooperation of various kinds). In the model, "Project coordination" mostly represents the monitoring of budgets and the projects' financial development.

A problem with Winch and Leiringer's model is that it represents not dynamic capabilities but rather only operational capabilities. Dynamic capabilities concern the second-order, routine changing learning of the organisation, according to Teece, Winter, and others (see the preceding discussion). Among Winch and Leiringer's categories, only the "Relational" one is aimed at transformative learning. In this context, a reasonable question to ask is how such learning otherwise can take place. However, the category is very wide-ranging and hence allows the gathering of knowledge from, for example, professional networks of various kinds outside the organisation, as well as from customers or from institutions and new policies.

An assumption underlying the work of Winch and Leiringer is that the client is not particularly involved in the implementation of a project. Here, the authors assume that outsourcing is apparent, which is reasonable considering the context of large-scale infrastructure projects and their clients on the national level; the "strong owner" idea argued for by Winch and Leiringer rather concerns capabilities beyond individual projects. We believe, though, that there is reason not to embrace this assumption for the common types of comparatively smaller municipal buildings that are in focus in the present study. From the work of Sporrong and Kadefors (2014) and our experiences from a preliminary study to the current project, we have reason to assume that a development towards complete outsourcing does not apply to our municipal actors. It is therefore sensible to complement the strategic capabilities that we have deducted from Winch and Leiringer to make a general analysis that focuses on effective strategic capabilities from the clients' perspective choosing different degrees of involvement.

Propositions regarding public clients' strategic capabilities for degree of involvement in specific projects are lacking in the discourse of construction management and are not particularly apparent in the literature in general.

Fine and Whitney (2002) present, though, a principal model on strategic knowledge and client involvement (see Figure 9.3). The model is derived from research on the automotive industry's organisation but appears to be applicable to several industries. Because the model allows for a reflection on dynamic capabilities of a municipal actor choosing different degrees of involvement, we believe it can serve as a starting point for an analysis and a discussion of the necessary strategic capabilities. The upper end of the model specifies the basic ability to identify qualified bidders, i.e. suppliers. This basic level of capability implies that the main actor is entirely dependent on the knowledge from others. At the lower end of the model, the main actor is independent of external knowledge but, at the same time, dependent on the binding of resources to produce the specific item/service in-house. It is possible to see the content of the left-hand side of the model as an extension of the model of Winch and Leiringer, especially for their category of "Contracting" capabilities. The right-hand side, however, is not the focus of Winch and Leiringer as they assume that the main work on projects is outsourced.

A major assumption of the model is that if you are able to do a job in-house, you have the capability to define production technically, which is consistent with Zollo and Winter's (2002) idea of how people working with their own resources over time strengthen their learning processes and capabilities.

From the work of Zollo and Winter (2002), learning by doing involves creating capabilities and integrating tacit knowledge (see also Nonaka and Takeuchi, 1995), which is important for creating operational and dynamic capabilities. Thus, in any assessment of strategic capabilities, it seems feasible to assess how such learning (i.e. learning by doing) helps create strategic capabilities.

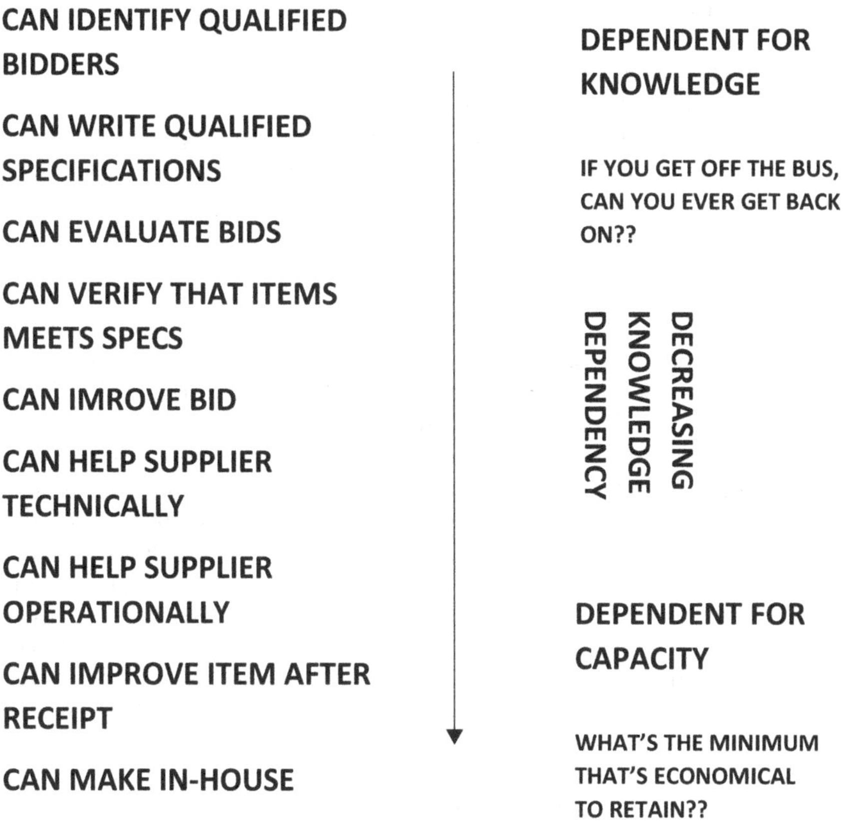

CAN IDENTIFY QUALIFIED BIDDERS

CAN WRITE QUALIFIED SPECIFICATIONS

CAN EVALUATE BIDS

CAN VERIFY THAT ITEMS MEETS SPECS

CAN IMROVE BID

CAN HELP SUPPLIER TECHNICALLY

CAN HELP SUPPLIER OPERATIONALLY

CAN IMPROVE ITEM AFTER RECEIPT

CAN MAKE IN-HOUSE

DEPENDENT FOR KNOWLEDGE

IF YOU GET OFF THE BUS, CAN YOU EVER GET BACK ON??

DECREASING KNOWLEDGE DEPENDENCY

DEPENDENT FOR CAPACITY

WHAT'S THE MINIMUM THAT'S ECONOMICAL TO RETAIN??

Figure 9.3 Knowledge in relation to different degrees of involvement by the purchaser (After Fine and Whitney, 2002)

One asset of Finn and Whitney's model is that it specifies a number of possible strategic knowledge items in relation to the degree of involvement of the client. Moreover, the model concludes that the actor might be dependent on the suppliers if deep technical knowledge of a specific production is not possessed by the client. The items in the model are also organised according to what Fine and Whitney perceive as a natural order for strategically important knowledge. For the case of public clients in the construction industry, it seems that most of the items could be of relevance, although one should acknowledge that the degree of involvement in practice could imply a variation with respect to the individual project.

By applying the model, emphasis is given to the municipal client's informed strategic decisions as regards knowledge and the client's degree of involvement. The model focuses on the distribution of required knowledge between the client and suppliers, but it does not address other possible sources of strategic learning.

In comparison, the broad "Relational" category of Winch and Leiringer (2016) portrays "learning from others" as potentially important, e.g. from colleagues representing other public clients and from market dialogues or from deliverers of technical solutions and building materials. Our basic assessment is thus that models of Winch and Leiringer and Fine and Whitney are complementary.

In the following analysis, we apply the core ideas underlying Fine and Whitney's model as well as the three categories of Winch and Leiringer's model that are relevant to our municipal client capabilities perspective.

The cases and their general context

The chosen cases in this chapter were all studied within the strategic research programme BioInnovation (bioinnovation.se). The programme was started in 2016 by the National Research Foundation VINNOVA in Sweden. As of 2018, BioInnovation is an industry-wide venture to develop strong, competitive, and innovative materials, products, and services based on renewable raw materials.

The project of the programme focusing on procurement and the conditions that enable more innovative wooden public buildings was initiated by the present authors, their respective universities, and the municipalities of Falun, Skellefteå, and Växjö. These three cities were co-founders of the national organisation Trästad, Sverige ("Wooden cities of Sweden", trastad.se), which aims at increasing the amount of "Green buildings" in the municipal stocks of Sweden. The three selected projects were the Norrskenet day care centre in Skellefteå municipality, Pär Lagerkvist school in Växjö municipality, and Brigaden students housing in the municipality of Falun.

All the projects were innovative, implying that new, strategically relevant knowledge was a prerequisite for the projects. The three projects had a load-bearing construction that was mainly made of wood, and they represented different levels of involvement with the municipalities in the building processes.

The three target cities are of medium size, with between 50,000 and 85,000 inhabitants, representing the northern, middle, and southern parts of Sweden. All three are situated within forested areas, and, not surprisingly, wood- and forestry-related industries have been of considerable importance for the local economies. The size of the three municipalities implied that they had the economic strength and capabilities to perform major design and construction management activities in-house.

The municipalities' involvement in the programme was a carefully planned effort to assess, evaluate, and distribute ideas about efficient procurement strategies to other municipalities of Sweden, particularly regarding innovative projects and project types that included wooden load-bearing components, which was consistent with the aim of the Trästad Sverige organisation.

The formal organisational structures of the municipalities were similar: all three municipalities had administrative units performing procurement and handling construction projects directly under the city council. Furthermore, the three municipalities had fully owned real estate companies. Technical staffs of five or six persons were involved when new buildings were designed and prepared for formal decision making by the council or the municipal company. Different consultants were typically hired for parts of the design work, but such work was also done by the in-house staff.

A characteristic aspect of the organisational units was that the technical staff's individual actors participated not only in the knowledge exchange that was implied by the formal organisation but also with the voluntary networks and organisations exchanging information of the purchases and conditions related to that process. Among these entities is SABO (sabo.se), a voluntary association for municipal real estate companies in Sweden. In this context, information about prices and ideas about standard construction models were typically exchanged.

The staff of Falun municipality were members and co-founders of ByggDialog Dalarna, a formal network joining construction actors who were interested in qualitatively enhancing construction in the local market, including the larger municipalities in the county (some 20 regional and national construction companies, Dalarna University, and architects and designers of the local market). The municipality of Falun expressed that it was an important forum for dialogue with market actors and potential main contractors. The activities largely concerned construction technology and were a forum for the presentation of new methods.

Concerning Växjö municipality, they annually organised information meetings about the municipality's upcoming projects. All stakeholders of the local construction businesses were invited to these meetings and did normally also show up.

Important for Skellefeteå's contacts with market actors in construction was its geographical position. This municipality has several major, nationally important manufacturers of load-bearing timber constructions in the region. These manufacturers were regarded as crucial for the local economy. Dialogues and meetings with these actors were arranged to gain a better understanding of how potential contractors viewed wood as construction material.

Data collection and analysis

A qualitative case study approach was applied for the BioInnovation project as a whole. In all, ten cases were selected for the project, and the data were mainly collected through interviews. The interviews were tape recorded and transcribed verbatim for each participant. We aimed to pay special attention to the study of knowledge formation and the strategic capability learning phenomena of public procuring organisations. Hence, we needed to study the phenomena of interest in a real-life context (Silverman, 2005; Patton, 1990). We therefore explored these organisations and their construction projects as cases (Yin, 2009).

Of the ten cases, three were chosen for the current study: one construction project carried out and led by the client organisation, one construction project conducted as a result of turnkey contracting, and one project representing an intermediate form of commitment from the client organisation representing a form of general contracting.

During the interviews, the respondents reflected on what constituted strategic knowledge and learning and how these features were stored, i.e. how they became embedded in organisational documents or other internal manifestations. They also reflected on how strategic knowledge is obtained.

The cases are presented in the form of a vignette case description that summarizes the main features of the respective cases and that allow comparative case analysis. In the analysis procedure, we looked for common and divergent patterns within and between the cases, as well as explanations thereto (Dubois and Gadde, 2002; Kirkeby, 1994). The approach should enable us to interpret and analyse the cases and allow a discussion of the purchasing organisations' competencies and capabilities as regards the chosen purchasing approaches (Eisenhardt, 1989).

The case: Project Norrskenet, Skellefteå

General features

The Project Norrskenet, initiated in 2010 and completed in March 2012, was developed to meet two pressing needs: the need for more day care centres in the municipality of Skellefteå and the need to develop and modernise kindergartens into larger and more effective facilities. The formal client of the building was the Board of Municipal properties. The total construction cost was SEK 24.5 million, which corresponds to SEK 26,000 per square metre. (See Figure 9.4.)

The project was done in-house and the design developed in close collaboration with Tyréns, a Swedish consultant firm. The major challenge was to construct a

Figure 9.4 Norrskenet day care centre (Reproduced with permission of Skellefteå kommun/municipality)

model that was extremely performative as regards energy consumption and air tightness. The intention was to develop a model for constructing day care centres in the future in the municipality. The initial idea was to arrange to have a design-and-build contract in place with an innovative contractor, but it was felt that the capabilities of the contractors, active on the local market, were not sufficient enough to deliver an acceptable solution. Hence, a decision was reached to manage the project in-house and to purchase a capacity-building advisor (consultant) for the design and construction management.

All contractors and entrepreneurs employed in the project underwent a common education to achieve the desired results in terms of energy consumption and air tightness. The contract with Tyréns required the firm to deliver special training to the contractors and the municipality regarding so-called passive house technology in general.

Case-related strategic capabilities

Concerning strategic knowledge and capability in use, the internal project manager and the head of the municipal department explain that the most important capability is to be able to generate technical specifications from the new type of construction and then use this knowledge to guide future contracts, preferably design-and build-contracts. Another essential aspect was the capability to assess market competence to decide as to whether the design phase is a major part of the obligation of the main contractor, i.e. establish whether the actors available on the local market have sufficient competence to manage a particular type of build, as well as to provide high-quality solutions at a reasonable price.

A third important aspect of strategic learning and capability formation pertains to dispersing the acquired strategic learning within the entire municipal organisation.

Storage of strategic knowledge

The acknowledged strategic knowledge base of the municipal organisation was developed and held by five or six experts (technicians, project managers, and a juridical expert) of the real estate department who regularly met to share and form a common discourse about procurement and construction management. It had become recognised that this engraving, or storage, was not sufficient and carried risks given that it was dependent on individual presence and participation. The municipal department was therefore working to document this knowledge in a formal manner. The first step involved letting the project managers structure important information and data derived from individual projects. The next step concerned forming a digitalised database, from the technical and soft data of the individual projects. The latter data concerned e.g. assessed qualities of contractors' work and their relational capabilities as shown during the design, contracting, and construction phases. However, the forms for this data storage were not yet fully worked out.

Sources of strategic learning

Inspiration concerning the innovative construction types of a new generation of school and day care buildings, was given by membership in the network energy-efficient building for climate, a committee of SABO in which the municipality was a member. Initial knowledge for using the particular technical solutions chosen was obtained through contacts with suppliers of building material. However, the most important knowledge for further procurement and/or construction was gained through the project itself and through the formal education given by Tyréns. The knowledge obtained through the project added to the accumulated knowledge of previous projects. This applied to both the technical know-how gained and the specific knowledge of the involved actor's capability to deliver a work of high quality.

The case: Pär Lagerkvist school, Växjö

General features

The project Pär Lagerkvist school was completed in the spring of 2017. (See Figure 9.5.) The client of the construction was VÖFAB, a company owned by Växjö municipality. The final cost of the building was about SEK 330 million, which corresponds to SEK 21,000 per square metre of building space. The chosen bearing structure was a combined construction of wood for the bearing part of the building and traditional concrete solutions for other parts of the building. The school building was an extensive construction (high school and preschool combined) and the project was complex with a variety of built-in functions.

Figure 9.5 Pär Lagerkvist school (Reproduced with permission of VÖFAB)

Because of the perceived complexity, VÖFAB chose to contract with a general contractor. The client considered the market not to be mature enough to handle the demanding complexity of the project. Moreover, there was a wish to test specific combinations of materials to ensure that each material was used where it was best suited for technical and environmental performance. Such an approach implied the testing of previously untested solutions. Hence, the client wanted to be directly involved and have control over the design phase, which included contacts with suppliers of the building material.

The usual set of consultants (architects, plumbing, electricity, land, etc.) was used for the project and hired by VÖFAB. As a complement, in-house competent technicians and project managers were engaged in the procurement as well as in the design phases of the project. For the part of the building with a bearing wood construction, special assessments were conducted in advance in which several alternatives were evaluated by the municipal company. For this phase of the project, contacts were also carried out with material suppliers.

Case-related strategic capabilities

The knowledge that was of particular importance for the organisation in terms of strategic competence was the ability to develop an understanding of the technical specifications derived from innovative projects (such as wooden constructions) and the long-term performance of such buildings.

Among the municipal experts in this case, there was a keen awareness that the construction market was very favourable in Växjö, as there were between five and ten small and medium-sized enterprises (SMEs) as potential main contractors with a steadily increasing capability for acting as design-and-build contractors of innovative wooden buildings at a relatively very low cost based on a national comparison.

Storage of strategic knowledge

The central staff at VÖFAB included a strategic development resource manager and a project manager, as well as several support functions aimed at the specific design areas. In total, the team included five or six people. In addition, the organisation had close contact with the two municipal real estate companies of the municipality and their respective experts. It was also acknowledged that the group of consultants used in many of the company's projects constituted an important entity that generated and stored large quantities of strategically relevant knowledge. This current project and all other projects implemented by VÖFAB needed to create a "feedback document". The purpose of this document is to record small and large technical errors that were made in the process and add this to the general experiences of previous projects. This process increased the capability to perform newer and better assessments and to develop and sharpen the capability to formulate technical specifications. This strategy was considered an important complement to the living discourse and collective memory carried by the handful of staff working with the purchasing/construction management at VÖFAB. The formally stored information was increasingly taking on the form of a technical manual.

Sources of strategic learning

In this project, there were not only contacts with the usual consultants but also with building material suppliers. The performance of the materials was thus discussed in order to ensure that the right material management knowledge was available to the construction company. An important source of learning for VÖFAB related to the internal network formed by the technical professionals of the real estate companies of the municipality; the network had extensive experiences of building in wood (wood construction). The municipal company was also involved in market dialogues preparing construction companies for upcoming tenders. These contacts were arranged through information meetings that served to gather all main contractors of the region annually. Contacts were also made through newsletters sent out to the potential main contractors. In addition, strategic knowledge generated and accumulated by previous projects were considered as an important entity to guide strategic decisions for procurement and construction management performed by the client.

The case: Brigaden, Falun

General features

The pre-studies for the project Brigaden (the Brigade) started in 2010, and the tender documents were launched in 2013. The project was completed in 2015.

Figure 9.6 Brigaden student housing (Reproduced with permission of Kopparstaden)

The purchaser of the building was Kopparstaden, a municipally owned public housing company in the city of Falun. The final cost of the work was SEK 98.2 million for a building containing 3,489 square metres of building space, which corresponds to SEK 28,000 per square metre. The building consists of about 90 flats primarily intended for student housing. In accordance with Falun municipality building policies, there was an emphasis on high energy performance and additional quality options to enhance maintenance performance. For the project's design work, the usually engaged consultants were called in for construction and architecture.

The innovative design solution included three sources of material: steel, wood, and concrete. The reason for choosing design-and-build contracting was that the municipal company determined that there was an opportunity to obtain an innovative idea on the design solution from a contractor, as well as to reduce functional risks. Although the municipal company typically procured buildings with design-and-build contracts, the general trend was that more of the design work should be done in-house by the client.

Case-related strategic capabilities

The major strategic capabilities concerned the ability to generate technical specifications and generate a deeper understanding of how different construction solutions perform over time. According to the respondents, accumulated knowledge contributed to the strategy of increasingly doing more of the design work in-house in collaboration with external technical consultants and, in this way, produce extensive documents as a basis for tenders. It was also important for the company to know and assess market competence apropos the potential option to engage consultants and construction firms.

Storage of strategic knowledge

Contractual-related information about the procurement, including "soft" information for strategic decision making, was stored in the PC of the purchasing manager responsible for storing all technical specifications and the procurement documentation. This information was also stored in the local server. Documentation about the process implementation itself was not extensive, and the strategic organisational learning that emerged would be stored and integrated into the living discourse of the professionals within the organisational unit. A process to create a general "cloud" solution for storage was in progress as a response to the experienced discontinuity between projects.

Sources of strategic learning

The most important source of knowledge for the strategic decisions was the experiences from earlier projects. In addition, knowledge generated from facility management was important for Kopparstaden to create ideas for technical specifications. This knowledge was analysed with reference to actual technical solutions and was particularly important for decision making: hence, internally created knowledge was an important source of knowledge creation. However, the knowledge base related to energy performance was also influenced by the SABO Energy Committee. Kopparstaden was very active and a respected national actor in that committee.

Information on new technical developments and knowledge about the competency of construction firms and consultants was gathered by the staff being active in external networks, mostly the regional network (ByggDialog Dalarna) and the national network (Trästad Sverige).

The professionals at Kopparstaden viewed the local market of contractors as being quite capable of providing innovative functional solutions to load-bearing wooden constructions. The assessment was mainly made through contacts during meetings with the regional network (i.e. ByggDialog Dalarna).

Comparative case analysis

As a result of the comparative analysis, a common operational capability (according to the theoretical ideas of Zollo and Winter, 2002 and Teece et al., 1997) can be observed. Thus, the operational capability to have a deep technical understanding of construction within the respective client organisations was an essential element. This understanding and knowledge, which represents first-order learning (Argyris and Schön, 1996), should primarily enable client organisations to specify functions and make evaluations of tenders in future projects.

The public client's emphasis on this capability is both logical and reasonable for organisations that largely act as procurers. It is important that the clients can acquire buildings that, from a technical standpoint, have high quality, represent a long-term functionality, and are economically and environmentally sustainable.

The second operational capability identified is to have knowledge to assess the technical and operational capabilities of the suppliers, mostly regarding potential main contractors and their network resources. It entails what the market can perform in terms of proposals for technical solutions and how market actors can handle the technical challenges in the construction process. Also, this capability was found in all three cases.

Maintaining the operational capability of generating technical specifications in the event there are changes in environmental conditions was also important and points to another capability observed through the interviews. Thus, in times of varying technology and new technological challenges, the clients are prepared to become more involved, even being builders themselves to engage in second-order learning processes (Zollo and Winter, 2002; Argyris and Schön, 1996). This ability to become more involved results in changing operating routines and upgrading operational capability, which, in turn, allow the generation of new technical specifications.

Being able to change the degree of involvement to engage in second-order learning processes constitutes a feature of dynamic capability shown by our municipal clients (Zollo and Winter, 2002; Teece et al., 1997). In practice, it means that they make different make-or-buy decisions that are situationally dependent on the competence of the assessed market and the need to actively get involved to secure second-order dynamic learning (Argyris and Schön, 1996). All three clients take into account the degree of involvement in a single project; these considerations depend on a combination of deliberations about what the market can do in terms of technical solutions and the possibilities of obtaining knowledge through own actions.

If the clients take the initiative to become more involved, the source of learning is naturally learning by doing (e.g., Finn and Whitney, 2002; Nonaka and Takeuchi, 1995); however, strategic learning about technical challenges and developments could also be obtained through other sources (see Table 9.1). Thus,

Table 9.1 Comparing case features

	Recognised strategic operational capabilities	Storage of strategic knowledge	Origins of generated strategic knowledge
Case 1, In-house production, Norrskenet, Skellefteå	Technical knowledge enabling thorough and detailed specifications Knowledge of market competence	Living discourse Ongoing discussion on common IT solutions	Learning by doing Learning through contacts with suppliers of building materials Learning through external networks Learning through consultants Learning from earlier projects
Case 2, General contracting, Pär Lagerkvist school, Växjö	Technical knowledge enabling thorough and detailed specifications Knowledge of market competence	Feedback documentation Creating a construction manual Living discourse	Learning through contacts with suppliers of building materials Learning by doing Learning through internal networks Market dialogues Learning through consultants Learning from earlier projects
Case 3, Design-and-build contracting, Brigaden, Falun		Emerging collective cloud solution Storage in personal computers according to formal responsibility Living discourse	Evaluation of external objects in other municipalities Learning through external networks Learning through consultants Learning from earlier projects

if the new upcoming projects differ only slightly from previous ones, the strategic "Learning from earlier projects" is highly valuable for future decisions and in forming a knowledge base that would be of value in terms of storage. In the pre-design phase, "Learning through contacts with suppliers of building materials" could be obtained, implying that clients are heavily engaged in design and even pre-design processes, which contradicts the findings of Sporrong and Kadefors (2014) and the assumptions of Winch and Leiringer (2016).

In our three cases, the strategic knowledge that is considered important has thus been generated in several ways: it is clear that learning also occurs through contacts with consultants and internal and external networks. However, these sources do not seem as important as the accumulated knowledge from direct engagement in previous projects. Actual involvement (i.e. learning by doing) potentially plays an important role for the clients. The municipalities are prepared to do much of the job themselves to gain the strategic learning benefits as well as to reduce the functional risks of the projects.

When it comes to the question of how to store the strategic learning that arises in the process of "engraving" as described by Argyris and Schön (1996), there is a general tendency for increased formalisation. Based on the cases investigated, it is also an obvious tendency to store strategic knowledge in order to become more proactive concerning strategic behaviour in relation to upcoming projects, i.e. to avoid discontinuity in the strategic decision processes. However, this does not mean that strategic learning stored in living discourse is less important, i.e. the knowledge stored in a formal way is complementary to the knowledge obtained and stored by the professionals themselves.

Comparing the preceding results with the model of Fine and Whitney (2002), it seems that several of the categories are relevant for assessing public clients' capabilities in construction. Obviously, the category "Can write competent specifications" is of utmost importance to our clients, although in the proposed model by Fine and Whitney, it is not ranked very high. In fact, according to the authors, the client does not need much strategic knowledge to have that capability. In our material, however, this category emerged as the most important strategic operational capability. We also noted that maintaining this capability drives the clients to be more involved through conducting construction work in-house or by being involved in pre-design in order to ensure a high-level competence as regards this operational capability.

In Fine and Whitney's model, the capability to assess market competence ("Can identify qualified bidders") does not require much client capability because it represents the initial strategic knowledge level of the model. Our results suggest this is also a crucial strategic competence for municipal clients: in combination with the expected capability to make specifications, it has guided the clients towards their chosen degree of involvement in the projects.

Our general interpretation of the cases, in comparison with the model of Fine and Whitney, is that deep strategically relevant technical knowledge is a prerequisite needed to perform most of the tasks of the model if applied to the construction sector and municipal clients. Yet it is difficult to pinpoint which task or activity requires most from the strategic knowledge base. From this perspective, the categories concerning evaluation of bids, verification of performed work by the supplier, and technical support or even cooperation with suppliers are relevant categories for public procurement in construction. Differentiating as regards relative importance of these features is, though, not evident or easily made from our case material.

There is a trade-off in Fine and Whitney's model between "Degree of knowledge dependence" and "Dependence on [production] capacity". Our analysis shows that all three clients have the operational capability to perform in-house production. Moreover, in two of the three cases, capacity has been allocated to do so. In one case, the client chose to run the whole construction phase in-house to ensure that strategic knowledge was obtained for the municipal organisation. The perception of the technical challenges and opportunities is of highest importance for the make-or-buy decision and the degree of involvement by the clients.

As stated in the theory section, several capabilities of Winch and Leiringer's (2016) model (the categories "Contracting", "Relational", "Project coordination", and "Packaging") might be worthwhile exploring when it comes to assessing strategic capabilities of municipal clients.

Concerning the "Relational" category, internally created capability in connection with the specification work of the technical specialists may be the most important source; however, inspiration with respect to the technical solutions of the upcoming projects was achieved through external and internal networks.

Important for the "Relational" category of the proposed model is that essential strategic learning can occur from discussions/contacts with the market of potential contractors. And, also, strategic learning from such contacts could be seen as potentially creating both operational and dynamic capabilities. In our three cases, relational contacts with potential contractors have not been fully used as made possible by the new EU legislation on public procurement, which would be a typical relation fitting into the category of Winch and Leiringer. However, it is clearly indicated by the material that assessments of the respective market capabilities of potential main contractors and others have been made by the municipal clients, as previously discussed. Thus, in the Falun case, market knowledge has been based on the contacts through ByggDialog Dalarna, which engages construction companies, consultants, and other clients. In the case of Växjö, contacts were made through annual meetings with contractors arranged by the municipality. In Skellefteå's case, continuous contacts with the important suppliers of building materials in the region were a fact, as well as direct and indirect assessments of potential contractor's capabilities. All these activities reflect the relational category of Winch and Leiringer (2016).

The "Contracting" capability, as suggested by the authors, contains "more than the transaction" according to them, i.e. general assessments of market conditions and market capabilities should be in place as regards the capabilities of the clients. Based on our results, this category is well motivated, encompassing both of our main found categories, as "Knowledge enabling thorough and detailed specifications" and "Knowledge of market competence", could be seen as subcategories of "Contracting".

Winch and Leiringer's category "Project coordination" relates to our cases in the sense that production could be achieved in-house, which would require such capabilities, although our clients' chief interest was to be effective procurers. In promoting the possibilities of having capabilities that enable project coordination, the Falun municipality organised all their work so that consultants and construction managers shared offices during the pre-design and design phases of a project, should it be performed in-house. In the Skellefteå municipality, close contacts were kept with good external project managers in order to engage them if a project was decided to be made in-house.

Concerning the category "Packaging", there are indications of its importance through the clients' engagement in pre-design work. Future studies are needed to comprehensively assess the importance of this category for our type of clients.

Concluding discussion

The main aim of this study was to assess whether there are strategic capabilities among municipal clients relative to municipal building projects in Sweden. Our intention was to identify eventual operational and dynamic capabilities and evaluate their core features, i.e. strategic knowledge and learning. Three research questions about strategic knowledge were posed. (1) What are the clients' perception of the features of strategic knowledge? (2) How do the clients store this knowledge? (3) What are the sources of strategic learning?

From our findings, we conclude that there is a focus on increasing strategic knowledge through altering the degree of involvement in individual projects. Our results demonstrate that the capability for altering the degree of involvement is in essence dynamic. The goal of the three organisations investigated in this study was to assess each upcoming project in terms of practical engagement in operations. This was done with respect to the technical novelty implied by the upcoming project.

The main strategic operational capability, as identified by our clients, reflects the understanding of the impact of technical solutions and the ability to generate technical specifications from that insight. The other significant operational capability evaluated through the case study entails clients having the knowledge to estimate the market's capability to generate proposals for innovative solutions and to be able to execute such solutions in practice.

Another conclusion we reached from the study is that there is a strong tendency to increase the structural storage of the procurement-related strategic knowledge that arises from each project. In the past, knowledge has mostly been stored as a living discourse in interaction between the professionals of the client organisations. The tendency towards modern data storage, which allows access for other organisational actors, is apparent and the empirical case material contains concrete manifestations of this trend.

For the sources of strategic learning, the clients' extensive (and intensive) involvement in the projects was essential. In addition, learning from previous projects is crucial for developing and establishing capabilities. Still, the present material suggests that learning could occur from other sources, including suppliers of building materials and through the clients' engagement in pre-design processes. Other paramount sources of strategic learning were the traditional consultants within the business and internal and external networks that the client organisations participated in at various times. All these latter sources indicate the importance of clients connecting to these sources to build a "Relational" capability as suggested by Winch and Leiringer (2016).

Our material suggests the rising importance of these latter sources, and it is obvious that the clients generally wanted to be in close association with the suppliers of the market. From the assessment of suppliers' capabilities, the clients are readily prepared to decide on the level of involvement in the projects to drive the development of market capabilities. The clients thus want to ensure that new strategic learning is generated and that this learning becomes not only internalised by the clients but also externalised in ex-post discussions with suppliers (who are directly linked to projects) and through network activities. Our clients therefore continuously strive to enhance their market capabilities by sharing strategic knowledge as a basis for reconnecting to the market and enabling more informed make-or-buy decisions in upcoming projects.

The idea of having a close relationship and frequently connecting with the supplier market and enhancing the suppliers' capabilities is important for the clients, as carrying out projects in-house is not the first choice of the clients given that they mainly regard themselves as procurers. This observation infers that the clients prefer some form of affiliation with suppliers that can provide high-quality solutions at a low cost rather than being heavily involved in various projects, which tends to tie up organisational resources; see the model of Fine and Whitney (2002). For the longer perspective, our clients believe that strategic learning and knowledge should be gained through regular contact with different actors and activities outside the frame of a given project. In all our innovative projects, such connections are already of importance and concern, for example, contacts with specialised consultants, experts on wooden constructions, various real estate firms, and traditional construction firms as main suppliers to the projects but also downstream connections all the way to suppliers of building materials. Another essential source for the clients in strategic learning is participation in external networks and member organisations (e.g., SABO, Trästad Sverige, and ByggDialog Dalarna). In addition, internal professional networks that exchange information and knowledge are of increasing importance for our client organisations. It is also noteworthy that, in the three present cases, the processes towards building innovative wooden constructions are initiated by politicians, which creates considerable pressure on the municipal organisations to become knowledgeable and innovative clients.

Contacts and connections between involved parties are increasing according to our respondents: all three main actors in the municipalities highlight the fact that contacts with contractors have increased and will likely continue to increase because of the new EU legislation, which allows competitive dialogues. This implies that decisions regarding future projects (among the active and innovative municipal actors) will largely be based on connectivity and strategic knowledge transfer from suppliers.

In the long run, it is possible that cooperation, knowledge transfer, and even mutual knowledge generation could become more common because of the higher dynamic capability of the actors. Two of the three municipalities in the study indicated that formal competitive dialogues (in accordance with the new EU legislation on public procurement) were already ongoing for impending projects. The municipalities introduce a new form of dialogue process that includes an information and discussion phase with several possible actors as main contractors/ suppliers that will eventually be transformed into a partnering phase enabling the parties to have shared and open knowledge generation. By implementing such a process, one can ideally take advantage of the overall technical knowledge historically accumulated by the parties in the creation of a new project. Such an arrangement is consistent with Prahalad and Ramaswamy's (2000) strategic idea of co-opting resources and creating innovation and value through the process.

However, this development is on the rise as to the types of object that are presented in this study. Moreover, it somewhat contradicts what is indicated in the study by Sporrong and Kadefors (2014), which renders the development among municipal actors as having become less active and less engaged in the process. On the contrary, our results suggest that our municipal actors exert their influence to become more involved and active and generally connected with actors of business.

How to interpret our results is therefore open to confirmation through further studies. However, we believe that attention should be given to the trend that innovative, ambitious municipality clients deliberately build strategic operational knowledge and have the dynamic capability to increase strategic control of the construction process. Such a position is in the spirit of Winch and Leiringer (2016). If correct, this would increase the link between different public projects, create connectivity, and reduce discontinuity. In essence, it connects the public projects through the strategic knowledge base and the strategic capability of the municipal actors.

We perceive the observed changes as well grounded in our studied clients. The clients' behaviour of interacting with producers of building materials to generate technical understanding as the basis for strategic decisions makes Kraljic's classic statement about the goal of developed purchasing relevant: "Purchasing must become Supply Management" (Kraljic, 1983). Our interpretation of the results is that our public actors are working precisely in that direction.

References

Adukpo, S.E. and Leiringer, R. (2016) 'Development of public sector client capabilities within the context of new public management', in *Proceedings, Engineering Project Organization Conference*. Cle Elum, Washington, USA, June 28–30.

Argyris, C. and Schön, D. (1996) *Organizational learning II: Theory, method and practise*. Reading, MA: Addison-Wesley.

Arnek, M., Karl-Markus Modén, K-M., Sidholm, S., Fredrik Tamm, F. and Wahlman, B. (2015) Den offentliga marknaden i Sverige. En empirisk analys av den offentliga sektorns samlade inköp UPPDRAGSFORSKNINGSRAPPORT 2015:4, KONKURRENSVERKET.

Arrowsmith, S (2012) 'Modernising the EU's public procurement regime: A blueprint for real simplicity and flexibility', *Public Procurement Law Review*, 21, pp. 71–82.

BioInnovation home page. bioinnovation.se. Accessed December 20, 2018.

Carrillo, P.M., Anumba, C.J. and Kamara, J.M. (2000) 'Knowledge management for construction: Key IT and contextual issues', in Gudnason, G. (ed.), *Proceedings of the International Conference on Construction IT*. Reykjavik, Iceland: Icelandic Building Research Institute, June 28–30, pp. 155–165.

Chen, J.C., Paulraj, A. and Lado, A.A. (2004) 'Strategic purchasing, supply management and firm performance', *Journal of Operations Management*, 22, pp. 505–523.

Davenport, T. and Prusak, L. (1998) *Working knowledge – How organizations manage what they know*. Boston: Harvard Business School Press.

Dewulf, G.M. and Kadefors, A. (2012) 'Collaboration in public construction – contractual incentives, partnering schemes and trust', *Engineering Project Organization Journal*, 2(4), pp. 240–250.

Dubois, A. and Gadde, L.-E. (2002) 'Systematic combining: An abductive approach to case research', *Journal of Business Research*, 55(7), pp. 553–560.

Eisenhardt, K.M. (1989) 'Building theories from case study research', *Academy of Management Review*, 14(4), pp. 532–550.

Fine, C.H. and Whitney, D.E. (2002) 'Is the make-buy decision process a core competence?' Sociotechnical Systems Research Center (SSRC), MIT.

Green, S.D., Larsen, G.D. and Chung-Chin Kao (2008) 'Competitive strategy revisited: Contested concepts and dynamic capabilities', *Construction Management and Economics*, 26, pp. 63–78.

Hartmann, A., Davies, A. and Frederiksen, L. (2010) 'Learning to deliver service-enhanced public infrastructure: Balancing contractual and relational capabilities', *Construction Management and Economics*, 28(11), pp. 1165–1175.

Itami, H. (1987) *Mobilizing invisible assets*. Cambridge, MA: Harvard University Press.

Kirkeby, O. (1994) 'Abduktion', in Andersen, H (ed.), *Videnskabsteori og metodelaere*. Frederiksberg: Samfundslitteratur, pp. 122–152.

Kraljic, P. (1983) *Purchasing must become supply management*. HBR September issue. Harvard University.

Lahdenperä, P. (2012) 'Making sense of the multi-party contractual arrangements of project partnering, alliancing and integrated project delivery', *Construction Management and Economics*, 30, pp. 57–79.

Lant, T.K. and Mezias, S.P. (1992) 'An organizational learning model of convergence and reorientation', *Organization Science*, 3, pp. 47–71.

Nonaka, I. and Takeuchi, H. (1995) *The knowledge-creating company: How Japanese companies create the dynamics of innovation*. New York, NY: Oxford University Press.

Pathirage, C.P., Amaratunga, D.G. and Haigh, R.P. (2004) 'Tacit knowledge and organisational performance: Construction industry perspective', *Journal of Knowledge Management*, 11(1), pp. 115–126.

Patton, M.Q. (1990) *Qualitative evaluation and research methods*. 2nd ed. Newbury Park, CA: Sage.

Prahalad, C.K. and Ramaswamy, V. (2000) Co-opting customer competence. *Harvard Business Review*, January. SABO home page. sabo.se. Accessed December 20, 2018.

Silverman, D. (2005) *Doing qualitative research*. London: Sage Publications.

SOU (2013) *Goda affärer – En strategi för hållbar offentlig upphandling. Upphandlingsutredningen, Slutbetänkande, SOU 2013:12*. Stockholm: Statens Offentliga Utredningar.

Sporrong, J. and Kadefors, A. (2014) 'Municipal consultancy procurement: New roles and practises', *Building Research and Information*, 42(5), pp. 616–628.

Teece, D.J., Pisano, G. and Shuen, A. (1997) 'Dynamic capabilities and strategic management', *Strategic Management Journal*, 18(7), pp. 509–533.

Terry, L.D. (2005) 'The thinning of the hollow state', *Administration and Society*, 37(4), pp. 271–281.

Trästad home page. http://www.trastad.se/

Vinnova home page. vinnova.se. Accessed December 20, 2018.

Winch, G. and Leiringer, R. (2016) 'Owner project capabilities for infrastructure development: A review and development of the "strong owner" concept', *International Journal of Project Management*, 32(2), pp. 271–281.

Yin, R.K. (2009) *Case study research: Design and methods*. 4th ed. London: Sage.

Zollo, M. and Winter, S.G. (2002) 'Deliberate learning and the evolution of dynamic capabilities', *Organisation Science*, 13(3), pp. 339–351.

10 Organising communities for construction innovation

Examples from the French and Swedish construction sectors

Florence Crespin-Mazet,
Malena Ingemansson Havenvid and Åse Linné

Introduction

The existence of organisational tensions in the interface between the temporary organisation of projects and the 'permanent' organisation of firms is well debated in the construction and project management literature. These interdependent organisational levels are at the heart of the apparent paradox of this industry, which, on the one hand lacks long-term innovativeness (Dubois and Gadde, 2002; Orstavik, Dainty and Abbott, 2015) and on the other constantly practices ingenuity and problem solving within individual projects.

Construction management and business scholars link the difficulties of exploiting project-based learnings (i.e. scaling them up to become innovations) to various factors such as the organisation of construction (Bresnen and Marshall, 2000; Harty, 2008), the adversarial and short-term nature of construction relationships (Miozzo and Dewick, 2004), the network-specificity of innovative project solutions (Havenvid, Hulthén, Linné and Sundquist, 2016a) and the lack of connections between the temporary environments of projects and the permanent environment of firms (Dubois and Gadde, 2002; Miozzo and Dewick, 2004; Winch, 2014; Hartmann and Dorée, 2015). To overcome these difficulties, several authors stress the need for more strategic leveraging of relationships through a longer-term, more cooperative approach (Skaates and Tikkanen, 2003). This suggestion echoes previous research in various industrial sectors establishing that strong couplings and high-involvement relationships stimulate learning and innovation (Håkansson, Ford, Gadde, Snehota and Waluszewski, 2009; Gadde and Dubois, 2010).

However, such contributions provide little insight on how to foster both internal and external relationships that overcome the tensions between the temporary and the permanent organisation. In this chapter, we mobilise the practice-based learning perspective and more specifically the literature on *communities of practice* (Wenger, 1998) to analyse this issue. This literature emphasises the role of communities in initiating and spreading learning and innovation based on the sharing of each member's individual practice. We believe this approach can provide fruitful insight on the dynamics of learning and innovation across such boundaries (across organisational levels within a firm *and* across several firms) for several reasons.

Firstly, this fluid form of organising (Dobusch and Schoeneborn, 2015) promotes communication processes outside hierarchical rules and constraints. It favours informal social exchange between individuals that transcends the various organisational boundaries of a firm, both at the internal level (boundaries between geographical units, functions or projects) and at the external level (boundaries with customers, suppliers, other partners, etc.). The focus on individuals rather than on the firm's structural units, enables the integration of both the project setting in which individuals develop innovative project solutions (temporary organisation) and the permanent setting where central units (such as R&D, corporate engineering or marketing departments) develop and market group-wide solutions. In this regard, the community of practice perspective provides a useful lens to investigate learning as boundary-crossing activities (Crespin-Mazet, Goglio-Primard and Grenier, 2017) and organisational connectivity (Teece, 1998).

Secondly, it views learning and innovation as a collective emergent endeavour anchored in social exchange, i.e. sharing the experiences and practices of community members (Wenger, 1998). Hence, it views learning as situated (Lave and Wenger, 1991), meaning that it depends on the context in which it takes place, which fits well with the characteristics of the construction industry.

Thirdly, this perspective has been proven relevant for analysing learning processes in project-based industries (Dubois and Gadde, 2002) and more recently in construction. As illustrated by Bresnen, Edelman, Newell, Scarbrough, and Swan (2003, p. 157): "processes of knowledge capture, transfer and learning in project settings rely very heavily upon social patterns, practices and processes in ways which emphasize the value and importance of adopting a community-based approach to managing knowledge". Although applying practice-based theory to learning in construction is still in its infancy, the recent literature review carried out by Kokkonen and Alin (2015) highlights that it has and can make novel claims as compared to traditional learning theory. For instance, studying the *practice* of partnering (Bresnen, 2009) raised the issue of time limitations to create knowledge through participation (Hällgren and Maaninen-Olsson, 2009) or the meaning of situated practices in partnering.

This chapter is structured as follows. The next section reviews theoretical insights about (1) the discontinuities of construction organisation and their consequences for learning and innovation, (2) learning through social practice in construction, and (3) learning in communities of practice introducing the two main concepts used for our case analysis – *participation* and *reification*.

We then present two contrasted cases of communities forming in France and Sweden, drawn from the authors' previous studies. The first case deals with the French construction firm Spie Batignolles and illustrates how an internal community supports the development of an innovative partnering concept branded as Concertance®. The second case deals with the development of new prefabricated concrete products in Sweden based on a mixed community formed between NCC Construction and its long-standing concrete supplier Abetong.

The cases were selected because of their complementarity, primarily regarding the communities of practice (henceforth referred to as CoP) emerging within a firm and across two firms but also in relation to the nature of the innovations (products vs. partnering practice) and the relational dynamics between the members of the permanent and temporary organisations. In the French case, a CoP emerged to connect the innovative concept launched by headquarters (the permanent organisation) to the context of use of its various operational units (temporary organisations) and managed to foster learning and users' adoption and to become a company-wide innovation (permanent organisation). The Swedish case depicts the reverse process where a group of individuals from project-based organisations formed a mixed CoP that was able to transcend the boundaries of their firms and various common projects to jointly develop new products and production processes (prefabricated frames and walls).

A qualitative method inspired from action research (Paillé, 2007; Mérini and Ponté, 2008) was used to conduct the French study. The researcher observed the creation of a CoP within the French main contactor (Spie Batignolles) and contributed to some of the debates as an external consultant. The study was conducted over seven years and involved numerous meetings, interviews with CoP members and top management, observations, production and analysis of several documents (memos, minutes of meetings, tools, project questionnaires, etc.). For the Swedish study, 11 in-depth interviews were conducted with key actors (site manager, sales manager, project managers, etc.) involved in the construction of seven related housing projects in the Uppsala area, as well as several on-site visits. The comparative analysis of these cases supports a discussion on the relevance of the concept of CoP and its various forms for understanding learning and innovation in construction.

The last part of the chapter proposes that CoPs can support three forms of connectivity between the temporary and permanent forms of organisation in construction and across the organisational boundaries of different firms (inter-firm relationships):

1   Linking the permanent organisation to temporary projects
2   Linking temporary projects to the permanent organisation
3   Linking temporary projects to other temporary projects

The conclusion summarises the main contribution of our chapter and discusses managerial implications and opportunities for further research.

The discontinuities of construction organisation

Several scholars in construction management, project management and the IMP (Industrial Marketing and Purchasing Group) community address the specificities of construction organisation and their consequences for learning and innovation (Winch, 1998, 2014; Hobday, 2000; Holmen, Pedersen and Torvatn, 2005; Havenvid et al., 2016a). These authors commonly stress several difficulties linked to the one-off nature of projects and to the number and variety of actors involved (design organisation, planning organisation, production organisation, etc.). Firstly, the introduction of any substantial change that goes beyond temporary problem solving requires intense interaction processes among actors. As expressed by Slaughter (1993, p. 227): "Innovation that requires even small modifications in other components, systems, or activities requires a degree of inter-organisational negotiation that is beyond the normal manufacturing requirements". Secondly, actors struggle to communicate across projects and develop a unified view on what needs to be changed. Thirdly, the one-off nature of projects requires specific constellations of resources and actors. While this specificity is regarded as positive for creativity and problem solving, it also implies that learning is highly task specific and restricted to the individuals involved (Lundin and Söderholm, 1995; Hobday, 2000; Principe and Tell, 2001). Thus, whereas the level of learning within the individual project is high, the exploitation of that learning across projects becomes unlikely (Ayas and Zeniuk, 2001; Scarbrough, Swan, Laurent, Bresnen, Edelman and Newell, 2004). Fourthly, the primary use of traditional tendering procedures (Bygballe, Jahre and Swärd, 2010; Håkansson and Ingemansson, 2013) hampers the industry's overall performance (Dubois and Gadde, 2002). While such buying practices favour the development of tight couplings in the temporary business networks (i.e. intense interaction in projects), they generate loose couplings in the permanent business networks (little interaction and limited long-term relationships across projects). This situation reduces learning and the transfer of project-based 'inventions' to permanent organisations and to the industry at large.

One suggested remedy for this problem is to adopt a long-term view on business relationships in order to 'bridge' projects (see Chapter 7 of this volume by Havenvid, Bygballe and Håkansson) and form 'channels' for knowledge that involve developing new solutions with a permanent network of actors (e.g. Holmen et al., 2005; Havenvid et al., 2016a). Various empirical studies highlight that business relationships can reduce perception of risk regarding challenging or innovative projects and enable reuse of specific resources across projects when working with the same counterparts (e.g. Crespin-Mazet, Havenvid and Linné, 2015; Havenvid et al., 2016a). This is one way of maintaining project-related learning and enabling further development of specific solutions:

> [As] learning is related to particular actors and to how particular resources are utilized, and activities organized, it becomes hard to diffuse and develop it further, unless the same set of actors, resources and activities are reutilized in subsequent projects. As such, learning in projects is 'network specific'
> (Havenvid et al., 2016a, p. 804)

In addition, the lack of long-term business relationships is deemed to generate different and disconnected forms of learning at different organisational levels. In their investigation of the use of explorative and exploitative learning (March, 1991), Bygballe and Ingemansson (2014, p. 24) state that "intense interaction during separate projects but little long-term interaction over several projects, enables explorative learning during projects but impedes exploration at other organisational levels, as well as exploitation of explorative solutions at project level". These studies thus unanimously call for a deeper analysis of the links between the temporary and the permanent organisations and how they support or impede learning processes in construction.

Learning through social practice in construction

The social theory of learning focuses to a large extent on the behavioural and performative aspects of learning by investigating the practices performed by individuals in a specific context (Lave, 1988). These practices are closely related to learning, as individuals need to learn how to act, how to reflect and how to execute certain practices. In doing this, individuals are dependent on the context of other individuals and groups of individuals, i.e. communities, where specific norms exist in terms of performance of execution practices (Nicolini, 2013). Learning is therefore a necessary part of performing practices. In addition, as practices depend on negotiation and interaction processes with other individuals and groups, learning and innovation are always situated and socially contextualised (Lave, 1988; Wenger, 1998).

Several construction management scholars have, during the last 10–15 years, recognised practices and social interaction as important vehicles for understanding learning, knowledge development and innovation processes in the construction sector. For Bresnen et al. (2005, p. 549), practices are an inherent part of learning: "learning depends upon the understanding of the social context within which it develops as well as the social practices in which knowledge is embedded, diffused and re-embedded". As knowledge is seen as "embodied and embrained . . . in members of the network of engineers within the firm" (Bresnen et al., 2003, p. 163), learning therefore requires the participation of community members (Bresnen, 2009) to support the development of "a shared vision. . . , as well as appropriate norms of knowledge sharing" (Bresnen et al., 2003, p. 164). In the same vein, Pink, Tutt, Dainty and Gibb (2010, p. 653) view learning and knowledge as something emergent, processual and interactive: "'knowing' is not a fixed body of knowledge, it is not attached to one locality, but it is learnt, adapted, modified, and engaged in practice by group(s) of practitioners who are in frequent contact with each other".

While Ruikar, Koskela and Sexton (2009) illustrated that CoPs can be actively encouraged and supported by top management, Styhre, Josephson and Knauseder (2006) highlighted the role of CoPs for communication on the construction site, based on the acknowledgement of the various verbal and non-verbal communication practices (and consequently learning practices) across CoPs. Schenkel and Teigland (2008) identified a positive correlation between CoPs and incremental improvement of performance in large construction projects but emphasised the relative lesser performance of geographically spread CoPs as compared to localised ones.

Based on an extensive literature review, Kokkonen and Alin (2015) conclude that "practice-based theory has been embraced somewhat sparsely in the empirical construction project literature to date" (ibid., p. 516). Out of 253 articles reviewed, only 15 were committed to practice-based theory (showing how learning and situated practices are intertwined). However, none of them dealt with boundary work between temporary and permanent organisations within firms as well as across them. Some contributions, however, emphasise the need to cross boundaries between groups and the importance of interacting with 'outsiders' (Ruikar, Koskela and Sexton, 2009) to improve learning and point to such boundary work as a space for renewal (Gustavsson and Gohary, 2012).

Three important results can be drawn from this earlier research. First, there is relevance in applying social theory of learning on construction as an empirical setting, as this industry "relies on a strong community of practice" (Dubois and Gadde, 2002, p. 10). Second, CoPs are arenas for problem solving, learning and diffusion of knowledge. Third, CoPs can create opportunities for learning and innovation *across* projects and firms as they are not necessarily framed by temporal project boundaries or the permanent organisational boundaries.

Learning in communities

Communities of practice refer to autonomous, self-emerging and *'tightly knit'* groups of individuals (Brown and Duguid, 1998), who share the same passion or interest (i.e. a practice such as the same job) and who learn by voluntarily communicating and exchanging with others (Wenger, 1998, 2000). This literature thus highlights the importance of social mechanisms of sharing between the individual members of a community based on their common interest in a given topic. Learning is part of forming relationships of mutuality, trust, solidarity and shared understanding over time between community members. Learning in CoPs relies on self-organising processes (Cohendet, Farcot and Pénin, 2006) that contrast significantly with traditional knowledge management mechanisms based on hierarchical, formal and well codified systems (Paraponaris and Rohr, 2015). The literature highlights two complementary processes that form the basis of our analytical framework. These two processes are complementary in the learning and creation of meaning for what community members do (Wenger, 1998):

- *Participation*: In pursuing their shared interest, members commit to engage in joint activities, to help each other (solidarity) and to share information (Wenger, 1998). They negotiate common actions, which create mutual responsibility ties. Participation therefore consists of constantly sharing, questioning and negotiating the meaning of the individual experiences of community members. As a result of participation, members constantly update ideas (Simon, 2009), sustain a common purpose and create a sense of shared identity. Participation is inherently local, since shared experiences and negotiation processes differ from one setting to the next, regardless of interconnections.

- *Reification*: In this process, CoP members produce material representations of their cumulated knowledge, such as stories, tools, symbols, rules, documents, artefacts and ways of addressing recurring problems (Wenger, 1998). This "shared repertoire of resources" facilitates brokering practices when community members exchange with other communities (through 'boundary objects'). Such brokering practices are key to avoid lock-in effects and to enable the community to be continuously fuelled with new ideas and knowledge. Beyond the simple transfer of knowledge, they often involve transformation.

Initially focused on communities made up of individuals, the practice-based perspective progressively extended its field application to communities existing within organisations, i.e. internal communities (Brown and Duguid, 1998; Cohendet and Diani, 2003; Amin and Roberts, 2008). Based on several company cases (such as Schneider Electric, IBM, Hewlett-Packard, British Petroleum or Caterpillar), research has highlighted the value that communities can bring to company performance: a more efficient way to create, share and stock knowledge; the relevance of their innovative ideas; or the capacity to generate radical innovations and cost reductions in the production and storage of knowledge (Sarazin, Cohendet and Simon, 2017). Internal communities are not permanent groups but are temporary and go through a "lifecycle" (Gongla and Rizzuto, 2001). The literature suggests two main reasons for the termination of a community: (1) its members no longer share the same passion, as there is nothing left to learn; (2) due to the high value that it has generated in terms of innovation for the firm, the community evolves into a formal organisation such as a project group or a new functional department (process of institutionalisation). Finally, several contributions reveal the existence of 'mixed communities' that stretch between the internal and external sides of the organisation, involving, for example, communities of product users (Sarazin and Couput, 2017) or even entirely 'external communities', such as Toyota's main suppliers. In this case, the focus of innovation for the group is the network, not the individual firm (Dyer and Nobeoka, 2000). This is particularly interesting to consider in relation to the construction industry, as construction projects are inter-organisational and demand high-intensity interactions. Next, we outline the two case studies, starting with the French and then moving on to the Swedish context.

The French case: internal communities

In the early 2000s, the contractor Spie Batignolles decided to offer partnering to private customers through a methodology called Concertance®. At the time, Concertance® promoted a drastic change from existing practices: development of trust relationships (open book), as opposed to transactional, adversarial practices; proactive sales approaches, as opposed to reaction to calls for tender; co-development of project specifications with customers and key project stakeholders (e.g. architects, specialised engineering firms or suppliers), as opposed to sequential working processes (Crespin-Mazet and Ghauri, 2007). At corporate headquarters, the sales VP, together with the marketing VP and legal manager, developed a preliminary set of guidelines and contract for Concertance® and asked all French regional units to promote it to their customers.

However, the initial reactions of the operational teams who tried to promote this approach to their customers highlighted several difficulties. Many local sales teams claimed that they were lacking appropriate sales material and internal skills to promote and execute such a partnering approach. As mentioned by one salesperson: "the problem is that we have people at the top level who engage in deep thinking, but who have no idea about commercial reality down here. It is purely unsaleable". They realised that their sales pitch around trust and open book was not convincing, as many of them did not truly believe in these methods and did not identify with the required change. Several customers also expressed doubts regarding the firm's true intent behind this method and its capacity to implement it and/or their attachment to work with architects during the design stage. This shows that headquarters' efforts to draft their innovative approach in a set of principles and rough guidelines were insufficient to ensure adoption. The desired innovation did not resonate with its target users. Hence, the lack of adoption of Concertance® depended on how it was received by its stakeholders (customers, project teams and design partners).

Step 1: The emergence of a CoP around Concertance® in a local unit

However, one sales and design team in the south-east region had a different reaction. Through their internal discussions about their sales experiences with Concertance®, they concluded that while Concertance® seemed to fit with the working culture of some private customers, others were naturally reluctant to partnering (e.g. public customers). Convinced of the need to be more selective in their sales calls, they decided to segment their market and managed to get the support of a regional manager – Paul – to hire an external consultant to structure their reflection. The segmentation process required their full commitment as it involved attending several meetings, completing questionnaires about their projects and customers (30 projects reviewed), exchanging with the consultant and sharing their cases with colleagues. The process then generated both engagement and division internally. Whereas some colleagues expressed their interest and decided to rally behind the group, others quit the process after the first meetings, realising their preference for more traditional ways of working. The whole process stretched over two years and involved 16 staff members (salespeople, design engineers, sales managers, supervisors and a sales assistant).

Thus, an internal CoP emerged spontaneously based on the initiative of a few motivated individuals who personally shared the method, values and principles of Concertance®. After two years, this CoP produced a first set of documents (reification process) summarising its collective learning about Concertance®: a typology of customers (seven customer segments), detailed descriptions of two target segments for Concertance® and a customer qualification grid to identify customers. This set of documents 'congealed' the learning acquired to date and served as a basis for training new salespeople locally.

Step 2: Growth of the CoP and reification of the sales process

Concertance® CoP members started to talk about their internal reflection with colleagues from the northern and western regions during sales conventions and common construction projects. As they discovered interest among colleagues in further sharing their work and practical tools, they received management support to organise a cross-regional seminar (2 days). This revealed an increased commitment of CoP members to Concertance®; they were happy to exchange and learn from one another and to acknowledge the value of their work to others. After this seminar, the regional teams from the west and north decided to also engage in a segmentation process with the same external consultant, with a view to capitalising on her pioneering experience. They informed headquarters, which expressed interest and encouraged them. Concomitantly, CoP members began to transfer their self-made sales presentations and brochures reifying their insights on how to implement Concertance®: its step-by-step method, the composition and organisation of the project team, the role of each party, the practical method for sharing costs and applying open book principles. As each member used these documents on specific projects, they asked for clarification from their colleagues and adjusted them. They also fine-tuned their sales approach, sales pitch and documents based on customer feedback. This resulted in the realisation of, for example, the central role of project managers for Concertance® projects and their lack of integration in the sales process.

Gradually, CoP members faced the need to share the same vocabulary (repertoire) to facilitate their exchange and to stabilise their tools to avoid duplications. By gathering, formalising and summarising all the experiences and productions of CoP members, the external consultant initially played a key role in this process. As she was involved in the operational work of the CoP from the start, she had developed a trust relationship with its members and was in the ideal position to help congeal their practice and transfer it to other members. However, as the CoP grew (with new members, comprised of staff from other regions), the consultant could no longer play this role: the CoP needed the formal resources of the corporate departments to engage the firm's responsibility through the issue of company brochures and sales presentations. Top management accepted that they needed to provide this support and appointed Michel – a member of the corporate marketing team – to carry out this community management task.

Michel had spent his entire career in the company in various operational teams (including 20 years in sales and construction supervision) and benefitted from a good reputation and internal network. His internal legitimacy helped him exchange openly with CoP members and to draft a common work agenda, including corporate brochures and sales presentations. This involved several discussions on the appropriate vocabulary to refer to Concertance® and its key attributes. Over time, the CoP members developed a full set of common resources to reify their practice, such as rules for classifying projects, a unified tool to target customers, reference lists and success stories. Michel created a formal reference guide and database. Thus, implicit knowledge progressively became explicit and accessible. Therefore, Michel naturally positioned himself as the Concertance® community manager.

Step 3: Testing their innovation on living labs

After having focused mostly on improving the sales process, CoP members started to work more precisely on the execution stage. From there on, several project managers and construction supervisors progressively joined the Concertance® CoP. Among other things, they highlighted the lack of training of 'Project Managers' (attitudes, methods and tools) and their ambiguous positioning towards Construction Site Managers. The CoP therefore worked for several months on defining this new function and convinced corporate management to recruit new staff for the job. They then designed and delivered specific internal training programmes for them. The feedback from Project Managers enriched collective learning, resulting in new customer relationship management tools for planning, cost and expense issues, organisation (suggestion of different committees) and decision-making processes.

All this learning would not have been possible without the detailed feedback from customers willing to openly share their perceptions about the Concertance® method during the execution stage and to suggest further ways of improving it in a win-win, co-development approach. To facilitate this process and learn faster, most local CoP members relied on pilot customers whom they trusted and with whom they had a close relationship. For example, in the north, the firm Le Creuset acted as a pioneer in testing the Concertance® approach. Thanks to the quality of their relationships with local teams on a first project, this customer continually pushed them to further develop and improve the method (five joint Concertance® projects carried out since 2010). Over the years, the customer had understood that Spie Batignolles was willing to bring them increased value through innovative solutions and therefore agreed to test new ideas with them and to provide feedback regarding their perceived benefits and operational value. As summarised by the local technical manager: "For us, this customer is a laboratory. We can test new ideas with this customer that we would not dare to test elsewhere. They are open and listen to us, they trust us". The feedback provided by Le Creuset proved essential, helping CoP members improve and finalise the company's innovations.

Step 4: Concertance® has a recognised brand

Headquarters recognised the value of the work produced by the Concertance® community and even decided to register the name as a brand to facilitate its promotion. Concertance® then became an integral part of the company's development project portfolio with well established methods. As summarised by the marketing director: "Through its level of service agreement, the brand undoubtedly defines a new standard in construction . . . A standard that will be constantly enriched by projects and practice, by mutualising experiences".

The Concertance® CoP thus enabled conversion of the initial innovation suggested by top management to an actual 'product', with its own set of tools, methods and procedures for the sales and execution processes. As the brand became more structured and widespread internally, its original management was taken over by the corporate marketing team, which hired new staff to that end. Thus the formal organisation progressively replaced the community. Since then, the company has capitalised on this experience to support the development of several other CoPs on varied issues such as Building Information Modelling (BIM) implementation, impact of digitalisation, future cities, legal issues or innovative solutions for specific market segments. We can thus observe within Spie Batignolles an evolution from a hierarchy management model to a network of communities model in which all existing CoPs are connected and form the basis of a learning organisation.

Analysing the forming of an internal CoP

This case concerns the development of innovative working and relational practices associated with partnering between a contractor, its customers and key project actors. Based on an open book policy and trust-based relationships, this partnering method involved major changes regarding Spie Batignolle's practices and highlighted various organisational difficulties linked to the initial lack of internal experience and staff to properly deliver partnering.

Initially, this idea developed and launched by corporate staff failed to be adopted by local units as it did not fit into their context of use, i.e. their traditional permanent network of customers and design partners. This difficulty echoes the failure of top-down approaches of innovation in construction exemplified in the literature. It is thanks to the birth of an *internal* CoP that emerged at the local level (south-east region) that Concertance® eventually developed into a full brand with a set of well established principles, guidelines and practices.

Participation: The CoP first emerged as a result of the active participation of several local colleagues, who were convinced that this concept could be turned into a successful solution. The sharing of their experiences in sales enabled them to enrich their practice through a better understanding and qualification of their customers (context of use). Following their positive initial results, the CoP was able to extend to other local units from the north and the west that were motivated to engage in a similar process. Through repeated trials and errors on different projects, this enlarged internal CoP went through a process of translation to make the approach their own and adapt it to their daily routine. The approach was regularly tested and improved repeatedly with various customers acting as 'living laboratories'. The case clearly demonstrates that the innovative idea started to make sense to local teams after they tested it and adapted it to their own market conditions.

Reification: The first reification of the CoP also developed internally and consisted of customer segmentation and a grid, enabling CoP members to qualify customers and projects (informing and directing their market practices). This innovative set of documents served as a basis for training newly recruited salespeople in the region. As the COP grew over the following years, CoP members developed several tools, methods, training materials and local sales documents freezing their collective learning process. But to go further in this reification process and position Concertance® as a core company offering, the CoP needed a protected brand name and logo (artefacts), company brochures, the creation of new functions with corresponding job descriptions and recruitment of new staff (e.g. project manager), a global data bank of reference customers and an approved contractual scheme. They therefore required the approval and involvement of top management. This shows how the learning developed at the local CoP level was transferred (back) to the global firm level. The corporate marketing team gathered these products of reification and created a formal reference guide that could be used throughout the company. Thus, implicit knowledge progressively became explicit and classified. Thanks to reification, the guide could be transferred to all geographical units and used throughout the company. While these products of reification reflected the specific practices and skills of CoP members, they also required the insights and feedback of pilot customers in their network who accepted to play an active role in this collective venture.

The Swedish case: a mixed community

Step 1: The birth of a community of practice

Project 1

In the early 2000s, Abetong, a Swedish supplier of prefabricated concrete products, saw the potential in convincing a customer, NCC Construction in Uppsala, to implement a new practice of using prefabricated frame solutions instead of manual on-site casting. It was initiated by a sales manager from Abetong – Alfred. At the time, NCC was launching the construction of a small housing project, Project 1 (60 apartments), with Lars as main site manager and supervisor of the production team (foremen, supervisor and assigned workers). Because of positive prior experiences, Alfred suggested that Lars should test a prefabricated solution on this project: a concrete flat base including steel aggregates. Whereas most site managers have little opportunity to choose suppliers, Lars enjoys "great influence on the end-product compared to other site managers" (according to Abetong) owing to his powerful position within NCC. As on-site casting is both time-consuming and pressing for workers, Lars saw great potential in prefabricated frames and decided, with Erik (NCC's main buyer for Project 1), to accept Abetong's test proposal. During the project, Alfred (Abetong) established a good relationship with Lars (NCC) thanks to frequent site visits, telephone conversations and the provision of assembly instructions. In turn, Lars provided detailed feedback on the solution and recommendations for improvements. As a result of these frequent interactions among Alfred, Lars and Erik, they established mutual trust and commitment to the relationship. At the end of Project 1, Lars and his production team declared their positive view of Abetong's new solution, which had proved to reduce both pre- and after-work at the site.

Project 2

Based on these improved practices, NCC decided to reuse Abetong's flat concrete base on a second housing project (Project 2). Lars and his production team were assigned to this project to capitalise on their experience with Abetong's products in Project 1. Convinced of the benefits of prefabricated solutions for construction, Lars saw the potential in developing his relationship with Alfred. However, this also meant that the production workers had to be able to incorporate a higher level of prefabricated materials and to change their on-site practices, e.g. production plans and coordination mode. This required reflection and investments that went beyond the scope of a single project. The managers from Abetong and NCC realised that they needed to intensify their cooperation to better grasp how prefabricated materials could contribute to more efficient on-site construction practices (joint interest). They understood that they could combine their idiosyncratic knowledge of the product and construction practices to transform the innovative solution developed in local projects (Projects 1 and 2) into a more widespread innovative construction practice.

Thanks to their initial experiences based on trust and mutual commitment, Lars, Erik and Alfred began to intensify their exchanges to adapt Abetong's prefabricated products and to imagine how to best assemble them during project execution. Alfred joined several on-site meetings and engaged with Lars and Erik in various exchanges and negotiations to jointly adapt assembly instructions, develop new routines for project execution and modify communication processes across parties (reification). Alfred initiated regular visits by Lars and his production team to Abetong's highly automated factory, reflecting the increased commitment and desire to engage in joint learning on both sides.

This increased participation marks the emergence of a mixed CoP consisting of individuals from both supplier and the customer (Alfred, Lars and Erik being its core members). The CoP emerged spontaneously during individual projects without any pressure or suggestion from top management. From then on, Lars's production team became a 'pilot customer team', helping Abetong improve their solutions and efficiently integrate them on-site based on renewed construction practices (reification).

Step 2: The development of the community of practice

Project 3

Thanks to the benefits obtained from prefabricated solutions on past projects, Lars and his team decided to incorporate Abetong's frame solutions during the planning phase of yet another large housing project. This time, the existence of the CoP accelerated the integration of an increasing number of prefabricated materials into the buildings: prefabricated flat concrete base, cellar walls and elevator walls but also new prefabricated inner walls (first installation on a project). Two new members from Abetong joined the CoP during this project: Hans, a new sales manager to replace Alfred (who left the company), and Karl, a new project manager. Thanks to his experience and work legitimacy, Lars was considered as a champion of this CoP and could therefore easily establish a common way of interacting within its evolving membership.

Projects 4, 5 and 6

Lars and his production team continued to apply prefabricated solutions in two subsequent projects (4 and 5). The integration of more sophisticated prefabricated wall systems and balconies required increased interaction between CoP members, including more informal contacts between Lars and Erik at the construction division at Abetong.

During the execution of the sixth project – managed by Lars – Hans and Karl suggested applying their new exterior wall solution containing lightweight concrete instead of organic materials. Lars saw the potential of this solution and accepted their suggestion in spite of tight time constraints. During execution, the CoP members had to adjust the wall solution and develop thinner concrete plates (reification). As summarised by Hans: "We actually sold one type of wall to NCC but delivered something else . . . it's a dynamic process [between NCC and Abetong]"; this was possible "as we signed a contract with NCC at an early stage and it was a long way to delivery and the development of the wall was ongoing".

Step 3: CoP members initiating and developing a new solution

Project 7

On this project, which involved the same production team at NCC, a foreman forwarded a request from Lars to use a prefabricated bathroom to replace the lengthy and tedious manual process based on mortar. Abetong did not have an existing solution, but Hans saw NCC's request as an opportunity to develop an innovative solution thanks to the trust they had in Lars and his team: "We cannot do this with anyone; it has to be someone that we trust".

Hans, Karl and Lars jointly adapted the specifications of the wall to minimise weight and enable tiling (reification). Hans and Karl communicated these improved specifications to various departments and individuals internally (Abetong) to make a first prototype (reification). This was not an easy task, as the new wall required a change in Abetong's production practices.

After inspection of the prototype, Lars and his team acknowledged its high quality and placed their order for Project 7. However, its actual application during the construction phase proved unexpectedly costly for both Abetong and NCC as a result of several unforeseen quality issues. As a consequence, Lars finally decided not to include the wall on subsequent housing projects and to continue with established prefabricated solutions from Abetong. Nevertheless, as a result of the developments regarding more efficient production processes of prefabricated frames, the two parties – NCC Construction and Abetong – established a long-term contract on a national level, making this a nationwide mode of production for concrete frames in NCC projects across Sweden.

Analysing the forming of a mixed CoP

The Swedish case describes the development of a CoP crossing the organisational boundaries of two firms and seven projects in relation to the development of a material component as well as prefabricated frames and related production processes. The corresponding practice is innovative as the customer (NCC Uppsala) had never used prefabrication in this way or to this extent. As summarised by NCC's project manager (Lars): "We have more prefabricated concrete solutions than anyone else in the Uppsala region". This new way of constructing frames thus significantly transformed the customer's production mode from traditional on-site construction to prefabricated manufacturing.

Participation: The community involved in this development transcends the organisational boundaries of individual firms to form a mixed community that includes members from the two organisations. Their participation deepened over time (seven projects) based on the mutual trust developed among its (varied) members. Working across projects enabled CoP members to develop what they referred to as a 'self-playing piano', i.e. a joint repertoire of resources and routines (reification) detailing how to plan and execute projects with a high degree of prefabricated solutions. Although some members entered and left the community as a consequence of leaving the company or not being assigned to a specific project, the participation of key individuals and intense interaction across several projects kept the overall community and its mission to work with prefabricated solutions intact.

Reification: The products of reification of CoP members involved both material (materials, production technology) and immaterial resources (know-how, methods of working) and implied renewal for both organisations: new combinations of materials and production technology for the supplier and a new production mode for the customer (prefabrication as opposed to on-site production). The efficiency with which these new material and immaterial solutions could be developed and used was based on mutual adaptations and learning achieved in a mutually beneficial way. This brought several subsequent changes in terms of (1) how the construction process was carried out within each project, (2) who was involved in frame-related construction activities, and (3) which other resources were involved. This ultimately led to the establishment of a formal long-term contract between NCC and Abetong on a national level. However, while these changes generated a more efficient production process, they also raised new difficulties for the customer and required major product and production developments.

Cross-analysis of the two cases: connectivity between the temporary and the permanent through CoPs

The two cases provide several insights regarding learning and innovation based on interactive processes across organisational levels and boundaries within construction. While they deal with different forms of development – material and organisational; product, sales and production methods – the two cases reveal how specific groups of individuals function as vectors for generating new ideas and/ or turning them into 'good currency' (Winch, 1998). Such groups take form as they share common interests and incentives to induce change (*joint enterprise*). As they communicate these common interests and start sharing their individual practices, they eventually turn into a *community*. This collective participation generates new or improved practices that are formalised and stored (*reification process*) in various forms: material solutions (such as a new wall, brochures) and marketing artefacts (such as a brand, logo) but also new working methods and principles (training documents, execution rules, job descriptions, production process). In both cases, community members act in their professional roles but imprint their specific understanding of this role. Thanks to their professional positions and profiles, these staff members consider their role as entailing continuous learning and improvement of their working practice through exchange with other individuals within or outside their organisation. Instead of learning through books or procedures or waiting for corporate management to design innovation, they proactively develop close interaction with selected individuals that share a common interest, concern and vision of their role to shape or spread new practices, knowledge and material solutions.

Based on the findings of the two cases, we argue that depending on how and where they arise, such CoPs can link the temporary and permanent forms of organisation within the construction sector in three types of process that connect:

1   *The permanent organisation with temporary projects*: The community takes on board change stemming from the permanent organisation, translates it to fit into users' settings (local temporary organisation) and spreads it among individual projects (other local temporary organisations).

2   *Temporary projects with the permanent organisation*: The community initiates change at the project level, transmits it and spreads it to the permanent organisation.

3   *Temporary projects with other temporary projects*: The community initiates and/ or reproduces the change within individual projects.

The first type of connectivity (the permanent organisation with temporary projects) is illustrated by the French case where the development of the partnering concept originally arose at top management level. However, the concept was not well received at first, as it was ill-adapted to the local context and to the users' abilities (no training of sales and execution staff), and customers expressed doubts about its effectiveness and benevolence. Instead, the members of a local geographical unit insisted that the method could work and devoted substantial effort to adapt it, with other local units, to their market conditions and anchor it within the organisation. This group formed a CoP through which the concept was reified in the form of specific documents and policies that spread across the firm at national level. Eventually this resulted in a redefinition of the concept within the organisation (new marketing artefacts; new functions, new corporate training programme) and developed into a permanent brand based on original sales and project management methods. Thus, through the persistent work of several individuals within the permanent organisation of Spie Batignolles (at the local and global levels), this became a widespread marketing concept across projects.

The second type of connectivity (temporary projects with the permanent organisation) is illustrated by the Swedish case, where the idea of the prefabricated frame and its further development was initiated at the project level. The development, which took place across a series of projects, enabled the construction firm to formulate a long-term national contract with its supplier, turning the use of prefabricated frames and other components into a 'permanent' production mode for NCC. Thus, through this mixed CoP involving members from a supplier and a customer, this project-specific solution became a regularly used production mode for NCC's permanent organisation.

The third type of connectivity (temporary projects with other temporary projects) appears in both cases. In the Swedish case, the further development of the prefabricated components across several projects turned into a standardised mode of production on a national basis. The mixed community operated across these projects to develop new materials and production technology, thus connecting individual projects over time. In the French case, testing the new partnering concept with specific customers in various 'live' projects (in different local regions) proved essential for developing it further and anchoring it both internally and externally. Thus, whereas the CoP that originated the new solution was internal, its further development and success depended on customers with which the firm had long-standing and trust-based relationships.

The cases illustrate that regardless of the organisational level where the community develops (in temporary or permanent organisations), projects work as 'laboratories' in which new solutions are tested and further developed in relation to external counterparts. However, this development depends on community members *actively* linking projects to other projects and/or to the permanent organisations (Ruikar et al., 2009). Thus, by transcending these different organisational levels in time and space, CoP can generate connectivity among specific actors, practices and material solutions that ultimately result in innovation; they allow knowledge and new solutions to spread outside the community and across the temporary and the permanent organisations of construction. The cases also illustrate that participation and reification are key mechanisms in moving from temporary learning to permanent solutions and vice versa. The active participation of specific individuals over time and the reification of practices, methods or material solutions are required to turn new solutions into widespread innovations, i.e. a set of experience-based formalised practices that are widely adopted and implemented.

In addition, both cases illustrate the need for specific counterparts and reinforce the importance of long-term and trust-based business relationships for learning and innovation in construction. Whether it is an internal or mixed community, the change or innovative solution that it promotes requires the involvement of its intended user(s), i.e. customers.

Concluding discussion and implications

This chapter has presented and analysed two cases of communities of practice (CoP) developing innovative solutions for construction. Based on the CoP lens on how learning is initiated, developed and spread through (local) participation of specific individuals and the way they formalise this learning into specific practices and solutions, this chapter provides several insights on how learning and innovation take place in construction.

In accordance with Dobusch and Schoeneborn (2015), this chapter confirms that communities are indeed a different, novel form of organising in construction. They are not restricted to the boundaries of firms or projects but transcend organisational boundaries in the pursuit of shared goals or interests. Learning is thus closely related to organisational connectivity and boundary-crossing activities. Viewing connectivity as both a requirement and a feature of learning aligns with earlier organisational literature that considers learning as a process related to previous activities and experiences (e.g. Teece, 1998). Thus, learning takes place over time and is related to specific contexts (Lave, 1988) and the experiences accumulated in those contexts (i.e. with particular individuals and through certain practices). However, what constitutes a context is not set in stone. As the cases have shown and also as argued by Pink et al. (2010), learning is indeed interactive, in the sense that it can spread among individuals and 'travel' to other groups or contexts through interaction. This is what makes CoPs such a powerful lever for learning and ultimately innovation: this form of organising explicitly promotes interactive learning processes and helps its members understand the implicit and tacit norms and knowledge of how things work.

While earlier contributions using practice-based theory demonstrated the importance of boundary work across groups for learning in construction (e.g. Gustavsson and Gohary, 2012) and the role of CoPs in such work (Schenkel and Teigland, 2008; Ruikar et al., 2009), we have shown how such communities relate not only to boundary work *within* firms (connecting the temporary and permanent organisations of the individual construction firm) but also across the organisational boundaries of *several* firms (inter-firm relationships). In our cases, this form of organising proved useful for spreading learning and new solutions both within and across firms on national levels (within the nationwide French and Swedish markets, respectively).

While such communities form the basis of sense making and shared identity, existing literature has shown that this form of organising may also generate barriers to outsiders (non-members). This may complexify the 'transfer' of learning from one community to another due to, for example, different forms of communication (Styhre et al., 2006). As expressed by Ruikar, Koskela and Sexton (2009, p. 443), communities face the risk of not learning from new insights occurring at the "boundary between communities". However, our studied cases clearly show that such pitfalls may be avoided and that communities can actively seek and manage to interact with outsiders either internally (from other locations) or externally (with external partners).

In this chapter, we have developed the idea that while business relationships have been shown to provide one arena for learning and innovation (e.g. Dubois and Gadde, 2002; Holmen, Pedersen and Torvatn, 2005; Havenvid, Håkansson and Linné et al., 2016b), the notion of CoPs captures different ways in which learning and innovation can take place in construction. We have considered temporary projects as particular settings and local environments and have illustrated that internal and mixed communities support three forms of connectivity between the temporary and permanent organisations: (1) spreading local inventions to the permanent organisation (standardisation or institutionalisation process), (2) adapting and implementing inventions stemming from the permanent organisation to individual projects, (3) developing and spreading local inventions across temporary projects. In line with previous insights on CoPs (Wenger, 1998) within the construction literature (e.g. Bresnen, 2005, 2009; Ruikar et al., 2009), this means that CoPs connect temporary and permanent organisational levels in construction but also local and global locations over time (Agterberg, van den Hoff, Huysman and Soekijad, 2010) by facilitating knowledge and practice development. They can also generate material solutions such as new components or production technologies.

We hope to have demonstrated that the notion of CoPs sheds new light on how learning and innovation develop in construction. It can provide rich insights on the way communities form and contribute to the development and implementation of new knowledge and a variety of innovative solutions. If confirmed by further research, this perspective has several managerial implications. Construction firms may reap benefits from favouring the emergence and development of internal or mixed communities based on internal motivated 'champions' who are willing to improve their work practice (such as increased sales or execution performance, increased customer satisfaction, internal motivation or improved margin). This could be based on encouraging self-emerging initiatives at the local level (accepting to give time and resources to that end), appointing sponsors at top management level to favour connectivity and transfer between the local and permanent levels, promoting best practices and CoP initiatives internally and externally, and creating opportunities for staff members to meet informally and exchange with others. Such activities develop best outside any formal authority or hierarchical control. In research terms, we call for further empirical investigations that take into account the notion of CoPs and its significance for connecting temporary and permanent conditions for construction.

218   *Florence Crespin-Mazet et al.*

References

Agterberg, M., van den Hoff, B., Huysman, M. and Soekijad, M. (2010) 'Keeping the wheels turning: The dynamics of managing networks of practice', *Journal of Management Studies*, 47(1), pp. 85–108.

Amin, A. and Roberts, J. (2008) 'Knowing in action: Beyond communities of practice', *Research policy*, 37(2), pp. 353–369.

Ayas, K. and Zeniuk, N. (2001), 'Project-based learning: Building communities of reflective practitioners', *Management Learning*, 32(1), pp. 61–76.

Bresnen, M. (2009) 'Living the dream? Understanding partnering as emergent practice', *Construction Management and Economics*, 27(10), pp. 923–933.

Bresnen, M., Edelman, L., Newell, S., Scarbrough, H. and Swan, J. (2003) 'Social practices and the management of knowledge in project environments', *International Journal of Project Management*, 21(3), pp. 157–166.

Bresnen, M., Goussevskaia, A. and Swan, J. (2005) 'Implementing change in construction project organizations: Exploring the interplay between structure and agency', *Building Research and Information*, 33(6), pp. 547–560.

Bresnen, M. and Marshall, N. (2000) 'Partnering in construction: A critical review of issues, problems and dilemmas', *Construction Management and Economics*, 18(2), pp. 229–237.

Brown, J.S. and Duguid, P. (1998) 'Organizing knowledge', *California Management Review*, 40(3), pp. 90–111.

Bygballe, L. and Ingemansson, M. (2014) 'The logic of innovation in construction', *Industrial Marketing Management*, 43(3), pp. 512–524.

Bygballe, L., Jahre, M. and Swärd, A. (2010) 'Partnering relationships in construction: A literature review', *Journal of Purchasing and Supply Management*, 16(4), pp. 239–253.

Cohendet, P. and Diani, M. (2003) 'L'organisation comme une communauté de communautés croyances collectives et culture d'entreprise', *Revue d'économie politique*, 113(5), pp. 697–720.

Cohendet, P., Farcot, M. and Pénin, J. (2006) 'Entre incitation et coordination: repenser le rôle économique du brevet d'invention dans une économie fondée sur la connaissance', *Management International*, 10, pp. 65–84.

Crespin-Mazet, F. and Ghauri, P. (2007) 'Co-development as a marketing strategy in the construction industry', *Industrial Marketing Management*, 36(2), pp. 158–172.

Crespin-Mazet, F., Goglio-Primard, K. and Grenier, C. (2017) 'Social collectives: A new form of organizing that sustains innovation'. *Management International*, Special Issue: 'Communautés et réseaux de pratique: Organisations innovantes et globalisation des connaissances', 21(3), pp. 33–44.

Crespin-Mazet, F., Havenvid, M.I. and Linné, Å. (2015) 'Antecedents of project partnering in the construction industry: The impact of relationship history', *Industrial Marketing Management*, 50, October, pp. 4–15.

Dobusch, L. and Schoeneborn, D. (2015) 'Fluidity, identity, and organizationality: The communicative constitution of anonymous', *Journal of Management Studies*, 52(8), pp. 1005–1035.

Dubois, A. and Gadde, L.-E. (2002) 'The construction industry as a loosely coupled system: Implications for productivity and innovation', *Construction Management and Economics*, 20(7), pp. 621–631.

Dyer, J.H. and Nobeoka, K. (2000) 'Creating and managing a high-performance knowledge-sharing network: The Toyota case', *Strategic Management Journal*, 21(3), pp. 345–367.

Gadde, L.-E. and Dubois, A. (2010) 'Partnering in the construction industry-problems and opportunities', *Journal of Purchasing and Supply Management*, 16(4), pp. 254–263.

Gongla, P. and Rizzuto, C.R. (2001) 'Evolving communities of practice: IBM Global Services experience', *IBM Systems Journal*, 40(4), pp. 842–862.

Gustavsson, T.K. and Gohary, H. (2012) 'Boundary action in construction projects: New collaborative project practices', *International Journal of Managing Projects in Business*, 5(3), pp. 364–376.

Håkansson, H., Ford, D., Gadde, L.-E., Snehota, I. and Waluszewski, A. (2009) *Business in networks*. Sussex: John Wiley & Sons.

Håkansson, H. and Ingemansson, M. (2013) 'Industrial renewal within the construction network', *Construction Management and Economics*, 31(1), pp. 40–61.

Hällgren, M. and Maaninen-Olsson, E. (2009) 'Deviations and the breakdown of project management principles', *International Journal of Managing Projects in Business*, 2(1), pp. 53–69.

Hartmann, A. and Dorée, A. (2015) 'Learning between projects: More than sending messages in bottles', *International Journal of Project Management*, 33(2), pp. 341–351.

Harty, C.F. (2008) 'Implementing innovation in construction: Contexts, relative boundedness and actor-network theory', *Construction Management and Economics*, 26(10), pp. 1029–1041.

Havenvid, M.I., Håkansson, H. and Linné, Å. (2016b) 'Managing renewal in fragmented business networks', *The IMP Journal*, 10(1), pp. 81–106.

Havenvid, M.I., Hulthén, K., Linné, Å. and Sundquist, V. (2016a) 'Renewal in construction projects: Tracing effects of client requirements', *Construction Management and Economics*, 34(1), pp. 790–807.

Hobday, M. (2000) 'The project-based organisation: An ideal form for managing complex products and systems?', *Research Policy*, 29(7–8), pp. 871–893.

Holmen, E., Pedersen, A.-C. and Torvatn, T. (2005) 'Construction relationships for technological innovation', *Journal of Business Research*, 58(9), pp. 1240–1250.

Kokkonen, A. and Alin, P. (2015) 'Practice-based learning in construction projects: A literature review', *Construction Management and Economics*, 33(7), pp. 513–530.

Lave, J. (1988) *Cognition in practice: Mind, mathematics and culture in everyday life*. New York: Cambridge University Press.

Lave, J. and Wenger, E. (1991) *Situated learning: Legitimate peripheral participation*. New York: Cambridge University Press.

Lundin, R. and Söderholm, A. (1995) 'A theory of the temporary organization', *Scandinavian Journal of Management*, 11(4), pp. 437–455.

March, J. (1991) 'Exploration and exploitation in organizational learning', *Organization Science*, 2(1), pp. 71–87.

Mérini, C. and Ponté, P. (2008) 'La recherche-intervention comme mode d'interrogation des pratiques', *Savoirs*, 16(1), pp. 77–95.

Miozzo, M. and Dewick, P. (2004) *Innovation in construction: A European analysis*. Cheltenham: Edward Elgar.

Nicolini, D. (2013) *Practice theory, work, and organization*. Oxford: Oxford University Press.

Orstavik, F., Dainty, A. and Abbott, C. (2015) *Construction innovation*. London: Wiley-Blackwell.

Paillé, P. (2007) 'La méthodologie de recherche dans un contexte de recherche professionnalisante, douze devis méthodologiques exemplaires', *Recherches Qualitatives*, 27(2), pp. 133–151.

Paraponaris, C. and Rohr, A. (2015) 'Communautés créatives et langage de codification, 1er séminaire de l'observatoire des communautés de connaissances', 1er séminaire de l'observatoire des Communautés de Connaissance, Strasbourg, Novembre.

Pink, S., Tutt, D.E., Dainty, A.R.J. and Gibb, A.G.F. (2010) 'Ethnographic methodologies for construction research: Knowing, practice and interventions', *Building Research and Information*, 38(6), pp. 647–659.

Principe, A. and Tell, F. (2001) 'Inter-project learning: Processes and outcomes of knowledge codification in project-based firms', *Research Policy*, 30(9), pp. 1373–1394.

Ruikar, K., Koskela, L. and Sexton, M. (2009) 'Communities of practice in construction case study organisations: Questions and insights', *Construction Innovation: Information, Process, Management*, 9(4), pp. 434–448.

Sarazin, B., Cohendet, P. and Simon, L. (2017) 'Les communautés d'innovation', in Sarazin, B., Cohendet, P. and Simon, L. (eds.), *Les communautés d'innovation*. Paris: Editions EMS-Management et Société.

Sarazin, B. and Couput, J.Y. (2017) 'Salomon reliance son innovation avec les communautés de sport', in Sarazin, B., Cohendet, P. and Simon, L. (eds.), *Les communautés d'innovation*. Paris: Editions EMS-Management et Société.

Scarbrough, H., Swan, J., Laurent, S., Bresnen, M., Edelman, L. and Newell, S. (2004) 'Project-based learning and the role of learning boundaries', *Organization Studies*, 25(9), pp. 1579–1600.

Schenkel, A. and Teigland, R. (2008) 'Improved organizational performance through communities of practice', *Journal of Knowledge Management*, 12(1), pp. 106–118.

Simon, L. (2009) 'Underground, upperground et middleground: les collectifs créatifs et la capacité créative de la ville', *Management International*, 13, pp. 37–51.

Skaates, M.A. and Tikkanen, H. (2003) 'International project marketing: An introduction to the INMP approach', *International Journal of Project Management*, 21(1), pp. 503–510.

Slaughter, S. (1993) 'Builders as sources of construction innovation', *Journal of Construction Engineering and Management*, 119(3), pp. 532–549.

Styhre, A., Josephson, P. and Knauseder, I. (2006) 'Organization learning in non-writing communities: The case of construction workers', *Management Learning*, 37(1), pp. 83–100.

Teece, D.J. (1998) 'Capturing value from knowledge assets: The new economy, markets for know-how, and intangible assets', *California Management Review*, 40(3), pp. 55–79.

Wenger, E. (1998) *Communities of practice: Learning, meaning and identity*. New York: Cambridge University Press.

Wenger, E. (2000) 'Communities of practice and social learning systems', *Organization*, 7(2), pp. 225–246.

Winch, G. (1998) 'Zephyrs of creative destruction: Understanding the management of innovation in construction', *Building Research and Information*, 26(4), pp. 268–279.

Winch, G.M. (2014) 'Three domains of project organising', *International Journal of Project Management*, 32(5), pp. 721–731.

11 The connectivity of domestic and international actors in product innovation

The case of Polish windows manufacturing

Milena Ratajczak-Mrozek

Introduction

The manufacturers of construction materials represent a significant part of the value of construction projects, but, "They [manufacturers] represent one of the most neglected research categories in the construction industry" (Sariola, 2018, p. 167). Hence this calls for more analysis of input products to the construction industry. An important input product to the construction industry are windows, which "are among the five most important technologies impacting energy use" (Koebel, McCoy, Sanderford, Franck and Keefe, 2015, p. 176). One of the leading manufacturers of windows in Europe and even worldwide is Poland. The Polish windows manufacturing industry is relatively large but very fragmented, as there are about 2,500 windows and doors manufacturers, both small carpentry workshops producing for the needs of local customers and well known large companies active on the international market (Polish Windows and Doors Association, 2015). The main advantage of these companies is still relatively low price combined with high quality. However, innovation in windows takes place, and the main part of innovation in windows is related to energy efficiency and thermal insulation.

It is said that the windows manufacturing industry is directly dependent on individual demand, on government orders, and on exports (Polish Windows and Doors Association, 2015). Traditionally, the mentioned factors are treated as demands of the market that cause supply changes. However these influences are not just a broad and nameless 'demand' expressed by a mass group of customers, but in business practice we can see them as particular information and expectation flows expressed in interactions with certain business actors. Interactions that are single instants of contact between particular business actors (Ford, Håkansson and Johanson, 1986) constitute a basis of business exchange (Håkansson and Snehota, 1995) and companies' development. In an industry where 35% of production is exported (Tomczak, 2017), the complexity of the mentioned interactions is additionally increased by a variety of involved international actors. These internationally embedded actors include, among others, foreign customers as well as interactions within supply networks that go beyond national borders.

Additionally, on the Polish market large international producers are present who use local cheaper production possibilities and export even 100% of this production. In this case, we can talk about international actors being part of domestic setting of Polish windows manufacturing industry.

The interactions between different domestic and international actors are not isolated but interconnected, which creates complex network structures and connectivity within the industry. This connectivity goes beyond the country of origin of a single focal company and its domestic setting, regardless of the scale of its activity (national or international). This fits into previous research according to which all business actors have some international connections (at least indirect ones) (Ratajczak-Mrozek, 2017, p. 9). From the perspective of a Polish windows manufacturer, this connectivity affects the business activities of the manufacturer, of which an important aspect are innovations understood as "a non-trivial improvement in a product, process, or system that is actually used and which is novel to the company developing it" (Slaughter, 2000, p. 14). Innovations ensure development both at the level of the company itself and that of the entire industry. Additionally, the different types of interactions with domestic and international actors create very specific flows of information, expectations and resources, which again influence both the picture of connectivity and the innovation pattern within the industry. Hence the two research questions arise:

1   What is the picture of connectivity among actors in the Polish windows manufacturing industry?
2   How do the different types of interactions between interconnected domestic and international business actors influence product innovation in the Polish windows manufacturing industry?

This chapter addresses the supply networks of an input product, windows, to the construction industry. It provides a picture of the input side of construction solutions and how this relates to product innovation on an industry level. The aim of the chapter is to discuss the role of different domestic and international actors and their connectivity in the product innovation based on the example of the Polish windows manufacturing industry, taking the perspective of the domestic windows manufacturer. The analysis focuses on innovations understood as non-trivial improvements and changes in a product that are novel to the manufacturer developing it. The chapter shows that innovation is partly pushed by connected indirect actors forming the network of interactions. The chapter addresses the connectivity dimension of innovation reflecting the existence of different types of interconnected interactions and different roles played by them in product innovation. It highlights which domestic and international actors are involved in the constant product innovation and what roles they play in this process.

The chapter is part of the current research perceiving the construction industry as industrial networks, which affect the development and introduction of innovations (e.g. Håkansson and Ingemansson, 2011; Wandahl, Jacobsen,

Lassen, Poulsen and Srensen, 2011; Bygballe and Ingemansson, 2014; Havenvid, Håkansson and Linné, 2016; Sariola, 2018). This chapter complements this research firstly by adding the perspective of an input product (windows) of the industry. Secondly, it presents a complex network picture of connectivity by including actors beyond the supply chain. This is important, as Sariola (2018, p. 167) states that "inter-organizational relationship research should consider all the parties involved in construction projects". Thirdly, it complements the previous research by adding the analysis of both domestic and foreign actors influencing product innovation in the windows manufacturing industry.

The analysis is conducted on the basis of secondary data, including empirical data on both the windows and the joinery industry in Poland (generally covering the period from 2009 to 2017) collected by the Polish Central Statistical Office, the Polish Windows and Doors Association, and industry publications. An important source of information was a survey conducted by the Chamber of Craft and Entrepreneurship in Warmińsko-Mazurskie Province (2011), devoted, inter alia, to the problem of innovation in the windows manufacturing industry. Based on the secondary data areas where conventional windows manufacturers are currently focusing, their development strategies were identified. Additionally, as supplementary data, information gained from websites of particular windows manufacturing producers were used to gain insights into operations of particular companies in the industry.

Based on the industrial network approach (Håkansson and Snehota, 1989, 1995), a taxonomy of different types of interactions and their role in product innovation is proposed. Also main actors in the windows manufacturing industry are identified, and the connections between them are assigned to one of the types of interaction from the proposed taxonomy. Additionally, by identifying the importance of the actors, their domestic or international origin is indicated. The taxonomy is used to reveal connectivity among actors within the industry and to assess the influence of this connectivity and particular actors on innovativeness of products offered by windows manufacturers. The interactions are assessed from the perspective of a domestic windows manufacturer, and the unit of analysis is windows offered by this manufacturer.

Theoretical framework

Research on innovations in the construction industry emphasises a number of features that determine the specificity of innovation in the industry. These include the complexity of the construction process (Miozzo and Dewick, 2002) and involved actors, the industry's project-based organisation (Gann and Salter, 2000), the tendency to resist change (Sariola, 2018) and being traditional (Wandahl et al., 2011). Both project organisation and the complexity of construction processes hinder the development of long-term relationships (Dubois and Gadde, 2002). These features of the construction industry are said to hinder innovation of the industry, which "is constantly accused of being non-innovative and conservative" (Bygballe and Ingemansson, 2014, p. 512).

However, the adoption of a network perspective on innovations in the construction industry is increasingly accepted as allowing to reveal the more innovative nature of the construction industry (e.g. Håkansson and Ingemansson, 2011; Wandahl et al., 2011; Bygballe and Ingemansson, 2014; Havenvid et al., 2016; Sariola, 2018). It is especially important as innovations in this industry are usually implemented within a project by a multitude of business actors from the whole supply chain who cooperate only for a limited time based on temporary contracts (Mlecnik, 2013), but the actors involved in a project may transfer their knowledge to new projects involving different participants (Bygballe and Inge-mansson, 2014). As Wandahl et al. (2011, p. 399) underline: "by adapting the network perspective new value-adding potentials became visible, which could have a huge impact on innovation". However, most of the research that adopts a network perspective, although acknowledging the importance of different actors for the innovation, concentrates on dyadic relationships within the supply chain.

The theoretical framework presented in this chapter acknowledges the importance of the network perspective for the analysis of innovation in the construction industry and hence is based on the industrial network approach (Håkansson and Snehota, 1989, 1995). According to this approach, interaction is a single instant of contact between business actors. Interaction includes any form of action and reaction, such as purchases, deliveries, business queries and payments. These interactions may be infrequent or frequent, irregular or regular, unconscious or conscious (Ford et al., 1986). Interaction usually forms part of the exchange process, although it may take place between actors "who are not engaged in any traditional exchange situations, but still relate to each other in certain areas" and it is "through interaction a company's structure and ideas are confronted by those of other companies" (Håkansson and Waluszewski, 2002a, p. 14). Interactions can lead to the development of relationships, which in turn are created by more long-term, interdependent sets of interactions (Ritter, Wilkinson and Johnston, 2004). Interactions and relationships may be defined as

> two distinct states of connection between companies (and/or other actors). Interactions refer to single episodes and need not (but can) be repeated. Relationships, in contrast, are formed as a result of numerous, repeated interactions between the same actors, which generate trust and commitment in addition
>
> (Ratajczak-Mrozek, 2017, p. 68)

Interactions and relationships to a different degree affect participating actors, resources, activities and both the requirements and the solutions offered (Håkansson and Waluszewski, 2002a). Therefore, interactions are said to be necessary for the creation of innovation (Håkansson and Waluszewski, 2002b; Havenvid et al., 2016) as single organisations do not have all the necessary resources to develop innovation. As companies need resources and capabilities of other business actors to develop innovation (Miozzo and Dewick, 2002), innovation is "the result of interaction processes among several parties that adapt their resources and activities in relation to each other in problem-solving and attempting to achieve increased efficiency" (Havenvid et al., 2016, p. 82). Innovation is an effect of interdependence and interactions between two or more actors (Håkansson and Snehota, 1995; Waluszewski and Håkansson, 2007), which means that it goes beyond a company's internal research and development (Håkansson and Waluszewski, 2013, p. 451). Such innovation is influenced by the interactions both within and outside the industry (Bygballe and Ingemansson, 2014).

With reference to interaction, Håkansson and Waluszewski (2013) distinguish six types of interaction: (1) pure exchange, (2) exchange with some social elements, (3) buying and selling, (4) producing and using, (5) cooperation and (6) networking. In a pure exchange, the purchasing and marketing processes are said not to affect any of the resources or actors involved directly. Exchange with some social elements affects only the business actors involved and their particular relationships but not the production and products involved. In practice, this usually concerns the exchange of standardised solutions. It is based on the assumption recognised in sociology that all human interaction has social consequences (Blau, 1968; Granovetter, 1985). In the case of buying and selling, the product becomes a result of the supplier–customer interaction and adaptation. This adaptation refers to transaction costs theory (Williamson, 1975, 1979). When it comes to producing and using, interaction affects production and resources and includes some changes in the product, which takes a longer time to proceed. This perception of change refers to the resource-based approach (Barney, 2001). Cooperation affects not only products but also how the actors are related to each other. It has been analysed in the research on strategic alliances (Doz and Hamel, 1998) and relationship marketing (Gummesson, 2002). As for the last type of interaction, namely networking, the aim is to create effects in the whole network, that is to influence the other actors (not only the one in the dyad relationships) in order to change them and their relationships.

These different types of interactions do not directly refer to the term *relationships*. However, considering that interactions and relationships are "two distinct states of connection between companies (and/or other actors)" (Ratajczak-Mrozek, 2017, p. 68), it can be acknowledged that the described types of interaction constitute a certain gradation of varying levels, from lower-level single interactions (pure exchange and exchange with social elements) to higher-level relationships (buying and selling, producing and using, cooperation and networking).

Making use of the presented types of interactions (Håkansson and Waluszewski, 2013) and referring to the study of Håkansson and Ingemansson (2011), who present the relationship between different types of learning and interaction within the construction industry, it can be assumed that different types of interactions have different effects on innovation. Therefore, a conceptual proposition of taxonomy of different types of interactions and their influence on innovation is presented (see Table 11.1).

If an interaction involves pure exchange, there is little room for learning. However, this does not mean that the pure exchange type of interactions do not

Table 11.1 Taxonomy of different types of interactions and their influence on innovation

Type of interaction		Influence on innovation
Pure exchange	Does not affect resources or actors directly	Impacts the ability to assess needs of customers; small degree of learning but in the long run can cause certain changes (e.g. the effect of EU regulations); affects the whole industry, which leads to the development of standard solutions; can provide an impulse for higher-level interactions with other actors
Exchange with social elements	Affects involved actors, not production and products; standardised solutions exchange	Improves the recognition of needs but leads to standard solutions ("similar to others")
Buying and selling	Affects products	Improves the recognition of needs (if the company is a seller) or stimulates the provision of new solutions (if the company is a buyer); can lead to the creation of new products (which are "similar to others")
Producing and using	Affects production, resources; includes changes in products that require longer time	Leads to the creation of a new way of production, new technology and new products
Cooperation	Affects not only products but also the way actors are related to each other	Leads to the creation of a new way of production, new technology and new products; in addition, thanks to a higher level of mutual learning and closer cooperation, stimulates the creation of customised solutions
Networking	Creates network effects; influences actors	Leads to changes and individualisation, not only in one relationship but also regarding many network participants

have any effect on innovation. More diversified solutions can be created if a pure exchange provides an impulse for higher-level interactions.

Exchanges with social elements that affect involved actors, not products, enable companies to better recognise customer needs. This process takes place at the social and interpersonal levels. But exchange with social elements still results in rather standard solutions and products, which are similar to those offered by industry competitors.

If interactions involve buying and selling, there are even more opportunities to get to know customer needs (if the company is a supplier) or learn about new solutions (if the company is a customer). In the second case, thanks to contacts with sellers, the company obtains information about new solutions or possible improvements of their product. This in turn leads to the creation of new products, which, however, are not individualised but still remain similar to products offered by competitors. This similarity is caused by the fact that the buying or selling type of interaction does not include close or individualised cooperation that constitutes a higher-level interaction type.

Interactions involving producing and using lead to changes in products that require more time to be developed and introduced. Such interactions lead to the development of a new way of production, new technology and new products, which in turn is associated with a more significant impact on innovation.

Cooperation affects not only products but also the way actors are related to each other, not only leading to the development of new ways of production, new technologies and new products but also enabling companies to develop more diversified solutions, thanks to a higher level of mutual learning and closer cooperation. Such diversified solutions enable companies to develop products that stand out compared to those offered by competitors, meaning exceptionally high influence on innovation.

The highest level of interaction, that is networking, gives rise to network effects. Interactions maintained in the context of networking not only lead to changes and diversification within a single relationship but also involve more cooperating actors, which should increase innovativeness at the whole industry level.

The level of interaction is related to the level of change within resources, involved actors and their activities and thus to which type of learning is achievable (Havenvid et al., 2016). A low level of technical and social exchange usually leads to relatively smaller learning, whereas cooperation can induce relatively more intense joint collective learning (Håkansson and Ingemansson, 2011; Havenvid et al., 2016). Hence, the type of interaction impacts what is possible to achieve in terms of innovation. When estimating the influence of particular types of interaction on innovation, it is necessary to refer to the definition of the innovation itself. If we take the Slaughter's (2000, p. 14) definition that "innovation is a non-trivial improvement in a product, process, or system that is actually used and which is novel to the company developing it" or the definition from *Oslo Manual* (OECD, 2005, p. 31) underlining that "[t]he minimum entry [of innovation] is that the product or process should be new (or significantly improved) to the company (it does not have to be new to the world)", then every distinguished type of interaction may lead to at least some innovation. However, it can be assumed that in order to 'stand out' among direct competitors, more radical innovations are needed "that can change the very nature of an industry" and lead to real novelty in the industry (Mlecnik, 2013, p. 103). Based on the conducted analysis and taxonomy of different types of interactions, it can be expected that higher levels of interaction can lead to a higher, more radical level of innovativeness.

The presented taxonomy of different types of interactions and their influence on innovation does not include the additional dimension related to different domestic and international origins of particular involved actors. Fletcher and Barrett (2001, p. 562) underline that "business transactions are embedded in networks of relationships that cross national borders and these relationships, in turn, are embedded in different national business environments (that is in each country of involvement)". In a similar vein, Ratajczak-Mrozek (2017, p. 377) states that "companies, their activities, and resources can be viewed as directly and indirectly embedded in domestic and international networks of relationships". Particular types of interactions can therefore occur with actors of different domestic or foreign origins. This different origin translates into different national contexts (settings) of these actors, which in turn also affects innovation. It is especially important for the construction industry, as Horta, Camanho and Moreira Da Costa's (2012) research indicates that in this industry, company performance is strongly affected by the national economic context. Interactions with foreign actors are a source of different information, knowledge or physical resources than those with domestic actors. This may be, for example, more advanced technology, information requiring product adjustment, or simply cheaper resources. It cannot be unambiguously determined whether the different national context always enhances innovation; however, the domestic and international dimensions add extra complexity to innovation-related processes.

Windows manufacturers in Poland: Industry background

Poland is one of the leading manufacturers of windows in Europe. The industry is very fragmented, as there are about 2,500 window and door manufacturers in Poland, ranging from small carpentry workshops that cater for the needs of local customers to large, well known companies that operate in the international market (Polish Windows and Doors Association, 2015). In 2011, the top five manufacturers accounted for 20% of the Polish window market, while altogether 35 companies generated half of its total value. In 2015, the annual window production in Poland amounted to 13 million units, of which 74% were plastic windows, 24% timber windows and the rest 2%, including aluminium and steel windows (Polish Radio, 2015). In 2016, the annual window production increased by 7% (Bereźnicki, 2017).

Poland is the second biggest exporter of windows in Europe, after Germany (Kwiatkowska, 2015). Windows produced in Poland are exported mainly to customers in the European Union (EU) countries. The main markets of expansion are Germany, United Kingdom, Czech Republic, Slovakia and Denmark. There is also growing interest in Polish products from Norway and Sweden. About 37% of the Polish production of windows and doors is sold to foreign markets, and the major manufacturers export up to 70% of their total output (Tomczak, 2017). Smaller companies produce unbranded windows and doors in response to orders from foreign distributors – retail chains or builder depots, which resell them under their own local brands (Kwiatkowska, 2015). The list of Polish window manufacturers, which are known internationally, includes companies like Drutex, Dovista Polska, Dako, Fakro (the main competitor of Danish Velux), or Oknoplast. For example, PVCu windows produced by Drutex were installed in the Hilton Hotel in New York (Consulate General of the Republic of Poland in Milan, 2014). Another fact is that the biggest European window manufacturers have located their production facilities in Poland. Examples include the Danish VKR Holding (manufacturer of Velux) (the Polish Windows and Doors Association Catalogue, 2015). These foreign manufacturers often export all of their production, which is an additional factor contributing to the growth of exports in this industry. Additionally, we have to mention changes that progress in the market related to the acquisition of Polish producers by foreign companies (including the acquisition of the Polish company Sokółka by the Swedish group INWIDO AB).

It is believed that the systematically growing demand for Polish products of the window manufacturing industry can be attributed to the long-standing tradition of this industry as well as its constant technological development (Biskupski, 2015). The main advantage of Polish window manufacturing companies is still a relatively low price, combined with high quality. The quality includes both quality in terms of the product offered and services such as well organised logistics and customer service (Bereźnicki, 2017). However, innovation is playing an increasingly important role (Polish Radio, 2015). A survey conducted by the Chamber of Craft and Entrepreneurship in Warmińsko-Mazurskie Province (2011) shows that in the years 2008–2010, the largest number of implemented innovations involved products, followed by organisational innovations, while the smallest number of innovations were made in processes and marketing solutions. The most common innovations are in the area of energy-efficient technologies and thermal insulation. The level of innovation can be increased by investments co-financed by EU funds and the impact the *EU energy efficiency directive* (for example in the case of roof windows). In addition, in many countries the sale of energy-efficient windows is subsidised by government programs. Window manufacturing companies have to comply with national and EU regulations concerning product quality and safety. There are increasingly stricter requirements and guidelines for the reduction of toxic emissions in the production of building materials, especially with respect to acoustic properties or the use of so-called safety glass, which crumbles into small granular chunks, like windows in passenger vehicles.

Diversity of actors and their connectivity influencing innovation within the Polish window manufacturing industry

In order to discuss the role of different domestic and international actors and their connectivity in window innovations, first main interconnected actors important for the industry are identified from the perspective of the Polish manufacturers. With the help of the introduced taxonomy of different types of interactions (see Table 11.1), the connectivities among actors are identified as certain types of interactions. The influence of these different interactions on product innovation is thereafter discussed. Next, the impact of the connectivity between identified actors on the innovation of the whole industry is analysed.

The group of main actors important for the windows manufacturing indus-try includes *customers*, *suppliers* but also *intermediaries, trade organisations* whose membership includes various competitors (such as Polish Windows and Doors Association) and *policy actors* (for example, European Union regulating bodies), as well as *architects* and *contractors*.

Customers buying windows are a highly differentiated group, which includes individuals, wholesalers and other intermediaries, property developers, construc-tion companies, and public property owners or government agencies. The largest group of windows customers in Poland consists of individual customers who build and repair their homes. "It is estimated that window replacement projects gener-ate about 58% of the entire demand in Poland, assuming that 30% of windows are exported" (Polish Windows and Doors Association, 2015). In 2011 "82% of Polish households have declared their intent to replace their current facade win-dows in the years 2012–2013, which corresponds to nearly 500,000 dwellings" (Polish Windows and Doors Association, 2015). For window manufacturers, it is difficult to maintain direct relationships with individual customers. From the perspective of a windows manufacturer, such business contacts can be classified as exchange interactions with certain social elements or simply buying and selling. Usually, products from large windows manufacturers are sold to intermediaries and then resold to individual customers. This explains the importance of inter-mediaries (further discussed later in the chapter), who are in direct contact with individual customers and who are involved in buying-and-selling interactions with producers. It makes dependent the innovativeness of a windows manufac-turer on intermediaries and indirect interactions with individual customers. It is important as innovation is perceived as dependent on relationships between users and producers (Bygballe and Ingemansson, 2014), and user-driven innova-tion is believed to increase the value of products (Wandahl et al., 2011). How-ever, as Wandahl et al. underline (2011, p. 400), "The current situation in the construction material industry demonstrates a lack of user knowledge as compa-nies rarely have explicit knowledge of how their products and services are in fact used by their end-users". Thus the indirect connections create limitations related to innovations, as they restrict the information flow between the windows manu-facturer and the customer (and the other way around). The described situation regarding indirect interactions with individual customers is different in the case of small window producers who tend to sell their products both directly to indi-vidual customers and to intermediaries. With direct contact with the customer, it is easier to have both a higher level of interaction and innovation. However, if resources are too small and limited, this direct contact with the customer can-not always be translated into innovation as the knowledge obtained cannot be transferred into expected activities.

Products can be sold to domestic and international customers. In order to enter international markets, manufacturers need to adapt to different expectations, even if the information and expectations are acquired only through exchange with social elements or buying-and-selling types of interaction. In Poland, one of the most important features is the thermal insulation of the window or the expected savings in the cost of heating (the same concerns as in the United States [Koebel et al., 2015]). In the German market, however, customers pay more attention to technical aspects – the product must function well, must be ergonomic, easy to operate and durable. In Italy and France, more so than elsewhere, consumers attach a lot of importance to the design of the product (Polish Radio, 2015). In the case of foreign sales to individual customers, the majority takes place through intermediaries. It makes innovation dependent on the flow of information between customers, intermediaries and manufacturers.

Another group of customers consists of property developers, who build and sell apartments, houses or non-residential buildings (for example, office buildings, shopping galleries, hotels). In Poland, this group of customers is smaller than the group of individual customers. "In the group of customers who install windows in new buildings, in 2011 the demand for facade windows was equal to 1.2 million; three out of every four windows were bought by individual homeowners and only 20% by property developers" (Polish Windows and Doors Association, 2015). Windows manufactures can establish long-term relationships and cooperation with property developers, but in this case, too, direct relationships are maintained only with large actors, which is a rather common way of interacting with customers. Such cooperation is possible with customers in both the Polish and the foreign markets, although in the case of foreign markets, it mainly concerns larger Polish window manufacturers who build their own brand, as opposed to companies that produce unbranded windows in response to orders from foreign distributors. Typically, the interactions with property developers (both domestic and foreign) are of a higher-level type than those with individual customers and thus enable more individual adaptations, leading to more individual solutions and thus higher innovation.

The presented analysis of interactions with various groups of customers has shown that these are often indirect interactions as they take place through *intermediaries*. This causes intermediaries to become important actors influencing the possible innovation pattern within the windows manufacturing industry. Moreover, this role of intermediaries (or builder merchants) is becoming more important in response to changes in the profile of the typical individual customer.

> We are dealing with a different type of customer than 10 years ago, when customers would merely choose a producer and leave the selection of technical parameters and solutions to its employees [. . .]. Nowadays, customers come prepared and know what they want. They compare product offerings of different manufacturers
>
> (*Trendy w stolarce okiennej*, 2016)

The intermediary becomes a customer adviser, who affects sales of windows manufacturer but also acquires information about customers' expectations. Thus, the quality of interaction between the windows manufacturer and the intermediary – the frequency and accuracy of the provided information, the willingness to take an individual approach – determines the possible level of innovation. Also in the case of sales to foreign markets, the importance of intermediaries is emphasised. Distributors on foreign markets "act on behalf of foreign customers and, for example, inspect the quality of the ordered goods before dispatching them abroad", which allows foreign customers to minimise the risk of purchase (Aikon Distribution of Poland, 2015). In this case, the interaction type can reach even a higher level between the intermediary (distributor) and the customer than between the intermediary and the windows manufacturer itself.

Important factors that exert a significant influence on customers and thus on the windows manufacturers themselves are architects and contractors. *Architects and interior designers* (both domestic and international, depending on the localisation of a customer) often look for unconventional solutions, which not only meet the technical requirements, ensure the comfort of users, but also match the sophisticated design (*Trendy w stolarce okiennej*, 2016). In this case, through information about trends expectations (for example, about colours), even pure exchange interactions between windows manufacturers and architects can lead to the development of new product solutions. However, such solutions developed as a result of a pure exchange type of interaction are likely to be similar to those offered by competitors. Closer cooperation with architects (interaction type: cooperation) can take place in the case of large and expensive projects, which can involve the development of individualised, innovative non-standard innovative solutions. Additionally, it should be noted that interactions between architects and windows manufacturers may also be indirect, when information from architects is passed on to manufacturers by customers or intermediaries when they demand new solutions or functionality. This introduces additional dependencies and possibilities to the picture of connectivity within the Polish windows manufacturing industry and again indicates the important role of intermediaries.

Especially individual customers, despite being aware of their expectations, are seeking support to find the solution best suited to their needs. They are looking for such support among *contractors*, that is business (a construction company) or self-employed individual workers who carry out and manage construction work, who very often recommend specific products. This is confirmed by the results of research, which indicate that 83% of contractors of facade windows and 93% of roof windows recommend specific brands to investors (Tomczak, 2017). Contractors (both domestic and foreign) are involved in the decision-making process of customers. Contractors play a key role in the development of innovation, as they deliver the projects to customers, give them recommendations and thus possess knowledge about the expectations, resources and activities of both the customer and of the actual building process (Sariola, 2018). As in the described situation, the contact between the windows manufacturer and the customer takes place indirectly, via interaction with the contractor, so the role of contractors for innovation resembles the role of intermediaries. This means that interaction type can reach even a higher level between the contractor and the customer than between the contractor and the windows manufacturer itself. However, contractors often do not work for one particular company, the window manufacturer, and are employed directly by the customers (especially individual ones). Therefore, in contrast to the interactions with intermediaries, who get a commission from the windows manufacturer, the manufacturer cannot 'force' the independent contractor to provide the information and feedback. This finding is confirmed by the research of Sköld, Fornstedt and Lindahl (2018), who show that the relations between customers and upstream suppliers being mediated by project-based contractors have "stolen the industry of important inter-organizational learning processes" (Sköld et al., 2018, p. 220). Although, on the contrary, Bygballe and Ingemansson (2014) show that contractors often provide construction companies with knowledge that they do not have. Indispensable incentives are needed to ensure that the interaction between the contractor and the manufacturer reaches a higher level and next that it has a higher impact on innovation. These incentives may include informal rewarding (Sariola, 2018) and may be supported by interpersonal relationships.

The next major group of actors important for windows manufacturers are *suppliers*. *Key material suppliers* include producers of glass, multiple-glazing units, PVCu and aluminium profiles and fittings (construction hardware). The group of suppliers also includes producers of gasket seals, paints, lacquers, foams and sealants and other chemical products for the construction industry and automation. All these suppliers provide not only key resources but also modern solutions important for innovation. For example, window pane producers are now offering insulated glass units with at least three panes separated by spacers, instead of doubled-glazed units, which are the current standard (*Trendy w stolarce okiennej*, 2016). In response to changing preferences, profile manufacturers are now offering profiles with rounded edges and angles, with oval-shaped elements that add a cosy feel to interiors. Another important aspect of the profile production is the range of available colours. Colour profiles account for between 30% and 80% of all profiles sold (*Trendy w stolarce okiennej*, 2016). Buying-and-selling interactions with suppliers enable windows manufacturers to offer new solutions and product innovation, which usually represent the industry standard and resemble products offered by other manufacturers. However, in some cases, closer cooperation with suppliers can lead to significant innovations that are unique to a given relationship. In general, suppliers' role for innovation is emphasised in the construction industry (Bygballe and Ingemansson, 2014; Sariola, 2018), and the analysis conducted by Mlecnik (2013) confirms that collaboration with suppliers is key for highly energy-efficient housing. Among the suppliers of resources, there are companies both with domestic ownership and international ones (especially global glass manufacturers, such as Guardian Industries Co.). However, it must be underlined that suppliers – companies with strictly domestic capital include also well known global actors (examples include glass manufacturer Press Glass and foams and silicones manufacturer Selena).

When identifying suppliers, we have to mention also *suppliers of machinery*, which is supplied mostly by foreign actors. Windows manufacturers invest in state-of-the-art machinery and production lines supplied by world-class manufacturers, for example Rotox, Elumatec, Urban (Aikon Distribution of Poland, 2015). The interactions with machinery manufacturers may be classified mostly as a producing-and-using type of interaction or cooperation. Such interactions are often focused on creating individual solutions, even if they are based on standard components. They lead to the creation of a new way of production, new technology and new products.

Among other suppliers that windows manufacturers rely on are *service companies and research institutions*. These are mainly consulting companies and companies offering promotion and exhibition services (Chamber of Craft and Entrepreneurship, 2011), as well as transport companies. Interactions with such companies mainly affect organisational innovation processes but do not usually contribute to product innovation. While when companies interact with research centres, the potential for product innovation increases. According to the survey conducted by the Chamber of Craft and Entrepreneurship in Warmińsko-Mazurskie Province (2011), the most commonly indicated area of cooperation between companies and research centres was the acquisition of information about new technologies and products (79% of respondents). Other areas mentioned in the survey included certification (42%), expert evaluations, technical consultations and consulting services (37%) and product quality assessment (32%) (respondents could indicate more than one area of cooperation). Respondents reported that the assistance of research units was rarely used in the process of product renewal. The survey results may be confirmed by the research of Bygballe and Ingemansson (2014), who prove that external sources of innovation such as universities and construction research bodies are generally considered by the construction industry to be of minimal value. In light of the survey just presented, most contacts with research units can be classified as buying-and-selling interactions, which are aimed at obtaining standard solutions or evaluating existing activities and products. Much less frequently, interactions with research units may be classified as the producing-and-using type and affect the production process, the technology used and innovation in this regard.

Window manufacturers are also motivated to innovate by *trade associations* (for example, the Polish Windows and Doors Association). The members of associations include various companies representing the window manufacturing supply chain, which are based in a given country (with strictly domestic or foreign capital), as well as supporting institutions. Members of the association are not only manufacturers with domestic capital. The large international manufacturers of windows in Poland can be members of the association as well. According to its own mission statement, the Polish Windows and Doors Association "sets out new directions for industry development, focuses on innovative solutions, represents and brings together the most powerful and best-growing Polish brands" and "its objective is to create for its members a forum for exchanging thoughts, sharing ideas, and holding discussions" (Polish Windows And Doors Association, 2017). In practice, the association provides information about developments and trends in the industry, organises training workshops, courses and consulting services. In addition, it represents the industry in contacts with various institutes, government agencies and the General Office of Building Control; it evaluates products and services offered by its members. While interactions within the association are intended to foster networking (interaction-type networking) by affecting many actors and creating network effects; in reality these are mainly buying-and-selling interactions and exchanges with social elements. This does not mean that the role of the association for innovations is insignificant but rather that it contributes to the spread of standard solutions across the industry.

Product innovations of windows manufacturers are also determined by *policy actors* (for example, European Union regulating bodies). Companies are forced to adapt their products to comply with new EU regulations. Another example of policy actors influencing window manufacturers are national institutions imposing regulations in the field of export and import or security, which are diversified especially if products are directed outside the EU. Such a type of interaction may be classified as pure exchange, which tends to result in product innovations that are similar across the industry. The importance of regulatory environment for innovation in the construction industry has been confirmed in earlier studies (Blayse and Manley, 2004; Testa, Iraldo and Frey, 2011). In this regard, Testa et al. (2011, p. 2136) proved that "a well-designed 'direct regulation' appears to be the most effective policy instrument for prompting the positive impact of environmental policies on innovation".

Based on the conducted analysis, Figure 11.1 presents the simplified picture of the connectivity of actors who are related to the window manufacturing industry and are influencing its product innovations. The location of particular actors within a Polish or international setting illustrates the domination of domestic or international business actors within a given group.

The conducted analysis indicates the diversity of actors that can affect the innovativeness of the Polish window manufacturing industry, including customers (individual, property developers and intermediaries); suppliers of resources, machinery and services; architects; contractors; the trade association; and policy actors (for example, European Union regulating bodies). Generalising, a large part of interactions maintained by window manufacturers may be classified as pure exchanges or exchanges with social elements or at most as buying-and-selling interactions. The question is whether such interaction types exclude the possibility of innovation. Interactions of a low-level type may lead to innovations as they may lead to significant improvements and innovative solutions, but at the same time they conform to accepted industry-wide standards and are similar to products offered by competitors. The result is that a large part of products offered in the whole industry are standardised solutions (even though still innovative). The picture and the connectivity of identified actors and the types of interactions they are linked with set the conditions on what is actually possible in terms of innovation related to the window as a product innovation on a local level in Poland. Assessing the picture of connectivity within the Polish window manufacturing industry we should especially stress the importance of indirect interactions that are important for innovation processes. This relates to the significant role of intermediaries and contractors who often mediate contacts with customers and thus can play a special role of knowledge broker for the manufacturer.

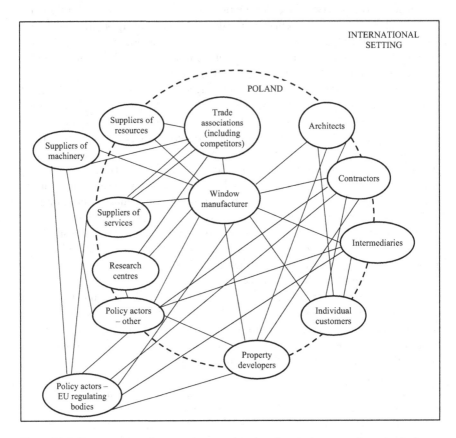

Figure 11.1 Connectivity of actors who are related to the window manufacturing industry and influencing its product innovations

In addition, the picture of identified actors and their connectivity must be imposed on different domestic and international settings in which they operate. This makes the picture the more complex, especially when we consider such aspects as the following:

- In the Polish market there are windows manufacturers with domestic (Polish) and foreign capital.
- Polish window manufacturers sell a large part of production to foreign customers (individuals, wholesalers and other intermediaries, other companies and institutions such as property developers).
- Suppliers with whom Polish window manufacturers cooperate are companies with both domestic and foreign capital; there are cases of suppliers with Polish capital but that are multinational enterprises embedded in global networks of relationships.

- Window manufacturers are forced to adapt their products to comply with the regulations of both international and domestic policy actors.

This international setting makes the connectivity of the industry even more complex. Thus it must be emphasised that the international origin of involved actors or resources does not mean by definition being better than domestic but rather 'different'. Therefore, foreign actors and the interactions with them do not automatically translate into a higher level of innovation. The complex international setting of the industry and international actors, through, for example, different knowledge, cheaper resources or other than domestic expectations, gives impulses to develop new solutions. This, in turn, if properly used, enhances innovation. However, this proper use of internationally embedded interactions is not straightforward as it requires international management capabilities.

Conclusions

The conducted analysis highlights the role of domestic and international actors in window innovation in Poland. It shows that innovation is crucially dependent on both more short-term interactions and long-term relationships within the supply chain that includes customers and suppliers. Both of these groups of actors are much diversified, also in terms of the type of interactions that they typically maintain. For instance, individual customers tend to maintain interactions involving exchanges with social elements or buying-and-selling interactions; in the case of property developers, such interactions frequently turn into relationships of closer cooperation. Another important conclusion that can be drawn from the analysis is that, regardless of the type of actor, the most common type of interactions are of the low-level type, that is pure exchanges, exchanges with social elements or buying-and-selling interactions. Thus the chapter shows how the different types of interactions between interconnected domestic and international business actors influence product innovation in the window manufacturing industry. Polish window manufacturers have to relate to a large variety of actors that are both domestic and international. The presented picture of connectivity is even more complex, taking into consideration the important role of indirect interactions held by Polish window manufacturers. Very important providers of information and experience are located both in Poland and abroad: intermediaries and contractors, who indirectly link manufacturers with customers.

The lower-type interactions with domestic and international actors enable companies to develop new and innovative solutions, which, however, tend to conform to certain industry-wide standards. The question with no simple answer is whether industry-wide standard solutions and products are sufficient. On the one hand, industry-wide standard solutions and products remain attractive both for many customers as well as for individual manufacturers and can significantly increase the innovativeness of their products. Low-level interactions can also motivate companies to look for other solutions and establish other (higher-level) interactions. For example, information about customer expectations (pure exchange) leads to the establishment of close cooperation with the supplier in order to develop a new production technology (cooperation). On the other hand, reliance on new but standard product solutions, including innovations, implies that a company may find it difficult to differentiate its products from similar products already offered by competitors and to succeed in the market.

The conducted analysis presents the complex picture of connectivity of the window manufacturing industry taking the perspective of interactions and connectivity. The picture reaches beyond the supply chain, including such business actors as customers, suppliers but also intermediaries, trade organisations whose membership includes various competitors (such as Polish Windows and Doors Association), policy actors (for example, European Union regulating bodies), architects and contractors. The presented analysis complements previous research adopting the network perspective on innovation in the construction industry by adding the analysis of both domestic and foreign actors influencing product innovation in the window manufacturing industry.

The conducted analysis shows that currently, one cannot speak only about the domestic impact on product innovation. Virtually all actors in the Polish window manufacturers network can be both domestic and international, although in the case of selected actors, we can indicate a certain domination of the domestic dimension (contractors, suppliers of services including research units, trade associations) or foreign dimension (EU regulating bodies). In the case of the Polish window manufacturing industry, we can clearly see that connectivity in the construction industry is not limited to a single country but spreads across national borders. The Polish windows industry is clearly not only Polish but indeed international. The presence of interactions with both domestic and international actors indicates the possibility of drawing on both domestic and international knowledge and other resources. For this, however, appropriate capabilities are needed, which should be the subject of further research. In addition, the analysis shows that part of the potential for increasing innovation as a result of interaction with other business actors is not appreciated by many manufacturers. This applies, among others, to contractors, suppliers of services and trade associations. The best window producers draw from the entire network, adapting to domestic and foreign interactions.

An important practical implication is that, to ensure that the product offering is sufficiently innovative and the innovation level is improved, window manufacturers need to engage in cooperation with diversified actors. Such diversified actors come from both domestic and international settings, which, especially in the case of the international setting, may additionally enhance innovation. The presented industry case shows that at the moment there are both fragmentation and connectivity at the industry level. However, in order to increase the level of innovation this connectivity should also be used to a higher extent by striving for close cooperation within and beyond the supply chain and by joint development of new products.

References

Aikon Distribution of Poland (2015) 'Benefits of importing windows from Poland'. www.windownews.co.uk/benefits-of-importing-windows-from-poland/. Accessed 15 September 2018.

Barney, J.B. (2001) 'Resource-based theories of competitive advantage: A ten-year retrospective on the resource-based view', *Journal of Management*, 27(6), pp. 643–650.

Bereźnicki, J. (2017) 'Branża okien i drzwi z PVC w UE kurczy się, ale w Polsce rośnie w siłę'. www.money.pl/gospodarka/unia-europejska/wiadomosci/artykul/branza-okien-i-drzwi-pvc,228,0,2354404.html. Accessed 15 September 2018.

Biskupski, Z. (2015) 'Stolarka okienna i drzwiowa to polska specjalność'. www.polskatimes. pl/strefa-biznesu/firma/a/stolarka-okienna-i-drzwiowa-to-polska-specjalnosc,10149334/. Accessed 15 September 2018.

Blau, P.M. (1968) 'The hierarchy of authority in organizations', *American Journal of Sociology*, 73(4), pp. 453–467.

Blayse, A.M. and Manley, K. (2004) 'Key influences on construction innovation', *Construction Innovation*, 4(3), pp. 143–154.

Bygballe, L.E. and Ingemansson, M. (2014) 'The logic of innovation in construction', *Industrial Marketing Management*, 43(3), pp. 512–524.

Chamber of Craft and Entrepreneurship in Warmińsko-Mazurskie Province (2011) 'Analiza Pt. Zwiększenie Potencjału Innowacyjnego i Konkurencyjnego Klastra Stolarki Otworowej – Kierunki Działań' Olsztyn.

Consulate General of the Republic of Poland in Milan (2014) 'Opis Sektora Stolarki Okiennej i Drzwiowej w Polsce, 2014, Konsulat Generalny Rezeczpospolitej Polskiej w Mediolanie'. www.mediolan.msz.gov.pl/pl/nasze_projekty/projekty_ekonomiczne/pol skie_firmy_we_wloszech/sektor_stolarki/opis. Accessed 15 September 2018.

Doz, Y.L. and Hamel, G. (1998) *Alliance advantage*. Boston: Harvard Business School Press.

Dubois, A. and Gadde, L.-E. (2002) 'The construction industry as a loosely coupled system: Implications for productivity and innovation', *Construction Management and Economics*, 20(7), pp. 621–631.

Fletcher, R. and Barrett, N. (2001) 'Embeddedness and the evolution of global networks: An Australian case study', *Industrial Marketing Management*, 30(7), pp. 561–573.

Ford, D., Håkansson, H. and Johanson, J. (1986) 'How do companies interact?', *Industrial Marketing and Purchasing*, 1(1), pp. 26–41.

Gann, D.M. and Salter, A.J. (2000) 'Innovation in project-based, service-enhanced firms: The construction of complex products and systems', *Research Policy*, 29(7/8), pp. 955–972.

Granovetter, M. (1985) 'Economic action and social structure: The problem of embeddedness Mark Granovetter', *American Journal of Sociology*, 91(3), pp. 481–510.

Gummesson, E. (2002) 'Relationship marketing and a new economy: It's time for de-programming', *Journal of Services Marketing*, 16(7), pp. 585–589.

Håkansson, H. and Ingemansson, M. (2011) 'Construction companies and how they acquire knowledge through business interaction', *The IMP Journal*, 5(2), pp. 67–78.

Håkansson, H. and Snehota, I. (1989) 'No business is an island', *Scandinavian Journal of Management*, 5(3), pp. 187–200.

Håkansson, H. and Snehota, I. (1995) *Developing relationships in business networks*. London: Routledge.

Håkansson, H. and Waluszewski, A. (2002a) *Managing technological development. IKEA, the environment and technology*. Oxon: Routledge.

Håkansson, H. and Waluszewski, A. (2002b) 'Path dependence: Restricting or facilitating technical development?', *Journal of Business Research*, 55(7), pp. 561–570.

Håkansson, H. and Waluszewski, A. (2013) 'A never ending story – Interaction patterns and economic development', *Industrial Marketing Management*, 42(3), pp. 443–454.

Havenvid, M.I., Håkansson, H. and Linné, Å. (2016) 'Managing renewal in fragmented business networks', *The IMP Journal*, 10(1), pp. 81–106.

Horta, I.M., Camanho, A.S. and Moreira Da Costa, J. (2012) 'Performance assessment of construction companies: A study of factors promoting financial soundness and innovation in the industry', *International Journal of Production Economics*, 137(1), pp. 84–93.

Koebel, C.T., McCoy, A.P., Sanderford, A.R., Franck, C.T. and Keefe, M.J. (2015) 'Diffusion of green building technologies in new housing construction', *Energy and Buildings*, 97, pp. 175–185.

Kwiatkowska, M. (2015) 'Stolarka za 5 mld zł. Polska jest potężnym eksporterem drzwi i okien'. www.forsal.pl/artykuly/867638,stolarka-za-5-mld-zl-polska-jest-poteznym-eksporterem-drzwi-i-okien.html. Accessed 15 September 2018.

Miozzo, M. and Dewick, P. (2002) 'Building competitive advantage: Innovation and corporate governance in European construction', *Research Policy*, 31(6), pp. 989–1008.

Mlecnik, E. (2013) 'Opportunities for supplier-led systemic innovation in highly energy-efficient housing', *Journal of Cleaner Production*, 56, pp. 103–111.

OECD (2005) 'Oslo Manual. The measurement of scientific and technological activities'. www.oecd.org/science/inno/2367614.pdf. Accessed 15 September 2018.

Polish Radio (2015) 'Polscy producenci okien i drzwi podbijają rynki europejskie'. www.polskieradio.pl/42/273/Artykul/1629066,Polscy-producenci-okien-i-drzwi-podbijaja-rynki-europejskie. Accessed 15 September 2018.

Polish Windows and Doors Association (2015) 'Members catalogue'. http://poid.eu/wp-content/uploads/2015/01/Aveex_POiD_katalog_ENG_2015_rgb.pdf. Accessed 15 September2018.

Polish Windows and Doors Association (2017) https://poid.eu/en/. Accessed 15 September 2018.

Ratajczak-Mrozek, M. (2017) *Network embeddedness. Examining the effect on business performance and internationalization.* Cham: Palgrave Macmillan.

Ritter, T., Wilkinson, I.F. and Johnston, W.J. (2004) 'Managing in complex business networks', *Industrial Marketing Management*, 33(3), pp. 175–183.

Sariola, R. (2018) 'Utilizing the innovation potential of suppliers in construction projects', *Construction Innovation*, 18(2). www.emeraldinsight.com/doi/abs/10.1108/CI-06-2017-0050. Accessed 15 September 2018.

Sköld, D., Fornstedt, H. and Lindahl, M. (2018) 'Dilution of innovation utility, reinforcing the reluctance towards the new: An upstream supplier perspective on a fragmented electricity industry', *Energy Policy*, 116(November 2017), pp. 220–231.

Slaughter, E.S. (2000) 'Implementation of construction innovation', *Building Research and Information*, 28(1), pp. 1–17.

Testa, F., Iraldo, F. and Frey, M. (2011) 'The effect of environmental regulation on firms' competitive performance: The case of the building and construction sector in some EU regions', *Journal of Environmental Management*, 92(9), pp. 2136–2144.

Tomczak, B. (2017) 'Stolarka otworowa -polski hit eksportowy'. www.buildercorp.pl/wp-content/uploads/2017/06/stolarka_otw.pdf. Accessed 15 September 2018.

Trendy w stolarce okiennej (2016) www.dom.pl/trendy-w-stolarce-okiennej.html. Accessed 15 September 2018.

Waluszewski, A. and Håkansson, H. (2007) 'Economic use of knowledge', in Håkansson, H. and Waluszewski, A. (eds.), *Knowledge and Innovation in Business and Industry. The Importance of using Others*. Oxon: Routledge, pp. 1–26.

Wandahl, S., Jacobsen, A., Lassen, A.H., Poulsen, S.B. and Srensen, H. (2011) 'User-driven innovation in a construction material supply network', *Construction Innovation*, 11(4), pp. 399–415.

Williamson, O.E. (1975) *Markets and hierarchies: Analysis and antitrust implications*. New York: Free Press.

Williamson, O.E. (1979) 'Transaction-costs economics: The governance of contractual relations', *Journal of Law and Economics*, 22(2), pp. 232–262.

12 Narratives of innovation that address climate change agenda in the construction sector

Natalya Sergeeva and Carmel Lindkvist

Introduction

This chapter explores narratives of innovation that address the challenges faced in the construction sector and associated firms in meeting climate change targets. Innovation is important to meet the targets, and there is an urgency reflected within continuously developing global strategies and policy initiatives. In this way, innovation must be sustainable with the specific objective to reduce carbon emissions in countries – we refer to this as 'sustainable innovation'. There is a temporal connection within the urgency to set ambitious climate change targets with specific deadlines and the need for industries like the construction sector to act. The UN Framework Convention on Climate Change advocates the necessity for countries to set targets to limit global warming to less than 2° Celsius above pre-industrial temperatures. Countries have set targets to meet emission goals with key years being 2020, 2030 and 2050. At the Paris climate conference (COP21) in December 2015, 195 countries, including Norway and the UK, adopted the first universally, legally binding global climate deal, which comes into effect in 2020. These continuous timelines to meet global/national goals to reduce emissions require support from industries such as the construction sector. Norway and UK are countries heavily promoting sustainable innovation to meet the construction sector targets set by policy. Since 2010, EU directives have guided the construction sector towards sustainability in Norway and the UK. In this chapter, we focus on this interaction process between climate change targets at the policy level and the action/reaction of the construction sector firms, both owners/clients and suppliers/main contractors. We also look into the way narratives of innovation are continuously promoted in textual forms – in Norway with the focus on working towards (nearly) 'zero emissions' and in the UK with the focus on 'low carbon'. Although maybe labelled differently in each country, we use the term *sustainable innovation* as the most commonly used in both contexts.

This chapter seeks to answer the main question: How do narratives of innovation that address the climate change agenda in the construction sector in Norway and the UK interact at the international, industrial policy and firm levels? We believe this is an important question to address that has important implications for policymaking. The performance of the construction sector rests upon a coalition of leading firms promoting narratives of innovation that address and who act on the climate change agenda (Orstavik, Dainty and Abbott, 2015). These firms and the people within them play an important role in creating a more systematic and holistic approach to 'low-carbon', 'zero-energy' innovation and changing organisational and industrial culture (Sergeeva, 2016; Winch, 1998). The industrial policy calls for stronger and more systematic links between narratives of sustainable innovation at industrial policy and firm levels (BIS Innovation Infrastructure Project: Working towards an Innovation System, 2010; Building our industrial strategy: Green paper, 2017). Yet little is known about how narratives of sustainable innovation interact: how they pull and push each other to be innovative for sustainable development in approaches and ambitions to reduce carbon emissions. Building upon the 'narrative turn' in the organisation studies (Czarniawska, 1997, 2010; Fenton and Langley, 2011; Rhodes and Brown, 2005; Vaara, Sonenshein and Boje, 2016) and innovation literature (Bartel and Garud, 2009; Garud, Schildt and Lant, 2014; Reissner, 2005; Seidel and O'Mahony, 2014), we demonstrate the ways textual narratives of sustainable innovation are continuously promoted in construction sector firms that address the targets set at industrial and international levels using specific examples. The narrative turn in innovation studies constitutes a shift in focus away from the material practices of innovation towards understanding how the meaning of innovation is socially constructed using narratives. In this chapter, we refer to the narrative of sustainable innovation as a discourse about the need to change and improve products, processes and services to meet the sustainability targets set by industrial policies and internationally and to deliver value for customers, which could be environmental, societal, economic etc. To date, there remains little consistency in terms of theoretical approach to narrative interactions in this area and scarce empirical investigation.

Norway intends to reduce energy consumption in general and to reduce reliance on fossil fuels. The aim in Norway is to reduce its emissions by at least 40% by 2030 compared with 1990 levels and be carbon neutral by 2050 through the reduction of domestic greenhouse gas emissions (Alonso and Stene, 2013; EU Emissions Trading System, 2016). Buildings account for about 40% of energy consumption in Norway, therefore the building industry is an important player when reducing the overall environmental impact of energy use. The Norwegian government strategy document "The Green Shift – Climate and Environmentally Friendly Restructuring" refers to policy that has led to stricter buildings regulations on reducing climate gas emissions (Lavenergiprogrammet, 2016). While a regulatory process is in place leading to standards such as TEK 17 and Passive House to reduce carbon emissions, there is no clear analysis on how these processes emerged.

In the UK Construction 2025 strategy sets the target of a 50% reduction in greenhouse gas emissions in the built environment by 2025, and the UK Climate Change Act sets the target of reducing emissions by 80% by 2025. The tasks set for companies in the wider construction sector in the UK are to (1) decarbonise their own businesses; (2) provide people with buildings that enable them to lead more energy-efficient lives; and (3) provide the infrastructure that enables the supply of clean energy and sustainable practices in other areas of the economy (Low Carbon Construction, 2010).

Whilst industrial policy and targets are in place to push the Norwegian and the UK construction sector firms to be more innovative and sustainable, it remains unclear how they respond to this push, as well as the interaction between innovation push and pull. This is the knowledge gap that we address in this chapter. In the following sections we examine the narrative turn in organisation and innovation studies; we present our empirical findings examining push and pull narratives of sustainable innovations between industrial policy and firms in both Norway and the UK; and finally, we discuss our conclusion that narrative interactions of sustainable innovation occur at multi-levels (international policy, national policy and firm levels).

'Narrative turn' in the organisation studies

We build upon the 'narrative turn' in organisation studies (Czarniawska, 1997, 2010, 2016; Fenton and Langley, 2011; Rhodes and Brown, 2005; Vaara et al., 2016) to explore the research question about how narratives of sustainable innovation interact at the policy and firm levels. By a narrative, we mean a discursive construction that embodies a degree of coherence and unity of purpose, together with connotations of performative intent (Boje, 2001; Cunliffe and Coupland, 2011; Humphreys and Brown, 2002; Sonenshein, 2010). Although rarely fixed or completely monolithic, narratives are nevertheless often repeated in organisations. Indeed, narrative repetition promotes innovation and/or then stabilises particular meanings (Buchanan and Dawson, 2007; Dailey and Browning, 2014). Narratives hence may carry important messages at the level of the firm and at a sectoral level. Narratives are frequently seen as an integral means of organising (Brown, Stacey and Nandhakumar, 2008). Organisational narratives tend to become institutionalised in textual forms on websites and firm reports. Industrial policy and international narratives are dominant in legitimising advocated actions by firms and individuals within them (Buchanan and Dawson, 2007).

Practising managers and policymakers play an active role in the construction of such narratives, as they are responsible for formulating and disseminating an organisational vision and strategies (Sims, 2003; Sonenshein, 2010). For example, Abolafia (2010) demonstrates the ways elite policymakers use plotted and plausible narratives to shape the reactions of those in their environment. Top managers sanction organisational values and identity through spoken and written narratives (Bourne and Jenkins, 2013). Sims (2003) further considers the special pressures on managers to tell narratives about their organisations to their superiors and subordinates, and, in addition, there is an expectation on managers to give coherent narratives of organisational performance to their staff. In this way, narratives play a prominent role in constructing organisational, industrial and national identities.

Time is key in how narratives (re)construct individual and organisational identities (Brown and Thompson, 2013). Dobusch and Schoeneborn (2015) emphasise that organisational identity is continually constituted in narrative texts and may be reflexively woven by organisational members. Whilst organisational identity narratives tend to be consistent, they can be modified over time (e.g. strategies are revised; firm reports are rewritten). Narratives hence have important implications for future (re)construction of identities and in the set-up of organisational visions and strategies. Narratives of sustainable innovation thus potentially play an important role of establishing an identity and image of 'innovative' and 'sustainable' construction sector. As such, the construction sector firms tend to promote themselves as innovative and sustainable, with these two terms being core organisational values (Opoku, Ahmed and Cruickshank, 2015).

Alvesson and Robertson (2015) address identity issues in relation to senior employees in the UK investment banking sector. Their study demonstrates that senior employees are far less sensitive to identity issues than existing research suggests. Other studies have examined the ways actors have interpreted the past in order to forge organisational identities (Hansen, 2007) and have set strategic directions (Schultz and Hernes, 2013). Gioia, Schultz and Corley (2000, p. 64) argue that organisational identity is commonly understood as an organisational members' collective understanding of the features presumed to be central and relatively permanent and that distinguish the organisation from other organisations. Expressed values often form part of an organisational identity. Bourne and Jenkins (2013) clarify that top management espouse organisational values through verbal and written statements and formal documents. Organisational values typically refer to the small number of values that are coherent and consistent. Changes in values do occur over time but are typically incremental.

'Narrative turn' in innovation studies

There is undoubtedly increasing interest amongst scholars of innovation in the importance of narratives (Beckman and Marry, 2009; Reissner, 2005; Seidel and O'Mahony, 2014). Bartel and Garud (2009) distinguish between narratives that portray innovation in a structured way using a plot and provisional narratives that capture individual perceptions without any clear plot. The purpose of the former is to promote a coherent viewpoint of innovation, whereas the latter acts as more personalised sense-making mechanisms. Structured narratives of innovation act as "cultural mechanisms for translating ideas across the organisation so that they are comprehensive and appear legitimate to others" (Bartel and Garud, 2009, p. 109). Denning (2005) also sees having the capability to develop narrative tools as essential to the promotion of innovation acting as sense-giving mechanisms. More specifically, narratives of innovation can be seen to carry important messages about organisational vision, directions and strategies (Doganova and Eyquem-Renault, 2009). Garud, Dunbar and Bartel (2011) further contend that structured narratives provide the organisational memory that enables people to translate emergent ambiguous situations associated with the innovation process into the meaningful present and future. In contrast, provisional narratives enable "real-time problem solving among individuals who must coordinate within and across different domains of activity" (Bartel and Garud, 2009, p. 112). This definition points towards a continuous process of social construction through which individuals ascribe meanings to innovation based on their social interactions.

The current literature is largely silent on the way in which innovation narratives interact at cross-levels and the implications of these interactions. Some scholars have taken a micro approach to studying individuals and teams to innovate within their specific contexts (Taylor and Greve, 2006). Others have taken a macro approach, offering insights on the role of national, regional and industrial contexts in inducing innovation (Lundvall, 2007). Several multi-level approaches have attempted to bridge the micro–macro boundary (Fenton and Langley, 2011; Vaara et al., 2016) but fall short in addressing the dynamics of this interaction and its implications for actions. This chapter uses insights borrowed from narratology to obtain a better understanding of interactions between narratives of innovation that address the climate change agenda at industrial policy and project-based firm levels. We believe this can offer a greater understanding of what drives innovation across different levels, in terms of the sustainability targets that are set and attempted to be met. It also has important implications for policymaking.

The interactions between narratives of sustainable innovation at industrial policy and firm levels

There is increasing recognition in the literature that the construction sector has progressed in the development of green building practices. Innovation as a process to implement new products, processes and/or management approaches with the intention to improve current practices is a means of achieving more sustainable green practices. At the same time, context plays an important role in understanding innovation (Orstavik et al., 2015). For example, for one firm, a practice may be perceived as new and innovative, but this practice may be more commonly used elsewhere. Previous research has shown an increased industrial and corporate focus on green innovation raises the quality of construction projects, sustains and enforces companies' positions in the market, and improves collaboration among the actors involved (Bossink, 2004). Government regulatory policies play an important role in shaping the direction of innovation and change in the construction industry (Blayse and Manley, 2004; Bossink, 2002). There is also consciousness that 'extensive' and prescribed regulations may stifle innovations, as parties have little incentive to improve (Rehan and Nehdi, 2005).

The directives from the EU focus on climate change targets, but it is up to individual countries to decide how these targets are realised. As noted in the construction innovation literature, building policy debates tend to have a narrow focus on value based on economics rather than on broader societal or environmental values, as well as paying little attention to motivation of the diverse range of stakeholders (Whyte and Sexton, 2011). European policies focus on improving the physical performance of building and market mechanisms (Baek and Park, 2012).

Concurrently, policymakers are aware of the importance of the non-technical dimensions of organisation, social and behavioural aspects within this area, but these dimensions are relatively under-explored (Schweber and Leiringer, 2012).

Increasingly, construction management literature has emphasised how the construction sector's identity is shaped by written narratives of innovation that address the sustainability agenda mobilised in government reports, structures and regulations, which include long-term processes (Gluch, 2009). It is clear that both industry and policy have narratives of innovation on how they address the climate change agenda, but how they influence each other is not always obvious. Innovation narratives shape how firm and project actors understand an innovation and reconstitute it through their discourses and actions. The project-based nature of construction sector firms reinforces the need for a consistent narrative of sustainable innovation (Hobday, 2000). Due to the project-based and diverse nature of the construction sector, the effective adoption of environmental innovation requires the collaboration of all the parties in the sector (Dewick and Miozzo, 2002). The importance to communicate ideas across the sector is increasingly recognised to broaden the adoption of green, sustainable innovations. As Gluch, Gustafsson, and Thuvander (2009, p. 451) state:

> For wider adoption of green innovations and ideas, for example solar panels, low emission glass, passive house design, extended life cycle thinking, and web-based analytical tools, it is important that the management group supports and communicates these ideas and innovations so that individuals perceive them as motivating.

We argue that narratives are the ways of communicating 'green' innovations and therein driving it across the sector. Both policy and leading construction firms play an important role in promoting narratives of sustainable innovation and motivating the construction sector to adopt green innovation and develop new solutions.

Methods

In our empirical investigation, we explore the ways Norwegian and UK construction firms respond to the dominant narrative about the need for sustainable innovation to meet climate change targets set nationally and internationally. The two countries are complementing each other in how they actively promote narratives of sustainable innovation. There are some structural differences, such as population size and climate, but we demonstrate the commonality in the ways narratives of sustainability innovation at sector-level connect with those at firm levels. The specific steps we followed in our empirical investigation are:

1 Analysis of textual narratives of sustainable innovation identified in the government and industrial policy reports;
2 Analysis of textual narratives of sustainable innovation identified in the selected firms' websites;

3   Analysis of the narrative interactions in terms of how firms respond to the national and international narratives of sustainable innovation.

In Norway, 18 Norwegian white papers, legislative acts and literary understandings of policy have been analysed to understand the policy perspective of reducing climate change. The white papers and legislative acts are listed in the Appendix (Table 12.4). This analysis focused primarily on sustainable policy directed at the building industry. In addition, websites of five construction companies leading in innovation of sustainable construction were analysed. These five companies were identified based on their role in pilot and demonstration projects to develop new solutions for the reduction of emissions in buildings.

In the UK, the textual narratives of innovation that address the low-carbon agenda at the policy level are identified and analysed from 15 reports published by government and professional institutions, which are publicly available. This is followed by the analysis of narratives of innovation that address low-carbon agenda at the firm level through corporate reports and strategies. For consistency purposes, five UK construction firms (both owners and suppliers) are selected and are extensively promoting sustainable innovations through textual narratives evident through firm websites (Table 12.3 in the Appendix provides more details about the Norwegian and UK companies' backgrounds).

Findings

Narratives of sustainable innovation in Norway

Constructing firm identities as leaders of sustainable innovation

Interaction between policy and industry appears intertwined in the role of transitioning to low-emission society on a policy level to already having leaders of low-emission building within the building sector. Norwegian policy identifies its roles of sustainability as becoming and transitioning. The "green shift" sums up the need for Norway to change over the next 30 to 50 years. Innovation and technology development are key elements of Norway's green shift to become a low-emission society by 2050 (New Emission Commitment for Norway for 2030, 2014; Innovation Norway: Financing of Environmental Technologies, 2017). While Norway positions itself within the global context, it also positions itself as a country that 'must find its own way'. The Norwegian government works with the UN and the EU to reduce climate emissions and advocates a long-term global objective of approaching net zero emissions by 2050. Norway's intended national determined contribution (INDC) includes the reduction of emissions to at least 40% by 2030 compared with the 1990 levels. These targets are ambitious and push industries in Norway to think innovatively to address targets. The five companies examined in this study indicate that they are not in transition but primarily identify themselves as 'leaders'. The companies use language of being "first", "leading", being "in front" or aims to be leading. This type of narrative indicates that companies, which are leading, do not need to go through the transition process as they are already ahead of other similar industries as illustrated in the following quote:

> [Firm B] is in the front on developing and building future homes which consider energy and environmentally friendly buildings.

The explicit intention illustrated through these narratives is the performative action that the building industry takes the responsibility to reduce carbon emissions seriously and include it as part of their corporate goals. They identify actions of what they do in their firm in sustainable future-oriented ways as opposed to the established practices within their field.

Authoritative narrative of advice giving on current standards and regulations

While the building industry narrative does appear to be acting on the call to meet targets, energy performance targets are not a specifically well established policy field in Norway's building industry (Knudsen and Dalen, 2014). Priority areas within the climate change agenda are:

- Reduction of emission from the transport sector;
- Development of low-emission industrial technology and clean production technology;
- Carbon capture and storage;
- Strengthening Norway's role as a supplier of renewable energy;
- Environmentally sound shipping (New Emission Commitment for Norway for 2030 – towards Joint Fulfilment with the EU, 2014).

However, the building industry is quite active in the development of legislation for the energy performance of buildings. The technical requirements in buildings, TEK 10 and TEK 17, address energy regulations primarily in new buildings and for very large renovations. The building industry was quite critical of TEK 10 but were active in providing input for TEK 17 (https://dibk.no/byggeregler/tek/). In 2012, the Passive House as a requirement changed to a voluntary initiative due to controversies within the industry (Müller and Berker, 2013) but was changed back to mandatory in 2017. There are two Passive House Standards in Norway: NS3700 for residential and NS3701 for non-residential buildings. The reason for this is that there was controversy on the requirement for energy supply for single-family homes and to what extent climate change mitigation should be included. Controversy also emerged due to calculated increased costs of constructing to the passive house standard, which hinders market penetration in Norway. However, those supportive of passive house approaches argue that the standard prescribes performance of the dwelling but leaves open the choice of solutions to achieve the standard. The openness indicates that it is up to the industry to find innovative solutions to sustainable building. Therefore, having leaders of sustainable innovation within the construction sector is important to reach passive house standards.

Being a leader and champion of innovation solutions for sustainable construction enables such companies to form a narrative of authority. This narrative is reflected in the advice-giving services offered to companies who are not leaders of sustainable building practices and who may be in a position of transitioning. Companies examined in this study can market their position of acting on green innovation to be authoritative figures not only to policymakers who integrate advice into standards but within their own industry. Therefore, companies who have a leader narrative embedded into a textual form on their website also enables an authoritative narrative to give advice to companies not at the forefront of sustainable building:

> [Firm E] is involved in a number of state and international institutions in connection with product development and certification. The requirements ensure that you as a customer or consumer make the right and proper choice.

Being a leader enables these companies to provide reassurances to potential customers that their experience leads to the "right and proper choices".

Shaping innovation solutions to meet environment and social demands

Policy initiatives support innovation solutions support Norway's climate change goals through a strong economic narrative. *Energiøkonomisering* – ENØK – is the Norwegian term that encapsulates how energy utilisation is directly associated with cost savings, profit or expense (Ryhaug and Sørensen, 2009). National policy instruments do not openly propose innovation but set up economic frames, e.g. funding bodies, in which innovation is attainable. Enova is an important actor in the implementation of new energy performance technologies to both private and public sectors. Enova, together with Energy Fund and Innovation Norway, offers subsidies and capital loans for development and demonstration of new and existing building projects related to energy reduction, but these loans often come with restrictions that reduce the scope of innovation (www.enova. no; www.innovasjonnorge.no). There is no clear guidance to industry on how to attain energy targets, but finances are available to reach them. Hence, the narrative of energy economising dominates Norwegian policy.

Policy does not indicate the use of specific energy solutions for the building industry, but legislation and regulation nudge the industry towards sustainable solutions. The firm websites in Norway do not refer to an economic narrative to any great degree. While research studies indicate financial profitability being a factor for developing sustainable solutions (e.g. Lindkvist, Karlsson, Sørnes, and Wyckmans, 2014), companies do not explicitly refer to an economic narrative but focus more on social and environmental narrative – specifically, in how sustainable solutions can benefit wider environment and social goals:

[Firm A] The [name] project uses new environmental technologies for renewable energy production in the Norwegian context; this includes a small-scale combined heat and power plant which is based on biomass gasification.

The type of "environmental technologies" mainly refers to renewable energy and energy reduction solutions. Companies also refer to technology in terms of preparing for the future but do so in terms of wider social issues. Firm B refers to developing 'welfare technologies' for 'future new buildings' that enable the "elderly and ill [to] live longer in their own homes"; this may allude to the need for the older population to live in their homes longer. Firm D use the green technology narrative as a form of 'defence against air, water and wasted energy' – elements that are impacted by climate change. The economic frames through policy level initiatives in Norway enable financing of social and environment visions within the building industry, primarily through green technology solutions.

Beyond ambitions: Technical narrative to innovation

The level of ambition in sustainable innovation projects is often decided by the technical energy performance of the building. The minimum requirements for the industry to meet are set by policy, so in this way policy is pulling industry to be sustainable in their building practices. At the same time, these minimum requirements allude to policymakers being heedful of energy ambitions. Policy does not push the industry to be more ambitious than the minimum standard. However, sustainable innovation in industry influences this technical performance standard as minimum requirements increase as technology facilitates further energy reductions in buildings. These minimum performance standards are in a constant state of flux, and requirements have become progressively tougher in line with technology development in sustainable solutions, such as TEK 10 in 2010 moving to TEK17 in 2017. The link between industry innovation in technology and policy is visible within companies who identify themselves as going beyond present ambitions:

> [Firm D's] Building Envelope offers solutions that meet or exceed codes, help extend building life, and help reduce fossil fuel consumption.

If these companies wish to maintain their leading narrative, thinking in terms of meeting standards is not enough. At the start of a project, there may be an ambition to meet current energy standards, but when that project is complete, a more ambitious standard could replace the original standard. Companies who are leading innovators of sustainable construction are prepared to go further to achieve as high result as possible.

The analysis outlines the narrative interactions between the Norwegian construction sector (which identifies itself within a green innovation narrative) and emission policy reduction from legislation on the one hand and regulations (based on related policy documentation) on the other. Table 12.1 provides an outline of the narrative interactions between documented policy narratives and building industry firm narratives. These narrative interactions are viewed in the way policy-setting sustainable targets lead firms with the expertise to meet these standards to construct their identity as leaders of sustainable innovation. The formalised policy-setting targets are developed in regulatory standards that facilitate firms who identify themselves within the narrative of being sustainable innovation leaders to further this narrative as authoritative and as givers of advice that they build into their services. The funding available from public bodies builds on the narrative of economising, providing economic frames to firms that work within their narrative of shaping innovation solutions to meet environmental and social demands. Finally, policy has a heedful narrative in meeting targets to reduce carbon emissions, while firms react within a narrative of either meeting or going beyond ambitions through the technical discourse of innovation.

Table 12.1 Narrative interaction between Norwegian building industry policy and firm levels

Industrial policy level narratives	Firm level narratives (Norwegian translation into English)	Narrative interaction
Setting ambitious emission targets	Firm A is the first member of the construction and management industry to build a zero-emission building at the highest currently defined level.	Constructing identities as leaders of sustainable innovation
	Firm B is in the front on developing and building future homes that consider energy and environmentally friendly buildings.	
	Firm C is Norway's' leading technical firm. . . . Firm C's technology competence and comprehensive service offerings, our experts prepare energy-efficient life-cycle solutions. . .	
	Firm D has been the industry leader since it invented [xxx] more than 30 years ago.	
	Firm E: It participates in [xxx] in order to be at the forefront regarding the development of sustainable and energy-efficient windows and doors.	
Regulatory	Firm A has advisors and concept developers who can recommend environmentally friendly use of resources, reduced land use and high environmental standards.	Authoritative: Advice giving
	Firm C: Our unique services covers the whole lifecycle: design, building and operations.	

Industrial policy level narratives	Firm level narratives (Norwegian translation into English)	Narrative interaction
	Firm E is involved in a number of state and international institutions in connection with product development and certification. The requirements ensure that you as a customer or consumer make the right and proper choice.	
Economic frames to attain innovative solution or green technology	Firm A: The (name) project uses new environmental technologies for renewable energy production in the Norwegian context; this includes a small-scale combined heat and power plant that is based on biomass gasification.	Shaping innovation solutions to meet environment and social demands
	Firm B: Welfare technology in new buildings: The 108 apartments are based on smart house technology that can control light and heat and that can easily be extended to other functions so that elderly and ill can live longer in their own homes. These experiences will be continued in our future new buildings as a foundation for smarter homes.	
	Firm D: Whether it's a skyscraper or a single-family home, the Building Envelope is an essential line of defence against air, water and wasted energy.	
Heedful ambitions: Minimum requirements	Firm A: The pilot project is characterised by green innovation, and it is likely that it will do more than achieve its ZEB-COM ambition.	Beyond ambitions: Technical discourse to innovation
	Firm B: For the moment we have lots of projects that focus on building passive house and low-energy homes. All our projects have low energy as a minimum requirement and are therefore better than the technical requirements.	
	Firm C: With our energy consulting services, you can be sure that we comply with all applicable laws, regulations and regulations. This includes current EU rules, which include the EU's climate and climate policy. As a result of the EEA agreement, large parts of the EU's environment and climate policy have been incorporated into Norwegian legislation.	
	Firm D's Building Envelope offers solutions that meet or exceed codes, help extend building life, and help reduce fossil fuel consumption.	

Narratives of sustainable innovation and their interactions at industrial policy and firm levels in the UK

The interaction between narratives of innovation at industrial policy and firm levels

As outlined earlier in the chapter, sustainable innovation is in the agenda of the UK construction sector. The UK construction sector policy reports set the target for the need for innovations that address the 'green', 'sustainable' agenda. There is a strong vision in the UK construction sector as a whole in meeting the sustainability targets for 2030 and 2050. This grand narrative of low-carbon, sustainable innovation at the macro level is highly visible. The analysis of corporate reports and strategies from both owner and supplier UK construction firms demonstrate the alignment with the macro-level narrative of sustainable innovation identified across a number of industry and government reports. Innovation and sustainability are recognised as key organisational values being represented in the form of firm brochures and symbolically evident in interior designs within selected firms. Some UK construction firms are already recognised as 'sustainable innovation leaders' through industry awards, as illustrated in the following quotation:

> [Firm F] Judges praised the company's 'exceptional progress on carbon reduction, which earlier this year included a pledge to halve carbon emissions by 2020, and the scale of ambition on sustainability. The company is already one of the only carbon neutral construction companies and also invests in communities.'

There are various industry sustainability awards through which UK construction firms become recognised by others as leaders in sustainable innovation.

A number of UK construction sector firms are in the process of becoming leaders of sustainable innovation:

> [Firm I] strives to deliver sustainable solutions guided by values. It strives to limit the environmental impact of activities.

In order to be recognised as sustainable leaders, UK construction firms take into consideration environmental concerns, reduction of carbon emissions, and improved efficiency through innovative technologies. These firms also recognise the need to become a more sustainable, more innovative sector as a whole.

More specific narratives of sustainable innovations in UK construction firms

The UK government and industrial policy not only set ambitious targets but also aims to incentivise the supply chain (e.g. through awards) to come up with and implement sustainable innovation solutions. The UK construction sector firms interact with the narrative of sustainable innovation at the national and industrial policy levels by constructing emergent narratives and acting on them. For example, firm H focuses on the following key activities:

- Management of environmental impact
- Materials and waste reduction
- Supply chain relationships
- Employee skill set
- Apprentices
- Engagement with local communities

The sustainability road map is used as a guidance that then becomes adjusted to different project types (e.g. highways, local projects, infrastructure, energy and power). Sustainability strategies have become publicly available. These are used for promoting themselves as sustainable leaders among competitors and for gaining market shares. Job roles with 'sustainability' in the titles have emerged in the UK construction sector firms. For instance, firm G has a long-term ambition to have a positive impact and reduce its own emissions as part of their journey. By working in collaboration with other suppliers and clients, they help to combat climate change and reduce costs of constructing and operating buildings:

> Our teams assist clients to identify, develop and then achieve their sustainable goals, focusing on issues such as in-use performance and cost-effective outcomes over the lifecycle of the building.

Firm G uses digital technologies for construction sites and started calculating and setting targets to reduce wider impact. Among other sustainability activities are employee training and attracting new talent in the sector. At the heart of the narratives of sustainable innovation of many UK construction firms are health and well-being.

The future-oriented narratives of innovation that address the climate change agenda

The narratives of sustainable innovation clearly connect the past with present and future. Companies promote sustainability and innovation in various ways: creating new job roles, formalising sustainability strategy, with an emphasis placed on the innovation. Of particular note is the future aspect of narratives of sustainable innovation. Whilst the UK construction firms self-present themselves as leaders in sustainability and innovation, they aim to become even more sustainable and innovative in the future. They develop the action plans encouraging innovation that delivers sustainable outcomes. For example, firm F developed an action plan to transform the firm to become more sustainable and innovative, which includes the following actions:

- Retain carbon standards.
- Develop a 'connected' sustainability reporting method to account for the value and impact of our strategy.

- Publicly report divisional performance through group review and client workshops.
- Collaborate and network across the industry to improve standards.
- Develop innovative solutions and bring them to the market.
- Identify and share learning and best practice internally and across the industry.
- Actively work to embed a culture of sustainability in our wider supply chain workforce and our customers, clients, householders and end users.

It is evident from the publicly available data (e.g. websites, corporate reports) that UK construction industry firms collaborate and network across owners, suppliers and users to work together in meeting the policy targets set at a national level. They aim to embed the culture of sustainability across the industry as a whole.

The analysis outlines the narrative interactions between the UK construction sector industrial policy reports in promoting the need for innovation that address environmental issues and how firms respond to the targets set, as presented in Table 12.2. It demonstrates how selected firms respond to the narratives of sustainable innovation identified at the industrial policy levels and how narratives interact through time and their implications for the future (e.g. strategising, constructing identities and images, shaping policy agenda).

Table 12.2 Narrative interaction between narratives of sustainable innovation at the industrial policy and firm levels

Industrial policy– level narratives	Firm level narratives	Narrative interaction
Setting ambitious carbon reduction targets	*Firm F* is recognised as a Sustainable Leader who received an industry award. The firm has made progress on carbon reduction. It aims to halve carbon emissions by 2020. It invests in communities. Formal sustainability strategy. The targets are: reduction of carbon by 50% by 2020, reduction of waste by 60% by 2020, and enhancement of the life chances of 10,000 young people by 2020.	Constructing identities as leaders of sustainable innovation Demonstrating leadership through the awards and performance improvement
	Firm G cares about a more sustainable future through vision and performance. It wants to contribute to the wider development and British economy. Sustainability is one of the key organisational values. The long-term target is to reduce emissions by working with the supply chain and clients.	Developing strategies to become sustainable innovation leaders
	Firm H: The main goal of the firm strategy is to become a sustainable leader to a	

Industrial policy–level narratives	Firm level narratives	Narrative interaction
	level that would push the market. They try to act beyond compliance so that they can step ahead of competitors. The sustainability road map is presented on the website, which is about global business strategy. All the activities come with an action plan that is communicated to all managers. There is a formal role of Heads of Sustainability.	
	Firm I aims to become a leader in sustainability. Sustainability strategy is published in the firm website with the specific focus on innovative solutions.	
	Firm J: Sustainability is how they do business every day. It is one of the organisational values.	
Pursuing a low-carbon agenda to stimulate innovation	*Firm F* sets ambitions under the themes of people, responsibility, energy/climate change, smarter use of natural resources.	Constructing more specific narratives of sustainable innovation
	Firm H works hard to engage with the whole supply chain to reduce waste through better design, better control of materials on-site. As an industry leader, they see sustainability responsibilities extending beyond their own business. It continues to improve efficiencies in the business through rigorous management as well as using new technologies for construction sites and starting to circulate and set targets for reducing wider impacts.	
	Firm G: We look at our sustainability strategy from both environmental and social perspectives and take a business approach to it.	
	Firm I focuses on five sustainability areas: Ethics, Environment, Health and Safety, Diversity and Inclusion, Corporate Community Investment. All of these activities are environmentally oriented.	
	Firm J is passionate about the world and is committed to protect and enhance the species. They use smart technologies to address industry targets. Smart technology events focus on how they use information and data in real time to make decisions.	

(*Continued*)

Table 12.2 (Continued)

Industrial policy–level narratives	Firm level narratives	Narrative interaction
Setting the future beyond present ambitions	Firm F is taking old buildings and turning them into new facilities for future generations.	Constructing strategies for the future
	Firm F published a sustainability development strategy about transforming tomorrow – an action plan with ambitions for 2020. They construct narratives of the future. The key ambitions are to demonstrate leadership, develop innovative business models and solutions, encourage innovation that delivers a sustainable outcome and lead cross-industry collaboration to share vision and innovation for the future.	Shaping identities as sustainable innovation leaders

Discussion

In this chapter, we found that narratives help to achieve consistency in establishing the alignment of innovation that address the sustainability agenda across industry, firm, and project levels through the connection to national and international policy. In our findings, the meaning of 'sustainable innovation' is constructed based on the interaction between a top-down policy approach for the construction sector to react to the climate change agenda and bottom-up in the way leading construction firms push the boundaries of climate change targets. In this way, innovation connectivity is prominently pushing and pulling in both directions between firms and policy levels.

The analysis indicates that there is a connectivity between Norway and the UK in how they understand sustainable innovation within a cross-level approaches from industrial policy and project-based firm narratives. International agendas to reduce carbon emissions are formalised in EU directives and translated into national policy. Our study in Norway and the UK exemplifies the interaction and connectivity between the policy narrative to reduce carbon emissions and the construction sector firms. The sustainable reduction of carbon emissions requires this connectivity at the global, national, industry and firm levels. It is evident from the data that the government initiatives in Norway and the UK do not go far enough with innovation for sustainability in the construction sector. Yet it is key to industry players, owners and suppliers who practice sustainable innovation, and our evidence shows that these players are willing to go beyond the expectations laid out in policy. These firms respond to the climate change agenda at the industrial policy level by formalising their sustainability strategies; using innovative and sustainable technologies; creating new job roles with sustainability and innovation in their titles; creating an environment and culture of sustainability and innovation that is built into their firm's narratives. In Norway, the focus on economy and sustainable innovation is prevalent in policy, which supports the perspective of earlier studies on innovation and policy perspectives (Whyte and Sexton, 2011). Economic frames incorporate financial incentives for sustainable innovation on the policy level and underpin these processes on the industry level. At the same time, building firms are pushing their strategy to benefit both the environment and society. In the UK, the construction/infrastructure sector creates an environment to incentivise sustainable innovations with emphasis on environment, society and not just economy. The emphasis is also placed on people's mindsets, behaviours and culture of being and becoming more innovative and sustainable firms and sector as a whole.

In both Norway and UK, a 'sustainable leader' means connecting other industries to the climate change agenda through an advice-giving narrative. This narrative comes from a perspective of a marketable authority offered in the form of a service. It supports the perspective that green innovation is aiming to increase the quality of construction projects and develop collaboration across the sector as described by Bossink (2004). However, this collaboration may not necessarily be equal as a distinction arises between leaders and novices. Both narratives from industries in Norway and the UK set themselves up as leaders of sustainable innovation, and the narrative in both countries connects to the narrative of policy using text such as 'reduce fossil fuel consumption' or 'zero emission' in Norway and 'carbon reduction' or 'reduce emissions' in the UK. Companies are aware of the need to meet climate change agendas within their own country and relate these agendas to their own narratives on the image of the firm. And it is through a continuous process of narrative interaction that shapes policymaking, strategising, identity and image construction.

Both the Norwegian and the UK governments have regulatory policies that play an important role in shaping the direction of innovation and change in the construction sector (Blayse and Manley, 2004; Bossink, 2002). At the same time, firms in the UK and Norway also appear to be pushing the boundaries of what is ambitious to reduce target emissions set at the national level. This is evident in our data under the narrative to go 'beyond ambitions' either by going beyond current standards in projects as in Norway or by developing strategies that incorporate action plans for 2020 through a future vision as in the UK. Companies that are setting themselves up as leaders of sustainable innovation legitimise themselves through connecting to policy by being authorities on the standards and regulations. They also do this by going beyond legislative requirements (e.g. adopting innovative sustainable technologies and approaches, creating new job roles with "innovation" and "sustainability" in their titles). Hence, narratives of innovation that address climate agenda in the construction sectors in Norway and the UK are being underpinned through connectivity to policy narratives.

Figure 12.1 presents an empirically derived model of interactions between narratives of sustainable innovation at international, industrial policy and firm levels and their implications for practice. Policy is pushing industry to innovate

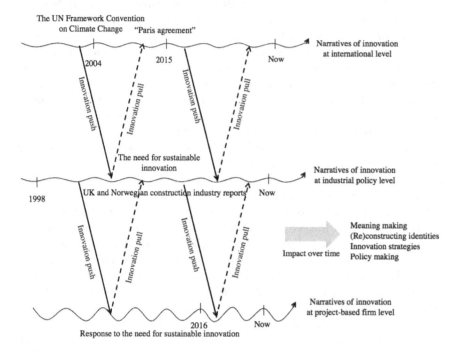

Figure 12.1 Interactions between narratives of sustainable innovation at multi-levels and their implications

in meeting the international climate change agenda, while project-based firms are incorporating this push as part of innovative product and service solutions (Barrett and Sexton, 2006; Winch, 2005). The figure shows a continuous interaction between narratives of innovation constructed at the international and industrial policy levels ('innovation push') and how project-based firms respond ('innovation pull') to the narrative at the policy level. The innovation push is exemplified by key moments in time such as the UN Framework Convention on Climate Change in 2004 and the Paris Agreement, which set international agendas to focus on climate change. In turn, this international agenda pushes national policy to focus on climate change within policy strategic documents, regulation and standards as illustrated in our studies in the UK and Norway. National climate changing strategies are translated into carbon-reducing targets to initiate an innovation pull in industry and, in our study, the building industry to react. This innovation pull does not come at once but evolves over time through reconstructing identities and creating innovative solutions that also influence policy to push industry to innovate further. The continuous process of narrative interactions has important implications for policy making, forming and updating policies and strategies, constructing identities and images.

Conclusions

This chapter has explored narratives of innovation that address climate change targets set in the construction sector on the international and national levels. Focusing mainly on textual narratives enabled an understanding of how a cross-level approach of innovation from policy and firm is connected. It is evident that narratives of low-carbon, zero-emission innovations have significant rhetorical ground internationally. Government policies, reports and regulations set the targets for low-carbon, energy-efficient industry towards 2020 and 2050. In response, construction sector firms come up with new innovative solutions to address the challenges faced with climate change. The innovation push and pull are in a continuous process of interaction that plays an important role in constructing 'green' and 'sustainable' construction sector identity and image. Policy is clearly setting the agenda to push industry to sustainable innovation, but firms go beyond ambitions by pushing policy to be less heedful and more ambitious in the energy-reducing targets. This type of interaction means that firms and their representatives need to be involved in the discussion with policymakers on what type of ambitious targets need to be set in the policy documents and agenda. In an explicit and interactive connectivity between firms and policy, both continue to push and pull each other but do so in more open discursive ways (e.g. forums, platforms, conversations). Industry and policymakers should work together to shape and promote sustainable innovation that goes beyond economising but incorporates social aspects and the connectivity of sustainable innovation to the local and global environments.

In this work, we have primarily focused on the link between narrative text in policy documents and industry text from websites and reports. However, further work is needed to look at best practice projects in how the narratives work amongst different building practices and construction projects. There is scope to go further with research into symbolic and spoken narratives of sustainable innovation represented in visual data, videos and conversation/interviews. Narratives of low-carbon, zero-energy innovations serve the purpose of making everybody aware of the sustainability agenda and of the need to adapt to changes in the climate. Examining innovation connectivity through narratives plays an important role in setting visions and strategies for the direction the construction sector is going to take in the future.

Acknowledgement

The authors would like to extend their gratitude to the editors of this book, Malena Ingemansson Havenvid, Åse Linné, Lena Bygballe and Chris Harty for their comments, as well as for the early comments from Finn Orstavik and input from participants of the ENRIC workshops. They are thankful also for the FP7 ZenN grant agreement no. 314363, which partially funded data collection in Norway, and Taru Uusinoka for assistance in gathering Norwegian policy documents. The authors also thank the ESRC grant (ref. ES/R011567/1) for supporting UK-based research.

References

Abolafia, M.Y. (2010) 'Narrative construction as sensemaking: How a central bank thinks', *Organization Studies*, 31(3), pp. 349–367.

Alonso, M.J. and Stene, J. (2013) *State of the Art of Nearly Zero Energy Buildings Country Report IEA HPP Annex 40 Task 1*. Norway – International Energy Agency/Heat Pump Programme.

Alvesson, M. and Robertson, M. (2015) 'Money matters: Teflonic identity manoeuvring in the investment banking sector', *Organization Studies*, 37(1), pp. 7–34.

Baek, C.H. and Park, S.H. (2012) 'Policy measures to overcome barriers to energy renovation of existing buildings', *Renewable and Sustainable Energy Reviews*, 16, pp. 3239–3947.

Barrett, P. and Sexton, M. (2006) 'Innovation in small, project-based construction firms', *British Journal of Management*, 17(4), pp. 331–346.

Bartel, C.A. and Garud, R. (2009) 'The role of narratives in sustaining organizational innovation', *Organization Science*, 20(1), pp. 107–117.

Beckman, S. and Marry, M. (2009) 'Design and innovation through storytelling', *International Journal of Innovation Science*, 1(4), pp. 151–160.

Blayse, A.M. and Manley, K. (2004) 'Key influences on construction innovation', *Construction Innovation*, 4(3), pp. 143–154.

Boje, D.M. (2001) *Narrative methods for organizational and communication research*. London: Sage Publications.

Bossink, B.A.G. (2002) 'A Dutch public-private strategy for innovation in sustainable construction', *Construction Management and Economics*, 20(7), pp. 633–642.

Bossink, B.A.G. (2004) 'Managing drivers of innovation in construction networks', *Journal of Construction Engineering and Management*, 130(3), pp. 337–345.

Bourne, H. and Jenkins, M. (2013) 'Organizational values: A dynamic perspective', *Organization Studies*, 34(4), pp. 495–514.

Brown, A.D., Stacey, P. and Nandhakumar, J. (2008) 'Making sense of sensemaking narratives', *Human Relations*, 61(8), pp. 1035–1062.

Brown, A.D. and Thompson, E.R. (2013) 'A narrative approach to strategy-as-practice', *Business History*, 55(7), pp. 1143–1167.

Buchanan, D. and Dawson, P. (2007) 'Discourse and audience: Organizational change as multi-story process', *Journal of Management Studies*, 44(5), pp. 669–686.

Building our industrial strategy: Green paper (2017) London: HM Government.

Construction 2025: Industrial strategy: Government and industry in partnership (2013) London: HM Government.

Cunliffe, A. and Coupland, C. (2011) 'From hero to villain to hero: Making experience sensible through embodies narrative sensemaking', *Human Relations*, 65(1), pp. 63–88.

Czarniawska, B. (1997) *A narrative approach to organization studies*. London: Sage Publications.

Czarniawska, B. (2010) 'The uses of narratology in social and political studies', *Critical Policy Studies*, 4(1), pp. 58–76.

Czarniawska, B. (2016) 'Performativity of social sciences as seen by organization scholar', *European Management Journal*, 34(4), pp. 315–318.

Dailey, S.L. and Browning, L. (2014) 'Retelling stories in organizations: Understanding the functions of narrative repetition', *Academy of Management Review*, 39(1), pp. 22–43.

Dewick, P. and Miozzo, M. (2002) 'Sustainable technologies and the innovation-regulation paradox', *Futures*, 34(9–10), pp. 823–840.

Denning, S. (2005) 'Transformational innovation: A journey by narrative', *Strategy and Leadership*, 33(3), pp. 11–16.

Dewick, P. and Miozzo, M. (2002) 'Sustainable technologies and the innovation-regulation paradox', *Futures*, 34(9–10), pp. 823–840.

Dobusch, L. and Schoeneborn, D. (2015) 'Fluidity, identity, and organizationality: The communicative constitution of anonymous', *Journal of Management Studies*, 52(8), pp. 1005–1035.

Doganova, L. and Eyquem-Renault, M. (2009) 'What do business models do? Innovation devices in technology entrepreneurship', *Research Policy*, 38(10), pp. 1559–1570.

EU Emissions Trading System (2016) https://ec.europa.eu/clima/sites/clima/files/factsheet_ets_en.pdf. Accessed 3 May 2017.

Fenton, C. and Langley, A. (2011) 'Strategy as practice and the narrative turn', *Organization Studies*, 32(9), pp. 1171–1196.

Garud, R., Dunbar, R.L.M. and Bartel, C.A. (2011) 'Dealing with unusual experiences: A narrative perspective on organizational learning', *Organization Science*, 22(3), pp. 587–601.

Garud, R., Schildt, H.A. and Lant, T.K. (2014) 'Entrepreneurial storytelling, future expectations, and the paradox of legitimacy', *Organization Science*, 25(5), pp. 1479–1492.

Gioia, D.A., Schultz, M. and Corley, K.G. (2000) 'Organizational identity, image, and adaptive instability', *Academy of Management Review*, 25(1), pp. 63–81.

Gluch, P. (2009) 'Unfolding roles and identities of professionals in construction projects: Exploring the informality of practices', *Construction Management and Economics*, 27(10), pp. 959–968.

Gluch, P., Gustafsson, M. and Thuvander, L. (2009) 'An absorptive capacity model for green innovation and performance in the construction industry', *Construction Management and Economics*, 27(5), pp. 451–464.

Hobday, M. (2000) 'The project-based organisation: An ideal form for management of complex products and systems?' *Research Policy*, 29(7/8), pp. 871–893.

Humphreys, M. and Brown, A.D. (2002) 'Narratives of organizational identity and identification: A case of hegemony and resistance', *Organization Studies*, 23(3), pp. 421–447.

Hansen, P.H. (2007) 'Organizational culture and organizational change: A narrative analysis of the transformation of savings banks in Denmark, 1965–1990', *Enterprise and Society*, 8(4), pp. 920–953.

Innovation System (2017) London: Nesta.

Innovation Norway: Financing of environmental technologies. www.innovasjonnorge.no/no/finansiering/miljoteknologi/. Accessed 1 March 2017.

Knudsen, J.K. and Dalen, K. (2014) 'Policy framework for the interaction between buildings and the energy system' in *Norway. Report WP4 INTERACT*.

Lavenergiprogrammet *Hva er et passivhus?* www.lavenergiprogrammet.no/artikkel/hva-er-et-passivhus/. Accessed 1 February 2016.

Lindkvist, C., Karlsson, A., Sørnes, K. and Wyckmans, A. (2014) 'Barriers and challenges in nZEB project in Sweden and Norway', *Energy Procedia*, 58, pp. 199–206.

Low carbon construction: Innovation and growth team (2010) London: HM Government.

Lundvall, B.-A. (2007) 'National innovation systems – analytical concept and development tool', *Industry and Innovation*, 14(1), pp. 95–119.

Maclean, M., Harvey, C. and Chia, R. (2011) 'Sensemaking, storytelling and the legitimization of elite business careers' *Human Relations*, 65(1), pp. 17–40.

Müller, L. and Berker, T. (2013) 'Passive House at the crossroads: The past and the present of voluntary standard that managed to bridge the energy efficiency gap', *Energy Policy*, 60, pp. 586–593.

New emission commitment for Norway for 2030 – towards joint fulfilment with the EU (2014) Norway: Norwegian Ministry of Climate and Environment.

Opoku, A., Ahmed, V. and Cruickshank, H. (2015) 'Leadership style of sustainability professionals in the UK construction industry', *Built Environment Project and Asset Management*, 5(3), pp. 184–201.

Orstavik, F., Dainty, A. and Abbott, C. (2015) *Construction innovation*. Chichester: John Wiley & Sons.

Rehan, R. and Nehdi, M. (2005) 'Carbon dioxide emission and climate change: Policy implications for the cement industry', *Environmental Science and Policy*, 8(2), pp. 105–114.

Reissner, S.C. (2005) 'Learning and innovation: A narrative analysis', *Journal of Organizational Change Management*, 18(5), pp. 482–494.

Rhodes, C. and Brown, A.D. (2005) 'Narrative, organizations and research', *International Journal of Management Reviews*, 7(3), pp. 167–188.

Ryhaug, M. and Sørensen, K.H. (2009) 'How energy efficiency fails in the building industry', *Energy Policy*, 37, pp. 984–991.

Schultz, M. and Hernes, T. (2013) 'A temporal perspective on organizational identity' *Organization Science*, 24(1), pp. 1–21.

Schweber, L. and Leiringer, R. (2012) 'Beyond the technical: A snapshot of energy and buildings research', *Building Research and Information*, 40(4), pp. 481–492.

Seidel, V.P. and O'Mahony, S. (2014) 'Managing the repertoire: Stories, metaphors, prototypes and concept coherence in product innovation', *Organization Science*, 25(3), pp. 691–712.

Sergeeva, N. (2016) 'What makes an "innovation champion"?', *European Journal of Innovation Management*, 19(1), pp. 72–89.

Sims, D. (2003) 'Between the millstones: A narrative account of the vulnerability of middle managers' storying', *Human Relations*, 56(10), pp. 1195–1211.

Sonenshein, S. (2010) 'We're changing – Or are we? Untangling the role of progressive, regressive, and stability narratives during strategic change implementation', *Academy Management Journal*, 53(3), pp. 477–512.

Taylor, A. and Greve, H.R. (2006) 'Superman or the fantastic four? Knowledge combination and experience in innovative teams', *Academy of Management Journal*, 49(4), pp. 723–740.

Winch, G.M. (1998) 'Zephyrs of creative destruction: Understanding the management of innovation in construction', *Building Research and Information*, 26(4), pp. 268–279.

Winch, G.M. (2005) 'Managing complex connective processes – innovation brokering', in Manseau, A. and Shields, R. (eds.), *Building Tomorrow: Innovation in Construction and Engineering*. London: Ashgate, pp. 81–101.

Whyte, J. and Sexton, M. (2011) 'Motivations for innovation in the built environment: New direction for research', *Building Research and Information*, 39(5), pp. 473–482.

Vaara, E., Sonenshein, S. and Boje, D. (2016) 'Sources of stability and change in organizations: Approaches and directions for future research', *The Academy of Management Annals*, 10(1), pp. 495–560.

Appendix

Table 12.3 Background of companies included in the analysis

Firm Code	Background
Firm A	Norwegian large property owner with a portfolio of 2.8 million square metres of buildings, as well as a number of buildings under construction
Firm B	Norwegian real estate developer that carries out all phases of building projects
Firm C	Norwegian firm that designs, builds, operates and maintains technical solutions for buildings, infrastructures and industries
Firm D	Norwegian firm that develops Building Envelop solutions
Firm E	Norwegian manufacturer of windows and doors
Firm F	UK leading construction and property services owner and operator
Firm G	UK construction provider of engineering solutions for rail, roads, water and land
Firm H	UK leading housebuilding, regeneration contracting firm
Firm I	UK construction and facilities firm
Firm J	UK project development and construction group

Table 12.4 Catalogue of Norwegian national policy relevant to sustainability in the built environment*

Land legislation	Energy efficiency legislation	Renewable energy legislation
Act (LOV-1999-03-26-17) on Tenancy www.regjeringen.no/en/dokumenter/the-tenancy-act/id270390/ Husleieloven (LOV-1999-03-26-17) In Norwegian: www.regjeringen.no/no/dokumenter/husleieloven/id270390/ Planning and Building Act In English: www.regjeringen.no/en/dokumenter/planning-building-act/id570450/ Plan og Bygningsloven (LOV-1985-06-14-77) In Norwegian: www.regjeringen.no/no/dokumenter/plan-og-bygningsloven/id570450/ Greenhouse Gas Emission Trading Act In English (for information only): www.regjeringen.no/en/dokumenter/greenhouse-gas-emission-trading-act/id172242/ Klimakvoteloven (LOV-2004-12-17-99) in Norwegian: https://lovdata.no/dokument/NL/lov/2004-12-17-99 Pollution Control Act In English (for information only): www.regjeringen.no/en/dokumenter/pollution-control-act/id171893/ Forurensningsloven LOV-1981-03-13-6 in Norwegian: www.regjeringen.no/no/dokumenter/forurensningsloven/id171893/ Climate policy www.regjeringen.no/contentassets/aa70cfe177d2433192570893d72b117a/no/pdfs/stm201120012021000dddpdfs.pdf	Regulations on Technical Requirements on Building Works English version (not approved by parliament): https://dibk.no/globalassets/byggeregler/regulations_on_technical_requirements_for_building_works.pdf Suggestion for new Technical Requirements on Building Works TEK17 In English (notification of regulations on Technical Requirements for Building Works –summary of the consultation paper): http://webcache.googleusercontent.com/search?q=cache:Ey2Nsx3luYgJ:ec.europa.eu/growth/tools-databases/tris/mt/index.cfm/search%3Ftrisaction%3Dsearch.detail%26year%3D2016%26num%3D9041%26Lang%3DEN+&cd=2&hl=en&ct=clnk&gl=no Suggestion for new building regulations (TEK17) https://svar.dibk.no/nb/docs/37731/Chapter/41072 Guidance on Technical Requirements for Construction Works, chapter 14: energy https://dibk.no/globalassets/endringshistorikk/byggteknisk-forskrift/kapittel-14-energi_byggteknisk-forskrift_2015.pdf Guide for Energy efficiency measures of buildings www.miljokommune.no/Temaoversikt/Klima/Tiltaksguide1/Energieffektivisering-i-bygg-og-eiendom/ Act on energy reporting In Norwegian only: https://lovdata.no/dokument/SF/forskrift/2012-12-07-1158 Regulations on energy reporting In Norwegian only: https://lovdata.no/dokument/SF/forskrift/2012-12-07-1158	Agreement between the Ministry of Oil Energy and Enova on supporting green energy technologies www.enova.no/download?objectPath=upload_images/8BC6BD7A24B2439DB806F987A2194B36.pdf www.enova.no/bedrift/bygg-og-eiendom/eksisterende-bygg/ List on predefined measures and minimum claim from ENOVA In Norwegian only: www.enova.no/download?objectPath=upload_images/DAA34327B94D449EB01B369EEC69AFDD.pdf The Norwegian Water Resources and Energy Directorate Rapport nr 47–2016 Regulations on plus-energy customers In Norwegian only: http://publikasjoner.nve.no/rapport/2016/rapport2016_47.pdf www.nve.no/elmarkedstilsynet-marked-og-monopol/nettjenester/nettleie/tariffer-for-produksjon/plusskunder/ Innovation Norway: financing of environmental technologies www.innovasjonnorge.no/no/finansiering/miljoteknologi/ Norwegian Standard NS3700 Criteria for passive houses and low energy buildings –residential buildings In Norwegian only: www.standard.no/nettbutikk/produktkatalogen/produktpresentasjon/?ProductID=636902

*Whenever possible, refer to the original Norwegian version.

13 Activity systems and innovation in project-based production

The case of construction

Finn Orstavik

Introduction

The specificities of construction production have often been overlooked in debates regarding construction innovation. The relevant business units have somewhat crudely been thought of in terms of "firms of the construction industry", and this otherwise unspecified genus and its assumed resident culture have taken blame for alleged rampant quality deficiencies, budget overruns and project delivery delays (e. g. Lepatner, 2007; Egan, 1998). As pointed out by Harty (2008), not paying attention to the internal complexity of the construction business has led to an inadequate grasp of the innovation challenges in construction. The objective of the present chapter is to consider innovation in construction starting out with an appreciation of what construction production on-site entails. The heterogeneity of firms in project consortia is highlighted, and the matrix of corporate and project organization of construction production considered.

Currently, while a generic concept of innovation can be defined adequately in a straightforward way, defining the concept of construction innovation is more challenging. Fundamentally, innovation is the transformation of established modes of production. Production as we know it (and as it has been analysed by Adam Smith and other classical social scientists) involves people with knowledge and skills working with materials and artefacts, learning by repetition efficient ways of operating (routines), as well as complying with codified and unwritten rules. Innovation generally impacts on what is produced and how. This implies technical change but also change in institutionalized modes of working. In practice, the latter creates many obstacles that are complex to deal with. In traditional business organizations, the lines of authority and spans of control present management with a set of levers to enact change, also in the face of internal resistance. In construction and the temporary matrix organization of a project, innovation can be more challenging.

Van de Ven, Polley, Garud and Venkataraman (1999) define innovation as *bringing a new idea into good currency*. This is in line with the definition of innovation presented here. Schumpeter's early theory of economic development inscribes and extends basic insights from classical economics (Schumpeter, 2006) and stresses the point that innovation has consequences for existing institutionalized production practices. Innovation in construction cannot be associated simply with novelty, such as the use of new technology; an original construction principle; or a unique design – without considering to what extent this novelty represents a new trend or a product or method that will be used again in the ensuing production of built objects. Considering innovation as *sticky* changes to established modes of production, neither creative ideas, inventions nor unique products can in themselves be considered innovations. Not, that is, unless these novelties will be used again in ensuing production efforts (Orstavik, Dainty and Abbott 2015). The way the relationships between different forms of novelty and innovation are construed here is shown in Table 13.1.

New ideas, novelty and innovation are not synonyms, and to understand how innovation happens in an industry, it is necessary to understand production. Hobday and colleagues see this and add the insight that it is unfortunate for the analysis of construction innovation that the idea of industrial mass production has had hegemony in innovation studies (Davies and Hobday, 2005; Hobday, 1998). Slaughter's pioneering efforts to analyse construction innovation introduces neo-Schumpeterian ideas into the debates regarding construction innovation but arguably remains true to the conventional mass production frame of reference (Slaughter, 1993a, 1993b, 1998, 2000). Looking for an alternative framing of the discussion of innovation, Hobday contrasts industrial mass production with industries that produce complex systems. When complex systems products are created, he says, innovation and production become one and the same. Complex systems products are bespoke and represent novel solutions that enter into the operations of existing industries. Hence, they represent sticky changes and are innovations.

However, Hobday (1998) does not consider the creation of built objects to be complex systems production, with the exception of particularly demanding projects such as airport and hospital construction. Notably, Winch makes the

Table 13.1 The specificity of innovation as a form of novelty

Novelty	Definition	Explanation
Creative idea	A cognitive construct that can be shared communicatively	A person or group having a vision or finding an answer to a problem and sharing this with others
Invention	A design for a practical solution or an actual construction – a functional solution	Implementing an idea in reality; creating a practical solution to a problem, maybe in the form of a unique device
Unique product	Something unique that is produced (and may be sold) once	A building with a novel and unique design, such as the Sidney Opera house
Innovation	Sticky changes in established forms of production	The changing of institutionalized production systems; by way of outcomes, processes, organization etc.

opposite suggestion at more or less the same time, claiming it is indeed appropriate to conceive of construction as a *complex systems*-producing industry (Winch, 1998). He does not, however, move on to substantiate this claim and admits that there is a need for further empirical and case-based research to clarify the issue.

Even though a large number of qualitative studies of construction practice have been made since Winch made this point (e.g. Chan and Räisänen, 2009; Clegg and Kreiner, 2014; Kreiner, 2015; Styhre, 2009a; 2009b; Styhre and Josephson, 2006), the specific issue as to whether construction should be considered a complex systems–producing industry has so far not been addressed head-on. This chapter is intended to provide a minimal first step in this direction by discussing what the nature of project-based construction production is and framing the construction innovation issue as one pertaining to the systemicness of construction.

Approaching construction innovation from this angle, the nature of organizational agency and the connectedness of agents become focal points. What entities enact innovation in construction and what relationships between entities are crucial for innovation to be embarked on and to succeed? Theorists of heterogeneous actor-network theory (ANT) have made a point of not being concerned with systems but with networks and with innovation as the outcome of network building (Callon, 1986; Latour, 2005). Employing ANT concepts, Harty has studied the reality of construction innovation qualitatively, throwing light on the challenges that emanate from the multi-firm coalition making up a construction project (Harty, 2008; Harty, 2010; Harty and Davies, 2013). He addresses the issues of innovative agency, contextual heterogeneity and connectedness, arguing that there are more obstacles to innovation in the project-based construction industry than in typical mass production industries. This is due to the project-based nature of construction production and the lack of a strong integrator that can promote an innovation across the various businesses and stakeholder interests involved.

To carry out a construction project, a temporary organization is set up on-site to ascertain the effective conjoining and interaction of construction project actors. The temporary production system on the construction site is particular in that it is not one integrated business organization but an agglomeration of many business organizations, each with its own identity as an independent firm. Any individual and team working in a construction project represents an employing firm and must heed this firm's business practices, including business plans and commercial strategies. At the same time, individuals and teams are parts of the temporary production organization of the project. The dual responsibilities and loyalties following from this particular kind of matrix organization is an important factor to consider when innovation in construction is analysed.

Theoretical framework: Activity systems

A construction site typically is a clearly delineated area of ground in which a multitude of firms contribute to the production of one or more built objects. Generally, the firms involved are represented by work teams tasked with specific activities within the construction project. The tasks, times and modes of involvement during the project lifecycle vary significantly.

Work teams and tasks

To analyse the production system established in a construction project, it is useful to focus on work groups and tasks. By conceiving of work teams as *activity systems*, I follow the lead of Trist and Bamforth and their path-breaking socio-technical analysis of coal mining work in the UK (Trist and Bamforth, 1951). Their perspective is that work is carried out by groups employing specific tools, machinery and equipment and performing work roles delineated by both unwritten codes of conduct (norms) and explicit rules (procedures, laws, regulations). Practices are routine-based, that is to say repetitive and shaped not only according to rules but also significantly by the technical and material means employed.

On a construction site, activity systems are dedicated to the production of well defined subsystems of the built object, such as the concrete structure, the facades, the internal walls, the plumbing, the electrical system, the ventilation system, the lifts, etc. Some activity systems are concerned with only temporary structures, such as scaffolding. Each worker is a member of a single activity system, and people in one such system are generally employed by a single firm.[1]

In theoretical terms, an activity system consists of the following elements:

- *People*: Team members and a designated leader; possessing knowledge, holding values, and with social resources such as relationships to others and a common language
- *Materials*: Encompassing the physical reality of the team's work situation, including the built object in its current state, building materials, tools, equipment and any machinery that is being used and more or less complex technical systems that are relied on in production
- *Routines*: Observable, repeating practices of the people in the team, such as carrying out operational runs in production; alternating between physical work and rest; handling tools and equipment; and dealing with safety measures
- *Rules*: The codified and explicit rules and procedures that apply to the production activity on-site, formulated as project-internal rules, for example on working hours and timekeeping; corporate rules regarding remuneration; and further laws and regulations imposed by regional or national government bodies
- *Communication*: The informal talk among team members and with people outside the team; transfers of information in scheduled meetings, as well as in written and otherwise codified form

The activity system is the basic unit of the production system on the construction site. Each unit combines selected inputs into specific outcomes. The group is also a social group with a culture, but the level of integration, cohesion and, hence, the strength of group culture varies across activity systems. A similar point can be made regarding the project: integration and cohesion and the strength of the project culture vary over time and across projects.

Activity systems, the temporary production system and innovation

It is important to note how the elements of an activity system are dynamic and mutually dependent. Change in one element generally depends on and can trigger changes in the other elements. For example, a new kind of tool can become useful only if team members learn how to use it and to the extent that routines, rules and knowledge are adjusted to allow for the new tool to be used as intended. Furthermore, mutual dependence applies also to people. What one person does or fails to do impacts on other people. The social reality of a project is essentially reflexive and emergent (Simpson, 2009).

Activity systems are living systems, and learning is part of everyday activities both on the individual and the organizational level. Individuals learn how to deal with tasks and colleagues, and the overall activity system is transformed as part of this. Change and learning can be triggered not only by new material elements entering as input but also by routine or rule changes introduced internally or imposed from outside (project management, corporate head office), as well as when people leave or new people enter a group.

As a social system, the activity system has members with *agency*, and the system is capable of innovation. New ideas can be developed by people in the group that can drive change. Informal rules for how to produce can be formed, for example regarding work intensity and pauses. Informal rules also develop regarding collaborative arrangements and ways of working together in the team and with other teams.

In theory, if output remains the same, change in one activity system (for example working hours) can be bounded to that activity system only. But on-site, change in one activity system generally will affect other activity systems and impact the input and output flows between systems. Typically, therefore, activity systems depend on one another in the construction project. Figure 13.1 is a simple illustration of the temporary production system in a construction project.

The figure is a highly stylized and, of course, incomplete rendering of realities in project-based production on-site. But it serves to show how different activity systems are mutually dependent and also to highlight that activity systems depend on the project management for information and rule setting regarding work. It also illustrates how activity systems are dependent on their "corporate homes" that serve both as suppliers to the project and as intermediaries for large, often multinational industrial firms in supplying industries. The corporate home is not only an important source of production resources (people and knowledge; materials and tools) but also of rules, norms and other constraints.

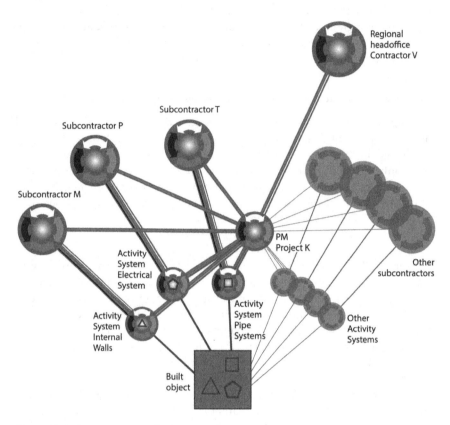

Figure 13.1 A temporary production system

Case research and ethnographic methods

The empirical analysis in this chapter is based on a field study that has been carried out within one specific construction project, here called Project K, which
was selected based on being a rather typical, run-of-the-mill project. About 80
flats were to be designed and built, all with veranda or balcony, in three separate
buildings up to six stories high, with a common underground garage, and outside park-like areas and playgrounds. After a project gestation and development
period that lasted several years, actual work on the site commenced in mid-2016
and was completed during 2018. The author carried out fieldwork in Project K
during 2017, gaining access after initial contact with the main contractor, here
called Contractor V, specifically managers at the head office and the director of
the relevant regional office during the winter of 2017. Non-participant observation on-site commenced in April and was concluded in December of 2017.

During the months of fieldwork, the researcher gained access to meetings
and had numerous informal conversations on-site, when work was ongoing. He

also visited offices and break rooms during office hours and generally had lunch with the people in management but sometimes also had coffee with workers during breaks. Access was granted to specific project information in the form of contracts with suppliers, internal communications including summaries of meetings, and regular updates of operational plans. Numerous visits on the construction site were made, generally two to four visits during each day spent in the project.

On these site visits, the main goals were to gain trust and obtain contact with all the categories of people involved and to discuss with them the main aspect of their work efforts. Doing this, the systems approach delineated in the previous section was used to direct and focus data collection. In observations, conversations and interviews, information was sought that was relevant for understanding ongoing work processes and the resources involved: first, regarding the technical content of the work, the materials, methods and tools used; second, regarding the work process, the daily routines and the collaborative practices enacted; third, the rules and technical specifications that had to be adhered to and what specific meanings the terms *high quality* and *sufficient quality* had in the activity system's practice. Finally, fourth, information was sought regarding the people themselves: their earlier work experiences; their educational background; their economic situation in terms of remuneration and employment; working hours, available facilities etc.; and the collegial relationships and group culture seen in their current work.

The results of visits and informal conversations were always recorded in field notes written up at the site, at a desk in the open environment of the project office. All the people in the project organization that were approached proved willing to contribute to the research. Key participants have been interviewed in depth, in thematically structured conversations generally lasting between 60 and 120 minutes. All scheduled interviews were recorded and fully transcribed. All meetings that were attended were recorded, and a selection of these meetings transcribed.

The research design is an ethnographic study of a milieu and of persons making up a project production organization on-site and goes beyond the conventional framework of a case study. The researcher is seeking to understand the reality of working lives of the main categories of employees contributing to project operations, both for people in administrative as well purely operational positions on-site.

Any project is unique, but information obtained on this project and its context indicates that this is a common type of project today in Norway. Hence, it is to be expected that findings from this project are relevant for are relevant for other analyses of the construction industry and could be relevant also for the study of projects in other European countries. At the same time, it is obvious that there are limits to the generalization possible from this research. Statistical generalization is impossible, and as always, analytical generalizations need to be corroborated in further research.

Firms, tasks and activity systems in Project K

A central finding from the empirical research is that production work on-site in Project K is functionally divided, based on a decomposition of the built object as a set of related subsystems. The division of labour between firms depends on what kind of services are to be offered, as this is agreed and inscribed in contractual arrangements. What this division of labour amounts to in specific terms in Project K is shown in Table 13.2.

The original intention was to put all important activities into a table of this kind. However, there proved to be a very large number of distinct activities and specialized activity systems, many of which were active in the project for only short periods of time. For this reason, what is presented in Table 13.2 is only an incomplete overview of activities in the project as a whole. The table does,

Table 13.2 Activities on site

Area	Operations
Foundation	Digging, trenching, filling, piledriving, sheet piling etc.; drainage
Concrete 1	Scaffolding construction, removal and hauling, concrete casting and curing support of walls, floors, roofs and balconies
Concrete 2	Rental and sales of formwork systems; columns, boards, beams, etc.
Scaffolding	Rental and sales of scaffolding systems; building, transport of scaffolding
Concrete 3	Prebar work
Concrete 4	Supply of shaped and cut prebars
Concrete 5	Specially designed and produced steel fasteners and struts for balconies
Concrete 6	Rental and sales of tools, fixtures, lasers, etc.
Timber 1	Wooden beam structures including parapet, windows and doors to the outside; outside wall panels, non-wovens, plastic sheeting and tape
Timber 2	Wood beams and other materials in standard dimensions
Timber 3	Rental and sales of tools, circular and other saws, fixtures, lasers, plastic sheeting, non-wovens, etc.
Windows	Supply of all aluminium framed windows, glass doors
Doors 1	Supply of all internal doors in flats and some for common areas
Doors 2	Main doors for entrances, etc.
Roof covering	Derbigum membranes on all roofs and parapets with sculptured, pre-cut isolation of Styropore and Rockwool; membrane on underground garage
Electrical system	Supply of all materials and necessary equipment and tools; layout and assembly of electrical system; floor heating in wet rooms; call system; power supply for lifts; power supply for ventilation fans
Pipe systems	Hot and cold fresh water supply; fittings and faucets (kitchen and bathrooms); showers, wet room drains; sewage pipe systems with connection to public sewage system; water-based heating of all floors except in wet rooms; central heating connected to public district heating system; roof drains and overwater drainage; sprinkler system common rooms, garage and apartments; central gas pressure tank, gas pipes for fireplaces

Area	Operations
Sprinkler	Mounting of sprinkler pipes and heads in apartments
Air circulation	Supply of all materials including pipes, fixtures and isolation materials; mounting of air ducts, isolation of air ducts, mounting of valve caps
Internal walls	Supply of all boards, steel sleepers and beams, tools and fixtures; supply of ceiling systems; walls layout, mounting of sleepers and beams; plywood and Wedi boards in wet rooms; ceiling systems.
Facade	Brick wall covering of facade; marezzo on facade; casting of wet room floors; tiling of floors and walls of bathrooms
Tinsmith work	Supply of materials and tools; fittings under windows etc.
Surfaces	All indoor plastering and painting
Floors	Supply of materials and mounting of floors
Hardwood flooring	Supplying and hauling materials and tools, foam sheeting, cutting materials; laying out floors and skirting
Fixed furniture	Kitchen, bathrooms wardrobe cabinet, bathroom cabinet with sink
Lifts	Supply of lifts components and parts, necessary tools and equipment, assembly and service

however, give a reasonably good overview of core activities carried out in the project.

Every firm involved in the on-site production operations over some time has their own team of workers and a designated team leader. The groups are subject to firm-specific organizational structures and cultures, salary systems, routines for quality control and for maintaining safety. Many of the workers, however, report that they are only loosely integrated in their employing company's organization. This is because they generally spend most of their hours of work in specific projects and building sites. Notably, there are several workers and whole activity systems that share their time between various projects.

An important exception from this general picture is that a significant proportion of workers on-site occupy temporary positions, in teams coordinated by the main contractor. These have employment in a recruitment company and are receiving salary from this company rather than from the company that they are contracted out to and that assigns them to a specific project, building site and task.

On the site, the team leader functions as the connecting link between project management and the work group. Team leaders take part in weekly meetings in which upcoming work is presented by project management and discussed by all meeting participants. In principle, teams of all firms contracted into the project by Contractor V should take part in the project meetings. However, some teams are small and tend not to take part. Amongst the reasons given for this is that attending meetings at times means that work has to stop, hence creating obstacles for other activity systems. Furthermore, some workers, specifically employed by subcontractors and subject to piecework payment, claim they are losing money when attending meetings.

Production work on-site is separated into work packages in the overall project plan and in the organization of the project. Importantly, the nature of activities is distinguished based on the actual subsystem of the built object that is being

Table 13.3 Examples of work areas and systemicness

Area	Systemicness
Foundation work	Piles and sheet piling are mechanical systems; fillings are layered materials with quality and quantity tolerances; drainage consists of pipe systems.
Concrete work	Formworks are systems made from fabricated parts. Prebar systems are layered structures with specific properties. Casting is done piece by piece to form the body of the built object. Pipes are built into and openings are made in this body to allow the construction of other systems. The body rests on a systemic piling structure.
Electrical system	The electrical system is calculated and designed based on specifications agreed with builder and is a self-contained system connected to the public electricity grid. Connections for other systems are generally offered as standard wall sockets.
Lifts	Lift are self-contained integrated, composite systems attached to the concrete body and the electrical system. Backup energy systems and GSM-based alarm systems are also part of the lift systems

constructed. This is illustrated in Table 13.3, where a few of the main operational areas in Project K and their systemic traits are shown.

Specific competence, technology, materials supply, work groups and firms are clustered around the construction of distinct systems, some of which are "primary" systems making up the built object and its technical and functional affordances (such as elevators, plumbing and ventilation). Other systems serve as interfaces (or functional bridges) between other systems (i.e. wood frames connecting concrete structures with windows), or they are temporary systems such as scaffolding, serving as intermediaries in the process of producing other systems.

For the discussion of the division of labour in the project to be anything near complete, not only production but the project in its entirety must be considered. The project forms a highly dynamic and heterogeneous system of systems, and many people are dedicated to creating, maintaining and changing the project organization.

Forms of connectedness in construction innovation

Innovation is sticky change in institutionalized forms of production, and in the model of the activity system, innovation entails not only change in output but accompanying and unavoidable changes in the configuration of the activity system's basic elements (people with knowledge, work routines, formalized rules and procedures, and materials and tools). This is the most basic sense in which innovation is connected in construction – it is carried out by people together in activity systems; by people who, to paraphrase Simpson, are reflexive and transactive and whose shared life-worlds are always emerging (Simpson, 2009). However, since construction production is project based, the construction project as a temporary coalition of activity systems must be considered in order to understand the issue of innovation in construction in a broader sense.

The project as an extended coalition of activity systems

A construction project obviously is much more than what goes on inside the construction site. Project K, like any construction project, has emerged as the outcome of a complex set of related activities earlier on. The first initiative in the Project K case was taken by professional property developers. The early phase encompassed a builder organization, a public regulatory agency, financing agents and investors, an architect, engineers, and potential buyers and residents. Based on this, a more comprehensive model of Project K is rendered in Figure 13.2.

When we consider the project as a whole, as in Figure 13.2, the dynamic nature of the temporary organization becomes a more salient issue. Based on the data acquired about Project K during the ethnographic research, it is known that this project was initiated "at the top" (by the builder) and that the full project organization only gradually emerged over a period of years. The interactions during the gestation period were in the form of protracted dialogues with authorities that over time provided a business rationale for Project K as one project in a programme of development that will extend over many years and move through several stages. Project K itself began to take form when Contractor V, Architect S and the Engineering Consultancy were selected and contracted in as partners by Builder C. Builder C is itself a rather newly established (and in itself probably temporary) subsidiary of a national property developer. Builder C is established specifically for the development effort that Project K is thought to be only a first part of.

Based on all this, Contractor V formed a Project K organization, and on-site foundation work could start in 2016. The building of the project production organization proved to be a challenge in itself: conflicts and troubled relationships were overcome only gradually and after personnel changes made in the project management team. During the research and data gathering in 2017, the temporary organization appeared to be both relatively stable and well functioning. In the winter of 2018, the project was approaching completion, and the organization was gradually dismantled.

Innovation on the level of activity systems

When construction innovation is seen through the lens of the activity system and project coalition model presented here, it is possible to discern different forms of innovation reflecting the various contexts within which innovation can take place. Such contexts can sensibly be distinguished on four levels: the activity system level, the project level, the corporate level, and the national industry level. In the following, primarily innovation on the activity system level and industry level will be discussed.

On the level of the activity systems in production on-site, problems are solved on a daily basis, and not seldomly more challenging problems are solved creatively

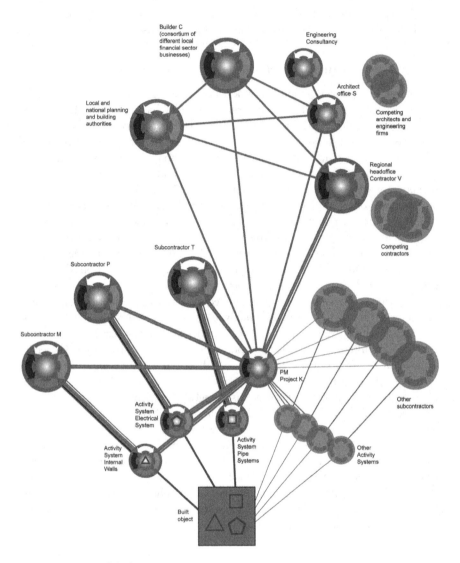

Figure 13.2 A model of Project K

with ingenious arrangements worked out to implement the solution. These creative solutions, however, do not represent innovation if no trace of them is found
when the work group is dissolved and the project completed. Referring back to
the earlier discussion of the specificity of innovation as novelty and to Table 13.1,
it is clear that creative implementations worked out by an activity system have to
become institutionalized at some level to represent innovation. That means that
other activity systems have to implement the same solution at later times, the

novelty in this way becoming an accepted feature of future construction production. This can certainly happen, not least if a corporate organization adjusts its operations and administrative systems to accommodate the novelty worked out in the activity system. This may happen in an even more significant and lasting way if matching changes are made in the overall system of production, including agencies, regulations and laws imposed on the industry in general.

Such occurrences do not appear to be very frequent, and why this is so becomes clearer when we consider some specific instances of innovation in construction. Examples of innovations observed in Project K are shown in Table 13.4.

All the innovations in Table 13.4 were observed in use in Project K. If nothing else, this makes a claim that construction is anti-innovative harder to defend. The general pattern here, however, is that construction is served by a large number of supplier industries that do technological innovation and product development within the logic of a mass production industry. This is in line with Pavitt's (1984) characterization of construction innovation as supplier-led. However, as pointed out by Harty (2008), this is only part of the picture. Harty introduces the concept of *relative boundedness* to pinpoint the reality that innovations in construction (and other industries) vary with respect to repercussions across firms and sectors and across stakeholders in general. The innovation in construction that Pavitt is concerned with primarily affects those activity systems on-site that have their corporate home in the industry in which innovation is taking place. Innovation is connected in the sense that innovative suppliers serve construction with industrial products and solutions that are conducive to innovation within their respective activity systems on-site. In Harty's terminology, this innovation is relatively bounded and is diffused because of the positive potential it represents for the firms and activity systems involved and because the innovation does not have significant negative effects on other firms and activity systems.

Based on the observations made in Project K, it appears that product development often consists in transforming generic materials into systems of standardized elements that are easily and efficiently assembled into complete systems on-site. Amongst others, this kind of product development applies to areas such as

Table 13.4 Examples of single-activity-system innovation in construction production

Area	Innovations
Foundation work	Built-in GPS-based map/BIM systems in machinery that makes paper drawings superfluous
Concrete work	(1) Lightweight, semi-automatic tools for binding prebars; (2) new formwork products making precision casting much easier to achieve
Electrical system	New components with properties that make them easy and fast to mount and that helps avoiding wrong connections being made
Lifts	Advanced automatic systems with built-in safety backup systems and GSM alarms

internal walls, facades, windows and doors, electrical systems, pipe systems of various kinds, formwork and scaffolding.

Construction innovation on the industry level

As shown in Figure 13.2, the builder, the architect, the consulting engineers, and planning and building authorities form separate activity systems that play important roles in the overall setting-up of the institutionalized system for production of the built environment. All these activity systems can innovate "on their own" to the extent that changes are insignificant for other activity systems. Business model innovation, the digitalization of architectural services and new ways of collaborating creatively across consultancy areas are all issues that may concern sticky transformations of practices inside such firms. However, as Harty has shown, these kinds of innovations tend to extend out of the single firms and project and to presuppose changes far beyond the single business units, not seldomly at the level of professions and other national and international institutions (Harty, 2008, 2010).

Innovation in construction is often challenging, one reason being that changes in one particular activity system tend to have real and (what at least is perceived as) negative consequences for other activity systems. This may be a reason why activity system creativity and problem solving relatively seldomly leads to innovation in construction. This argument corresponds closely to Harty's findings in his discussion of implications of the lack of boundedness in construction innovation. In Project K, an ongoing and relatively unbounded process innovation pursued by Contractor V could be observed both in production on-site and in the administrative activities of project management. Data from interviews and observations in meetings show that those involved in the project were concerned with the novel way of working endorsed and implemented on the corporate level in Contractor V. High-level management in Contractor V have over several years become involved in academic and professional settings discussing and researching "Lean Construction" and are in a process of implementing work practices based on such ideas across all Contractor V projects.

As a consequence, also Project K management was seen to participate in courses to learn the new principles in order to be able to develop and implement new routines and administrative techniques locally. This Contractor V process innovation cuts across practically all activity systems in the firm's projects and in particular impacts those involved in the day-to-day operations on-site. The innovation, therefore, is of concern for all the firms (or corporate homes) represented by activity systems in the Contractor V on-site production. The innovation is not exclusively an intra-organizational challenge; it is an inter-organizational challenge. This makes the innovation a long-term effort, and eventual success is still coming, depending on continuing engagement from top management and "believers" on other levels of the organization of Contractor V and its many projects.

Another example of innovation that is susceptible not to take hold because it cuts across activity systems and firms in the industry is Building Information Modelling (BIM), as discussed by Harty and Davies (2013). While Contractor V management voice some interest also in employing novel information technologies, BIM is not used in Project K and is not used as a spearhead to realize a "leaner" approach to project management in the company. Contractor V allowed the different activity systems in Project K to rely on their own versions of drawings, based on the architect's original sketches. Work is ongoing, however, in Contractor V to integrate software development into the overall process innovation effort, the hope being that technology can become an additional lever and a resource for efforts to transform current working methods into the new and "leaner" ways of working.

Conclusion

Project-based construction production is carried out by way of a temporary organization in which activity systems representing both an external firm and the project as such, are basic production units. The organization is both dynamic and complex, as tasks and preconditions for work are changing throughout the lifecycle of the construction project. Complexity is reduced by unequivocal definitions of tasks being made based on a systems conceptualization of the product: the built object. Activity systems deal with one or more specific subsystems of the built object and produce this system (or these systems) largely independently, in structural terms. The work process has to be collaborative, however, as each activity system must coordinate efforts with other activity systems and in accordance with the overall project plan. Operational dependencies are dealt with by way of dialogue and negotiations as well as managerial decision making.

Innovations in construction are of many kinds. Distinctions can be made regarding the extent to which innovations affect many other activity systems and regarding the extent to which innovation going on in an activity system is dependent on its corporate home outside the project organization.

The most common form of innovation in construction is product innovation sourced from the mass production industry with the corporate home of an activity system serving as the intermediary. Generally, this form of innovation can be relatively bounded. This means that other activity systems are affected only in a minimal way by the innovation.

Another important form of innovation, the relatively unbounded type, affects other activity systems in much more notable ways. Examples of such innovations discussed here are the introduction in construction production of Lean Principles and of Building Information Models. Such innovations affect activity systems across a project and across Contractor V projects. For this reason, such innovations are much harder to realize, and typically take much longer to carry out. These innovations are dependent on involving significant stakeholders and getting their commitment to carry their part of the burden related to operational and professional redesign. For this reason, even if connectedness invariably is a feature of any innovation process, connectedness takes on a new and increased significance in construction innovations of the unbounded kind. For these, trust-based collaboration is essential, and the innovations have to be brought forth through co-creation.

Note

1 Observations on the site and interviews with key personnel indicate that the interfaces between activity systems are generally clearly defined and that the main reason for this is that clarity on operational tasks entails clarity on responsibility. Being unequivocal on the boundaries around one's own role reduces complexity in the everyday work situation and is effective in reducing risk.

References

Callon, M. (1986) 'The sociology of an actor network: The case of the electric vehicle', in Callon, M., Law, J. and Rip, A. (eds.) *Mapping the Dynamics of Science and Technology: Sociology of Science in the Real World*. Basingstoke: Macmillan.

Chan, P.W. and Räisänen, C. (2009) 'Editorial: Informality and emergence in construction', *Construction Management and Economics*, 27(10), pp. 907–912.

Clegg, S. and Kreiner, K. (2014) 'Fixing concrete: Inquiries, responsibility, power and innovation', *Construction Management and Economics*, 32(3), pp. 262–278.

Davies, A. and Hobday, M. (2005) *The business of projects: Managing innovation in complex products and systems*. Cambridge: Cambridge University Press.

Egan, J. (1998) *Rethinking construction. The report of the Construction Task Force to the Deputy Prime Minister, John Prescott, on the scope for improving the quality and efficiency of UK construction*. London: Department of the Environment, Transport and the Regions.

Harty, C. (2008) 'Implementing innovation in construction: Contexts, relative boundedness and actor-network theory', *Construction Management and Economics*, 26(10), pp. 1029–1041.

Harty, C. (2010) 'Implementing innovation: Designers, users and actor-networks', *Technology Analysis and Strategic Management*, 22(3), pp. 297–315.

Harty, C. and Davies, R. (2013) 'Implementing "Site BIM": A case study of ICT innovation on a large hospital project', *Automation in Construction*, 30, pp. 15–24.

Hobday, M. (1998) 'Product complexity, innovation and industrial organisation', *Research Policy*, 26(6), pp. 689–710.

Kreiner, K. (2015) 'Built-in innovation and the ambiguity of designing accessibility', in Orstavik, F., Dainty, A. and Abbott, C. (eds.), *Construction Innovation*. Chichester: Wiley Blackwell, pp. 29–45.

Latour, B. (2005) *Reassembling the social: An introduction to actor-network theory*. Oxford: Oxford University Press.

LePatner, B.B. (2007) *Broken buildings, busted budgets. How to fix America's trillion-dollar construction industry*. Chicago and London: University of Chicago Press.

Orstavik, F., Dainty, A. and Abbott, C. (eds.) (2015) *Construction Innovation*. Chichester: Wiley Blackwell.

Pavitt, K. (1984) 'Sectoral patterns of technical change: Towards a taxonomy and a theory', *Research Policy*, 13(6), pp. 343–373.

Schumpeter, J. (2006) *Theorie der wirtschaftlichen Entwicklung*, Nachdruck der 1. Auflage von 1912. Berlin: Duncker and Humblot.

Simpson, B. (2009) 'Pragmatism, mead and the practice turn', *Organization Studies*, 30(12), pp. 1329–1347.

Slaughter, E.S. (1993a) 'Builders as sources of construction innovation', *Journal of Construction Engineering and Management*, 119(3), pp. 532–549.

Slaughter, E.S. (1993b) 'Innovation and learning during implementation: A comparison of user and manufacturer innovations', *Research Policy*, 22(1), pp. 81–95.

Slaughter, E.S. (1998) 'Models of construction innovation', *Journal of Construction Engineering and Management*, 124(3), pp. 226–231.

Slaughter, E.S. (2000) 'Implementation of construction innovations', *Building Research and Information*, 28(1), pp. 2–17.

Styhre, A. (2009a) *Managing knowledge in the construction industry*. London and New York: Spon Press.

Styhre, A. (2009b) 'Tacit knowledge in rock construction work: A study and a critique of the use of the term', *Construction Management and Economics*, 27(10), pp. 995–1003.

Styhre, A. and Josephson, P.-E. (2006) 'Revisiting site manager work: Stuck in the middle?' *Construction Management and Economics*, 24(5), pp. 521–528.

Trist, E.L. and Bamforth, K.W. (1951) 'Some social and psychological consequences of the Longwall Method of coal-getting: An examination of the psychological situation and defences of a work group in relation to the social structure and technological content of the work system', *Human relations*, 4(1), pp. 3–38.

Van de Ven, A.H., Polley, D.E., Garud, R. and Venkataraman, S. (1999) *The innovation journey*. New York: Oxford University Press.

Winch, G. (1998) 'Zephyrs of creative destruction: Understanding the management of innovation in construction', *Building Research and Information*, 26(4), pp. 268–279.

14 Tracing the connectivity of innovation in construction across time and space

Malena Ingemansson Havenvid, Åse Linné, Lena E. Bygballe and Chris Harty

Introduction

The chapters of this book represent approaches to empirically trace connectivity as a way of unpacking the interactive elements of learning and innovation processes within and between construction-related organisations over time. This tracing cuts across single and multiple projects, different sectoral levels and transnational networks. The renewal processes have entailed both learning and innovation practices and outcomes of everyday work, as well as explicit innovation attempts. So what do these studies and examples tell us about innovation and about connectivity? Can any dominating patterns that govern innovation processes in construction or innovative behaviour be identified? Are there mostly opportunities or obstacles, friction or smoothness, stability or dynamics, long-term or short-term goals, deliberate or emergent practices and strategies? Is there mainly continuity or discontinuity? In describing how and why renewal processes succeed or fail, or why an industry appears to be innovative or non-innovative, the use of such dichotomies is quite common. However, this type of binary opposition serves little purpose when trying to grasp a complex reality and a multidimensional phenomenon such as innovation. Are things necessarily either/or? Is it success *or* failure? Is the construction industry innovative *or* non-innovative?

The organisation of the construction business is often described as problematic due to a dominating pattern of fragmentation – temporally and structurally. In forming an eclectic research network to investigate this from a different viewpoint – finding out how and why it may be connected – we have not set out to show *one* picture of how the organisation of construction relates to learning and innovation, or one specific pattern, but a more nuanced and multiple view. This work has entailed dealing with a number of paradoxes, or tensions, that reside in this organisational or *organising* pattern. Tensions often arise in the interface of seemingly contradictory forces, structures or goals and as such may appear as paradoxical. In the words of Lewis (2000), paradoxical tensions are intrinsic to organisational life, and by revealing them as researchers, we may address "*what* tensions exist, *why* they may actually fuel reinforcing cycles, and *how* actors may manage paradoxes to foster change and understanding" (p. 774).

Paradoxes are defined as social constructs that come to life as actors try to deal with a complex reality. As a result, such constructs are often simplified into dichotomised *either/or* aspects but in fact represent a reality of complex interrelationships (ibid.). Simplifying reality is a must in order to cope as a human being, as a manager or as an organisation. In many ways it helps us to grasp what is going on in terms of providing a manageable space and scope for action; how should we act in particular situations or scenarios? But it may also limit our understanding of our surroundings, the options we have to act and the developments that lie ahead. Should we act as individuals or as collectives? Should we steer or be steered? Are things improving, or are they worsening?

For some time, management scholars have advocated the potential of a paradox perspective (i.e. paradox theory) as a way of progressing management and organisational research beyond dealing with either/or states of organisational, social and cognitive contradictions, such as long-term vs. short-term, centralise vs. decentralise, direct vs. follow (Smith and Lewis, 2011; Jules and Good, 2014). We believe this might be a fruitful lens to further investigate the tensions and contradictions of innovation in construction. As a meta-theoretical perspective, a paradox approach advocates viewing contradictory forces or conditions as existing simultaneously and re-enforcing each other, i.e. taking a stance of things being *both/and* (Lewis and Smith, 2014). The idea is that by addressing such conflicting forces, structures or goals as co-existing and co-evolving, new understandings and theories of why things are as they are and why they may or may not change could materialise. This relates to Giddens' (1984) structuration theory and the idea of seeming opposites functioning as *dualities*; i.e. human agency and structure (or context) are essentially interactive and interdependent aspects of socio-economic systems, rather than one dominating or opposing the other. In this very vein, Kolb (2008) explores the notion of connectivity (defined as socio-technical interaction) through the idea of dualities and as such discusses disconnections as an inherent part of a socio-technically interconnected society: "If we think about connectivity as a theoretical duality, we can see independent categories, namely 'connects' and 'disconnects' (being disconnected is antithetical to being connected), which are often, if not always, intertwined in interdependent relationships" (Kolb, 2008, p. 131).

Inspired by these notions, this edited volume does not describe the construction business and its social and technical entities as *only* connected. Rather, connectivity is revealed as one aspect of an inherent duality (connectivity–disconnectivity) that will require further scrutiny in order for us to grasp the interactive elements and interdependencies of this, as well as other dualities of the industry. Therefore, in this final chapter, we find it suitable to address the learnings from the chapters from the perspective of renewal processes including a set of paradoxical tensions, or dualities, that individuals and organisations try to deal with when trying to achieve (or avoid) change. Reflecting the way construction business is organised to deal with innovation and how connectivity is part of that equation, we will focus on the duality of boundaries and connections and how this relates to different spatial and temporal conditions of construction organisation and ultimately innovation. As such, we place this final chapter about construction innovation in the context of organisational arrangements of individuals, organisations and markets where tensions arise in simultaneous conditions of boundaries and connections and of temporary and permanent structures. This has implications for the inherent transformative nature of technology and knowledge and the tensions arising from trying to transfer what is being learnt, renewed or innovated to different contexts over time.

Boundaries and connections are here addressed as part of the organisational set-up of the industry in terms of representing a wide set of different professions, competences and organisations and in being project based. On the one hand, this can be described as extensive fragmentation, i.e. resulting in a complexity of boundaries. On the other, it can be seen as creating conditions under which different kinds of connections are and need to be made for this set-up to function as a whole aligned towards particular goals. The issue of boundaries and connections relates to different temporalities of construction organisation. A well recognised temporal duality is that of the temporary project organisation and the 'permanent' firm. These organisational forms represent different logics for how practices can be initiated and evolve, which among other things relates to the different time horizons and types of task at hand. However, a variety of other organisational structures and temporalities influence what is, and they can be developed from an industry, firm and project point of view. There is an institutional context including international and national policy organisations and associations, but there are also structures of business relationships and networks connecting firms, projects and nations over time. This indicates a complexity of both boundaries and connections that cut across different organisational levels and temporalities.

How organisations and individuals manage to navigate among and across these boundaries and connections but also influence them has consequences for how they learn and innovate – intentionally and unintentionally – as well as how we may describe these processes. From an interactive and inter-organisational perspective, learning and the development and use of new solutions are context-dependent processes. This means that how, when, where and for what purposes knowledge and material solutions are applied matters for how it can be part of value creating activities (or not) and for whom. As such, investigating the boundaries between contexts as well as the connections between them is important to understand how knowledge, as well as technology, 'travels' and how it can or cannot become embedded in different contexts over time.

Next, we address the issue of boundaries and connections based on how this paradox can be interpreted drawing on the chapters in this collection, as well as its consequences for spatial and temporal conditions of construction innovation. From this we generate a set of analytical questions concerning the challenges and opportunities of tracing learning and innovation processes as multidimensional phenomena across a connected and disconnected business landscape, over time. Based on these challenges and opportunities, we suggest a research agenda for considering connectivity as an inherent and paradoxical part of organisational life in construction.

Understanding the role of boundaries and connections for innovation in construction

The preceding chapters have illustrated a number of different boundaries that individuals and organisations in the construction business need to operate within and across as part of everyday work and in efforts to induce change and innovation. Boundaries are interesting because they indicate that there is an inside and an outside and that there is a border to something else. In some situations, boundaries need to be overcome or worked around. In others, renewal is possible due to the very existence or intersection of boundaries. Looking into the involvement of technology providers in construction projects, Hughes and Stehn (Chapter 4 of this volume) address the problem of specific competences entering the construction process at a time when innovative solutions are difficult to introduce into the final product. The organisational boundaries separating a diversity of competences across the construction process and the timing of their involvement are regarded as a main obstacle to introducing technological innovation. The authors point to the narrowly defined contractual boundaries that this induces, which place focus on only limited tasks and goals rather than what should be the 'real' objective of the project: satisfying the client's needs. Overcoming these organisational and contractual boundaries, i.e. discontinuities, through vertical and (foremost) horizontal integration is presented as a way of creating continuity across the construction process and technological innovation. Connectivity between actors and their involvement in the construction process can in this way be interpreted as attempts of erasing or reducing the influence of boundaries. However, boundaries can also be a positive force for innovation. The study by Tzannis, Biraghi and Gambetti (Chapter 6) of an innovative hospital construction project in Italy –Vimercate hospital – illustrates how a multitude of competences and the temporary integration of them during the project were necessary for a new innovative hospital design to emerge and to gain legitimacy from the regional authorities. Thus, the multitude of interfaces between different competences can here be viewed as an enabler of innovation. A constellation of actors was instigated within the larger project constellation – a technical board – that could communicate the different needs of the hospital wards into the hospital design. In this case, boundaries were inevitable, even necessary, in order to obtain the right diversity of competences within the project. It was also a necessity to find a way of intersecting them to reach consensus. This work illustrates connectivity as a way of taking advantage of the existence of boundaries and what they represent in terms of different competences.

In a similar vein, Chapter 3 by Linné shows how boundaries are an intrinsic part of creating connections through inter-organisational relationships over time and how this facilitates the use and development of BIM within a large-scale project – the New Karolinska Hospital (NKS) in Stockholm. She demonstrates how the practice of using BIM in particular ways for particular purposes, develops across a network of actors that interacts both within and across projects. New and innovative BIM practices are related to how this network has been operating over a long period prior to the project. The study illustrates connectivity as a way of using and developing technology across the organisational boundaries of both firms and projects.

Boundaries also give rise to friction. Simon, Révész, Mandják, Szalkai and Hetesi (Chapter 8) address boundaries in terms of conflicts. They examine a number of disagreements arising during the early phases of two different hospital construction projects in Hungary and the resulting use of the buildings by the end users – the medical professionals and the patients. In some cases hindering and in some cases supporting renewal in terms of a new patient-centred hospital design, in each of the projects these conflicts arose at the interfaces of different professions and networks. More specifically, the conflicts arose both within and between the public network consisting of the respective universities and health care institutions on the one hand and the private network of contractors and construction-related suppliers on the other. This illustrates two important things: firstly, boundaries may exist on and influence multiple levels. In this case, it is between professions operating within the same type of network (public or private) and between different networks (public vs. private). Secondly, friction that arises at the intersection of boundaries can work as both a hindrance and a driver of renewal processes. Connectivity is here revealed in the way actors are bound to different networks of interdependencies, which in turn creates both resistance and capitulation to change.

These studies show that while some boundaries or boundaries in some instances can work as constraints to innovation, others create important interfaces at which learning and innovation can take place. In their Chapter 7, Havenvid, Bygballe and Håkansson point to the apparent dilemma of the need for setting boundaries around a project and being sensitive towards its embedded nature. Based on revisiting previous studies of construction projects in Sweden, they use the term *bridging* to refer to how construction actors create bridges between project 'islands' by systematically using and changing interdependencies that exist between a project and its context and thereby enable innovation. They demonstrate the dual nature of projects in terms of being bounded and connected at the same time. While there are economic and contractual boundaries that have clear implications for the specific project, there are socio-material interdependencies that will both influence and be influenced by the way firms and individuals choose to use or include them. As such, connectivity is both a state under which projects are executed (the project context) and a way of actively using that context within and across individual projects (bridging) to learn and innovate.

Taking a sectoral perspective, Sergeeva and Lindkvist (Chapter 12) reveal boundaries and connections through the narratives of innovation that are being communicated regarding the sustainability achievements and ambitions of the industry. Looking into the narrative interactions between international and domestic policy and firm levels in Norway and the UK, they argue that narratives are a central way of establishing an identity and image as a green and sustainable sector. Despite numerous organisational boundaries existing on multiple levels across the industry (policy, firm and project), they identify pull and push effects of international and domestic policy narratives and firm-level narratives regarding complying with regulations and recommendations on the one hand (push) and moving beyond them on the other (pull). Some of the obvious effects are the translations and interpretations of narratives across these levels, resulting in new approaches, technologies and job roles. However, multiple boundaries also hinder more effective and efficient communication about future goals and actions, indicating the need to collaborate and interact across these boundaries and levels in order to legitimise and intensify the green innovation agenda. In turn, this could create further opportunities for construction to act as a 'sustainable leader' towards other sectors. Here, connectivity is the narratives of sustainability developed and used across multiple levels of construction sectors. Such narratives may also be part of creating connectivity to other sectors.

With the ambition to grasp why some forms of innovation are harder to implement than others, Orstavik (Chapter 13) depicts the construction business as a set of interconnected and yet bounded activity systems involving national, industry and firm and project levels. The firm and project levels are analysed as permanent and temporary activity-based systems consisting of people, materials, routines, rules and communication. A distinction is made between innovation in activity systems compared to that across them, pointing to different types of innovation depending on the boundary around the involved actors and artefacts. Renewal can take place within the boundaries of one activity system over time (i.e. changing the way one system of people work, their routines and the materials they use) or across several such systems. Innovation of an unbounded nature, such as Lean Principles or BIM, requires cutting across such system boundaries, which may explain why this form of innovation is more difficult to implement than that which is confined to one activity system. This relates directly to Chapter 5 by Hulthén and Sundquist, which also adopts an activity-based view of firms and projects. By investigating how the involvement of a logistics service specialist causes a major reorganisation of logistics and other activities both on and off the project site, they point to the driving and hindering effects of activity interdependencies on innovation. On the one hand, the interrelation among a set of coordinated activities that cut across different types of activities (logistics and other) makes change difficult. On the other hand, when change is instigated, it will have far-reaching effects on several activities and on the actors and resources connected to them. In their case study, the transformation of a distributor into a service provider can be seen as innovation by taking parts of a network that require coordination and reducing them (for the contractor in this case) to one simple outcome. Bundles of services comprised of heterogeneous products and processes (that might be seen as 'outside' projects) are developed to be delivered at a specific place and time. Together, these chapters illustrate connectivity as activity-based interdependencies by the 'unbounded' nature of some innovations.

Chapter 11 by Ratajczak-Mrozek relates to boundaries and connections on a transnational level by displaying domestic and international actor structures of Polish window manufacturing. The author concludes that there are no actors within this supply network that can be considered either domestic or international;

such boundaries are blurred in that they are interacting across national borders and thus basing their operations on both domestic and international resources. Consequently, innovation related to the production and supply of windows as an input product to the construction industry is a distributed process across transnational borders. Here, connectivity is the interrelated distribution of actors and resources across transnational boundaries. In turn, this illustrates the distributed nature of product innovation processes across international borders.

The chapters that have been addressed so far illustrate that boundaries and connections are a way of describing not only how construction is organised but also how this duality influences the paths that learning and innovation processes may take. However, although we can identify that this duality is a central feature of construction organisation and innovation, it is also clear that there are no simple answers to how it will affect learning or change processes in each particular case. Rather, the most important insight may be that in the investigation of specific paths and patterns of learning and innovation, the simultaneous influence of boundaries and connections is a way of understanding what is going on and the tensions at play, as well as the dynamics of their influence over time. Next, we move on to the issue of time and how this relates to boundaries and connections.

On the temporalities and spatial aspects of innovation in construction

A well rehearsed theme in the construction management literature on learning and innovation is the divide between the temporary and permanent forms of organising. While this form of temporal boundary is often stated to hinder the exchange of learning and solutions over time, less is known about the connections between these different temporal ways of organising. In Chapter 2 on the construction of "the most sustainable building in the world" (the Evenstad campus of the Inland Norway University of Applied Sciences), Hugosson, Stevik, Søberg and Tryggestad illustrate a process of transforming an initially ordinary project into a highly innovative one. This was done through an intricate process of using material and technical devices to gain political legitimacy and funding. In the process of reformulating the project, the interaction between particular actants (individuals, organisations and artefacts) connected not only to policy, firm and project levels but also different temporalities. Including wood (an 'old' material) into the building as a way of creating an innovative and sustainable building in the present forged connections between the past and the present. The way in which the project also generated a biogas plant at the campus, as well as new public policy targets for sustainability, connected the past and present to future sustainability states, visions and goals. Thus, while the project was a temporary occurrence of a particular set of actants to construct a campus, the way these actants interacted created connections between established materials and knowledge with present and future sustainability targets and goals that went beyond the single project. Chapter 9 by Hugosson and Nord investigates knowledge development in public client organisations regarding strategic make-or-buy decisions in construction procurement. Investigating such decision making in innovative construction projects in three Swedish municipalities, they show that public clients can take an active part in framing the projects as well as in developing their own operational knowledge across projects. In this way, projects are actively used as a way of developing the strategic and dynamic capabilities of the municipalities. Temporary projects are used as a way of learning and developing capabilities within the permanent organisation, as well as in relation to others, such as suppliers. As the authors conclude, this enables more informed make-or-buy decisions in upcoming projects. These chapters illustrate how different temporalities can be taken advantage of in order for development, both material and immaterial, to take place.

The divide and connections between temporary projects and the more permanent structure of firms is also an apparent theme in Chapter 10 by Crespin-Mazet, Havenvid and Linné. By addressing how the practices of collectives of individuals – communities of practice – may transcend the organisational boundaries of projects and firms, their studies show the connections that can be made between these different temporalities. They argue for the relevance of establishing communities of practice on various levels to overcome the long recognised problem of scaling up innovations on the project level to the wider organisations. In the establishment and preservation of new practices and solutions, communities can function as time capsules of knowledge that may then be tested and further developed in other contexts, i.e. across the organisational and temporal boundaries of firms and projects. In some instances, the interdependence between the temporary and permanent structures becomes more apparent than the divide between them, as also shown by the two case studies by Simon, Balazs, Mandják, Szalkai and Hetesi (Chapter 8). These authors reveal how the discrepancies between decision-making practices of public and private actors resulted in particular project team structures in attempts to bridge the two types of decision system. These cross-disciplinary teams operated according to a 'third' decision-making logic, which combined the business competence of the private sector with the expertise of the public health care system: hence, the temporary coalitions of actors needed to relate to two different types of decision-making structures outside the boundaries of the projects. In addition, in order to complete the projects, these teams enabled a merged system combining the two different competences and decision-making practices. This illustrates how temporary project coalitions not only represent combinations of different permanent organisations but rather are *mergers* of them and as such represent a temporal and organisational logic of its own.

In reconsidering innovation in construction as that of changes within and across activity-based systems, Orstavik (Chapter 13) points to the different boundaries and temporalities around innovations, for instance how unchanged activity systems are integrated differently in different temporary projects. Thus, although the boundaries may remain the same, it can be the way that they intersect with one another that creates innovation. Chapter 5 by Hulthén and Sundquist more specifically addresses how the finely balanced activity interdependences at play within projects make moving from temporary to permanent organising a difficult thing to do. The shifting role of a material delivery firm (deliveries in projects) to a logistics provider (facilities off site) reveals the fragility of changing such interdependencies and ultimately of service/network coordinating innovations. This reveals the importance of appreciating time and the meaning of incremental change. By looking into the interactivity between how firms implement sustainability goals set on international and national industry levels and how such goals in turn are pushed further, Sergeeva and Lindkvist (Chapter 12) reveal an incremental development of narratives over time. While sustainability goals and requirements are being heard, their implementation evolves over time through processes of reconstructing firm and job role identities, and the development of innovative solutions in turn create a pull from the industry to raise the policy ambition to stricter or new targets. As such, industry narratives on sustainable innovation are described as being shaped and reshaped through continuous interaction processes between narratives on the international and national policy levels and project-based firm level connecting the past, present and the future.

What is illustrated through these chapters is that time is not an easy matter. It is a dimension that influences processes of renewal in different ways. The past will in one way or the other be present in contemporary ways of doing or interpreting things and in the artefacts that are used. Ideas or plans of what the future may look like will also merge into the present, and, consequently, in each moment different temporalities will influence what can be changed and how. It is also shown that organisations try to find ways of dealing with different temporalities and time horizons, for instance by organising in communities that cut across different temporalities or shifting roles that create new temporal states of organising activities and resources. By tracing development processes across different spaces and over time, the chapters illustrate how the distributed nature of innovation influences what knowledge and technology can be applied, as well as how it can be further developed. For instance, in showing how the use of a technology, BIM, triggers the development of a new and innovative digital platform, Chapter 3 by Linné addresses the different innovative effects that a technology can have depending on where and when it is applied and for what purposes. Chapter 8 by Simon, Révész, Mandják, Szalkai and Hetesi shows that using innovative methods in one sector, i.e. construction, may support innovation in another, i.e. health care. However, ultimately, whether the final construction product (i.e. the building) is used for the intended purposes or not is a matter of how well it integrates and can become an integrated part of both the established and planned activities of the end users. The construction project as a vehicle for (societal) innovation is thus ultimately a matter of *use* and not production – or, more specifically, the interaction between production and use.

Analytical questions and research agenda: investigating innovation in construction as distributed processes across time and space

Engwall (2003) reminded us that in the assessment of the events and outcomes of a project, one must consider its historical and organisational context. Thus, while projects as a way of organising represent deliberate attempts of demarcating some activities from others in both an economic and organisational sense, i.e. creating boundaries, they are still dependent on historical, parallel and future events. In turn, this makes them related to the participants and technologies involved in those events.

In this volume, we have used the concept of connectivity to describe and analyse the implications of this embedded nature of projects for innovation. The chapters demonstrate that connectivity, as well as innovation itself, is a processual phenomenon (Langley and Tsoukas, 2016). A process relates to events taking place over *time*, and, as events can be connected in several ways, one or several particular events can be stated to matter for innovation in different ways. Events have a historical development, they can depend on or affect other parallel events and they can have an impact on future actions. Mobilisers and participants of events, as well as the technologies and knowledge they use to be part of them, are thus also directly and indirectly connected across time. From a development point of view, they may also be dependent on one another.

Several of the chapters have taken on a network view of the conditions for learning and innovation. This means that in their analysis of why learning and innovation processes unfold in particular ways, they place focus on the interplay among different actors, processes and resources within and across projects. The view of construction organisations as actors, or *actants*, operating within networks in which they are highly affected by and even dependent on the actions and reactions of others, brings a certain understanding of what is possible to achieve as a single organisation, as a project organisation and as an industry. As has been shown throughout the chapters, these connections, or interdependencies, are established over time as individuals, firms and organisations choose to deal with each other in separate projects, collaborate to solve problems or simply because they have no choice!

A central part of such type of network analyses (e.g. actor-network theory or industrial network theory) is the agency of materiality and the interplay between the material and immaterial (Orlikowski and Scott, 2008). Thus, what is possible or not possible to change or innovate and how it can be done are not necessarily "simply" a matter of what individuals or organisations want or do not want to do. It is not necessarily just a struggle between different stakeholder interests, perspectives, cultures and goals. Rather, material representations, technologies and infrastructural arrangements will also greatly affect what can be innovated, in what way and how long it will take (if it will work at all). It will also greatly matter how such material solutions have become interconnected over time and across organisational spaces. Thus, trying to replace one solution with another is indeed primarily an issue of understanding how things are connected.

Projects are also part of forming particular structures, or *spaces*, for innovation. Interestingly, the chapters report studies from various empirical spaces, ranging from single projects in individual countries to multiple projects involving comparative analyses between countries, in addition to international- and sector-level analyses involving transnational construction-related networks. Tracing connectivity across different organisational, national and international spaces has provided us with several interesting observations. The most interesting one is probably that, despite the variety observed, there is consistency in showing that innovation in construction can be understood as a distributed process over time and space, in which connectivity and disconnectivity play key roles, and analysed as the tracing of connections being made, translated and broken. This is particularly interesting given the outset of the ENRIC network, and initial intentions of doing comparative studies in a joint research project. Even if this idea soon proved problematic, the chapters, based on the authors' autonomous research, nevertheless illustrate common and comparable patterns of innovation processes in these construction sectors.

So what avenues for future analytical questions and research agenda(s) can we derive from this reasoning and insight from the presented work? A general call for further processual studies of construction innovation, grounded in understanding it as the dynamics of connectivity, is a given. But if there are boundaries and connections and different temporalities, and if learning and innovation processes are distributed over time and space, what kind of questions should be pursued, and how do we go about finding answers to them?

Methodologically, there are some interesting challenges. Most of the contributions in the book adopt some form of case study approach, where the boundary of the empirical space is set by the organisation or project. But where should we draw boundaries around innovation? How can we find the 'edge' of the network of connections that produce it? How far beyond the case, project, organisation and sector should we stop? This is further complicated if we move beyond the spatial or structural into the temporal. At what point does innovation stop and 'normal' start? How far back in time do we trace connections in order to understand the existing mechanisms that facilitate new innovation? Another issue is tracing the agency of materiality. We generally collect data by engaging with actors – interviews, written texts and so on, but how do we interrogate the material and technological parts of networks? Whilst we have concepts such as Gibson's (1977) affordance or Latour's (1992) delegation, moving beyond anthropomorphism is a methodological challenge for network-oriented approaches.

Research agendas should also stretch our analytical concepts, as well as add to our understanding of particular phenomena. This book shows how innovation can be positioned as connections forming, activating, breaking, transforming, but does the concept of 'connectivity' have enough granularity to explain, for instance, differences between success and failure, or could it be developed to explain how and why some innovations extend beyond the space or context in which they are formed and others remain rooted in one context? Successful innovation is not just the continual extension of a network, so, for example, what are the conditions through which complex connectivity is separated out or bundled up into a more simple connection? Are there further patterns around when innovation activity is about making connections or about drawing boundaries?

The notion of connectivity is potentially a fruitful one to begin to move beyond cases, or 'stories' of innovation, to move beyond describing change and innovation into a perhaps more analytical and forensic mode of studying innovation. We would not claim to have the tools ready to be able to do this but might tentatively suggest that it is in this testing of concepts that more robust comparative analyses of innovation lie. We believe we have come some part of the way by elaborating on the idea of dualities and more specifically, on the notion of construction innovation being influenced by simultaneous conditions of connection and disconnection over time. As such, construction is not operating under either/or states of being innovative or non-innovative. Rather, there is a pattern of connections and disconnections forming and re-forming over time that create specific opportunities and challenges for innovation. Based on these fundamental questions of conducting processual research and the notion of innovation as a distributed process of connectivity and disconnectivity over time, we suggest the following three overarching questions for further research, a research agenda for tracing innovation in construction as connectivity in a systematic way.

What are the types of connectivity that can be observed across different scales of construction organisation, i.e. project, firm, sector, national, transnational levels?

In considering innovation as that of involving different scales of connectivity (as proposed by Orstavik in Chapter 13), we might have a great deal to learn from systematically observing, describing and theorising the interplay between the innovation process and its distribution across such scales. There might be explanatory value in such descriptions in providing opportunities for investigating the paradoxical tensions at work in driving and hindering particular processes. Some related aspects might be if connectivity appears differently across these different organisational scales of construction or if there is a change in types of connectivity, or types of innovation across these scales. This type of inquiry would require a systematic identification of types of connectivity and innovation and their relation to context. Studies could include both single-scale and cross-scale analysis.

What is the influence of types of connectivity on what is or can be learnt and innovated over time?

The contributions of this volume have described how learning and innovation takes place in an industrial setting characterised by connectivity and disconnectivity (as a duality). However, this is just a first step in understanding the dynamics between connectivity and innovation as interrelated states and processes. An inquiry further scrutinising types of connectivity and the relation to particular forms of innovation process could not only be fruitful in better grasping the dynamics between connectivity and innovation as intertwined phenomena but also be a step towards more fine-grained conceptualisations of connectivity as well as innovation in construction. It could potentially lead to studies of various types of connectivity and the related innovation processes across scales.

How does innovation influence connectivity over time?

While connectivity is part of the context in which innovation takes place, innovation is also part of reshaping that context. Thus, while we try to grasp the nature of innovation, we must also be aware of the changing context in which it takes place and how innovation is part of that transformation. Over time, what is the relationship between innovation and the (re)configuration of connectivity? More precisely, how is innovation part of influencing what connections are forming, activating, breaking and transforming across construction sectors? This type of inquiry requires both an in-depth and a longitudinal type of approach scrutinising the relation between process and context. It could involve single-scale and cross-scale analysis and would benefit from international research collaboration and comparisons.

We believe these three overarching inquiries are broad enough for the benefit of applying different theoretical perspectives and methods, which is essential for investigating innovation as a multidimensional phenomenon (e.g. Orstavik, Dainty and Abbott, 2015). Theoretical and methodological variation will be important ingredients in further developing our notion of past, present and future developments of this industry. Yet they are (hopefully) specific enough for a consistent research agenda through which knowledge can be drawn from a multitude of studies and approaches. The goal of such a research agenda would be to inspire international research collaborations and by extension making cross-sectoral type of analyses. This could potentially result in mapping patterns of what we here have referred to as paradoxical tensions or dualities and, more specifically, how construction sectors operate under simultaneous conditions of connectivity and disconnectivity. One main point of this would be to shift the debate about the construction business as *either* innovative *or* non-innovative to consider it as *both* innovative *and* non-innovative and to further investigate the related spatial and temporal types of pattern underlying this duality.

References

Engwall, M. (2003) 'No project is an island: Linking projects to history and context', *Research Policy*, 32(5), pp. 789–808.

Gibson, J.J. (1977) 'The theory of affordances', in Shaw, R. and Bransford, J. (eds.), *Perceiving, Acting, and Knowing: Toward an Ecological Psychology.* Hillsdale, NJ: Lawrence Erlbaum, pp. 67–82.

Giddens, A. (1984) *The constitution of society: Outline of the theory of structuration.* Oxford: Polity.

Jules, C. and Goods, D. (2014) 'Introduction to special issue on paradox in context: Advances in theory and practice', *The Journal of Applied Behavioral Science*, 50(2), pp. 123–126.

Kolb, D.G. (2008) 'Exploring the metaphor of connectivity: Attributes, dimensions and duality', *Organization Studies*, 29(1), pp. 127–144.

Langley, A. and Tsoukas, H. (2016) *The Sage handbook of process organization research.* London: Sage.

Latour, B. (1992) 'Where are the missing masses? The sociology of a few mundane arte-facts', in Bijker, W. and Law, J. (eds.), *Shaping Technology/Building Society: Studies in Sociotechnical Change*. Cambridge, MA: MIT Press, pp. 225–258.

Lewis, M.W. (2000) 'Exploring Paradox: Toward a more comprehensive guide', *The Academy of Management Review*, 25(4), pp. 760–776.

Lewis, M.W. and Smith, W.K. (2014) 'Paradox as metatheoretical perspective: Sharpening the focus and widening the scope', *The Journal of Applied Behavioral Science*, 50(2), pp. 127–149.

Orlikowski, W.J. and Scott, S.V. (2008) 'Sociomateriality: Challenging the separation of technology, work and organization', *Academy of Management Annals*, 2(1), pp. 433–474.

Orstavik, F., Dainty, A. and Abbott, C. (2015) *Construction innovation*. London: Wiley-Blackwell.

Smith, W.K. and Lewis, M.W. (2011) 'Toward a theory of paradox: A dynamic equilibrium model of organizing', *The Academy of Management Review*, 36(2), pp. 381–403.

Index

Note: Page numbers in *italics* indicate a figure and page numbers in **bold** indicate a table on the corresponding page.

Printed in the United States
by Baker & Taylor Publisher Services